And They Lived Happily Ever After

And They Lived Happily Ever After

NORMS AND EVERYDAY PRACTICES OF FAMILY AND
PARENTHOOD IN RUSSIA AND CENTRAL EUROPE

Edited by
Helene Carlbäck, Yulia Gradskova
and Zhanna Kravchenko

CEU PRESS

Central European University Press
Budapest–New York

© 2012 by Helene Carlbäck, Yulia Gradskova
and Zhanna Kravchenko

Published in 2012 by
Central European University Press

An imprint of the
Central European University Limited Company
Nádor utca 11, H-1051 Budapest, Hungary
Tel: +36-1-327-3138 or 327-3000
Fax: +36-1-327-3183
E-mail: ceupress@ceu.hu
Website: www.ceupress.com

400 West 59th Street, New York NY 10019, USA
Tel: +1-212-547-6932
Fax: +1-646-557-2416
E-mail: mgreenwald@sorosny.org

All rights reserved. No part of this publication may be reproduced,
stored in a retrieval system, or transmitted, in any form or by any means,
without the permission of the Publisher.

ISBN 978-615-5053-57-3

Library of Congress Cataloging-in-Publication Data

And they lived happily ever after : norms and everyday practices of family and parenthood in Russia and Central Europe / [edited by] Helene Carlbäck, Yulia Gradskova and Zhanna Kravchenko.
    pages ; cm
  Some papers were presented at the conference "Family, Marriage and Parenthood in Eastern Europe, Russia and Sweden" held September 2008 in Sweden.
  Includes bibliographical references and index.
  ISBN 978 6155053573 (hardbound)
 1. Families Russia (Federation) 2. Families Soviet Union. 3. Families Baltic States. 4. Families Europe, Eastern. 5. Family policy Russia (Federation) 6. Family policy Soviet Union. 7. Family policy Baltic States. I. Carlbäck, Helene, 1947 , editor, author. II. Gradskova, Yulia, editor, author. III. Kravchenko, Zhanna, editor, author.

HQ638.A53 2012
306.850947 dc23

2012000307

Printed in Hungary by
Prime Rate Kft., Budapest

Table of Contents

LIST OF ABBREVIATIONS vii
PREFACE ix
INTRODUCTION | Helene Carlbäck, Yulia Gradskova and
Zhanna Kravchenko 1

PART I | 1940s–1980s THE FAMILY AS A "BASIC UNIT OF SOCIALIST SOCIETY"

CHAPTER 1. *Lone Motherhood in Soviet Russia in the Mid-20th Century—In a European Context* | Helene Carlbäck 25

CHAPTER 2. *Family, Divorce, and Comrades' Courts: Soviet Family and Public Organizations During the Thaw* | Elena Zhidkova 47

CHAPTER 3. *A Life of Labor, a Life of Love: Telling the Life of a Young Peasant Mother Facing Collectivization* | Ildikó Asztalos Morell 65

CHAPTER 4. *East German Women Going West: Family, Children and Partners in Life-Experience Literature* | Christine Farhan 85

CHAPTER 5. *Why Does Public Policy Implementation Fail? Lithuanian Office of State Benefits for Mothers of Large Families and Single Mothers, 1944–1956* | Dalia Leinarte 105

CHAPTER 6. *The Latvian Family Experience with Sovietization 1945–1990* | Maija Runcis 123

PART II | 1990s–2000s SOCIAL TRANSFORMATION IN THE MIRROR OF FAMILY LIFE

CHAPTER 7. *"Two children Puts You in the Zone of Social Misery:" Childbearing and Risk Perception among Russian Women* | Anna Rotkirch and Katja Kesseli 145

CHAPTER 8. *"Supporting Genuine Development of the Child:" Public Childcare Centers Versus Family in Post-Soviet Russia* | Yulia Gradskova 165

CHAPTER 9. *Everyday Continuity and Change: Family and Family Policy in Russia* | Zhanna Kravchenko 185

CHAPTER 10. *Single Mothers—Clients or Citizens? Social Work with Poor Families in Russia* | Elena Iarskaia-Smirnova and Pavel Romanov 207

CHAPTER 11. *Welfare Crisis and Crisis Centers in Russia Today* | Aino Saarinen 231

CHAPTER 12. *Marriage and Divorce Law in Russia and the Baltic States: Overview of Recent Changes* | Olga A. Khazova 251

CHAPTER 13. *Doing Parenting in Post-Socialist Estonia and Latvia* | Ingegerd Municio-Larsson 273

CHAPTER 14. *Gendered Experiences in Entrepreneurship, Family and Social Activities in Russia* | Ann-Mari Sätre 297

NOTES ON CONTRIBUTORS 319
INDEX 323

List of Abbreviations

CEDAW	Convention on the Elimination of All Forms of Discrimination Against Women
CoE	The Council of Europe
GARF	Gosudarstvennyi Arkhiv Rossiiskoi Federatsii (State Archive of the Russian Federation)
GEM	Gender Emplowerment Measure
GDR	The German Democratic Republic
HDI	Human Development Index
HDR	Human Development Report
ICVS	International Crime Victim Survey
KP RSFSR	The Communist Party of the Russian Soviet Federal Socialist Republic
KPSS	The Communist Party of the Soviet Union
LCVA	Lithuanian Central State Archives
LSSR	Latvian Soviet Socialist Republic
MDGs	Millennium Development Goalsn
NCRB	The Network for Crisis Centres for Women in the Barents Region
NGO	Non-Governmental Organization
OSI	The Open Society Institute
RACCW	The Russian Association for Crisis Centers for Women
RSFSR	The Russian Soviet Federal Socialist Republic
SOGASPI	Samara Regional Archive of Social and Political History
TsGASO	The Central State Archive of Samara Region
TFR	Total Fertility Rate
USSR	The Union of Soviet Socialist Republics
VAW	Violence Against Women
WB	The World Bank
WGA	Welfare, Gender and Agency

Preface

The collection of texts in the present book started with a conference held in September 2008 at the Centre for Baltic and East European Studies (CBEES) at Södertörn University. Titled "Family, Marriage and Parenthood in Eastern Europe, Russia and Sweden," the symposium sought to gather scholars from various parts of Europe to discuss topics having to do with the family, marriage, childhood, and parenthood from a contemporary, historical and comparative perspective. It was also part of the research project "The Family vs. the Strong State in Eastern Europe and the Baltic Sea Region: Freedom or Coercion?" The project and the conference were funded by Östersjöstiftelsen (the Foundation for Baltic and East European Studies), established by the Swedish government to support research and the training of researchers dealing with the Baltic region, Russia, and Eastern Europe at Södertörn University.

We are grateful to the foundation for the financial assistance that made this book possible and to the Publication Committee at CBEES for their support and encouragement. We also thank the members of the abovementioned research project for their important commentaries to the introductory chapter of this volume. Finally, we express our gratitude to Charles Rougle (University at Albany) for copyediting the English text in the final manuscript and Peter Isotalo for editing the English text in parts of the book at an earlier stage.

We recommend this volume specifically to scholars and students of the Baltic Sea region and Eastern Europe with a particular interest in social, gender and family issues, and to specialists in social and welfare policies on a broader level. The book is also well-suited as a reader in sociology, gender studies, history, and other academic disciplines within the humanities and social science.

Introduction

HELENE CARLBÄCK, YULIA GRADSKOVA
AND ZHANNA KRAVCHENKO

This book is about various aspects of family life in some countries of Central and Eastern Europe and Russia. It deals with issues of marriage, parental strategies, single motherhood, and absent fatherhood, as well as family policies, legal rules, and popular discourse. Because of the interdisciplinary character of the contributions and the wide spectrum of family-related phenomena they analyze, this introduction will attempt to link the chapters by outlining some important parameters of social life in the region and contextualizing the volume within the body of existing research. There is also a description of the overall structure of the volume and a brief presentation of each chapter individually and in relation to the others.

The book has several goals. The first goal is to critically analyze family norms as captured in legislation and public-policy regulations and partly also to study the implementation of policies, particularly in social work and public childcare in the last two decades. The book's second goal is to provide an account of changing discourse and norms with respect to gender roles, the gender division of labor, parental duties, and state intervention in family life. Third, drawing on everyday family practices, the book conceptualizes actual patterns of reproduction, the division of household labor, and childcare. At the turn of the millennium, a significant number of publications on gender issues in Eastern Europe appeared that include the subject of the family in their analysis (Asztalos Morell et al., 2005; Björnberg and Sass, 1997; Gal and Kligman, 2000; Haney and Pollard, 2003; Robila, 2004a). However, we would still argue that, compared to politics and economics in the region (Robila, 2004b, p. 5), the family is a little-studied topic. We see issues of family and family-related policies as crucial for an understanding of change in the life of contemporary societies and individuals, including developments in labor market strategies, educational choices, and the promotion of democratic values among the younger generations.

As editors of this book, we recognize the wide scope of approaches to the study of the family over time, and we appreciate the fact that images and interpretations are constantly in flux. We therefore encouraged the contributors to this book to take a wide range of theoretical and methodological approaches. The title *And They Lived Happily Ever After* refers to the established idealized image—so familiar to all from popular fiction—of the harmonious, stable, and prosperous life that begins after the wedding. For researchers of family life, the moment a family union is formed is usually just a starting point in their work. Historical, sociological, and gender studies translate this ideal image into reality, revealing how aspects of general societal organization and dynamics are embedded in family life. Throughout the last century, the family in Eastern Europe and Russia faced a number of dramatic social transformations that came with the promise of a better life but have not necessarily lived up to the expectations of the people who had to endure their results. This book explores various aspects of experiences in family life and family-related policies at different historical moments in the twentieth century in various countries of the region.

Contemporary Eastern Europe is frequently defined by scholars and others from the perspective of its recent past as "former communist countries" or "post-Soviet countries." Yet in spite of this, many publications focus mainly on what has happened in the region after the changes of 1989/1991 and thus do not pay much attention to the past of the state socialist system. This often creates a lack of understanding of what the legacy of this system has meant for today's policies and practices. By this legacy we are referring to particular characteristics of the state socialist system such as official norms of women's emancipation, predominantly female responsibility for family matters in everyday life, and a strong emphasis on an all-embracing welfare state of a specific authoritarian kind.

Although this book is about family life and policies in countries of the former socialist bloc, we do not see these issues in that part of Europe as being isolated from ideas and practices on the other side of the traditional East-West divide, not even before the fall of the Berlin Wall and the demise of the Soviet Union. On the contrary, we attempt to provide a comparative perspective that indicates similarities and potential mutual influences with respect to legal rules, popular norms, and everyday practices in both Eastern and Western Europe. Thus even though this book addresses different aspects of family life and policies in Russia, Hungary, the Baltic countries, and the former East Germany, many of the authors contextualize their cases by referring to models of family policies and practices in countries such as Sweden, Finland, and the former West Germany.

In the following we will address several dimensions of the social transformation that Central and Eastern Europe experienced throughout the period after World War II, particularly after the fall of socialism. The dimensions we want to focus on are family patterns in a changing social context, welfare and social security, and gender aspects of family relations. Changes in each of these dimensions have been substantial and crucial to understanding the overall processes in the region.

FAMILY PATTERNS IN A CHANGING SOCIAL CONTEXT

Since World War II, general demographic behavior has changed dramatically in the industrialized world, although specific patterns of partnership and reproductive practices and the timing of their formation have fluctuated significantly between countries and regions. These trends include a substantial decline in fertility rates, the postponement of first marriage and childbirth, increasing non-marital cohabitation and extramarital births, a rise in divorce rates and voluntary childlessness, and the common use of a wide range of contraceptives. Historians of the family in Europe have used the theory of "demographic transition" to trace the reasons for the decrease in the birth and death rates further back in history, to the processes of industrialization, urbanization, and secularization (Chesnais, 1992). Recent demographers (such as van de Kaa, 1996) have conceptualized the continuing trend toward a destandardization of the life course and a diversification of living arrangements and family forms as "the second demographic transition." This theory regards the increasing trend towards "thinner," "de-institutionalized," and "non-co-resident families" (Hantrais, 2006, p. 12) as a result of modernization (Inglehart, 1990; Sobotka, 2008; van de Kaa, 1996) or of socialization through globalization.

The demographic transition reflects and contributes to changes in societal beliefs and attitudes and in economic development and scientific and medical knowledge. The statistical data usually used in demographic analysis provide equally rich ground for sociological interpretations. They present the process of change in family relations as a transition from the traditional family with strict gender-specific roles to a relationship in which men and women maintain a high degree of autonomy in pursuing their own individual interests both outside and within unions. Furthermore, the statistics point to the fact that young people are less subject to family control and social norms and can freely decide whether and when to cohabit, marry, divorce, or have children (Coleman, 1996; Tahlberg, 2003).

Eastern Europe and Russia went through these transitions at a different pace. The first radical changes in the family there were caused by the institutional transformation introduced after the establishment of the communist regime in Russia in 1917 and then in Eastern Europe over half a century ago. State control over economic production, geographic and social mobility, and the secularization and ideological rejection of traditional gender roles forced a faster transition to the nuclear dual-earner family form. Organization of the education system and transitions from school to work, systems of housing allocation, and provision of health care created opportunities for a rather universal pathway through the life course (Katus et al., 2007). This standardized biography was marked by obligatory employment, early marriage that usually was not preceded by cohabitation, and relatively early childbearing. Although the pattern of early and nearly universal entry into marriage continued to dominate in the region up until the early 1990s, a tendency toward decreasing birth rates, increased numbers of divorces, and postponed first births started much earlier (Philipov and Dorbritz, 2003, pp. 13–14). It is especially noteworthy that at the same time, the family and sometimes also religion played an important role in sustaining national/ethnic identity, despite the domination of communist ideology (Pilkington and Yemelianova, 2003; Titkow and Duch, 2004).

The post-socialist transformation in Eastern Europe and Russia had important implications for the demographic development of the region. The developments outlined above were accompanied by increased mortality, morbidity, and out-migration, trends that were not compensated for by in-migration. The scope of these problems led researchers to speak of a rapid depopulation phenomenon with low interregional differences affecting, for example, the Baltic states, Hungary, and Russia (Bucher and Mai, 2005; Philipov and Dorbritz, 2003). In the current political discourse, demographic changes are increasingly perceived as a crisis and are often identified as a threat to the nation (Kis, 2005; Rivkin-Fish, 2010; Zhurzhenko, 2004a).

Socioeconomic transformation caused high levels of poverty and social exclusion to recur and be compounded in subsequent generations. The risk of poverty is significantly higher for households with children, especially those run by lone parents. On the one hand, socially disadvantaged children inherit poor social and economic capital, while on the other, limited resources may discourage childbirth and sustain low fertility in the long run (Szivós and Guidici, 2004). As we look at these new aspects of family development, it is also important to recall that there were not infrequently gender and racial/ethnic undertones in the way welfare policies under state socialism encouraged or discouraged the growth of specific populations, such as the Roma (Varsa, 2010, p. 178).

Research on family relations suggests that the family, marital partnerships, and parenting are highly valued throughout the region and that intergenerational support remains an important source of social and economic stability. After the collapse of the state socialist regimes, a revitalization of religion and traditional life rituals accompanied a re-traditionalization of family ideology (Robila, 2004b; Zhurzhenko, 2004b). At the same time, Eastern European countries started developing some heterogeneous patterns in family formation. The retreat of the ideological domination of the ruling parties stimulated differences in normative perceptions of suitable timing for entry into marriage and childbearing (Philipov, 2002; Tahlberg, 2003). Juang et al. (1999) have aptly summarized the recent tendencies as diversifying individual biographic trajectories within the former socialist bloc yet also converging life paths with those in the West at a different pace.

As mentioned above, institutional framework and policy measures had a considerable influence on demographic behavior. Thus state concern with population dynamics was strong in many parts of Europe in the past century. The history of state intervention in nuptial and reproductive behavior included both punitive measures such as a ban on abortion and stimulative measures such as privileges related to childbirth in the form of special assistance to pregnant women and unmarried mothers. For instance, the punitive and stimulative practices began in Germany, France, Sweden, and the Soviet Union during the interwar years and in some countries in Eastern Europe after World War II. It is also interesting to note that demographic policies in Europe sometimes took sharp turns depending on the perceived needs of a certain period in one or another country. The most illustrative example is the development of legislation on abortions under the Soviet regime, where the liberalization of marriage and divorce laws in the 1920s was accompanied by the legalization of abortions, only to be completely rejected in the 1930s and 1940s in favor of more limited opportunities for dissolving marriages and the criminalization of abortions (Goldman, 1993; Carlbäck, 2005). In the 1970s the legal framework in the Soviet Union was reversed again, and reproductive rights were liberalized anew, in line with the practices established by that time in most of the Eastern European countries, with the exception of Romania.

In more recent decades, the persistence of demographic problems was openly acknowledged. The measures set up to deal with them ranged from intensified propaganda promoting traditional family values and roles (Gradskova, 1997; Rotkirch et al., 2007; Zhurzhenko, 2004a) to family-friendly social policies such as maternity/parental leave regulations and extended social guarantees for mothers. We shall return in more detail below to some aspects of the changes in family policies and gender roles. Here we want to emphasize that studies of public policies often focus on administrative regulations and treat norms and practices of everyday family life as secondary in importance. Furthermore, such studies are usually centered on contemporary welfare policies and do not pay much attention to past practices under state socialism. Moreover, when norms and practices are brought up in studies on the socialist (particularly Soviet) family and its distribution of gender roles and childrearing, they are often presented as unique (Aivazova, 1998; Buckley, 1989; Kelly, 2007).

Several contributions in the present volume add to our existing knowledge of the development of family patterns throughout the region by examining norms and practices with respect to several types of demographic characteristics of families across nations and time periods—marriage and divorce (Khazova), childbearing (Rotkirch), childrearing after divorce (Municio-Larsson), and mortality and morbidity connected with the issue of interpersonal violence (Saarinen). Moreover, state pronatalist policies aimed at stimulating an increase in childbirth and promoting lifelong marital commitments are analyzed from a historical perspective (Carlbäck, Leinarte). The authors draw upon individual life stories and memories, policy documents, and aggregated statistics to bring together past and present and indicate tensions between everyday family practices and public policies.

WELFARE AND SOCIAL SECURITY

The second important dimension of social transformation with regard to the family in Eastern Europe and Russia is the development of welfare and social security. Historically, changes in family legislation in late nineteenth- and early twentieth-century Europe were among the first steps in creating the possibility to influence patterns in family formation by means of public welfare policies. These changes led to the abolishment of the ancient tradition of providing the male head of the family—the *pater familias*—with extensive and exclusive power over other members of the family and household. They also led to the secularization and individualization of marriage and simplified divorce procedures. Later in the twentieth century, legislation in many European countries facilitated a growing state interference in family matters. Marriage became a popular institution among all classes of society, partly because such laws made it easier to enter and to leave a union and partly because the state attached a range of incentives to registered marriage, including better access to housing, in-kind services, and cash benefits. Not only did social norms support the tradition of marriage, but the state as well regarded the institution of marriage as a means to produce the next generation of citizens (Therborn, 2004; UNICEF, 1999, p. 43).

The twentieth century, more specifically the period after World War II, witnessed an upsurge of publicly financed welfare measures in many spheres of everyday life. State socialist regimes in Eastern Europe had their own distinct and consistent approach to welfare issues. This created a common model of social security and protection characterized by the integration of social insurance into state budgets; highly centralized, standardized, and institutionalized forms of service provision, including universal health care; and the extension of welfare provision to all workers through the enterprise, which distributed a substantial portion of the resources (Manning, 2004; Voirin, 1993). Despite these commonalities, however, important differences between the countries persisted. Even in the Soviet Union, where both pressure and opportunities for standardization were the strongest, significant discrepancies could be observed in living standards and social policy realization between the union republics (George and Manning, 1980).

Compared to social policy in general, family-related policies were normally less uniform in design and implementation. Family policy played an important role in the provision of social security in most of the Eastern European countries and the Soviet Union (Voirin 1993). All countries provided job protection for women and income compensation during maternity leave. The size of benefits during parental leave varied among the countries, but in the 1980s all benefits gradually and systematically entitled men as well to receive this type of leave. The public-policy agenda and the discourse on fatherhood, however, were largely shaped by the absence of a discussion on the need to distribute parental responsibilities for small children equally. This is one reason why the implementation of the laws on the rights of fathers to be paid as caregivers was considerably more extensive in, for example, Scandinavia than in the Eastern European countries (Ohlander, 1992).

The forms the benefits have taken, especially from the late 1960s and on, have differed from country to country. One set of countries, including Hungary and Poland, had a system of predominantly contribution-based cash benefits, while benefits in others such as the GDR, Bulgaria, and the Soviet Union were mostly in-kind, through the distribution of services and exemptions. Finally, in some countries, most notably Czechoslovakia, both types of provision were present in equal measure (Borowczyk, 1986).

After the fall of state socialism, the social security system of the Eastern European countries was deeply affected by acute cuts in state budgets.

Even before that, however, a considerable percentage of the population was actually living at the poverty line. Because of various reasons—including an emphasis on full employment as a social right—the state socialist regimes in Eastern Europe did not prioritize the reduction or abolishment of poverty as a core function in their social security systems (George, 1991, p. 61). Thus in the mid-1980s, 6–7 percent of the population in Czechoslovakia and 20 percent in Poland were living below the social minimum level, and in 1989 the USSR statistical office estimated the corresponding figure there to be 40 million, or 14 percent of the population (UNICEF, 2001, p. 31).

With the overall political, economic, and social transformation after 1989/1991, the social security systems were scrutinized, re-evaluated, and redesigned under both internal and external pressures. Neo-liberal ideas of a free-market economy were strongly encouraged by international financial organizations such as the International Monetary Fund and the World Bank and endorsed by national leaders (Fajth, 1999). Thus the quality and quantity of the social security and public social protection structures deteriorated significantly, which meant that the existing system was not able to meet the challenges of new or previously ignored social risks such as mass unemployment and inflation.

Consequently, all Eastern European countries initiated a series of reforms in the field of social security (Manning, 2004; Rys, 2001). There is no agreement among researchers as to what long-term direction the development of social policy has taken and which welfare model should be favored. During the fiscal crisis of the late 1990s, some analysts expected that poverty relief measures would be given priority and lead to the emergence of a neo-liberal, "residual" welfare model along lines specifically advocated by researchers associated with the World Bank (Barr, 1994). Others have suggested that a majority of the countries, including Hungary and Estonia, were developing into one or another variant of the Western European welfare state model, which combines a mix of social insurance and public financing, while others like Ukraine and Romania attempted "to retain something of the past social contract between workplace and worker" and to postpone significant reforms altogether (Deacon, 2001, p. 151).

With regard to the transformation of family-related policies, a few common trends can be observed. First, the system of maternity and parental leave as introduced before major reforms was maintained in most countries. Second, family allowances, the budget for which was cut significantly, ended up being transformed into means-tested benefits (UNICEF, 1999). Thus the economic activity of both men and women is still critical for family survival. Although the gender pay gap is lower than in many Western

European countries, there was a decline in female employment, which subsequently threatened the long-term economic well-being of families (Pascall and Manning, 2000).

Of the provision for public childcare, it can be noted that, according to a recent study of eight Eastern European countries, only Hungary and Lithuania preserved and further developed a system of available and high-quality childcare services (Szelewa and Polakowski, 2008). A majority of the post-socialist countries have attempted to apply policies that explicitly or implicitly support the allocation of care responsibilities within the family, but there are still considerable differences among them. Thus more than 80 percent of children aged three to five attended preschool in the Czech Republic in 2004, compared to less than 49 percent in Poland (Saxonberg and Szelewa, 2007, p. 357). Although the data on childcare availability in Russia are ambiguous, one could also include this country among those that cut financial support for this part of the public sector in the 1990s (Teplova, 2007).

Family life in Eastern Europe today takes place in a complex institutional setting that includes family legislation and the regulation of labor market relations, parental leave, and childcare provision. The analysis of welfare policies in contemporary Eastern Europe and Russia in the present volume takes into consideration the specifics of their development under state socialism. Several elements of welfare provision are discussed in more detail: interrelations between discursive norms on the one hand and the practices of social assistance and childcare provision in Russia on the other (Gradskova, Iarskaya-Smirnova and Romanov). The implementation of state policies toward families is explored in a more historical perspective (Zhidkova, Carlbäck) and examined through a juxtaposition of family policies and family practices (Kravchenko). The authors indentify continuity and change in legislative practices and in the construction and negotiation of social problems.

GENDER ASPECTS OF THE FAMILY

Gender aspects constitute the third important dimension of social transformation with regard to the family in Eastern Europe. Although the Eastern European state socialist regimes widely advertised their efforts to eliminate the patriarchal family order, one of the basic findings of feminist research in this area is that many elements of patriarchy remain. Why did the state socialist project of gender equality result in comparatively high degrees of traditionalism in popular attitudes and practices? To grasp this question, it is crucial to understand the idea then prevailing—that if only private property and its undemocratically distributed control over the means of production were abolished and a public system for the upbringing of children were introduced, the problem of the subordination of women to men, and children to parents, would be solved. Unlike Western feminist thinking, which from the 1970s onward was dominated by the idea of the social nature of gender and its key role in the construction of social inequalities, communist gender ideology from the 1917 Russian Revolution to 1991 was a blend of essentialist social outlooks that viewed the relationship between the sexes as naturally predetermined (Ashwin, 2000) on the one hand, and socially constructed, rooted in the mode of economic production, on the other. In fact, state socialist regimes did not eliminate patriarchy but transformed it into a system in which the state filled the role of a new kind of parental figure (Verdery, 1996) by keeping men out of the sphere of domesticity (Ashwin and Lytkina, 2004) and creating a contradictory mix of traditionalism and egalitarianism.

Other researchers have pointed to similar conflicting features in gender relations in the region. On the one hand, the state socialist regimes actively brought women into the public sphere by providing them with education, full-time employment, and public social assistance. On the other, gender relations in the private sphere remained unreconstructed and thus created the double burden, one of the key notions in the theory of a gender contract based on the realities of working mothers (Zdravomyslova et al., 2009, pp. 13–14; Zdravomyslova and Temkina, 2006). These contradictions under state socialism between public and private spheres, and women's inability to challenge the power of men in the former and induce them to accept more responsibility in the latter, may be related in part to the fact that the dominant state-imposed ideology remained unchallenged by the international women's movement (Pascall and Kwak, 2005).

At the same time, it is important to note that there were substantial differences in the gender regimes of the state socialist countries. Thus different governments acted differently, for example, when it came to policies aimed at promoting increased birth rates. The former East Germany and Hungary did so by providing generous allowances for parental leave, while others, such as the regimes in the USSR in the 1930s–1950s or in Romania after World War II, used punitive measures such as criminalizing abortion. Other examples of differentiation include divergent attitudes toward divorced women and single mothers (Funk and Mueller, 1993, p. 9) and the significant diversity of family practices and policies among different ethnic and religious groups (Pilkington and Yemelianova, 2003; Sorokina, 2011;

Stewart, 2001; Temkina, 2008). Recent scholarship has also discovered social and generational differences in attitudes toward reproduction and intimacy (Rotkirch, 2004; Semenova, 2002). Studies of sexuality in particular have shown that, in spite of the absence of a sexual revolution in the USSR, Soviet generations growing up in the 1970s and afterward expressed the importance of sexual pleasure and demonstrated diminishing gender differences in sexual experiences (Rotkirch, 2004).

As for the most recent trends in research on gender relations in Eastern Europe and Russia, the situation of "working mothers" in the new market economy environment has been elucidated recently by scholars who point to the obvious difficulties women experience in balancing productive and reproductive activities (Ashwin, 2006; Saxonberg and Sirovatka, 2007; Saxonberg and Szelewa, 2007). New discourses have replaced old ideological models by emphasizing ideals of motherhood for the sake of the nation instead of enhancing the image of the professional woman (Zhurzhenko, 2008: Rivkin-Fish, 2010). If before it was emancipatory ideals that pressured women to work outside the home, today we see women compelled to work simply in order to survive (Funk and Mueller, 1993; Haney, 2002; Zhurzhenko, 2008). Furthermore, studies of long-term changes and continuities in family policies and practices in the region have challenged any simplistic dichotomy between the socialist past and the capitalist present (Haney, 2002, pp. 237–238; Olah, 2003).

Gender research on the family in Eastern Europe has expanded into new areas. Thus studies on masculinity and fatherhood have addressed the stressful situation of men faced with expectations of being main breadwinners and difficulties in acquiring a caring role in the family (Kay, 2006; Zdravomyslova et al., 2009; Zdravomyslova, 2006). Two more issues that have long been central to Western gender research, namely the problem of domestic violence (Johnson, 2009) and limits of heteronormativity (Vorontsov, 2004), have caught the attention of scholars of Eastern Europe.

Gender structures and dynamics are inherent in studies on the family and are therefore addressed in all chapters of this volume. In their discussion of gendered aspects of family policies and family life, they focus on regional specifics with respect not only to the forms of gender inequality but also to local attempts to overcome it. With regard to the unequal distribution of power resources in public and private life between men and women, special attention is given to the mechanisms through which the role of fathers is constructed in various aspects of family life—in the internalization of fatherhood norms (Municio-Larsson) and their translation into attitudes and demands for policy reform (Carlbäck), in the process of deciding whether to have children (Rotkirch), and in changing family care responsibilities (Sätre). The role of gender norms in the process of creating national and individual identity is discussed through analyses of narrated life stories in Latvia (Runcis) and Hungary (Asztalos Morell). Furthermore, a study of women's biographical texts (Farhan) discusses the German experience in restructuring the gender order at a pivotal period in its recent history.

INTRODUCING THE VOLUME

The studies in this book are based on a variety of sources. However, as the primary materials for their analyses, most of the authors use personal documents of various kinds such as letters, collected life stories, interviews, Internet forum entries, and memories. Unlike official papers, personal documents afford a look at the family through the eyes of its own members, something that allows the scholar to find "invisible" but still important components of family practices such as stereotypes, motivations, and strategies. Since part of the book is devoted to family policies and practices during the period of state socialism, we feel the following observation by two Estonian scholars to be highly relevant:

> The turn towards autobiographical sources such as life stories, memories, letters, and diaries has taken place in areas where the accessibility of documentary historical sources has been difficult, where the sources have become fragmented or destroyed, or where they are one-sided and biased. (Hinrikus and Köresaar, 2004, p. 30)

It is true that the use of these sources does not always allow for a study of more far-reaching societal processes, but it certainly makes it possible to include different voices (Bertaux et al., 2004, pp. 19–20; Pet and Waaldijk, 2006, p. 19) and to approach the historical or contemporary family in its full complexity.

To organize these theoretically and methodologically diverse contributions, we have grouped them into two parts. The first part includes studies that tackle the overarching goals of the book by presenting a critical analysis of family norms, an account of discourse on gender roles and state intervention in family life, and finally, a discussion of patterns of reproduction and the provision of public childcare. All this is done from a historical perspective, providing the reader with an analysis of family practices and policies of the decades preceding the collapse of socialism in the region.

The second part of the volume tackles the same goals, only now in the light of more recent times, and reflects the political, economic, social, and ideological transformation that the region underwent from the late 1980s to the early 1990s. Still, most of the contributions to this second part also place the present-day family-related phenomena into a broader historical context.

In the introduction thus far, we have pointed out the contribution of the present volume to the corpus of existing knowledge of family patterns, social welfare, and the construction and reproduction of gender relations. Below, the content of the book is presented in more detail in order to highlight the multiple connections between different chapters across time and space and shed light on how the authors deal with different aspects of the same issues, the methods they use, and the results they have achieved. Several chapters offer a deeper understanding of how family-related policies have been shaped and subsequently restructured and the role they have played in the lives of families with children. This theme covers a rather long period of time, from the mid-1940s to recent years. In her chapter on attitudes in society and politics on marriage and the family in mid-twentieth-century Soviet Russia, Helene Carlbäck examines how both ordinary citizens and politicians regarded some pertinent issues of lone motherhood against the background of more general discourses on motherhood and fatherhood. She identifies a number of dominant yet competing discourses on children's rights, women's morals, and men's responsibilities and argues that some of the discourses differed from many parts of Europe at the time, while others were similar to them. With a similar ambition to relate policy framework attitudes and everyday practices, Maija Runcis discusses the degree to which family privacy could be a shelter against the Sovietization of Latvia after the establishment of the Soviet regime. In an attempt to sustain individual national identity, in their life stories Latvian women construct a traditional Latvian lifestyle and ideal of the Latvian woman strongly contrasting with official communist images of the time. These two analyses are followed by that of Olga Khazova, who demonstrates how the revision of family law in Russia and the Baltic states after 1991 has led to the creation of two very different trends—the preservation of a liberal approach to marriage and the family on the one hand (Russia), and the restoration of religious marriage as a means of overcoming the Soviet legacy on the other (the Baltic states). The author emphasizes that these tendencies reflect the wider institutional context in which the legislation was redesigned. This context needs to be taken into consideration in the analysis of any phenomenon related to marriage, divorce, family property, and spousal maintenance.

A comparative conclusion on the provision of family support in Soviet and Russian history can be drawn from a reading of Dalia Leinarte's chapter on Lithuania from the 1940s to the 1960s and Elena Iarskaya-Smirnova and Pavel Romanov's chapter on contemporary Russia. The authors analyze the process through which public policies are being implemented in two very different contexts, focusing on inter-institutional responsibilities (Leinarte) and social work activities on the local level (Iarskaya-Smirnova and Romanov). These chapters discuss the stigmatization of specific social policy target groups in Soviet Lithuania and contemporary Russia, respectively. They point out that social norms assigned to needy families in general and lone parents in particular may cause policies aimed at elevating the recipients from poverty to backfire when they are implemented. Thus Leinarte demonstrates that the provision of financial allowances to single mothers and large families encountered institutional challenges in the form of bureaucracy and incompetence. More importantly, however, this assistance contradicted traditional family norms, according to which these types of family failed to live up to acceptable moral standards. This was something that in fact deprived them of their right to public support. Iarskaya-Smirnova and Romanov in turn stress the importance of the "un/worthy citizen" discourse and its influence in determining the effectiveness of social assistance to poor female-led families.

Elena Zhidkova and Zhanna Kravchenko examine the extent to which public policies intervened in the private lives of families. On the basis of archival materials of the Soviet Communist Party and the trade unions, Zhidkova examines various organizations at the lower levels, including enterprises, that participated locally in the implementation of family policy in the 1960s. This policy sought to mobilize citizens to exert moral control and distribute welfare. Through the prism of everyday family life, Kravchenko examines the role of institutionalized public financial transfers and services to Russian families in the first few years of the twenty-first century. By focusing on the ways explicit forms of public control become internalized by public and private actors, these two chapters are particularly important for scholarship on family protection. On the basis of publicly discussed philosophical and moral principles, Zhidkova focuses on changes in cultural and social patterns during the "Thaw" period in the Soviet Union (the late 1950s and early 1960s) and shows how these changes contributed to a crystallization of ideas on the new Soviet citizen and family norms. Although Kravchenko does not focus specifically on public debate, she reveals that the normalizing structure of contemporary family policy lacks moral monitoring of the reconciliation of work and care, which allows for considerable variation in everyday family practices.

Two chapters in this volume explicitly address current childbearing and childcare norms and practices. Thus Anna Rotkirch examines perceptions of the optional timing and number of childbirths among Russian women, key elements in the construction of adulthood and femininity. The author asserts that reproductive norms in Russia differ substantially from those in the West: the orientation toward motherhood is rather strong, and there is a discrepancy between the desired and actual number of children. While most of the mothers have only one child per life course, the two-child norm that prevails today can be instrumental in solving the problem of fertility rates falling over the past several decades. Gradskova explores the transformation of discourse on parenthood and early childcare and education by looking at pedagogical publications and Internet discussions among parents about various issues of day-care services. The author argues that the pedagogical discourses in post-Soviet Russia have preserved a certain uniformity from the Soviet era, while the ways in which parents interpret advantages and disadvantages of public preschool centers are more diversified and depend largely on differing understandings of children's well-being. The authors indicate that shared parenthood and family-friendly policies are important in order to secure the well-being of children.

Both chapters cut across all three goals of the volume, relating the aspirations and practices of mothers to the existing framework of family and demographic policies, meaning economic incentives for childbearing embedded in the most recent policy initiatives and the scope of childcare provision. Gender norms with regard to parenting are also discussed at length. Rotkirch, for example, emphasizes the mother-centered focus of the discourse on childrearing: male partners were almost completely absent in the discussion of factors determining when and how many children a woman would have. Similarly, Gradskova reveals that only women, as the most involved parents, participated in the discussions on early childcare and education, thus reconfirming the norm of a symbiotic relationship between mother and child.

Several contributions further develop an understanding of gender policies in the sphere of work and care under state socialism. Ildikó Asztalos Morell examines differences in the experiences of Hungarian men and women occupied in family farming prior to the collectivization of private farms and after their integration into co-operative labor organizations during the period between 1959 and 1968. The author elucidates how the project of collectivization integrated the task of emancipating women with the aim of radically transforming the traditional peasant family household. The analysis of the oral history material gives new arguments for a discussion on "the emancipation of women" under state socialism. As a matter of fact, the attempts to free women from patriarchal dependency by integrating them into the labor force resulted in a loss of autonomy and the creation of new inequalities that were concealed by a formally equal gender contract. Farhan's study focuses on how women in the former GDR have reflected upon their own life stories through the prism of the then-dominant gender norms that affirmed women's right to gainful employment and at the same time gave them the main responsibilities for childcare. Like Asztalos Morell, Farhan chooses an important historical moment of radical social transformation in the reunification of Germany and uncovers how sometimes conflicting norms and values, such as the gender contract of the working mother on the one hand and the housewife ideal on the other, are being re-evaluated in a situation marked by radical social change. Like Asztalos Morell, Farhan pays attention to women's agency and shows that the authorities' attempt to "emancipate" women in the former GDR is remembered by many women as contributing to their autonomy.

By looking at their objects of study from a contemporary perspective, three of the authors—Aino Saarinen, Ingegerd Municio-Larsson, and Ann-Mari Sätre—note that the gender order established during state socialism is still quite resilient despite substantial institutional changes. In their respective chapters they look at interpersonal violence (Saarinen), childcare responsibilities after divorce (Municio-Larsson), and entrepreneurial activity (Sätre). Saarinen cross-examines official documents used in correspondence between the Russian Federation and the UN, reports on violence against women conducted by international organizations, and finally, the results from a survey carried out with representatives of crisis centers in northwest Russia. On the basis of these documents, the author shows that contemporary official political discourse on violence against women in Russia has distorted and concealed the scope and depth of the problem. Instead, the author finds, that discourse has created a very different gender interpretation of demographic problems with regard to men and women at the price of women's reproductive rights and right to safety and personal integrity. The chapter highlights Russian policymakers' inattentiveness to the problem of domestic violence.

Municio-Larsson studies the discursive context of social change in Estonia and Latvia, focusing on how family rights and obligations of divorced parents of minor children, as well as other family members, are formulated after the marriage is dissolved. Based on interview materials, the analysis reveals very different ways of constructing the rights and obligations of women and men. While the responsibilities of the mother are seen as permanent irrespective of her relationship to a male partner, those of the father appear to be interchangeable. The former is expected to resume full responsibility for care and economic support of the children, while the latter is given the right to move on to new relationships, and his role as a father may subsequently be taken up by his former wife's new partner or other members of an extended family network.

Finally, Sätre looks at persisting gender norms that ascribe tasks of work and care to women and free men, in their role as main breadwinners, from domestic responsibilities. Sätre examines how these norms are being implicitly challenged by individuals employed in the rising sector of private enterprise. The author explores new aspects of how masculinity is constructed in the context of a highly competitive market economy, an issue which has been studied relatively little in contemporary research on gender and family. This chapter is also an important contribution because it illuminates the prospects for new market-based forms of care provision that can potentially relieve women's double burden.

Although certain themes are central to the contributions, with cross-references and intersections in the theoretical and empirical treatment of different issues, the authors demonstrate how aspects of the organization of everyday life and the design and implementation of policies become interwoven in the fabric of the family and parenthood, with gender norms as the structuring threads. All chapters relating to the domain of social policy demonstrate that objectives, policy implementation, and the process of provision and reporting are necessarily dependent on how normative family life is conceptualized in the public discourse. The chapters dealing with the social construction of gender norms insist that studying how these are actually enacted in everyday life-partnership and parenting is essential to understanding the transformation/continuity of the roles of men and women in contemporary society.

We hope that the interdisciplinary character of the present volume and its attempt to introduce a comparative perspective will bring us closer to understanding similarities and differences between central components of family life before and after the fall of state socialism in Eastern Europe and Russia.

References

Aivazova, Svetlana. 1998. *Russkie zhenshchiny v labirinte ravnopraviia* (Russian women in the labyrinth of equality). Moscow: RIK Rusanova.

Ashwin, Sarah. 2000. *Gender, State and Society in Soviet and Post-Soviet Russia*. London: Routledge.

———, ed. 2006. *Adapting to Russia's New Labour Market: Gender and Employment Behaviour*. London and New York: Routledge.

Ashwin, Sarah, and Tatyana Lytkina. 2004. "Men in Crisis in Russia: The Role of Domestic Marginalization." *Gender and Society* 18, no. 2: 189–206.

Asztalos Morell, Ildikó, Helene Carlbäck, Madeleine Hurd, and Sara Rastbäck, eds. 2005. *Gender Transitions in Russia and Eastern Europe*. Eslöv, Sweden: Gondolin.

Barr, Nicholas. 1994. "Income Transfers: Social Security." In *Labour Markets and Social Policy in Central and Eastern Europe: The Transition and Beyond*, ed. Nicholas Barr, 192–225. Washington, DC: World Bank.

Bertaux, Daniel, Paul Thompson, and Anna Rotkirch, eds. 2004. *On Living through Soviet Russia*. New York and London: Routledge.

Björnberg, Ulla, and Jürgen Sass. 1997. *Families with Small Children in Eastern and Western Europe*. Aldershot, UK: Ashgate.

Borowczyk, Ewa. 1986. "State Social Policy in Favour of the Family in East European Countries." *International Social Security Review* 39, no. 2: 164–182.

Bucher, Hansjoerg, and Ralf Mai. 2005. *Depopulation and its Consequences for the Regions of Europe*. Strasbourg: Council of Europe.

Buckley, Mary. 1989. *Women and Ideology in the Soviet Union*. Hemel Hempstead, UK: Harvester Wheatsheaf.

Carlbäck, Helene. 2005. "Tracing the Roots of Early Soviet Russian Family Laws." In *Gender Transitions in Russia and Eastern Europe*, eds. Ildikó Asztalos Morell, Helene Carlbäck, Madeleine Hurd, and Sara Rastbäck, 69–84. Eslöv, Sweden: Gondolin.

Chesnais, Jean-Claude. 1992. *The Demographic Transition*. Oxford: Clarendon Press.

Coleman, David, ed. 1996. *Europe's Population in the 1990s*. Oxford: Oxford University Press.

Deacon, Bob. 2001. "Eastern European Welfare States: The Impact of the Politics of Globalization." *Journal of European Social Policy* 10, no. 2: 146–161.

Fajth, Gaspar. 1999. "Social Security in a Rapidly Changing Environment: The Case of the Post-Communist Transformation." *Social Policy and Administration* 33, no. 4: 416–436.

Funk, Nanette, and Magda Mueller, eds. 1993. *Gender Politics and Post-Communism: Reflections from Eastern Europe and the Former Soviet Union*. New York: Routledge.

Gal, Susan, and Gail Kligman. 2000. *The Politics of Gender after Socialism: A Comparative-Historical Essay*. Princeton, NJ: Princeton University Press.

George, Vic. 1991. "Social Security in the USSR." *International Social Security Review* 44, no. 4: 47–64.

George, Vic, and Nick Manning. 1980. *Socialism, Social Welfare and the Soviet Union*. London: Routledge.

Goldman, Wendy. 1993. *Women, the State and Revolution: Soviet Family Policy and Social Life, 1917–1936*. Cambridge: Cambridge University Press.

Gradskova, Youlia. 1997. "Novaia ideologiia sem'i i ee osobennosti v Rossii" (The new ideology of the family and its peculiarities in Russia). *Obshchestvennye nauki i sovremennost'* 2: 181–185.

Haney, Lynne Allison. 2002. *Inventing the Needy: Gender and the Politics of Welfare in Hungary*. Berkeley: University of California Press.

Haney, Lynne, and Lisa Pollard, eds. 2003. *Families of a New World: Gender, Politics, and State Development in a Global Context*. New York and London: Routledge.

Hantrais, Linda. 2006. "Living as a Family in Europe." In *Policy Implications of Changing Family Formation: Study Prepared for the European Population Conference 2005*, eds. Linda Hantrais, Dimiter Philipov, and Francesco C. Billari, 11–18. Population Studies, no. 49, Strasbourg: Council of Europe Publishing.

Hinrikus, Rutt, and Ene Köresaar. 2004. "A Brief Overview of Life History Collection and Research in Estonia." In *She Who Remembers, Survives: Interpreting Estonian Women's Post-Soviet Life Histories*, eds. Tiina Kirss, Ene Köresaar, and Marju Lauristin, 19–34. Tartu, Estonia: Tartu University Press.

Inglehart, Ronald. 1990. *Culture Shift in Advanced Industrial Society*. Princeton, NJ: Princeton University Press.

Johnson, Janet. 2009. *Gender Violence in Russia: The Politics of Feminist Intervention*. Bloomington: Indiana University Press.

Juang, Linda P., Rainer K. Silbereisen, and Wiesner Margit. 1999. "Predictors of Leaving Home in Young Adults Raised in Germany: A Replication of a 1991 Study." *Journal of Marriage and the Family* 61: 505–515.

van de Kaa, Dirk. 1996. *The Ideas of a Second Demographic Transition in Industrialized Countries*. Paper presented at the Sixth Welfare Policy Seminar of the National Institute of Population and Social Security, Tokyo, Japan, January 29, 1996, http://www.ipss.go.jp/webj-ad/WebJournal.files/population/2003_4/Kaa.pdf.

Katus, Kalev, Allan Puur, Asta Poldma, and Luule Sakkeus. 2007. "First Union Formation in Estonia, Latvia, and Lithuania: Patterns Across Countries and Gender." *Demographic Research* 17: 247–300.

Kay, Rebecca. 2006. *Men in Contemporary Russia: The Fallen Heroes of Post-Soviet Change*. Aldershot, UK, and Burlington, VT: Ashgate.

Kelly, Catriona. 2007. *Children's World: Growing Up in Russia, 1890–1991*. New Haven: Yale University Press.

Kis, Oksana. 2005. "Choosing without Choice: Predominant Models of Femininity in Contemporary Ukraine." In *Gender Transitions in Russia and Eastern Europe*, eds. Ildikó Asztalos Morell, Helene Carlbäck, Madeleine Hurd, and Sara Rastbäck, 105–136. Eslöv, Sweden: Gondolin.

Manning, Nick. 2004. "Diversity and Change in Pre-Accession Central and Eastern Europe since 1989." *Journal of European Social Policy* 14, no. 3: 211–232.

Ohlander, Ann-Sofie. 1992. "The Invisible Child? The Struggle over Social Democratic Family Policy." In *Creating Social Democracy: A Century of the Social Democratic Labour Party in Sweden*, eds. Klaus Misgeld, Karl Molin, and Klas Åmark, 213–236. University Park: Pennsylvania State University Press.

Olah, Livia. 2003. "Gendering Fertility: Second Births in Sweden and Hungary." *Population Research and Policy Review* 22, no. 2: 171–200.

Pascall, Gillian, and Nick Manning. 2000. "Gender and Social Policy: Comparing Welfare States in Central and Eastern Europe and the Former Soviet Union." *Journal of European Social Policy* 10, no. 3: 240–266.

Pascall, Jillian, and Anna Kwak. 2005. *Gender Regimes and Transformation in Central and Eastern Europe*. Bristol: Polity Press.

Pető, Andrea, and Berteke Waaldijk. 2006. *Teaching with Memories: European Women's Histories in International and Interdisciplinary Classrooms*. Galway: University of Ireland.

Philipov, Dimiter. 2002. *Fertility in Times of Discontinuous Societal Change: The Case of Central and Eastern Europe*. Max Planck Institute for Demographic Research. Working Paper 2002–024, June 2002, http://www.demogr.mpg.de/papers/working/wp-2002-024.pdf.

Philipov, Dimiter, and Jürgen Dorbritz. 2003. *Demographic Consequences of Economic Transition in Countries of Central and Eastern Europe*. Population Studies, No. 39, Strasbourg: Council of Europe Publishing, May 2003, http://www.coe.int/t/e/social_cohesion/population/Publications/index.asp.

Pilkington, Hilary, and Galina Yemelianova, eds. 2003. *Islam in Soviet and Post-Soviet Russia*. London and New York: Routledge.

Rivkin-Fish, Michele. 2010. "Pronatalism, Gender Politics, and the Renewal of Family Support in Russia: Toward a Feminist Anthropology of 'Maternity Capital.'" *Slavic Review* 69, no. 3: 701–725.

Robila, Michaela, ed. 2004a. *Families in Eastern Europe: Contemporary Perspectives in Family Research*. Vol. 5. Amsterdam: Elsevier JAI.

———. 2004b. "Families in Eastern Europe: Context, Trends and Variations." In *Families in Eastern Europe: Contemporary Perspectives in Family Research*, ed. Michaela Robila, 5:1–14. Amsterdam: Elsevier JAI.

Rotkirch, Anna. 2004. "What Kind of Sex Can You Talk About? Aquiring Sexual Knowledge in Three Soviet Generations." In *On Living through Soviet Russia*, eds. Daniel Bertaux, Paul Thompson, and Anna Rotkirch, 93–119. London and New York: Routledge.

Rotkirch, Anna, Anna Temkina, and Elena Zdravomyslova. 2007. "Who Helps the Degraded Housewife? Comments on Vladimir Putin's Demographic Speech." *European Journal of Women's Studies* 14: 349–357.

Rys, Vladimir. 2001. "Transition Countries of Central Europe Entering the European Union: Some Social Protection Issues." *International Social Security Review* 54, no. 2–3: 177–189.

Saxonberg, Steven, and Tomas Sirovatka. 2007. "The Re-Familisation of the Czech Family Policy and its Causes." *International Review of Sociology* 17, no. 2: 319–341.

Saxonberg, Steven, and Dorota Szelewa. 2007. "The Continuing Legacy of the Communist Legacy? The Development of Family Policies in Poland and the Czech Republic." *Social Politics: International Studies in Gender, State and Society* 14: 351–379.
Semenova, Victoria. 2002. "Two Cultural Worlds in One Family—The Historical Context in Russian Society." *History of the Family* 7: 259–280.
Sobotka, Tomás. 2008. "The Diverse Faces of the Second Demographic Transition in Europe." *Demographic Research* 19: 171–224.
Sorokina, Sofia. 2011. "Nadzor ili besprizornost'? K probleme gosudarstvennogo paternalisma v otnoshenii korennykh narodov severa" (Supervision or neglect? On the problem of state paternalism in relation to the indigenous peoples of the north). *Zhurnal issledovanii sotsial'noi politiki (Journal of social policy studies)* 9, no. 1: 79–98.
Stewart, Michael. 2001. "Communist Roma Policy 1945–1989 as Seen through the Hungarian Case." In *Between Past and Future: The Roma of Central and Eastern Europe*, ed. Will Guy, 71–92. Hatfield, UK: University of Hertfordshire Press.
Szelewa, Dorota, and Michal Polakowski. 2008. "Who Cares? Changing Patterns of Childcare in Central and Eastern Europe." *Journal of European Social Policy* 18, no. 2: 115–131.
Szivós, Péter, and Cristina Guidici. 2004. *Demographic Implications of Social Exclusion in Central and Eastern Europe: Population Studies, No. 46*. Strasbourg: Council of Europe.
Tahlberg, Sara. 2003. *Demographic Patterns in Europe: A Review of Austria, Germany, the Netherlands, Estonia, Latvia and Lithuania*, http://www.framtidsstudier.se/filebank/files/20051201$133737$fil$2Ti7LOh51kI7NHnB7T9u.pdf.
Temkina, Anna. 2008. *Seksual'naia zhizn' zhenshchiny—mezhdu podchineniem i svobodoi* (Sexual life of women: Between submission and freedom). St. Petersburg: Izdatel'stvo Evropeiskogo universiteta.
Teplova, Tatyana. 2007. "Welfare State Transformation, Childcare, and Women's Work in Russia." *Social Politics: International Studies in Gender, State and Society* 14, no. 3: 284–322.
Therborn, Göran. 2004. *Between Sex and Power. Family in the World, 1990–2000*. London: Routledge.
Titkow, Anna, and Danuta Duch. 2004. "The Polish Family: Always an Institution?" In *Families in Eastern Europe: Contemporary Perspectives in Family Research, Vol. 5*, ed. Michaela Robila, 69–86. Amsterdam: Elsevier JAI.
UNICEF. 1999. *Zhenshchiny v perekhodnyi period. Regional'nyi monitoringovyi doklad No. 6.* (Women in transition. Regional monitoring report No. 6). Florence: UNICEF.
———. 2001. *A Decade of Transition, Regional Monitoring Report, No. 8*. Florence: UNICEF Innocenti Research Centre.
Varsa, Eszter. 2010. "Gender, 'Race'/Ethnicity, Class and the Institution of Child Protection in Hungary, 1949–1956." PhD diss., Central European University, Budapest, Hungary. http://www.etd.ceu.hu/2011/gphvae01.pdf (accessed May 20, 2011).

Verdery, Katherine. 1996. *What Was Socialism, and What Comes Next?* Princeton, NJ: Princeton University Press.

Voirin, Michel. 1993. "Social Security in Central and Eastern European Countries: Continuity and Change." *International Social Security Review* 46, no. 1: 27–65.

Vorontsov, Dmitrii. 2004. "'Semeinaia zhizn'—eto ne dlia nas': mify i tsennosti muzhskikh gomoseksualnykh par" ("Family life is not for us:" Myths and values of male homosexual couples). In *Semeinye uzy: modeli dlia sborki (Family bonds: Models to assemble)*, ed. Sergei Oushakine, 576–607. Moscow: Novoe Literaturoe Obozrenie.

Zdravomyslova, Elena, Anna Rotkirch, and Anna Temkina. 2009. "Vvedenie. Sozdanie privatnosti kak sfery zaboty, liubvi i naemnogo truda" (Introduction). In *Novyi byt v sovremennoi Rossii: gendernye issledovaniia povsednevnosti* (The new way of life in contemporary Russia: Gender studies of the everyday), eds. Elena Zdravomyslova, Anna Rotkirch, and Anna Temkina, 7–32. St. Petersburg: EUSPb.

Zdravomyslova, Elena, and Anna Temkina. 2006. "Istoriia i sovremennost'. Gendernyi poriadok v Rossii" (The past and the present: Gender order in Russia). In *Gender dlia 'chainikov'* (Gender for dummies), 55–84. Moscow: Zven'ia.

Zdravomyslova, Olga. 2006. "Sem'ia—iz proshlogo v budushchee" (The family: Out of the past into the future). In *Gender dlia 'chainikov'* (Gender for dummies), 141–160. Moscow: Zven'ia.

Zhurzhenko, Tatiana. 2004a. "Families in Ukraine: Between Postponed Modernization, Neo-Familialism and Economic Survival." In *Families in Eastern Europe: Contemporary Perspectives in Family Research*, ed. Michaela Robila, 5: 187–209. Amsterdam: Elsevier JAI.

———. 2004b. "Staraia ideologiia novoii sem'i: demograficheskii natsionalizm Rossii i Ukrainy" (Old ideology of the new family: Demographic nationalism in Russia and Ukraine). In *Semeinye uzy: modeli dlia sborki (Family bonds: Models to assemble)*, ed. Sergei Oushakine, 268–296. Moscow: Novoe Literaturoe Obozrenie.

———. 2008. *Gendernye rynki Ukrainy: politicheskaia ekonomiia natsional'nogo stroitel'stva* (Ukraine's gender markets: The political economy of nation-building). Vilnius, Lithuania: EGU.

PART I
1940s–1980s
THE FAMILY AS A "BASIC UNIT OF SOCIALIST SOCIETY"

CHAPTER 1

Lone Motherhood in Soviet Russia in the Mid-20th Century—In a European Context

HELENE CARLBÄCK

INTRODUCTION

For a long time the phenomenon of unmarried mothers and children born out of wedlock was excluded from the dominant discourse on motherhood and relations between men and women. According to this discourse, sexuality was to be practiced only within marriage. Still, as early as the late eighteenth century, practices began to change in Europe. The number of extramarital births grew considerably in the following centuries, a change in demographic behavior that scholars predominantly attribute to the vast migration processes taking place in connection with industrialization, urbanization, and the restructuring of agricultural life (Laslett et al., 1980; Therborn, 2004, pp. 148–150).[1] It must be stressed, however, that demographic change occurred at different rates in different regions of Europe. In most parts of Western Europe, the industrialization and urbanization process developed during a relatively protracted period of at least a century or more. However, in many parts of Eastern Europe, as a result of the state socialist project of forced industrialization and agricultural collectivization, this process was drastically accelerated.

Shifting constructions of unmarried or "lone" motherhood[2] have influenced social and family policies in different ways in different European countries. For example, in Britain and the Netherlands, which used to have relatively few unmarried mothers, the negative attitude in public discourse on lone mothers was accompanied by a tightfisted and manifestly moralistic state policy (Lewis and Welshman, 1997). By contrast, the Scandinavian countries adopted a more generous welfare policy toward unmarried mothers as early as the beginning of the twentieth century. Furthermore, Sweden's policy sought to make biological fathers take more responsibility for their children born out of wedlock (Elgán, 1990, pp. 491–493). The statistical evidence helps explain that ambition, for during the early twentieth century, Swedish illegitimacy rates were among the highest in Europe (Bergman and Hobson, 2002).

At the beginning of the twentieth century, Russia, like most of Eastern Europe, had few children born out of wedlock[3]—less than 3 percent as compared to 11 percent in Sweden. Early age at first marriage and the high marriage rates explain this aspect of demographical behavior. By the 1950s, however, circumstances had changed drastically. The figure for children born out of wedlock in Soviet Russia rose to an average of 24 percent in 1945. As with other countries involved in World War II, in Russia many of the extramarital births were due to the vast loss of young and middle-aged men (Zhiromskaya, 2001, p. 240). Moreover, changes in marriage legislation that allowed men to avoid the consequences of extramarital relations created a new social group of "lone mothers."[4] Before 1944 an unmarried woman could ask the court to establish the paternity of her child, a process that often went in her favor regardless of whether she lived in a steady relationship with the biological father or had more casual relations with him.

In this chapter I will analyze discourses on lone motherhood in Soviet Russia in the mid-twentieth century. The issue of lone motherhood has caught the interest of scholars since the 1970s, due to its potential for revealing discourse and norms about a group considered to have been outcasts in the traditional family context. Lone mothers in Soviet Russia have been researched to a lesser degree, and so this chapter aims to elucidate some aspects of this problem.

Background

The new Soviet government in post-revolutionary Russia started off in 1917 by passing a series of laws on various issues. The legislation on the family and marriage reflected an ambition to modernize Russia and place it on a par with more advanced European societies of the time such as France and Germany (Antokolskaia, 2003). Modernization was achieved by making marital matters basically a private issue, especially when it came to decisions about starting and ending marriages, decisions that lawmakers felt ought to be taken by the couples themselves without interference from the state or the church. Thus it became easier to marry and easier to divorce. The "semifeudal"[5] social system that placed family matters under the authority of the Orthodox Church was abolished; procedures for registering marriages were simplified and individualized, the minimum requirement being registration with the civil authorities. A further sign of this modernizing ambition was putting gender relations on an equal footing. This manifested itself in the abolishment of the centuries-old exclusive right of the man in the family to social and economic power over his wife and children (Carlbäck, 2005).

However, on a few legal positions the Soviet Russian regime of the 1920s went far ahead of most of Europe, trying to prepare for a more advanced stage of development—communist society. This was expressed in a law provision that placed children born out of wedlock on a legal par with children born within marriage. Soviet Russia differed from most of Europe by, for instance, simplifying the divorce procedure to the point that it was popularly called "postcard divorce"[6] and recognizing cohabitation as legally valid unions comparable to officially registered marriage. The result of the new legislation was a drastic drop in the number of registered marriages and a sharp increase in divorces (Aralovets, 2009, pp. 96–97; Goldman, 1993, pp. 297–298; Vishnevskii, 2006, pp. 129–130).

Accordingly, although a decree issued in 1944 made an about-face from the revolutionary legislative norms by severely complicating the process of divorce and providing that only officially registered marriage would guarantee fathers' rights and obligations vis-à-vis their children, the idea of marriage as such had already lost much of its pre-revolutionary value. It can therefore be assumed that the 1944 decree did not provide the degree of marriage stability the authorities intended, even if the number of divorces fell considerably. People, mostly men, left their partners for new ones, but without officially divorcing and remarrying. To my knowledge, no reliable statistics on this phenomenon have been published yet in Russia, but efforts have been made to estimate its extent (Vishnevskii, 2006, pp. 104–105).

Consequently, it is hard to say to what degree the increase in the number of children born out of wedlock really reflected a corresponding increase in the number of "lone" mothers. We do not know how many parents were living together but not registered as married. According to the 1944 decree on marriage and the family, biological fathers were not registered as such on the child's birth certificate unless they were officially married to the mother. Although it may not be possible to know the exact number of women who raised their children alone, they existed, and their voices can be heard from historical sources such as citizens' letters to the authorities.

Contextualizing the study: Norms on motherhood and fatherhood
Asearly as the nineteenth century, "motherhood" had become the most significant denominator in the characterization of femininity in European discourse on the family and gender. Women were allotted the main responsibility for homemaking and for the care and upbringing of children, but legal

rules and public norms still gave men the ultimate say over material and educational matters for their children. The ideal family model in the nineteenth century and well into the twentieth presupposed the husband and father to be the sole breadwinner, although the practices of the vast majority of the population did not coincide with these ideals.

With the revolution in Russia in 1917, the Bolshevik rulers sought to create new norms and ideals. Legal rules on the family and marriage were influenced by ideas in, for instance, Aleksandra Kollontai's writing on women and motherhood. Family planning was regarded as crucial to women's emancipation, and thus abortion was legalized. Although Kollontai considered motherhood a natural thing for a woman to experience, women's right and duty to take part in gainful employment and other public endeavors was of extreme importance and was in no way to be infringed upon by traditional duties of motherhood that could easily be handed over to collectively run institutions (Ashwin, 2000; Clements, 1979; Rotkirch, 2008). This balanced women's reproductive and productive missions, but with time the Soviet regime gradually developed legal rules and produced public discourses that more explicitly enhanced the reproductive roles and tasks. Thus, for example, the 1936 amendment to the marriage and family law state introduced allowances for women after childbirth, and another in 1944 provided for honoring mothers of large families with medals and compensated them financially (Goldman, 1993; Schlesinger, 1949).

Hence the officially stated norms sought a certain re-naturalizing of the gender order, something that took place in an era when several states in Europe also introduced various measures on protecting and supporting mothers and children (Koven and Sonya, 1993). At the same time, however, because industrialization created an urgent demand for labor, Soviet women were strongly encouraged to enter the market in order to engage in waged work. Also, potential taboos on letting women into traditional male spheres had been removed by the widely proclaimed objective of the Communist Party and the state to emancipate women by giving them access to the public sphere of paid labor and social engagement (Goldman, 2001; Ilič, 1999).[7] Thus the "working mother" became a solid official norm that strongly influenced Soviet gender policies (Rotkirch, 2004). It would not be questioned in public discourse until perestroika in the 1980s (Attwood, 1999; Buckley, 1989).[8]

In comparison to research in Europe and elsewhere on the discourse and practice of motherhood and women's role in family life, fatherhood was a little-studied topic until the 1980s. Since then, however, a considerable number of books and articles have appeared. One prominent position in research on fatherhood has been the notion that as the status of motherhood was enhanced, the importance of fatherhood in European family life decreased. Thus, for example, fathers' authority as educators was downplayed (Gillis, 1997). As to the role of fathers in Russia, scholars have stressed its specifically weak position during Soviet times. Factors explaining a weakening of this role include "extended motherhood," in which members of the elder generation of women take care of their grandchildren, and the reduction of the father's role during the Soviet period (Chernova, 2008; Isupova and Kon, 2009; Rotkirch, 2001). Historically, this institution of fatherhood—weak in comparison to the *pater familias* tradition influential in, for example, German or French family norms—can also be traced back to the "Eastern European family pattern." This pattern is characterized by extended peasant families with generational power relations—that is, the young couple normally lives with the husband's family, where the elder generation is in a position of power (Hajnal, 1965; Laslett, 1983). Finally, two traditional pillars of male power within the family realm were demolished when private property was virtually abolished during the Soviet era and almost all women entered the labor market.

Discourses on Lone Mothers: Time Frames, Sources, and Themes

The time frame for my study is the 1950s and the early 1960s, a period that saw extensive law revision in Soviet Russia (Juviler, 1976). In this connection Soviet citizens were encouraged to voice their opinions on matters of marriage and family legislation.[9] Furthermore, this period is interesting for the purposes of this chapter, since it brought a degree of relaxation of the previously strict control of what topics could be exposed in the mass media, such as criticism of various everyday life aspects in society (Zubkova, 1998). The sources for my study are of three different kinds. First, I have done a selective reading of so-called citizens' letters (*pis'ma grazhdan*) to the law commissions of the USSR Supreme Soviet in the 1950s and 1960s. Since the demise of the Soviet Union, a considerable amount of research has focused on citizens' letter-writing as a communicative strategy and as a literary genre (Bogdanova, 2006; Fitzpatrick, 1996; Livshin et al., 2002). It is worth noting, however, that opinions on the family and marriage have not been examined in depth in this research. Thousands and thousands of letters are stored in a collection called "Suggestions from Citizens Regarding Marriage and Family Law" in the State Archives of the Russian

Federation (GARF) in Moscow. Reading through this vast number of documents to determine the frequency of topics and the social strata, profession, age, and location of the letter-writers presents obvious difficulties. Furthermore, the fact that many of the letters are handwritten makes it an even more laborious task, and even assuming that all the correspondence filed in archives is available, there is still no way of knowing whether every letter sent to the authorities has been preserved. Of assistance in my search for frequent discourses and typical topics were the recurring overviews of incoming letters compiled at the Supreme Soviet's "correspondence department" (*otdel pisem*), which provide some idea of the total number of the letters, indicate what topics were most frequent, and sometimes quote letters at length.

Second, I have used unpublished minutes of meetings with members of the above-mentioned law commissions that worked in different constellations from the late 1940s up until the early 1960s on revising the existing legislation on marriage and the family. The commissions of the Supreme Soviet were made up of people with legal training as well as of ordinary citizens, representatives of various state and party institutions, and the press.[10] The law on marriage and the family dated back to 1926, but it was amended and revised several times during the 1930s and 1940s.[11] The minutes of the commissions' meetings, stored in the GARF archives, were made accessible to researchers only in the 1990s. Finally, in order to identify public discourse controlled by the state, I have also read through the women's magazine *Rabotnitsa* (Female Worker) and the family journal *Sem'ia i shkola* (Family and School) for the period 1947–1970, as well as some other media publications such as the weekly journal on cultural and social issues *Literaturnaia gazeta* (Literary Gazette) and the law journal *Sovetskoe gosudarstvo i pravo* (The Soviet State and Justice).

In the letters there are two dominant themes. A majority are about *children of divorced parents* or *children born out of marriage*. Many writers address the heavy financial burden divorced men must bear for child support and others argue that the children of lone (unmarried) mothers should be morally and legally acknowledged on a par with other children. Letters pleading for lowering child support obligations were written predominantly by men, but a few also came from present wives complaining about the meager portion of the husbands' income left to the new family. Conversely, letters that brought up the problem of "fatherless" children from a legal and social viewpoint were written mainly by women. They were critical of the fact that the financial and other support that the state provided for these children[12] was less than what divorced men were paying for their children from former marriages. Increasingly over the years letters brought up the moral suffering of children who were not entitled to a legal father. Now and then men brought up the issue, albeit often as a more general matter of principle. With further respect to the gender of the letter writers, the proportion of female authors seems on the whole to have grown considerably over time, concurrently with the increased openness in society and the growing concern of the authorities for the issue of "fatherless children" and their lone mothers.

The second most important theme to be identified in the citizens' letters on marriage and the family is *divorce*. Here the authors complain about the complicated and costly divorce procedure, a result of the 1944 decree. In this study, however, I will deal solely with the theme of lone mothers and their children,[13] within which I have identified three dominant but competing discourses on "children's equal rights," "lone mothers' morals," and "fathers' responsibilities."

Children's Equal Rights

> Please forgive me, but I can no longer refrain from expressing my views on behalf of myself and hundreds of other Soviet women, the unmarried mothers. My child is two-and-a-half years old. The father deceived me, and as a result I am left alone with my child. He was "born illegitimately" and doesn't have a father registered on his birth certificate. So does this mean that my child was not really born in the USSR? Is there no article in the constitution stipulating that all citizens have equal rights? In real life we all know that there is no such thing as a child without a father. Please forgive me for my frankness, but I consider the current law a huge political mistake.[14]

This is an extract from a letter sent by an anonymous "Soviet woman" in 1951. It is fairly typical of those dealing with issues of restoring children's right to a father and thus to proper legal status as citizens. At this time in the early 1950s, however, criticism of existing laws was restricted to talks behind closed doors and letters not intended for publication.

A few years later, in 1953, the new post-Stalin leadership opened up the public space for talks on several hitherto silenced matters. The issue of lone mothers and children born out of wedlock had to wait longer to be exposed more broadly, but the issue surfaced publicly a few times in the following decade. It happened first in 1954–1955, when some press articles criticized the existing legislation for not letting children born out of marriage carry their fathers' name (Carlbäck, 2009, pp. 93–96), and then in the immediate aftermath of the Twentieth Congress of the Communist Party in the spring of 1956, when new Communist Party leader Nikita Khrushchev, with his "secret" speech, sought to de-Stalinize certain areas of politics and society. Thus in autumn 1956 the law journal *Sovetskoe gosudarstvo i pravo* published two articles calling for a substantial revision of the existing legislation on marriage and the family, one of them under the title "The Official Status of Illegitimate Children Must Change" (*Sovetskoe gosudarstvo i pravo*, 1956, no. 9, pp. 65–66). By this point the number of citizens' letters to the authorities with suggestions on marriage and the family law had increased significantly. A report from the correspondence department of the Supreme Soviet chancellery stated that the law commissions had received almost 8,000 letters in the first half of 1958 alone.[15] Furthermore, several other state institutions, as well as Communist Party organs, Soviet newspapers and journals, and various cultural and social dignitaries received letters on the same matter.

The next time the matter was brought up in the press, this time more widely, was in connection with the Twenty-second Communist Party Congress in 1961, in which the country's leadership declared it would consider popular opinion when taking political decisions on everyday matters. In contrast to some other parts of the press, the women's magazine *Rabotnitsa* and the family journal *Sem'ia i shkola* had been silent on the issue of lone mothers up until then, in spite of the fact that almost half of the readers' letters commented on the law on marriage and the family.[16] However, in the March 1961 issue of *Sem'ia i shkola*, the young lawyer and writer Arkadii Vaksberg told a story about Katia, a young mother who was abandoned by Sergei, the father of her child, and the negative attitudes that she encountered from colleagues and society (*Sem'ia i shkola*, 1961, no. 3, p. 40). Two years later Vaksberg wrote that "hundreds and hundreds" of readers had reacted to the story, with the overwhelming majority supporting the author's criticism of the existing legislation that deprived children the right to an acknowledged father. Now Vaksberg said Sergei had returned to Katia after an unhappy marriage. "Thus all's well that ends well?" the author asked. No, far from it, problems still remained. Due to the strict marriage law, Sergei had not managed to divorce his former wife. Consequently, although he had turned to the authorities claiming he was the father of Katia's child and was prepared to accept all the responsibilities involved, the child was not allowed to carry his name. Thus the birth certificate read "father unknown,"[17] all according to the 1944 decree

(*Sem'ia i shkola*, 1963, no. 2, p. 25). This open criticism of the 1944 legislation in *Rabotnitsa* was preceded by discussions within the Soviet authorities. Thus at a meeting with the Supreme Soviet law commission in 1959, a government legal expert emphasized that all children must carry their father's names: "Thereby the child will have a father;" there was a strong need for restoring "the earlier prevailing Leninist principle of full equality between children," he explained to the commission members.[18]

One widespread political discourse in Soviet Russia declared that it was the most democratic country in the world and defended the rights of its citizens according to the constitution, very much in contrast with its main Cold War adversary, the United States (especially concerning the suppressed civil rights of black people). We have already seen a letter in which a woman referred to the Soviet constitution to buttress her plea for children's right to a father. Among the writers there were also a few male authors who supported the case by using the discourse on citizens' rights:

> The younger generation must get access to the same rights; get the same upbringing and education. This requires that all children receive equal material and moral support. In the Soviet Union there ought not to be children who are illegitimately born, since in reality all children have a father, but the father is not held responsible.[19]

This discourse on children's civil rights often merged with a post-Stalin discourse on the need to return to Leninist principles, which was a forceful argument of the Khrushchev regime in various political and economic campaigns, since Lenin's ideas had been distorted during the Stalin regime. Similarly, a group of women from the city of Lvov demanded "the restoration of Leninist norms of full equality for all children and the equal distribution of responsibilities between both parents for supporting and raising their children."[20] Considering that most of the letters contained pleading for changed financial measures, leaning towards officially approved political discourses could well be regarded as a wise strategy.

LONE MOTHERS' MORALS

During the 1950s and 60s, the Supreme Soviet law commissions frequently discussed how to implement the principle of equal rights for children born outside and inside marriage. Several members of the commissions did not support a draft law that would return the country to the situation before 1944, when women "too easily could take men to court."²¹ The same attitude was expressed from the very start in several citizens' letters reacting to the marriage and family law. Thus in 1950 one man writes that previously, "before the really bad regulation was done away with in 1944, any woman who had given birth to a child was entitled to call any citizen the 'father' of her child, even if this person did not have any connection at all to it."²²

Obviously the members of the commissions were concerned about the moral aspects of lone motherhood. Thus the dominant view was that the fathers of children who were the result of "casual relations" should not be acknowledged. Or, as a lawyer from the USSR prosecutor-general put it: "It is important that casual relations not be encouraged. Thus let us try to find the right wordings for the law, so that in most cases the father of the child will be identified in the court procedure, but so that children of casual relations are excluded from this procedure." In connection with this, he remembered how female constituencies he had met on a recent election tour around Soviet Russia had urged him not to allow the state to impose child-support payments on men for children born out of a casual relation:

> Thus I visited Dagestan and met with 600 women from factories and kolkhozes and, in unison, they told me: "Don't make them pay support in instances of casual relations—this will just send us women the wrong signals."²³

We also find cases in the letters of unmarried mothers who referred to moral behavior, declaring that they themselves—unlike some other women—were not promiscuous, and that their relation to the father of the child had not been "casual:"

> I therefore ask you to insert the following regulation into the legislation: A child born out of wedlock should be eligible to get support from the father—not, however, if it is the result of casual relations.²⁴

Moreover, it was not only women who were accused of low morals in these letters. Quite a few of the female authors mention that the Communist Party had punished non-paying fathers by excluding them from the ranks of the party. The glimpse we get from the following letter is interesting because it tells us something about the party's ambitions to control and oversee the moral behavior of men as well. It also indicates an apparent conflict between party interests and the written law:

> Although my husband was excluded from the party for not paying for his child, no one can make him pay, since we lived together without being officially registered as husband and wife—this in spite of the fact that I can show documents signed by the neighbors that we lived together at that time.[25]

A few women in the commissions objected when the others expressed fear of encouraging women to have free relations with men. They pointed to the fact that according to the existing law, men too easily escaped responsibility. Below is an extensive quotation from a speech by Aleksandra Pergament, a well-known lawyer at the time, in which she urges the commissions "finally, after forty meetings," to take a firm stance on the issue of establishing paternity for children born out of wedlock:

> We say that the woman should have the right to demand that the court establish the paternity of her child. However, unlike the situation before 1944, the burden of proof will be on the woman. This sounds fair, but in fact there will be very few cases where women will succeed, because we, the members of the commissions, have decided that we require the woman to have lived together with the man under the same roof and to have shared the household at the time the child was conceived. This means that all married men will go free. This draft law encourages men to be together with whomever they wish. As long as they are married, they won't have to take any responsibility for their actions. A woman, on the other hand, is a cautious creature, and the very thought of the consequences the situation of a lone mother would bring prevents her from consciously getting into a casual relationship.[26]

Thus it was a delicate task for the commissions to offer a law proposal that would convey a feeling of respect for lone mothers and at the same time restrain what was considered immoral behavior in relations between men and women.

Quite a different angle on the issue of the status of lone mothers was expressed by some letter-writers who did not at all see the women as victims. Thus one man wrote that he considered the law obsolete:

> Every citizen in our country has the right to work, and this work is well-paid, and therefore every single mother capable of working should be able to support one child. Thus I propose that state

allowances to single mothers be abolished and the money be used instead to strengthen our country.[27]

Other authors expressed similar views to the effect that unmarried mothers, like all other citizens of the socialist state, had the right to work and in fact earned enough to provide for their own children. This opinion fit well into the heady official discourse of the time on Soviet citizens' rapidly and steadily increasing income level. This discourse proclaimed that, in contrast to the capitalist world and as a characteristic feature of socialism, every Soviet citizen enjoyed the right to gainful employment.

Fathers' Responsibilities

"Fathers' responsibilities," the third prominent discourse in my study, cannot, of course, be clearly distinguished from the discourses on "children's equal rights" and "lone mothers' morals." They are all intertwined. The context in which citizens expressed their attitudes towards fathers' responsibilities and members of the law commissions discussed the draft legislation on this point was, in short, the following. In comparison to the legislation of the 1920s, the 1944 decree radically changed the legal duties of biological fathers to children born out of wedlock by stipulating that women no longer could demand that the court establish paternity and order the father to pay child support. Unmarried mothers would now get financial support from the government instead of the biological father, but normally they would receive less money and only until the child was twelve years old. Additionally, children born out of wedlock would get special benefits when it came to places in kindergarten and free attendance at boarding schools. Further, the name of the father was not to be stated on the child's birth certificate; so, this spot on the document was left blank. The rationale for the 1944 law obviously had to do with the vast losses of Russian men as a result of World War II. Thus the legislation actually encouraged men to father children, and not only within marriage (Nakachi, 2006).

The discourse on fathers' responsibilities stands out as rather contradictory. Some letter-writers plead that fathers be required to pay for their children to alleviate the heavy burden of unmarried mothers. As indicated above, these writers are most often women. Several authors express anger over the regulations that released men from all responsibility for their offspring. In the following two excerpts from letters, we find typical pleas for financial relief and calls for men to do their duty as fathers.

In the name of the life we give, we the mothers call for the abolishment of this regulation; we beg you to meet our demand for the protection of our future children. Single mothers have a very hard time; so let them be granted support through court decisions in the future [said one collective letter].[28]

Every mother wants a stable family, but they are deceived by men earning three or four thousand rubles. Oh, it is so humiliating when the father of the child lives in luxury in a fine apartment, and he can eat and dress any way he wants! He gets a lot of money, but the woman who gave birth to his child gets fifty rubles from the government[29] and he goes on living, the bastard! [writes another female author][30]

On the other hand, some citizens express quite different views. A man simply should not have to take responsibility for children conceived "by mistake."[31] Again we find the attitude that men were not obliged to take responsibility for "casual relations." Some of the writers in the early 1950s who had children they were supporting according to the pre-1944 situation complained bitterly about their heavy financial burden. Thus one writer argues: "During the war I made the mistake of engaging in a casual relation with a woman who got pregnant. I pay 25 percent of my salary to this woman, while the members of my family get only 9 percent each. Why should a casual relationship ruin my family?"[32] Another typical complaint is as follows: "When a man pays for children from a casual relationship, very little of his salary is left for his real family."[33]

The issue of men's responsibilities was frequently discussed in the law commissions of the Supreme Soviet. As already pointed out, it was the female members who were most critical of the way the existing legislation freed men from responsibilities towards their children, giving examples such as the following:

I work in a medical institute with male students who live in dormitories with young girls that they promise to marry, but when they have completed their studies they leave, and the girls are already pregnant. It is good that the Komsomol[34] organizations deal with these things, but we need formal legislation as well.[35]

Like the issue of lone mothers, the subject of fathers' responsibilities was slowly creeping into the mass media in the early 1960s. Furthermore, the topic of fatherhood as such was raised widely in the women's magazines. In the 1950s men in their role as fathers had been almost invisible in articles and short stories on the family and the household in *Rabotnitsa* and *Sem'ia i shkola*. When they did come into sight, it was frequently as troublemakers and drunkards who left their families without paying for the children. However, beginning in the early 1960s, men were more often made visible as fathers. Thus a young father holding his baby boy in his arms graced the cover of the August 1961 issue of *Sem'ia i shkola*. *Rabotnitsa* organized debates with the readers of the magazine under headlines such as "It's Not Awkward [for men to take care of the household]" or "When Men Finally Start to Understand" (*Rabotnitsa* 1963, no. 2; 1964, no. 1).

Finally, it is an open question to what extent the flow of letters influenced the lawmaking process. The new political regime after Stalin's death considered this interaction of citizens and authorities as "one of the most effective ways of establishing trustful relations between the people and the authorities" (Kabashov, 2010, p. 135), and various official Communist Party and Soviet government resolutions furthering this process were issued from the late 1950s onward. The law commissions referred to the need to take into consideration citizen reactions. Thus one representative of the Soviet government at a law commission meeting in 1959 noted that since the issue of lone mothers and their children had "evoked an unprecedented flow of letters and suggestions from the working people," it was necessary to make changes to the existing law.[36]

In the 1958 edition of a standard work for university students on marriage and family legislation by the law professor Georgii Sverdlov, the concept "children born of lone, unmarried mothers" (Sverdlov, 1951, p. 124) was changed to "children born of unmarried mothers" (Sverdlov, 1958, p. 194). Many of the letter-writers complained specifically about the use of the word "lone," stating that the women were not alone at all, since they had their children! Also, there are reasons to believe that public calls for actions to restore the constitutional rights of children born out of wedlock emboldened people to make demands on the authorities. One example of such a public call was published in the prestigious *Literaturnaia gazeta*. It was signed by prominent composers and writers like Dmitrii Shostakovich and Ilya Ehrenburg, who urged the authorities to follow the Leninist principle of equal rights for all children (Carlbäck, 2009, p. 94).

Concluding Remarks

Until recently, researchers did not have access to archival materials permitting a reconstruction of the discourse on lone motherhood in Soviet Russia. Furthermore, printed public sources such as newspapers, magazines, and books on marriage and the family were almost silent on the subject, which was thus a non-issue in the public space. Between 1946 and 1968, however, the Supreme Soviet commissions and other state authorities and institutions received a multitude of citizen letters addressing the question.

In this chapter I have analyzed attitudes of Soviet citizens toward the existing laws on the family and marriage in the mid-twentieth century. I have focused on opinions in citizens' letters and discussions in the relevant law commissions and identified three dominant discourses on the subject—children's equal rights, lone mothers' morals, and fathers' responsibilities. The views on children's rights can be divided rather clearly into two groups. One group maintains that children should have full constitutional rights regardless of the conduct of their parents, although it is not fully obvious what these rights should include—is it mainly financial support, and should it be provided by the state or the biological father? Or do constitutional rights mainly refer to the right of being an acknowledged citizen of the USSR in the sense of having both parents visible and present? The other group of letters does not take up children's rights at all, but concentrates on either the mothers or the fathers.

The discourses on mothers and fathers are both more closely intertwined and more contradictory. Thus the woman is often viewed as a victim of the situation, yet at the same time, because she has failed to uphold the sexual mores of society, she is held responsible for that situation. Conversely, the man is regarded as the victim of casual relations for which he is not held accountable, yet he is also asked to share financial responsibility with the poor woman.

Furthermore, a view of fatherhood as something conditional is evident from the many letters conveying the message that fatherhood loses its meaning when the man and child live separately. Thus sometimes openly, but more often between the lines, one detects the opinion that children from previous relationships do not really belong to their biological fathers. In this respect Soviet Russia did not differ from the rest of Europe. The need for tight bonds between biological fathers and their children was something that would appear much later in public discourse, and then not so much in Russia as, for example, in the Scandinavian countries. The attitude to motherhood in many ways was similar in most places in Europe at this time to the one in Soviet Russia. The underlying norm in many of the citizens' letters is that women have the overwhelming responsibility for children, a position that also makes them vulnerable in situations where sexual morality is evaluated ("casual" relations resulting in pregnancy). Again, women are seen as having the ultimate responsibility for avoiding situations leading to unwanted pregnancy.

Still, with respect to attitudes toward lone motherhood, Soviet Russia may have differed from dominant discourses in many parts of Europe. The degree of shame often attached to the civil state of "unmarried mother" seems to have been less.[37] At any rate, we do not find in the letters much condemnation of women who ended up with a fatherless child. This may have to do partly with the severe shortage of men after the war, but it is also explained partly by the fact that the official norms as reflected in previous legal rules had supported the right of unmarried women to turn to the court to have paternity established and that the value of marriage was deflated by the legal norms that dominated in the interwar period.

When the German scholar Elizabeth Heinemann researched the discourse of lone mothers in divided Germany in the postwar decades, she found that in the German Democratic Republic the state promoted a wider variety of options for mothers, including unmarried mothers. This contributed to a popular discourse of greater tolerance towards women with children born out of wedlock in comparison to the discourse on unmarried mothers in West Germany (Heinemann, 2000). At the same time, in the socialist GDR the issue of single motherhood was not a topic for public debate but on the contrary was more of a non-issue. This is reminiscent of the Soviet Russian case.

The models of fatherhood and motherhood that emerge from these letters are not uniform. Viewed in retrospect, mid-twentieth-century Soviet Russia stood between two historical eras with regard to official norms and legal rules pertaining to the family. The radical thinking behind the revolutionary family laws clearly changed when the regime replaced ideas of the fading away of the family with the perceived need to develop a stable family. In practice the state authorities had to deal with various concrete challenges such as destabilized families due to the social, political, and economic turbulence of the 1930s and the enormous loss of life due to war. The legislative norms from the late 1960s and on, as seen below, expressed a concern for a stable family supported by the state, yet recognizing the family as unit of a certain degree of private.

Epilogue

After two decades of legislative processes in which the Supreme Soviet law commissions took part, a new law on marriage and the family was issued in 1969. The new law abolished the procedure of noting the absence of a father on the child's birth certificate. Either the name of the biological father would be registered, or the mother could come up with some other (fictitious) name, in order to give the child a proper patronymic. Furthermore, a mother who gave birth out of wedlock would now be entitled to ask the court to establish the child's paternity. Although the law seemingly returned to the pre-1944 legal position, the burden of proof laid on the women was in fact greater than before. With the help of witnesses if need be, she would have to prove that she had lived with the man under marriage-like circumstances (*Kodeks zakonov...* 1986, pp. 18–19).

Notes

1. For a brief historiographical account of the discussion among scholars of the main reasons for the sharp increase of extramarital births during this period, see Clark (2006, pp. 64–67). This highlights the divergences between Edward Shorter's (1975) ideas on an early sexual revolution as an important factor and other scholars' focus on factors such as industrialization and urbanization.
2. I prefer the term "lone motherhood," since it corresponds better to the Russian term *odinokie materi*.
3. In this case Moscow and St. Petersburg differed from the rest of the country, with rather high numbers of children born out of wedlock (Therborn, 2004, p. 149). For a study on the system of foundling houses in these cities where lone mothers could leave their children anonymously, see Ransel (1988).
4. Research has treated the issue of lone mothers as a special group in various ways. Thus Rudolf Schlesinger (1949) compares the Soviet policy to the contemporary ideas of the Swedish social democrat and feminist Alva Myrdal. In Myrdal's efforts to support lone mothers financially and socially, Schlesinger finds positive similarities with Soviet Russia, and he even predicts the possibility of the development of a "social group representing a really new conception of the profession of motherhood." At the same time, however, he stresses that Soviet Russia's economic resources do not measure up to Sweden's (ibid., pp. 4–7). A researcher of a much later period, Mie Nakachi (2011), on the other hand, views the Soviet policy much more critically, stating that the legal system created an underprivileged group of single mothers and their children in terms of health, financial, and moral conditions and that the new legislation had evoked a fierce "battle of the sexes" (ibid., p. 110).
5. This expression was used by Marxist lawyers, as cited in Schlesinger, 1949.

6 The expression goes back to the fact that it sufficed for one spouse to send a card notifying the registration authorities of his or her intent to ask for a divorce.
7 In her article Goldman analyzes the gender conflicts due to the new situation with women entering the labor force in record numbers.
8 For a study of women in Sweden and Soviet Russia caught between motherhood and wage work, see Carlbäck (2007).
9 Initiatives from above to mobilize popular reactions to law matters were taken already in the 1920s and can be regarded as a specific state socialist form of referendum (Schlesinger, 1949; Goldman, 1993).
10 GARF, f. 7523, op. 45, d. 213, pp. 70–71.
11 For the full text in English of the laws from 1918 until 1944, see Schlesinger (1949).
12 According to law provisions issued in 1944, children of unmarried mothers would be given priority for places in kindergarten and would also have the right to free places in boarding schools.
13 I have dealt with divorce in Soviet Russia in a more general way in earlier works, e.g. Carlbäck (2005), and I am presently doing a study on "Divorce à la Russe" within the research project "Family and the Strong State—Coercion or Emancipation?" financed by the Baltic Sea Foundation. For an informative study in courts' dealings with divorce in the 1950s and 1960s, see Field (2007).
14 GARF, f. 7523, op 45, d. 229, Letter 28/3–51.
15 GARF, f. 7523, op. 45, d. 270, Overview of citizens' proposals 18/8–58.
16 GARF, f. 7523, op. 45, d. 270, Overview of citizens' proposals 18/8–58.
17 In practice, this was expressed on the birth certificate by leaving the space asking for the father's name blank.
18 GARF, f. 7523, op. 45, d. 274, Minutes 29/6–59.
19 GARF, f. 7523, op 45, d. 229, Letter 30/4–51.
20 GARF, f. 7523, op. 45, d. 439, Overview of citizens' proposals, 1963.
21 GARF, f. 7523, op. 45, d. 274, Minutes 29/6–59.
22 GARF, f. 7523, op. 45, d. 215, Letter 25/6–50.
23 GARF, f. 7523, op. 45, d. 357, Minutes 14/12–62.
24 GARF, f. 7523, op 45, d. 215, Letter 7/3–52.
25 GARF, f. 7523, op 45, d. 273, Letter 27/2–56.
26 GARF, f. 7523, op. 45, d. 357, Minutes 14/12–62.
27 GARF, f. 7523, op 45 a, d. 229, Letter 4/7–52.
28 GARF, f. 7523, op. 45, d. 217, Letter 14/3–55.
29 To start with, in 1944, lone mothers got 100 rubles per child per month until the child turned twelve. From 1949, however, this sum was reduced to fifty rubles. The average income of a worker at the time was about 1,000–1,500 rubles.
30 GARF, f. 7523, op 45, d. 217, Letter 23/11–52.
31 It should be pointed out that from 1936 to 1955, abortion was not an obvious solution to the problem of unwanted children, since abortion was illegal during this period.
32 GARF, f. 7523, op. 45 a, d. 229, Letter 2/2–50.
33 GARF, f. op. 45 a, d. 229, Letter 28/12–50.

34 The Komsomol, the youth organization of the Communist Party, was supposed to deal with various moral issues among its members. For a recent study on the way the Communist Party and the "social organizations," *obshchestvennye organizatsii*, dealt with family conflicts in workplaces and neighborhoods, see Zhidkova (2008; this volume).
35 GARF, f. 7523, op. 45, d. 357, Minutes 14/12–62.
36 GARF, f. 7523, op. 45, d. 274, Minutes 29/6–59.
37 For two studies on the issue of lone mothers in Britain and Finland, respectively, in the mid-twentieth century, see Lewis and Welshman (1997) and May (2003).

References

Archive documents
Gosudarstvennyi Arkhiv Rossiiskii Federatsii (GARF) State Archive of the Russian Federation in Moscow, f. 7523 (Verkhovnyi Sovet SSSR- Supreme Soviet of the USSR), op. 45 and 45.

Journals, newspapers, serials
Literaturnaia Gazeta (Literary Gazette)
Rabotnitsa (Female Worker)
Sem'ia i shkola (Family and School)
Sovetskoe gosudarstvo i pravo (The Soviet State and Justice)

Literature
Antokolskaia, Maria. 2003. "Development of Family Law in Western and Eastern Europe: Common Origins, Common Driving Forces, Common Tendencies." *Journal of Family History* 28, no. 1: 52–69.
Aralovets, Natalia. 2009. *Gorodskaia sem'ia v Rossii, 1925–1959 gg.* (Urban family in Russia, 1925–1959). Tula, Russia: Grif i K.
Ashwin, Sarah, ed. 2000. *Gender, State and Society in Soviet and Post-Soviet Russia*. London: Routledge.
Attwood, Lynne. 1999. *The New Man and Woman: Sex-Role Socialization in the USSR*. Basingstoke, UK: Macmillan.
Bergman, Helena, and Barbara Hobson. 2002. "Compulsory Fatherhood: The Coding of Fatherhood in the Swedish Welfare State." In *Making Men into Fathers: Men, Masculinities and the Social Politics of Fatherhood*, ed. Barbara Hobson, 92–124. Cambridge: Cambridge University Press.
Bogdanova, Elena. 2006. "Obrashcheniia grazhdan v organy vlasti kak opyt otstaivaniia svoikh interesov v usloviiakh pozdnesovetskogo obshchestva (1960-e-1970-e gody)"(Citizens' appeals to authorities in defense of their interests in the conditions of late-Soviet society). PhD diss., European University in St. Petersburg, St. Petersburg: EUSPb.
Buckley, Mary. 1989. *Women and Ideology in the Soviet Union*. Hemel Hempstead, UK: Harvester Wheatsheaf.

Carlbäck, Helene. 2005. "Tracing the Roots of Early Soviet Russian Family Laws." In *Gender Transitions in Russia and Eastern Europe*, eds. Ildikó Asztalos Morell, Helene Carlbäck, Madeleine Hurd, and Sara Rastbäck, 69–84. Eslöv, Sweden: Gondolin.

———. 2007. "Wives or Workers? Women's Position in the Labour Force and in Domestic Life in Sweden and Russia during the 1960s." In *Gender, Equality and Difference during and after State Socialism*, ed. Rebecca Kay, 85–104. Basingstoke, UK: Palgrave.

———. 2009. "Lone Mothers and Fatherless Children: Public Discourse on Marriage and Family Law." In *Soviet State and Society under Nikita Khrushchev*, eds. Melanie Ilič and Jeremy Smith, 86–103. London: Routledge.

Chernova, Zhanna. 2008. *Semeinaia politika v Evrope i v Rossii: gendernyi analiz* (Family policy in Europe and Russia: gender analysis). St. Petersburg: Norma.

Clark, Anna. 2006. "Female Sexuality." In *The Routledge History of Women in Europe since 1700*, ed. Deborah Simonton, 54–92. London: Routledge.

Clements, Barbara Evans. 1979. *Bolshevik Feminist: The Life of Aleksandra Kollontai*. Bloomington: Indiana University Press.

Elgán, Elisabeth. 1990. "En far till var kvinnas barn? Politik och debatt angående män, kvinnor och oäkta barn i Sverige och Frankrike vid seklets början" (A father for every woman's child? Policy and debate on men, women and illegitimate children in Sweden and France at the beginning of the century). *Historisk tidskrift* 4: 481–504.

Field, Deborah A. 2007. *Private Life and Communist Morality in Khrushchev's Russia*. New York: Peter Lang.

Fitzpatrick, Sheila. 1996. "Supplicants and Citizens: Public Letter-Writing in Soviet Russia in the 1930s." *Slavic Review* 55, no. 1: 78–105.

Gillis, John. 1997. *A World of Their Own Making: Myth, Ritual and the Quest for Family Values*. Cambridge, MA: Harvard University Press.

Goldman, Wendy Z. 1993. *Women, the State and Revolution: Soviet Family Policy and Social Life, 1917–1936*. Cambridge: Cambridge University Press.

———. 2001. "Babas at the Bench: Gender Conflict in Soviet Industry in the 1930s." In *Women in the Stalin Era*, ed. Melanie Ilič, 69–88. Basingstoke: Palgrave.

Hajnal, John. 1965. "European Marriage Patterns in Perspective." In *Population in History: Essays in Historical Demography*, eds. David V. Glass and David E.C. Eversley, 101–143. London: Edward Arnold.

Heinemann, Elizabeth D. "Single Motherhood and Maternal Employment in Divided Germany: Ideology, Policy, and Social Pressures in the 1950s." *Journal of Women's History* 12, no. 3 (2000): 146–172.

Ilič, Melanie. *Women Workers in the Soviet Interwar Economy: From "Protection" to "Inequality."* Basingstoke, UK: Palgrave, 1999.

Isupova, Olga and Igor Kon. "Materinstvo i ottsovstvo. Sotsiologicheskii ocherk (Motherhood and fatherhood. Sociological essay)." In *Gender dlia "chainikov" (Gender for 'dummies')* Moscow: Zven'ia, 2009.

Juviler, Peter H. *Revolutionary Law and Order: Politics and Social Change in the USSR*. New York: Free Press, 1976.

Kabashov, Sergei. *Organizatsiia raboty s obrashcheniiami grazhdan v istorii Rossii* (The organization of work with citizens' appeals in the history of Russia). Moscow: Flinta, 2010.

Kodeks zakonov o brake i sem'e (The family and marriage code). Moscow: Iuridicheskaia literatura, 1986.

Koven, Seth and Michel Sonya, eds. *Mothers of a New World: Maternalist Politics and the Origins of Welfare States*. New York: Routledge, 1993.

Laslett, Peter. "Family and Household as Work Group and Kin Group: Areas of Traditional Europe Compared." In *Family Forms in Historic Europe*, eds. Richard Wall, Jean Robin, and Peter Laslett, 513–563. Cambridge and New York: Cambridge University Press, 1983.

Laslett, Peter, Karla Oosterveen, and Richard Michael Smith, eds. *Bastardy and its Comparative History: Studies in the History of Illegitimacy and Marital Non-Conformism in Britain, France, Germany, Sweden, North America, Jamaica and Japan*. Cambridge, MA: Harvard University, 1980.

Lewis, Jane, and John Welshman. "The Issue of Never-Married Motherhood in Britain, 1920–1970." *Social History of Medicine* 10, no. 3 (1997): 401–418.

Livshin, Alexander, Igor Orlov, and Oleg Khlevniuk, eds. *Pis'ma vo vlast', 1928–1939. Zaiavlenia, zhaloby, donosy, pis'ma v gosudarstvennye struktury i sovetskim vozhdiam* (Letters to the authorities, 1928–1939. Declarations, complaints, denunciations, letters to state institutions and Soviet leaders). Moscow: Rosspen, 2002.

May, Vanessa. "Lone Motherhood Past and Present: The Life Stories of Finnish Lone Mothers." *NORA* 1, no. 11 (2003): 27–39.

Nakachi, Mie. "N.S. Khrushchev and the 1944 Soviet Family Law: Politics, Reproduction, and Language." *East European Politics and Societies* 20, no. 1 (2006): 40–68.

———. "Gender, Marriage, and Reproduction in the Postwar Soviet Union." In *Writing the Stalin Era: Sheila Fitzpatrick and Soviet Historiography*, eds. Golfo Alexopoulos, Julie Hessler, and Kiril Tomoff, 101–116. New York: Palgrave 2011.

Ransel, David L. *Mothers of Misery: Child Abandonment in Russia*. Princeton, NJ: Princeton University Press, 1988.

Rotkirch, Anna. *The Man Question: Loves and Lives in Late 20th Century Russia*. Helsinki: University of Helsinki, 2001.

———. "'Coming to Stand on Firm Ground:' The Making of a Soviet Working Mother." In *On Living Through Soviet Russia*, eds. Daniel Bertaux, Paul Thompson, and Anna Rotkirch, 146–175. London and New York: Routledge, 2004.

———."Rakare, friare, friskare. Kollontajs vision för kvinnokroppen (Straighter, freer, healthier: Kollontai's vision of the female body)." In *Revolusjon, kjærlighet, diplomati: Aleksandra Kollontaj og Norden*, ed. Yngvild Sørby, 83–104. Oslo: Unipub, 2008.

Schlesinger, Rudolf. *The Family in the USSR: Documents and Readings*. London and New York: Routledge, 1949.

Shorter, Edward. *The Making of the Modern Family*. New York: Basic Books, 1975.

Sverdlov, Georgii. *Sovetskoe semeinoe pravo* (Soviet family law). Moscow: Gosudarstvennoe izdatel'stvo iuridicheskoi literatury, 1951.

———. *Sovetskoe semeinoe pravo* (Soviet family law). Moscow: Gosudarstvennoe izdatel'stvo iuridicheskoi literatury, 1958.

Therborn, Göran. *Between Sex and Power: Family in the World, 1990–2000*. London: Routledge, 2004.

Vishnevskii, Anatolii, ed. *Demograficheskaia modernizatsiia Rossii 1900–2000* (The demographic modernization of Russia 1900–2000). Moscow: Novoe izdatel'stvo, 2006.

Zhidkova, Elena. "Praktiki razresheniia semeinykh konfliktov. Obrashcheniia grazhdan v obshchestvennye organizatsii i partiinye iacheiki" (Family conflict resolution. Citizen's appeals to social organizations and party cells). In *Sovetskaia sotsial'naia politika: stseny i deistvuyushchie litsa, 1941–1985 (Soviet social policy: scences and actors, 1941–1985)*, eds. Elena Iarskaia-Smirnova and Pavel Romanov, 266–289. Moscow: Variant, 2008.

Zhiromskaya, Valentina, ed. *Naselenie Rossii v XX veke: istoricheskie ocherki* (The population of Russia in the 20th century: Essays in history). Vol. 2. Moscow: ROSSPEN, 2001.

Zubkova, Elena. *Russia after the War: Hopes, Illusions, and Disappointments, 1945–1957*. Armonk, NY: Sharpe, 1998.

CHAPTER 2

Family, Divorce, and Comrades' Courts: Soviet Family and Public Organizations During the Thaw

ELENA ZHIDKOVA

INTRODUCTION

The 1950s and 1960s in the Soviet Union were notable for several social reforms dealing with the education, pension, and welfare systems. Although it witnessed the last Soviet antireligious campaign, Khrushchev's tenure was called the "Thaw" because of the significant loosening of cultural and social restrictions that took place in these years. It also brought on a debate over a wide range of social problems, from child upbringing to the family crisis (Zubkova, 2008, p. 134). It was a period of liberalization in many senses, and not just politically, since the concept of "private life" was rehabilitated somewhat. On the other hand, it was also a time of decisive struggle for a communist lifestyle. In practice, by adopting the "Moral Code of the Builder of Communism" at the 1961 Party Congress, the Communist Party sanctioned the strengthening of public control of citizens' actions, both at work and in private. Ordinary people were encouraged to take an active role in public affairs and to volunteer for social and community work. Thus some voluntary organizations like the women's councils and volunteer people's patrols made a comeback after almost three decades of inactivity. In my chapter I will use regional archive materials to reconstruct the expectations authorities placed on the activities of various voluntary organizations—women's councils (*zhensovety*), volunteer people's patrols (*druzhinniki*), comrades' courts (*tovarishcheskie sudy*), trade unions (*profsoiuzy*), and people's controllers (*narodnye kontrolery*)—that emerged in Khrushchev's time and were involved with family matters.

The social history of the Khrushchev era is now beginning to receive more focused attention. British historians have published a series of important publications on Soviet women as a cultural phenomenon (Ilič, 2001, 2004, 2009). Ilič, a leading researcher of Soviet history, has stated that "in the late 1950s and early 1960s, the women's councils were no longer simply regarded as the facilitators of women's emancipation; they were now looked upon as the very markers of women's equality in the Soviet Union" (Ilič, 2009). Gradskova's book *Soviet People with Female Bodies: Performing Beauty and*

Maternity in Soviet Russia in the Mid 1930–1960s provides new insight into the ways in which Soviet women dealt with the everyday practices of maternity and beauty. It was thought that women would be the main benefactors of the Soviet social reforms. As the author argues, however, many of them found it difficult to adjust to the new conditions (Gradskova, 2007).

The voluntary organizations in Russia, as agents of social surveillance and control, have barely been examined. A general overview of the Khrushchev period, with an emphasis on cultural aspects and the history of everyday life, can be found in the works of Lebina (2006), Leibovich (2008), and, in particular, Kozlova (2005), who has consistently focused her research on the role of social policy in the formation of postwar Soviet society. All of these authors, however, are interested in the broader sociocultural context of the era and do not devote specific attention to the theme of social regulation and control. Other sources suggest a different reality and call for a different methodological approach. Based on the research of a team of anthropologists in rural areas of northern Russia, Kushkova's studies (2006, 2007) have provided useful firsthand accounts not only of women's lives but also of the social ferment of the 1960s and how it affected female participants. Through a series of qualitative interviews, she examines the testimonies of female activists who participated in the women's councils. My contribution to the research on voluntary organizations brings a new perspective by focusing on thus-far rarely studied family and gender issues.

This chapter examines the theme of social control and the promotion of socially approved behavior in private life. A concurrent topic is the destruction of the traditional social order of the Russian peasantry, ideas about the family, and expectations related to age and gender in agrarian cultures under the influence of urban lifestyles. The notion of public assistance to the family will be examined through the prism of the dramatic realization of what Temkina and Rotkirch have called the "working mother gender contract" (2007, pp. 179–181). This gender contract involved many social actors and revealed a widening gap between everyday practices and official ideology. Although it was the dominant gender contract of the Soviet period, it has almost disappeared in post-communist Russia. The theoretical framework in my chapter is set by interpreting the Soviet gender order as an "etacratic" (French *état*—the state) order. In their discussions of the state's central role in the formation of the Soviet gender system, Zdravomyslova and Temkina (2007, pp. 97–98) point out that family relations and configurations and the related discourses were predominantly determined by state policy. The state interfered in almost all aspects of human life. Thus the state acted as the primary agent both in the formation of gender relations and in the regulation of women's employment and social policy towards family and women. Here Zdravomyslova and Temkina develop the ideas of the Marxist philosophers Gramsci and Althusser on the repressive role of state ideological structures in the reproduction of social inequality and stratification (ibid., pp. 98, 128). The gender contract "working mother" functioned as a principal part of the etacratic gender system throughout almost all of Soviet history, allowing millions of women to combine full-time employment with family duties.

The geographic area of my study is the Middle Volga region, especially Kuibyshev (now Samara) Oblast. Between 1935 and 1991, this oblast was named after the famous Soviet Communist Party leader Valerian Kuibyshev. Like many other industrial areas in the country, the region experienced a high population increase and economic growth accompanied by an intense urbanization. In 1962 the population in the Kuibyshev region reached 2,424,000, 65 percent of whom settled in towns and only 35 percent of whom settled in the countryside. Kuibyshev city had a population of over 800,000 (SOGASPI, f. 656, op. 130, d. 498, l. 24). By Khrushchev's time the region was rather typical in terms of demographic and industrial development. Since the war years several enormous plants of national significance had been located there. Some of these enterprises were closed to outsiders, since they were producing for the military and aircraft and airspace industries and were therefore considered to be "special classified," meaning secret, enterprises. In fact, Kuibyshev's status as a "closed city" might have had an impact on human-resources policies.[1] In contrast to the old city center, with its well-established commercial and religious traditions, "socialist towns" (*sotsgorodki*) were built around the enterprises in the suburbs, fulfilling both the housing needs of the labor force and the ideological mission of forming the proletarian social base (Kotkin, 1995).

My study is based on the analysis of archival records from two regional archives: the Central State Archive of the Samara Region (TsGASO) and a former local branch of the Communist Party Archive, now the Samara Regional Archive of Social and Political History (SOGASPI). The available source material is rather conventional for historians, although it is somewhat limited. For example, there are few records relating to the work of the women's councils or the comrades' courts at the lower levels in medium-size enterprises or apartment blocks. Records of their activities and some reports can be found in the documents on the workings of trade unions and the district and city-level Communist Party committees responsible for their supervision and control. Here we have a perfect combination of surveys and case materials that is sensitive to general trends. Needless to say, only with some reservations could these organizations, or any other public structures in the Soviet Union, be described as "volunteer" ventures. Like many other initiatives, they could exist only under the supervision of the Communist Party. I am well aware of the limitations that ideologically charged documents from party archives might have. But taken together, they can represent the official discourse while also providing an understanding of the role of such organizations in the process officially known as "the building of communism." Thus the present study does not explore everyday practices but rather provides an analysis of representation and discourse on the Soviet family developed in connection with the activities of volunteer organizations. The introduction and functioning of these organizations can be viewed as part of a state effort to create new norms and impose state ideology. In addition, I attempt to examine what a "normal" family model and family gender roles looked like as reflected in the dominant discourse of the period.

Soviet Society in the Khrushchev Era — Analytical Problems and Contradictions

Control over various aspects of human life was part of the forced modernization of the economy and society that was launched by the Soviet regime. When discussing the role of voluntary organizations in the debate on family issues, one should keep in mind that the surveillance of sexual and reproductive behavior within the family domain was considered a political question (Kharkhordin, 1997) and therefore a matter of state interest. The war had resulted in a devastating decline in population, which in turn dramatically impacted the labor force. Official discourse emphasized the crucial role that educated and professional women could play in promoting communist values and in taking part in what was labeled "the building of communism."

Among the most characteristic features of the etacratic gender system to play a vital role in Soviet social policy was the wide-ranging network of state childcare institutions, which included kindergartens and nurseries, boarding schools, and extracurricular activities like after-school clubs. The role of the state was particularly noticeable in its increasing impact on the social sphere. Thus the state widely supported women by providing maternity leave, financial assistance for single mothers, and benefits for mothers with multiple children. In 1955 Stalin's strict law on abortion was changed. All these measures were intended to encourage Soviet women to fulfill various social roles as mothers, workers, and activists. By providing housing, childcare, work, and regulated wages, the state to a certain extent took the role of father and breadwinner that in the traditional gender contract was normally assigned to men. Voluntary organizations also took part in upholding the etacratic gender system.

The official discourse on family, sex, and communist morality was very different from the discourse of sexual revolution in the West (Temkina and Rotkirch, 2007, pp. 171–172). Moreover, women remained responsible for the preservation of the family and the "salvation" of men. And according to Reid (2004, p. 382), women's mentor role was part of their "biologically predetermined mission." It was the responsibility of women of all social classes to bring up children, regardless of whether they worked or had adequate housing. Working-class husbands were too often negligent in their own performance of family duties to be considered suitable for these tasks (Fitzpatrick, 1999, pp. 156–163).

THE ACTIVITIES OF VOLUNTARY ORGANIZATIONS

The involvement of the local community in the lives of families was nothing extraordinary for a society with old traditions of subjugating the individual to a collective formed by the peasant family or the Orthodox parish. Contemporary concepts of private life and the inviolability of the private space are hardly relevant to a study of Soviet history, where the acceptable limits of social interference were very different from those of today. In the postwar period most Soviet urban residents were former peasants with strong ties to kin and family. As Oleg Kharkhordin (1997, 2001) stresses in his detailed studies of Soviet collectivism, the mechanism of disciplinary surveillance was deeply rooted in Russian Orthodox culture. Furthermore, it was not limited to the control of juniors by seniors, but also included peer control within the same status group.

From the earliest period of the Soviet regime, the peasantry as a class was considered backward and ignorant of the ideological and political agenda of the day. The peasant inferiority complex was intensely exploited by the party propaganda machine. The Communist Party seems to have thought it important to make society in general and "backward" groups like peasants in particular more "cultured." In line with the observations of contemporaries, some researchers have pointed out that former peasants turned urban workers were highly susceptible to slogans and propaganda (Kozlova, 1996, pp. 166–167). It is worth noting here that, due to a special propaganda campaign in rural areas, in the late 1950s *kolkhoz* peasants constituted a higher proportion of Communist Party membership than they had in the first half of the decade.[2]

Although it obviously was not a priority of the regime, traditional peer control—at least at the rhetorical level—had found new forms and had established a new agenda. One example would be the activity of the voluntary sector in the post-Stalin years: during this time people were encouraged to take part in volunteer work in their free time. This encouragement was part of the ongoing ideological promotion of building communism and the gradual withering away of the state. As party leaders promised in their speeches, many state functions were supposed to be transferred to citizens and citizen coalitions (Lebina, 2006, pp. 160–161). That is why volunteer people's patrols appear along with the police, comrades' courts along with law courts, and people's controllers along with state institutions that had official control functions. Between 1958 and 1961, nearly 840 voluntary organizations with large memberships (more than 6,800), of which women's organizations were an important part, were set up in the city of Kuibyshev (SOGASPI, f. 714, op. 1, d. 2395, l. 91). A volunteer movement that included women's organizations certainly existed earlier, in the interwar period, but during the Khrushchev era it experienced a revival.[3]

The Industrial Enterprise as a Center of Social Life

Industrial enterprises—at the time the hubs of Soviet social life—were made responsible for everyday work with the population. The mobilizing character of economic activity, in which people were attached to their workplaces, contributed to this state of affairs. The Soviet workplace was the key spot for the interaction of various social structures, including party cells, police, trade unions, educational and medical organizations, and labor inspection (Kotkin, 1995). Industrial enterprises supported everyday life and served as distributors of material resources and social benefits. Because of the way the enterprises operated, an individual's life could be controlled not just within but also outside the confines of the factory. The range of issues employers dealt with may surprise readers today. They ranged from safety issues to legal advice and aid to low-income families. Soviet enterprises assigned flats, put children in kindergarten, arranged group tours, and even organized food supply and public transport.

The company had to teach its employees to be workers as well as city dwellers, since the overwhelming majority of migrants to urban areas (as much as 80 percent) came from neighboring villages (Repinetskii and Rumiantseva, 2005, p. 206). This goal was certainly very difficult, given that the lifestyle of former peasants was very different from the disciplined regime of industry. The cyclical order of life was broken. Peasants counted time in terms of tasks and assignments finished rather than as a given number of working hours, and the completion of tasks on farms was marked by festivities. The social composition of the population had an impact not only on their working habits but also on their sense of morals and ethical principles. A low level of self-control and lack of required qualifications among workers compelled factory administrators to educate them and take measures against "unhealthy conduct in everyday life:" drunkenness, wife-beating, domestic violence, and brawling. Not surprisingly, these were sometimes classified as breaches of labor discipline and the work code, even if they occurred outside the factory. Many educational programs of this time "enlightened" and bestowed "culture," teaching how to cook, what to read, how to bring up children, how to build up family relations, and even about the everyday use of chemicals (TsGASO, f. 4187, op. 1, d. 27, l. 2). For example, in 1963 one of the district committees on the atheistic education of youth reported: "The library hosted the public party debate 'Who Can Be Brought into Communism.' In addition, a poster advertising anti-religious books was displayed, together with a list of recommended books for reading, such as *Soviet People in Space* and *Towards Communism without God*" (TsGASO, f. 4187, op. 1, d. 28, l. 41).

Indeed, disciplinary measures had the pragmatic goal of consolidating the labor force. The dense settlement of workers in apartment blocks and communal flats, along with the construction of housing and cultural and social infrastructure, meant that everything, including everyday life, leisure time, and social life, was supervised and controlled. Michel Foucault defines any closed environment or space as a social institution of power. According to him, a new type of surveillance, hierarchized, continuous, and functional, "ran right through the labour process [and] did not bear—or not only—on production [...]; it also took into account the activity of the men, their skill, the way they set about their tasks, their promptness, their zeal, their behaviour" (Foucault, 1995, p. 174). Such control was possible in the Soviet Union due to specially designed worker suburbs. For example, one of the huge machine building plants in Kuibyshev ran eight kindergartens, nine shops, a secondary school, a vocational school, a hospital with an ambulance, a sports club with a stadium and swimming pool, a café, and several canteens.

For several hundred years, until the turn to collectivization of agriculture at the end of the 1920s, the patriarchal family and the rural agricultural commune (or *mir*) were the basic institutions of the Russian peasantry, which accounted for more than 80 percent of the population in the pre-revolutionary period (Mironov, 1994, pp. 54–55). Within the traditional social order, peer control served to ensure that the stability of social groups and peasant institutions such as families, communes, and religious groups was upheld. Very often it was a simple question of these groups' physical survival. With the introduction of Soviet forced modernization, "care" became a slogan of state social policy. Even in the late 1950s, "care," which Bogdanova (2005, p. 78) has described as "an official codified rule of relations within Soviet society," reflected the logic of socialist paternalism. Everything—not just groups one might expect, like invalids, the elderly, orphans, or the socially marginalized—became the subject of "care." By the mid-1950s every stratum of society, every social, professional, and age group, was being taken care of. People were subjects and objects of care. The Communist Party "cared" about every city and enterprise, all enterprises cared about their employees, and everyone cared about colleagues, friends and the ordinary Soviet citizen. In Mironov's words (1994, p. 72), authoritarian interpersonal and social relations of the peasant family and commune later "served both as fertile ground and as socio-psychological prerequisites for the creation of an authoritarian regime within the country."

As is evident from the archive material, everyday disciplinary offenses were the normal type of cases reviewed by the various voluntary organizations of the 1950s and 1960s. The "enemies of the people" of previous decades were now replaced by other themes and characters such as "social parasites," "hooligans," vagrants, alcoholics, and idle youth. Very often men exhibited what was considered "inappropriate conduct," which usually meant separation from the family, neglect of the family and children or an "inappropriate" attitude towards the family, the humiliation of women, and especially "moral degradation." Those who demonstrated such vices could be expelled from the party. Extramarital relations, seen as breaches of legitimate gender norms, were perceived as defying Soviet ethical principles. It is not a coincidence, then, that the newspaper *Trud* (Labor) in 1959 published for "public discussion" the draft Code of Procedure of Comrades' Courts and included an item called "the undignified treatment of women and parents and the inadequate upbringing of children" (SOGASPI, f. 714, op. 1, d. 2367).[4]

Prior to legal action it was possible to settle family disputes by an appeal to a local party committee or voluntary structures, women's councils or comrades' courts, who acted as elective bodies. By 1964, out of a total of 2,621 comrades' courts in the Kuibyshev region, 1,219 were established in companies and organizations and only 447 within housing management committees (SOGASPI, f. 8755, op. 2, d. 90, l. 10). While the former dealt with minor thefts, disciplinary offenses, and violations of industrial safety, the latter handled communal affairs, immoral behavior, and neglect of children. Comrades' courts generally had a pre-emptive function. The decisions they took were usually backed up by persuasion, social disapproval, reprimands, and warnings. Guided by the principle "educate, don't punish," the courts suggested measures such as disciplinary penalties, fines, reductions of bonuses or summer vacation, eviction, dismissal from work, removal of parental rights, and cancellation of urban residential registration, to be undertaken by the respective authorities. Nevertheless, the most common practice was intervention by a collective body to educate the individual. Discussions of morals and the conduct of individuals were very typical of comrades' courts. Complaints were lodged with them at the prompting of enterprise administrations or as a result of signals from comrades and complaints from individuals: the latter was regarded as the responsibility of neighbors and co-workers.

The Revival of Women's Councils in the Thaw Years

In contrast to the emancipation rhetoric of the radical 1920s, women were no longer treated as a generally backward group. But the notion of the backward village woman lived on. Thus peasant women were treated as comrades who needed special guidance and who were very difficult to mobilize for the creation of women's councils in collective farms in rural areas (SOGASPI, f. 714, op. 1, d. 2394, l. 19). The sphere of Soviet women's responsibility constantly expanded. A woman was expected to be not just a worker, but a front-rank worker; not merely a mother, but a mother of many children; not a mere social activist, but a people's deputy. A massive increase in the creation of women's councils began just after the 1960 party decree "On the Goals of Party Propaganda in Contemporary Conditions," which suggested boosting output by increasing women's role in production and social work. The leading activists from district councils were delegated to city and oblast councils. According to an account from a local archive, by 1962 there were 400 women's councils operating in industrial enterprises in the transport and construction sectors, and in medical and educational establishments, research institutions and housing management committees. Close to 3,000 women from different social groups had been elected to work in these councils (SOGASPI, f. 714, op. 1, d. 2346, l. 102). This number is comparable to the women's councils from the neighboring city of Saratov: a total of 1,713 people from several backgrounds had been involved there (Ilič, 2009). So the situation in Kuibyshev was rather typical.

Most of the issues discussed by women's councils have been perceived as purely "women's issues." However, these councils were usually composed of several sections or committees working, for example, with production, activities with children, housing, food and nutrition, and culture and entertainment. Councils in factories and plants reported that "there were many petitions requesting intervention in family life. In particular, there were too many complaints about how husbands behaved towards their families" (SOGASPI, f. 714, op. 1, d. 2346, l. 38 ob). It is hardly surprising to come across cases with the following heading: "On Abnormal Relations between Husbands and Wives, the Incorrect Collection of Alimony, on Assistance for Single Mothers and Women with Large Families" (ibid., l. 49). True, the councils and comrades' courts could not take legal decisions affecting families or individual family members, but proceedings were initiated on their requests, and administrative measures were taken. For instance, in one case a council was able to banish a woman from the city for five years for "immoral conduct" (SOGASPI, f. 714, op. 1, d. 2394, l. 31). In 1957 housekeeping and home economics classes were reintroduced into the secondary school after a twenty-year absence. Mothers who worked full-time did not show daughters how to cook or clean. While the traditional method of passing on skills from the older to the younger was lost, the council's activities did include classes for young mothers and lectures on cooking (SOGASPI, f. 714, op. 1, d. 2394, l. 21). The councils taught women how to become informed consumers, advised them on how to "dress nicely and inexpensively," and helped arrange flowers for Women's Day. Therefore, councils focused mainly on maternal concerns and reproduced quasi-family relations within workers' collectives, like a family at work.[5] Women activists cooked for enterprise festivities, helped organize children's holidays, made sure that sanitary and hygienic norms were upheld, and issued satirical papers.

Complaints and petitions to various official bodies or citizen's associations became a powerful means for intervening in family and neighbor relations. The archive material shows how women took full advantage of privileges granted to war veterans[6] and women: "I am the wife of a soldier who died while defending his Motherland," "As a Soviet woman I cannot tolerate such an offense," "This petition comes from a woman worker, the wife of a disabled soldier of the Patriotic War, and a mother of two underage children" (SOGASPI, f. 7614, op. 12, d. 111, ll. 15–16, 132–136).

The state family policy can clearly be detected in the way the moral ideal of a "solid Soviet family" was used. Fighting for the family meant first of all combating divorces. Women's councils made every effort to keep the Soviet family intact. In 1958 a party decree was issued entitled "How to Fight Drinking and How to Deal with the Sale of Strong Alcoholic Beverages." It is interesting to note that alcohol consumption was considered not a personal concern but an economic problem (leading to disruptions in productivity) and a political issue (potentially leading to espionage and sabotage). In reality, however, alcoholism became a serious and widespread social malaise. Archival documents indicate that male alcoholism was a leading cause of divorce. Wives' and mothers' appeals regarding drunkenness constituted the majority of the complaints to voluntary organizations. These were women who saw themselves as moral agents tasked with saving marriage and observing the norms of Soviet morals: "Citizen Toporova has complained to the headquarters of the volunteer people's patrol that her husband gets drunk and brawls. As a result of several visits and repeated talks, he stopped drinking, and the family is well" (SOGASPI, f. 714, op. 1, d. 2370, l. 4).

No gathering or party could be imagined without alcohol. For example, the consumption of Zhiguli brand beer was measured in buckets. Popular anecdotes and jokes like the following responded to the issue at the time: "Why can't Russian women walk on high heels? Because they drag heavy bags on one side, kids on the other, their drunk husbands behind them, and have a Seven-Year Plan ahead of them" (Dushechkina, 2007, p. 153). This joke reflected gender stereotypes that were popular not only in the Khrushchev period but throughout the entire Soviet era: a weak husband who badly needs to improve his character and a woman who is struggling against male degradation with state assistance.[7] To support the symbolic value of fatherhood, meetings of fathers were introduced in the early 1960s, and the best fathers were awarded honorary certificates in what was similar to a competition to improve production rates.

The Struggle against Divorce and Child Neglect as an Important Task of Women's Councils

According to statistical data, the demographic situation remained problematic. For example, there were three times as many single women as single men in the Middle Volga region. Divorces were increasing, and the birth rate seemed to be steadily declining. In the decade 1955–1965 it dropped 1.5 times. From 1950 to the mid-1960s, the number of divorces in the Russian Federation increased almost tenfold (Repinetskii and Rumiantseva, 2005, pp. 58, 144, 203), despite the fact that the government had made divorce procedures more expensive and lengthy with the aim of preventing premature decisions. To complicate matters further, housing problems for divorced people remained unresolved. Dividing flats was very difficult at that time, and the actual separation of couples was often delayed by several years. Officially, a housing market did not exist. A witty question about "where to bring a bride after the wedding" posed by one listener during an anti-religion lecture was interpreted as an ideological provocation, since it seemed to hint at the lack of housing in the Soviet Union (SOGASPI, f. 714, op. 1, d. 2406, ll. 34–45).[8] In villages the bridegroom brought the bride to his household, but in the Soviet urban context this gender pattern did not work.

The problems of family life were rooted not only in the consequences of a late modernization and industrialization but also in the absence of a positive, alternative role model for men. A lack of options for male self-realization, either in their traditional role of breadwinner or in any alternative role, resulted in the exclusion of men from the private sphere. The state, after all, was providing housing, kindergartens, and schools and was distributing food and goods. The workings of the women's councils testify that men's position was not inside the family, but outside of it—a position often likened to that of a naughty child. For instance, "Worker K. has misbehaved towards his family for a long time. He was rude to his wife and did not treat his children well" (SOGASPI, f. 714, op. 1, d. 2283, l. 18). Another example: "Worker M. drank a lot and did not spend his salary on his family. Following his wife's request, the women's councils had a special conversation with him. After questioning, he quit drinking and regularly provided the family with money" (ibid., d. 2346, l. 9).

The late 1950s were a period of intense discussion about the involvement of various participants in the upbringing of Soviet youth. In contrast to earlier pedagogical debates that played down the parents' role in the upbringing of children, the new discourse called for an upgrading of parental responsibility. There were lectures on parental authority in factories and enterprises during lunch breaks, and women's councils would monitor women who "did not bring up their children appropriately." The patriarchal subordination of family members had disappeared. Instead, parental authority was to be supported by experts (war veterans, teachers, doctors) and assisted by neighbors and co-workers.

One of the signs of the times was the renewal (since the 1920s) of a broad discussion on child neglect. In the countryside, any elder person could look after children while the parents were busy, but in the city, because both parents were employed, children were left to themselves. Child neglect was considered to be a consequence of the urban lifestyle. As Melanie Ilič points out in her study on leading Soviet women's magazines in the Khrushchev era, the "Soviet family was sustained through many decades via reliance on the network of the extended family. The grandmother *(babushka)* was an essential component of domestic childcare arrangements" (Ilič, 2004).

But not all families had a grandmother. In the postwar period retirees and housewives had been asked to fulfill a social duty as volunteers and public tutors. They joined citizen's associations in the apartment blocks or residential areas where they lived. In 1958 the Communist Party issued a decision on involving retired people in "active social work." As a result, in the Kirovskii district of Kuibyshev, a group of fourteen pensioners studied how children lived and examined potential causes of neglect. In 1960, thanks to their efforts, 335 neglected children were identified, and sixty-nine letters were sent to their parents' workplaces (SOGASPI, f. 714, op. 1, d. 2144, l. 8). Although the veteran movement was not officially supported until 1965, the first pensioner clubs appeared under Khrushchev. In the spirit of Soviet enthusiasm, senior citizens everywhere took volunteer positions as teachers, agitators, and coaches.

Still, we should not forget that the status in Soviet society not only of retirees but also of housewives (a group defined as women with children) was rather uncertain. Due to the official goal of total involvement of women in production, by the 1960s the percentage of the population that was fully employed had reached its limit (Repinetskii and Rumiantseva, 2005, p. 205). The results of the 1959 national Soviet census led to nonworking housewives being identified as a possible source for wage labor (Ilič, 2009). In 1946 only 14.3 percent of mothers with three or more children worked at the industrial enterprises of the Volga region; by 1961 this figure had increased to 57 percent (Repinetskii and Rumiantseva, 2005, pp. 111, 199). The 1961 Soviet government decree "For Intensification of the Struggle against Persons Avoiding Socially Useful Work and Leading an Anti-Social Parasitic Way of Life" put housewives in a difficult situation. According to Sheila Fitzpatrick (2006), citizens were concerned that the measures to be taken in this struggle would affect women belonging to this group. This nuance was skillfully used in complaints: "the handicapped working woman of the working class" was contrasted with "an idler who does not work anywhere and just hangs around gossiping" (SOGASPI, f. 7614, op. 2, d. 19, l. 63 ob-64).

The portrayal of weaknesses in family upbringing was restricted mainly to single-parent families, although the attitude toward single mothers and extramarital relations became more tolerant in the difficult demographic situation of the postwar years. Children from single-parent families were given increased attention by voluntary organizations and were increasingly seen as a risk group. A note saying "no father, single-mother child" was viewed as an extenuating circumstance when reviewing disciplinary offenses. Members of volunteer people's patrols were also supposed to identify problematic families. They detained children on the streets, visited families with delinquent teenagers, and observed housing conditions. From numerous protocols and reports, we can see how this kind of work was organized: "On weekdays from eight to twelve in the evening and on Saturdays and Sundays from six p.m. to two a.m., a group of seven to ten members of a volunteer patrol makes the rounds in an effort to stop teenage delinquency. Children who have been guilty of mischievous activity were asked to come with their parents to headquarters. Later, notification letters were sent to the parents' offices" (SOGASPI, f. 714, op. 1, d. 2370, l. 2). Local campaigns were organized to identify cases of child neglect. For instance, a similar approach was used by the volunteers making sanitary inspections (*sanupolnomochennye*) who were supposed to identify sick people in the apartments they visited and were tasked with organizing outings for children whose parents were busy working.

CONCLUSIONS

This chapter has focused on the numerous public family policy initiatives in the 1950s and 1960s, which existed mainly as a supplement to legal procedures but were nevertheless quite influential and widespread. Discussion has also touched on the ideological mobilization of families and the pressure on women as responsible for the social institution of the family. Various voluntary organizations such as women's councils, housing committees, and comrades' courts dealt with family issues. They were supposed to resolve the problems of deficient parental attention that appeared as a consequence of the "working mother" gender contract. As part of the Soviet gender order, external involvement in family affairs was seen as a form of care and protection. The issue is illustrated using archive materials belonging to regional voluntary organizations, the trade unions under whose auspices they functioned, and the Communist Party.

The voluntary organizations assisted families and schools, and they participated in campaigns for improved health, harmonious families, and divorce prevention. The public (*obshchestvennost'*) functioned as an intermediary and a conductor of activities typical of an etacratic gender order. Faith in the decisive role of the public in educational and enlightening activities was generated along with the power that collectivism had over people's minds. Thus one could say that the voluntary organizations—as they were intended to do—demonstrated some success in taking over some functions of the state.

The period of Khrushchev's reforms, the Thaw, led to wide-ranging changes in Soviet cultural and social patterns. Intellectuals and dissidents raised questions about the private life of the Soviet citizen. Highly polemical new literary trends, names, journals, and films turned the focus of interest towards the private sphere, gender relations, and new cultural trends. The influence of Western trends in urban living and daily culture (including housing, living conditions, fashion, and childcare) became a defining feature. Nevertheless, the new moral order declared by the Communist Party after Stalin's death and the new social policies towards the Soviet citizen disregarded gender and were based, as before, on class background. The idea of emancipating the Soviet people demanded a system of social control. Taking into account surviving traditions of social control in Russian peasant culture, I have in this chapter used provincial archival materials authored by both men and women to illustrate the intervention of the state in all spheres of life.

I have also focused on the language of public discourse relating to gender and family issues. With regard to shaping the history of totalitarian culture, we have to keep in mind that Soviet-style "emancipation" did not rigidly distinguish between public and private. As Mironov (1994: 73) concludes in his study of the origins of Soviet authoritarianism, the socialization of private life (when labor collectives took responsibility for the moral character of their members vis-à-vis official organs, resolved family problems, and looked after health needs) was characteristic of communal relations. But in the end, it was the Thaw generation that crystallized ideas about the new Soviet citizen and a new mentality on the basis of publicly discussed philosophical and moral principles. Traditional gender roles and the division of labor in families, however, were not questioned during this period. On the contrary, they were supported by state policy.

Notes

1 This meant that the area could not be visited by foreign citizens or tourists. To keep military secrets and thwart espionage, enterprises in such areas did not have any official names or trademarks, but rather were given a post office number where correspondence could be sent. For instance, in Kuibyshev there were plants named "P.O. Box 24" and "P.O. Box 76."
2 I am very grateful to Melanie Ilič for this comment.
3 On the housewives' movement in the interwar period, see also Fitzpatrick (1999, pp. 156–163) and Buckley (2001).
4 In Russian: *"О недостойном отношении к женщине и родителям, выполнении обязанностей по воспитанию детей"*
5 For a more detailed examination of Soviet discourses on maternity, see Gradskova (2007).
6 After World War II the state social policy provided some support for war veterans.
7 For a deeper analysis of the strong women/weak men dichotomy in socialist countries, see Christine Farhan's chapter in this volume.
8 On the last Soviet, state-sponsored anti-religious campaign, see Zhidkova (2008) and Paert (2004).

References

Archive Documents

Samarskii oblastnoi gosudarstvennyi arkhiv sotsialno-politicheskoi istorii (SOGASPI), Samara Regional Archive of Social and Political History

Fond 656 (Kuibyshevskii oblastnoi komitet KP RSFSR), op.130, ed. khr. 498.

f. 714 (Kuibyshevskii gorodskoi komitet KP RSFSR), op. 1, ed. khr. 2144, 2283, 2346, 2367, 2370, 2394, 2395, 2406.

f. 7614 (Novokuibyshevskii gorodskoi komitet KP RSFSR), op. 2, ed. khr. 19; op. 12, ed. khr. 111.

f. 8755 (Kuibyshevskii promyshlennyi obkom KPSS), op. 2, 1963–1964 gg. - ed. khr. 90.

Tsentralnyi gosudarstvennyi arkhiv Samarskoi oblasti (TsGASO), Central State Archive of Samara Region

f. 4187 (Upolnomochennyi Soveta po delam Russkoi pravolslavnoi tserkvi pri Sovete ministrov SSSR po Kuibyshevskoi oblasti) op. 1, 1962 g. - ed. khr. 27, 1963 g. - ed. khr. 28.

Literature

Bogdanova, Elena. 2005. "Sovetskaia traditsiia pravovoi zashchity, ili v ozhidanii zaboty" (The Soviet tradition of legal defense). *Neprikosnovennyi zapas* 39, no. 1: 76–84.

Buckley, Mary. 2001. "The Untold Story of the Obshchestvennitsa in the 1930s." In *Women in the Stalin Era*, ed. Melanie Ilič, 151–172. Basingstoke, UK: Palgrave.

Dushechkina, Elena. 2007. *Svetlana: ulturnaia istoriia imeni* (Svetlana: The cultural history of a name). St. Petersburg: EUSPb.

Fitzpatrick, Sheila. 1999. *Everyday Stalinism: Ordinary Life in Extraordinary Times; Soviet Russia in the 1930s*. New York and Oxford: Oxford University Press.

Foucault, Michel. 1995. *Discipline and Punish: The Birth of the Prison*. Translated by Alan Sheridan. New York: Vintage.

Gradskova, Youlia. 2007. *Soviet People with Female Bodies: Performing Beauty and Maternity in Soviet Russia in the Mid 1930–1960s*. Stockholm: Acta Universitatis Stockholmiensis.

Ilič, Melanie, ed. 2001. *Women in the Stalin Era*. Basingstoke, UK: Palgrave.

———. 2004. "Women in the Khrushchev Era: An Overview." In *Women in the Khrushchev Era*, eds. Melanie Ilič, Susan E. Reid, and Lynne Attwood, 5–28. Basingstoke, UK: Palgrave.

———. 2009. "What Did Women Want? Khrushchev and the Revival of the Zhensovety." In *Soviet State and Society under Nikita Khrushchev*, eds. Melanie Ilič and Jeremy Smith, 104–121. London and New York: Routledge.

Kharkhordin, Oleg. 1997. "Reveal and Dissimulate: A Genealogy of Private Life in Soviet Russia." In *Public and Private in Thought and Practice: Reflections on a Grand Dichotomy*, eds. Jeff Weintraub and Krishan Kumar, 337–363. Chicago: University of Chicago Press.

———. 2001. "Fuko i issledovanie fonovyhk praktik v Rossii" (Foucault and the study of background practices in Russia). In *Misel Fuko i Rossiia*, ed. Oleg Kharkhordin, 46–81. St. Petersburg: EUSPb.

Kotkin, Stephen. 1995. *Magnetic Mountain: Stalinism as a Civilization*. Berkeley: University of California Press.

Kozlova, Natalia. 1996. *Gorizonty povsednevnosti sovetskoi epokhi: golosa iz khora* (The horizons of everydayness of the Soviet era: Voices from the choir). Moscow: RAN, Institut filosofii.

———. 2005. *Sovetskie lyudi. Stseny iz istorii* (Soviet people: Scenes from history). Moscow: Evropa.

Kushkova, Anna. 2006. "Derevenskii tovarishcheskii sud perioda 'razvitogo sotsializma': vvedenie v problematiku i metodologiyu izuchenia" (The village comrades' court during the period of "developed socialism:" Introduction to problematics and methodology). In *Pravo v zerkale zhizni: issledovaniia po yuridicheskoi antropologii* (Law in the mirror of life: Studies in legal anthropology), ed. N.I. Novikova, 320–334. Moscow: Strategiia.

———. 2007. "Phenomenon of 'Comrades' Courts:" Between Customary and Official Justice (Based on Contemporary Field Materials from Northwestern Russia)." Manuscript.

Lebina, Natalia. 2006. *Entsiklopediia banal'nostei: sovetskaia povsednevnost'. Kontury, simvoly, znaki* (Encyclopedia of banalities: Soviet everydayness; Contours, symbols, signs). St. Petersburg: Dmitrii Bulanin.

Leibovich, Oleg. 2008. *V gorode M. Ocherki sotsialnoi povsednevnosti sovetskoi provintsii v 40–50-kh gg.* (In the city of M: Sketches of social everydayness of a Soviet province in the '40s and '50s). Moscow: Rossiiskaia politicheskaia entsiklopediia (ROSSPEN).

Mironov, Boris. 1994. "Peasant Popular Culture and the Origins of Soviet Authoritarianism." In *Cultures in Flux: Lower-Class Values, Practices, and Resistance in Late Imperial Russia*, eds. Stephen P. Frank and Mark D. Steinberg, 54–73. Princeton, NJ: Princeton University Press.

Paert, Irina. 2004. "Demystifying the Heavens: Women, Religion and Khrushchev's Anti-Religious Campaign, 1954–64." In *Women in the Khrushchev Era*, eds. Melanie Ilič, Susan Reid, and Lynne Attwood, 203–222. Basingstoke, UK: Palgrave.

Reid, Susan E. 2004. "'Byt—ne chastnoe delo': vnedrenie sovremennogo vkusa v semeinuyu zhizn'" ("Everyday life is not a private matter:" Introduction to contemporary taste in family life). In *Semeinye uzy: modeli dlia sborki (Family Bonds: Models to Assemble)*, ed. Sergei Oushakine, 1:360–391. Moscow: NLO.

Repinetskii, Alexander, and Maria Rumiantseva. 2005. *Gorodskoe naselenie Srednego Povolzh'ia v poslevoennoe dvadtsatiletie. 1946–1965 gg.: ocherki demograficheskoi istorii.* (The urban population of the Middle Volga region in the postwar decades 1946–1965: Sketches of demographical history). Samara, Russia: NTTs.

Temkina, Anna, and Anna Rotkirch. 2007. "Sovetskie gendernye kontrakty i ikh transformatsiia v sovremennoi Rossii" (Soviet gender contracts and their transformation in contemporary Russia). In *Rossiiskii gendernyi poriadok: sotsiologicheskii podkhod (Russian gender order: sociological approach)*, eds. Elena Zdravomyslova and Anna Temkina, 169–200. St. Petersburg: EUSPb.

Zdravomyslova, Elena, and Anna Temkina. 2007. "Sovetskii etakraticheskii gendernyi poriadok" (The Soviet etacratic gender order). In *Rossiiskii gendernyi poriadok: sotsiologicheskii podkhod*, eds. Elena Zdravomyslova, and Anna Temkina, 96–137. St. Petersburg: EUSPb.

Zhidkova, Elena. 2008. "Antireligioznaia kampaniia vremen 'ottepeli'" (The anti-religious campaign of the Thaw period). In *Neprikosnovennyi zapas* 59, no. 3, http://magazines.russ.ru/nz/2008/3/zh12.html (accessed August 11, 2011).

Zubkova, Elena. 2008. "V kruge blizhnem. Chastnaia zhizn' sovetskogo cheloveka" (In the intimate circle: The private life of the Soviet individual). In *Rodina* 7, http://www.istrodina.com/rodina_articul.php3?id=2675&n=130 (accessed August 11, 2011).

CHAPTER 3

A Life of Labor, a Life of Love: Telling the Life of a Young Peasant Mother Facing Collectivization

Ildikó Asztalos Morell

Introduction

This was when the cooperative started. I will never forget how horrible it was. I was taken home from the [maternity] hospital, and there they were: the agitators, as we used to call them. One was a Mrs. Bözsi. She was a stern captain. I went to her to cry. I said: "They took me home with my little baby. This is Magdi [her first child]. She is to turn two in July. What shall I do?" "We'll solve it!" she said. But we could not take her to day-care. There was no crèche. There was nothing we could do. [Katalin, who was a young peasant woman in the early 1960s]

The household of a peasant family in the pre-collective period was a unit of production and consumption, but collectivization disrupted the production function. The aim of state socialism in agrarian matters was to dissolve the traditional peasant household radically through collectivization. Women's emancipation and collectivization of the agrarian sector were two of the alleged "humanization" agendas of state socialism. This chapter seeks to shed light on the experience of these two interconnected "humanization" projects as reflected in the life history of Katalin, a young, married mother with a former "middle peasant" background. While accounts of collectivization typically focus on the organization of production, this chapter applies an intersectional perspective to focus on family relations and the relations of reproduction. The impact of collectivization (the class transition from peasantry to collective workers) is scrutinized from the perspective of a cross-section of class, gender, and generational relations in family life. These three intersecting aspects are viewed not as additive but as articulated with each other (Walby, 2007; Yuval-Davis, 2006).

Intersecting Class, Gender, and Demographic Relations through Life History Analysis

Rural women's lives were shaped by two interrelated communist projects: the collectivization of the agrarian sector and the emancipation of women. According to the rhetoric of state socialism, women were to be liberated by participating in paid labor, thereby cutting the ties of personal dependency on a patriarchal system of bondage that was condemned as "domestic slavery." Putting this ideal of emancipation into practice did, in fact, alter the gender contract (Asztalos Morell, 2007b; Fodor, 2002; Goven, 2002; Haney, 2002) by weakening both men's ability to be the main breadwinners and women's economic dependency. Nonetheless, women continued to be the main caregivers, while men's freedom from caregiving responsibility was not challenged. The state was supposed to create institutions that would release women from their care duties. This would both create the preconditions for liberating women from "domestic slavery" and provide professionalized care based on scientifically approved methods. It has been argued that contrary to the ideals, women were caught in a dependent relationship to the almighty state as a *pater familias* providing for its citizens. Thus women were in explicit debt to the state (Goven, 2002). In the Stalinist 1950s the masculinized woman was an ideal. The widely propagated figure of the tractor-driving woman contributed to a politicized image of rural women that collided with common rural perceptions of femininity, which led to conflicts in the process of implementing emancipatory ideals in the countryside (Farkas, 2003).

Following the de-Stalinization politics of 1956, a "renaturalization" of the gender contract strengthened the nurturing role of the family and women's maternal role within the family. As a consequence, a comprehensive childcare subsidy was introduced in 1967 that allowed working mothers to take paid leave (Asztalos Morell, 1999; Haney, 2002). In Hungary the collectivization of agriculture was completed relatively late, in 1961, and was thus accomplished in a period when the gender regime was moving away from the Stalinist paradigm (which was characterized by a strong image of the state as the *pater familias* and a masculine ideal of women's emancipation) towards a renaturalized paradigm characterized by a reevaluation of the family as a nurturing institution and women as caregivers (Asztalos Morell, 2007b).

Instead of leading to a production organization of equals, collectivization created a hierarchy based on social differentiation (Juhász, 1976). Based on the integration of women into subordinate positions of paid labor and on a gender-differential division of caregiving, the new post-1956 gender contract in Hungary led to new forms of subordination for women within the cooperative production machine and signaled women's incorporation into what we can call—applying Walby's term (1997)—a system of public patriarchy. In this organization men obtained core positions that brought with them full co-operative membership, year-round employment, and highly skilled jobs that provided power and prestige. Women became integrated as working family members in seasonal unskilled manual labor. Moreover, since women were less than full members of the collective and thus only marginally integrated, they were only partially incorporated into the benefit systems of the welfare state (Asztalos Morell, 1999). The three-year childcare subsidy system GYES was introduced in 1967, but the integration of women who worked in collectives was delayed. This meant that rural women were less supported and therefore less dependent on the welfare state than their urban sisters. Meanwhile, private dependency on male breadwinners weakened but was not superseded. Inequalities rooted in the public and private systems of patriarchy were articulated with each other.

The Hungarian experience of collectivization differs somewhat from the process elsewhere. The horrors of Soviet collectivization in the 1930s claimed eight million lives (Denisova, 2010). Women became the majority of the kolkhoz labor force, which performed mainly manual labor. Like the early collectivized labor force, they were not covered by social security schemes or guaranteed wages. The Soviet economy prioritized the expansion of heavy industry and resource extraction (in the form of both products and men's labor) from agriculture. During the collectivization of the 1930s, Stalin sought to base agriculture on women's labor. This aim was reflected in the iconographic representation of agriculture in Mukhina's famous 1937 sculpture, which portrays a peasant woman holding a sickle (Bonnell, 1997; Waters, 1991). By contrast, although rural men were considered a labor reserve for heavy industry in Hungary as well during the collectivization of the 1960s, agriculture was not perpetuated as a female sphere. Women were instead integrated as a secondary labor category.

While radical societal transformations set the outer frames for individual life experiences, they are also formed by the individual's shifting existential positions, which evolve along the demographic stages of life within ever-changing constellations of intergenerational relations. These in turn are related to specific gender and social positions (Asztalos Morell, 2008; Melberg, 2005; Sireni, 2008). The key formative periods of life are related to personal phases such as birth, childhood, and marriage, as well as to formative periods of working careers. A person's identity and ability to experience, understand, and form his or her life conditions is formed along the intersection of class, gender, and demographic positions (Walby, 2007).

Power, Autonomy, and Personal Agency in the Interpretation of Life Histories

The individual's potential to form his or her personal life is circumscribed by the hegemonic power relations of the given historical moment. According to Hobson (1990), however, agency prevails even in subordinated situations when it comes to choosing among voicing, accepting, or exiting. Thus even awareness of the unjust conditions of one's existence does not necessarily entail the loss of agency in forming life opportunities. This is not to imply that those in positions that can theoretically be seen as subjugated view their position that way themselves. Skeggs (1997) has pointed to working-class women who find pride and respectability in identifying with maternal and domestic roles normally characterized by lack of control over the economic resources of life. In different research contexts Eriksson (2003) and Björnberg (2005) also point to the paradox within family negotiations where women make fully autonomous decisions that nonetheless lead to positions in which they become economically dependent within their partner relations. Harmony achieved in the relationship is deemed to be more important than personal achievement. Thus paradoxically, personal feelings of harmony and satisfaction can be derived from a feeling of agency in decisions concerning life choices, even if these choices lead to subjugation and dependency in the relations that determine life opportunities.[1]

Consequently, the forms of agency differ depending on the individual's own perception of more or less blatant forms of subjugation. Power can be perceived as more blatant in a public relationship compared to a private one, since it can obstruct individual possibilities for self-realization in more or less obtrusive ways. In some cases private dependency can be a consequence of injustices suffered in the public sphere, caused, for example, by an imposed division of labor associated with collectivization rather than with an informal contract within the family.

Agency can also be problematized as private versus collective. During the Soviet collectivization of the 1930s, peasant women expressed their discontent in collective protest actions. These organized *bab'i bunty* ("women's riots") argued for production based on the household rather than the collective (Viola, 1986). Women had a central role in household-based production following collectivization in Hungary as well. Organized women's protest actions, however, did not play a central role in the "silent revolution" that led to an increase in the importance of this form of production (Szelényi, 1988). It is of interest to see how individuals are presented as part of the collective through self-representations in life stories. How do they position their own agency into the context of a collective?

Life histories provide interpretations of the individual's own past as empowering or disempowering. Personal understandings of past life events as enriching or impoverishing express ambiguities arising both from shifting positions of control over these events and from available possibilities for self-realization. Thus concepts of autonomy, abilities, power, and agency emerged also as interpretative constructs from an inductive analysis of the interviews. This chapter attempts to unravel whether the understandings presented in Katalin's life history express empowerment and/or disempowerment in the formative events of life, which crystallized along constellations between her shifting class, gender, and demographic positions.

Oral History and Interpreting Life Experiences

The fall of state socialism radically changed the possibilities for scholars of this period. Not only did the archives open up, offering various written documents of the past, but peoples' recollections of their past were also unlocked in a way that had been unthinkable before, when memories were actively censored and the legitimated code of history writing was safeguarded. Collecting memories of ordinary people is thus of the utmost importance today, when the generation that experienced collectivization firsthand has reached an advanced age. However, postmodern history writing has called attention to diverse flaws in interpreting life histories as sources of historical documentation (Hansson and Thor, 2006). Although the large-scale societal transformations of this historical period affected, among others, women's lives, history itself was created by the way these women performed and experienced their lives.[2]

This study explores the historical period from an individual perspective by focusing on the ways in which women reflect on their lives and their ability to realize themselves both in working life and in family relations. Life histories, then, are viewed as self-construals (Öberg, 1997) and as stories about a self-realization process. Thus they are not scrutinized as historical sources in the traditional sense (Hansson and Thor, 2006) but are used to elucidate the ways women understood and found meaning in their lives.[3]

I see life histories as ways in which participating actors convey an understanding of how social transition (in this case to state socialism) was experienced and made sense of, and how these experiences and the emerging understandings were contextualized in the diverse social, gender, demographic positions that these actors occupied. Personal memories are seen as subjective reconstructions of the past. However, they are also viewed as produced collectively through negotiations in different arenas. They are produced in the context of an interview situation that takes place in a certain time and space in history, which means that they are created from the horizon of an understanding of more recent experiences. Furthermore, memories of the past are understandings of personal experiences formed in the context of macrosocietal events such as collectivization and dominant public discourses on the one hand, and in the context of personal events on the other. The interpretations of past or present events constitute socially situated knowledge, since they are formed from a certain social position of the actor. The public voicing of memories that creates socially "accepted" discourses is a negotiated process and an expression of power. The end of socialism altered the terms of voicing memories and alternative interpretations of collectivization.

Through the analysis of one life story, the story of Katalin, this chapter attempts to give voice to the life experiences of one actor during collectivization. The interview with Katalin was recorded in 2007 in Hungary as a part of a broader investigation into the social origins of rural entrepreneurs in post-socialist Hungary. A sample of families was identified from a set of interviews conducted with fifty farm families living in villages in a fifty-kilometer radius from Budapest who succeeded in establishing viable farms after the reprivatization of agriculture. In this sample of six families, the elderly generation was also interviewed. The sample was chosen to exemplify different rural social strata. Katalin belonged to the elderly generation of a family with roots in the middle peasantry prior to collectivization. Her fate can be considered representative of the fate of women of her generation and social standing. While members of kulak families suffered harsher repressions and were often excluded from the collectives, middle peasant women were actively recruited as the "foot soldiers" of the collective labor force prior to the comprehensive mechanization that expanded by the 1970s and made these women's manual work superfluous.

The study's main purpose is to interpret personal life experiences as part of a collective memory of a period that was nonetheless formed distinctly depending on the social, gender, and demographic position of the actors.

Personal life experiences involve recollections of a life and also an evaluation of key events. The chapter seeks to improve our understanding of the value systems that can be identified as operative while the narrator reflects on the formative events of personal life histories and how these form the basis of gender-differential identities.

The analysis of the interviews was inspired by grounded theory (Glaser and Strauss, 1967; Mella, 2007). The interview text was coded into emerging themes that constituted the basis for interpretations. Expressions of value statements arose early on as a systematic way of sorting experiences into positive and negative. Thus life experiences were constructed in such polarities, and I have utilized them to elucidate the life experiences of my informant. I have sought to explore which events were narrated as negative and which were seen as positive. These value statements guided the formation of theories on how certain historical periods are perceived as "empowering" or "disempowering." Katalin's narrative evolves along evaluative understandings of formative moments in her life. She depicts her life as characterized by experiences that she perceived positively or negatively. Events of large-scale social transformation emerge interwoven with life experiences of a more personal nature.

Establishing the Family Farm as a Narration of Positive Life Experiences

Feelings of satisfaction are mixed with recollections of hardship in Katalin's narration of memories of the time when the family farm was established. Katalin describes positively the efforts to establish the new family farm with her husband:

> We worked to be able to buy out [my husband's] siblings and my mother-in-law. This took a lot of effort... The truth is that we were also very satisfied when we took over the land from his mother and siblings and were able to pay them. It was so good to be able to compensate them.

Thus Katalin and her husband had to work hard to end their economic dependency on her husband's family. She emphasizes the hardships involved by indicating that the terms of freedom were dictated by a harsh economic contract:

> Because everything was counted out in deciding how much one sister or the other, or the mother or my husband would [receive]—the horse, the cart and so on. The only thing that was not [counted] was the land. We took it on lease. There was an agreement about how much wheat and corn we had to give for it. Not money.

Taking over the farm would provide their subsistence. The opportunity to do so arrived when Katalin's father-in-law unexpectedly died. In 1954 her husband was to take over, but he was performing his military duty. One of the married sisters filled in for him temporarily, but she was not considered suited for the task, especially since her husband worked in the city. This meant that they were short a male hand:

> The daughter of my mother-in-law lived with her husband at her mother's place, but they did not know how to manage with all the work at home, since he [the husband of the sister-in-law] was working in Pest.

The family agreed that Katalin's husband should buy out the other siblings and take over the farm after finishing his military service. According to the inheritance practices of the time, all siblings received their share from the father's estate, while the mother kept her share.

Katalin's position was that of a *menyecske* (young farm wife) moving into the family of her husband. This position was the consequence of another aspect of inheritance, according to which daughters typically did not inherit land at the time of marriage and consequently entered the family of the husband without any landed property of their own to contribute. She described her position at marriage by saying she came with only a dowry:

> My husband's parents had 15–16 hectares. I left four siblings at home. At that time I did not take anything with me, only the lot that girls used to get.

The land transfers in her family of origin and in her family of marriage are both depicted in a non-conflicting manner. What instead comes to the fore in her story is the satisfaction she got from the control and autonomy achieved by buying out the siblings. She depicts herself as a participating agent, heroizing herself and her husband for the hard work leading to independence.

Thus, as discussed above, life histories reflect on the past through the filter of events both in the past and at the time of narration. Katalin's story about how her and her husband's family farm was established should be interpreted not only in its own historical context but also as an event that got its meaning through the filter of later experiences of collectivization. Furthermore, narrated memories are integrated into the self-construal of the narrator and can also be perceived as fulfilling a function within the narrated life history as a whole. Katalin's heroizing story serves as a statement about herself as a person with agency, but it also serves as a contrast to her actions later on.

Forced Collectivization

In contrast to the narrative about the establishment of the family farm as an empowering event, collectivization was depicted as disempowering, even victimizing. It is portrayed both as forced recruitment and as a process of incorporation into the labor organization of the cooperative. The female agitator "Mrs. Bözsi" embodied the brutality of recruitment. The event is told from the experience of the young mother. Katalin had just returned from the hospital with her newborn baby when Mrs. Bözsi came to their home to implement the forced collectivization. Katalin did not know how to arrange care for the children if she joined the collective. Seeking aid in a vulnerable situation as a mother, she turned for help to Mrs. Bözsi, the harsh agitator: "I went to her to cry." The total lack of empathy she encountered could only strengthen Mrs. Bözsi's inhuman image, and by extension, that of collectivization as well.

> "Did they try to coerce people?"
> "Indeed they did. I was crying so badly. I think you can imagine. Two little children, and this big, powerful communist woman, Mrs. Bözsi, would not stop bothering me. She had no compassion for anybody in this world."

The way the family and the children were deprived of their means of subsistence is central to Katalin's description of the brutality of the event:

> We had a cow that my husband and I had already bought. Since we had two children, we would really have had good use of it. But we had

to give even the cow away; they took everything we had—the crops, the hay, and everything. We used to have big stacks of alfalfa.... We thought we could give away half of the alfalfa and sell the other half to get some money for food, since we had no other source of money. But they took even that.

Collectivization also deprived the family of their means of production, and they were not given any economic compensation. The value of these assets could have been used to build a house for the family:

They came with their tractor and packed up whatever they could find, the cornstalk cutter, the harrow, just anything [...] We could have built a house for that. They took it all, and we received absolutely nothing. Not even an advance payment to make our life a little easier.

Thus the very act of forced recruitment is remembered from the young mother's standpoint as an event that deprived the family of its traditional subsistence base and assets and also undermined traditional solutions to the problem of childcare.

Family Strategies in the Face of Incorporation into the Collective

During the establishment phase of the collective production system, Katalin, like most women from her village, was employed as a manual worker in the cultivation of vegetables. She was allotted a certain amount of land for plants such as cucumbers and sugar beets. She was to organize the cultivation, which meant both hard physical labor and unreliable and low returns. They allotted the land without taking into account whether people were able to cultivate it:

They didn't care if you had a family or not. You got one *hold* [acre] of cucumbers [...] They didn't care whether we had the resources to harvest or not. If we didn't manage to harvest it, they would shout at us.

Katalin needed her husband and children's help to be able to carry out the work that was expected from her in the cooperative:

So my husband had to come home from work. And he wouldn't get any sleep. He came home and immediately he started to hoe and so on. He knew that all my chores were waiting for me [...] So he would come home around six. And then he would often stay out [on the fields] until ten.

Thus the work duties were all very demanding. It meant hard physical labor, including fieldwork, gathering crops by hand, loading manure and fertilizers, seeding grass... Apart from the fixed responsibility of cultivating a certain area for a certain product, women were also expected to help with all kinds of manual labor. The workload was experienced as dangerous to one's health. Katalin considered herself lucky compared to women who had no family to help them out:

There were women who were already 50–55 years old. Their children had already left the family to start their own families, so they could not help. Those unfortunate women, oh, how much they worked! All of them are crippled now. There is not one healthy woman in the village.

The system did not allow for sick leaves, since deliveries had to be made on an individual basis:

Fate has been hard on us. Even if we had problems, we could not take sick leave. We could go to a doctor, but he would never give us a shot or anything. Whatever happened, we had to go out on the fields, since the cucumbers had to be picked whether we had the strength or not.

Furthermore, the system did not allow women to work the year round. Yet although they were registered for only half the year, they were expected to be prepared to work all year. The unreliable and seasonal character of the work and the uncertain pay forced women to depend on a stable breadwinner. That this was a model intended and expected by the cooperative is clear from Katalin's recollections:

I had to join the cooperative with all our property, and my husband had to find a job to provide for the family, since we didn't get any money from the cooperative, even though we had given away everything!

Katalin's life, like that of other young mothers, was burdened by caregiver duties. Despite the emancipatory rhetoric promising that the state would provide care, cooperatives did little to live up to these goals. Instead, according to Katalin's story, the collective expected relatives to help young mothers to solve their childcare problems. What young mothers faced was insensitivity to their situation, both from the cooperative leaders ("solve it with your family, with your mother!") and from the local day-care center's teachers:

> Magdi started in day-care when she was three. When Józsi turned three, he was also accepted there [...] But he used to fall asleep all the time, sometimes even at 10 a.m. So they kicked him out. Then it was Kati, and there was no place for her. They decided themselves whom to accept. If they didn't want a child, they wouldn't accept it.

In the traditional system of family farms, a young mother could rely on the different generations to help each other. The young generation helped the parents with the physical work in the fields, and they could in turn expect help with childcare. However, collectivization made these mutual bonds of help obsolete:

> They always told me to solve my problems together with my family and with my mother. My mother was not a co-op member, but my mother-in-law was. But still she had a household plot with grapes to take care of... We had no time to help her cultivate her vineyard. She could not take the children.

Katalin explains the deterioration of the standard of life of the children as resulting from the dissolution of traditional patterns of mutual aid. One consequence of this was that children were forced to follow their working mothers to the fields: "There were so many children who grew up in the fields." Also, due to their mothers' workload, the children had to help:

> I will never forget one occasion. We had half a hectare of cucumbers, the normal thing. Then the children grew up a little and we had our third one, a daughter. She had to carry the cucumbers with us from the age of three.... We poured two buckets of cucumbers in a sack. My mother sewed a little sack for her. And she placed it by the side of the buckets and poured them into it. The children worked a lot.

Another aspect of the deterioration was that more distant relatives were also called upon to help, but they could not provide regular and reliable assistance, since they were also bound in various ways to their own duties. One of the relatives was Katalin's ten-year-old sister. She never finished school, most likely because of all the work she had to do. Katalin comments:

> The truth is that, as I said, my sister was ten years old when we joined the co-op. She is the one who didn't finish eighth grade. She came home from school [and took care of my children]. Then my husband has a sister. She was a seamstress. But poor her, she could not do anything else [but help them]. She saw that we were in trouble, that we didn't have any place to leave the children. "Leave them with me!" she said, "until Marika [Katalin's ten-year-old sister] comes to fetch them."

Although she appreciated her relatives' extraordinary help, Katalin also realized that these ad hoc arrangements did not provide a satisfactory solution for childcare:

> Poor children, they were pushed from one place to another. They were carried all over. My heart was bleeding for them. They did not have a place of their own. We really had very hard times.

Working in the cooperative meant that people were forced to solve their care problems privately. Katalin, however, did not have a sustainable solution. Besides her female relations (sisters and sister-in-law), she was supported in this difficult situation by her husband. However, rather than helping her out with care duties, he made her labor duties in the cooperative easier: "So my husband would come home from work. And he wouldn't get any sleep. He would come home and immediately he would start to hoe and so on." Consequently, despite the burdens that the cooperative put on women, the traditional gender division of labor that assigned care duties to women was reinforced. Thus in Katalin's narrative the solidarity of the family and relatives was juxtaposed with the brutality of the cooperative as manifested in its complete indifference toward women's childcare problems.

Agency and Victimization

The forced recruitment to the cooperative was depicted as a brutal, victimizing experience. However, the degree of victimization is diminished by Katalin's outcry. She did voice her anxiety, and she did cry on account of her children's fate, which made visible the involuntary nature of the event. Thus the cooperative's refusal to meet her outcry enhances her agency in this desperate situation.

Katalin contextualizes her continued enrollment in the cooperative in relation to her life situation and formulates it as a "choice" made under restrictive circumstances. She explains that as the mother of three children, she remained primarily because of their needs. She had to take a job in the village in order to be there for the children, for other jobs were not available:

> "Couldn't you have left the cooperative?"
> "Now, listen to me! I couldn't leave because of my three children! I couldn't take a job in a factory or in Pest. My husband was commuting, so I had to stay at home to get them ready for school and other things. To pay attention to them, make them do their homework, everything."

Katalin turns her self-sacrificing motherhood from a subjugated condition into a virtue. Despite the discontent she experienced because she could not arrange her children's care in the way she wanted, motherhood gives her life meaning and pride. Choosing motherhood to suit the perceived interests of children was not really an alternative to full-time motherhood for Katalin. It was instead a rhetorical resource that allowed her to maintain her self-respect under sub-optimal working conditions that prevented her from raising her children according to desired standards. Thus by representing herself as a self-sacrificing mother, she morally justifies accepting her dehumanizing working conditions. Remaining in the cooperative did not mean that she lost her critical stance on collectivization. As time passed, she stopped voicing critique by protesting and crying and shifted to a more passive strategy. She depicted this passivity as characterizing cooperative members at large and therefore positions herself as acting in the context of a common strategy:

> If we weren't ready with the picking, they would shout at us. Mrs. Bözsi would scream and curse. God, what a rude person she was! Nobody could deal with them, not even my father, though he was a

very able-bodied man, decisive and hard-working and all that. It all had to be according to their commands. Everybody got accustomed to the fact that it had to be as they decided.

Thus a kind of acceptance superseded the voicing of dissatisfaction as a choice based on reasoning about available alternatives. Having elected to stay with the cooperative in order to be there for the children, Katalin chose the least burdensome way to normalize conditions. An alternative strategy in my sample of life histories was to leave the cooperative. These two options (accept and exit) stand in contrast to the organized protest of *bab'i bunty* (Viola, 1986) in the Soviet Russia of the 1930s. These peasant women collectively organized protest actions demanding household-based production. Rather than organized protest, Katalin exercised her passive resistance in the context of a collective strategy that silently transferred the focus to the private plots that collective agriculture allowed its members (see Szelényi, 1988).

While explaining her choice as the result of maternal inclination, she also indicated that the women who joined the cooperative received a household plot that could be cultivated by the family and became very important for their subsistence. As time passed, the cooperative as a production form normalized, and social and economic conditions improved for both the workers and the cooperative, an improvement that Katalin noted when she recalled later periods of her life.

Conclusion: Feelings of Deprivation, Loss of Autonomy and Forms of Historical Agency

In summary, the experiences that Katalin recalls of the early cooperative period sharply contradict the self-professed commitment of the socialist state, which according to the ideology of women's emancipation was to raise women from patriarchal dependency on the family and provide childcare to help them participate in supposedly emancipatory paid work. Collectivization was to bring about the empowerment of women by integrating them into the labor force. This was to secure women an independent income and thereby end their economic dependence on their husbands and patriarchal families.

Instead, the analyses of change in both productive and reproductive roles narrated by Katalin indicate that due to forced collectivization, what she experienced was vulnerability and loss of control. This event was epitomized by the leaders in charge (such as the harsh agitator referred to as Mrs. Bözsi). Thus in this narrative, those in power, the beneficiaries of collectivization, were held personally accountable for the cruelties in the early phase of the process. The autonomy and control of the individual over production gradually diminished—first control over the yields of production, then over the means of production and the forms, timing, and extent of remuneration, followed by powerlessness over the degree of exploitation of labor. Women were forced to perform tasks for which they were traditionally not considered to be suited—physical labor done by elderly women, for example. Katalin's dependency on her husband's help remained strong both for subsistence needs and the performance of daily tasks. It was difficult to combine working in the collective fields of the cooperative and childcare. It was easier to coordinate childcare with work on the household plot. The importance of this land is emphasized both in the above-mentioned uprising of the Russian peasant women and in some of the life stories in my Hungarian sample as well. It provided a key source of livelihood, especially for women and during a period in which there were no guaranteed wages from the cooperative. One of the informants in the sample chose to quit the collective because she was denied a plot.

Katalin's life history depicts a similar process of loss of autonomy over organizing and providing care. Her loss of autonomy was most acutely expressed when it came to childcare. She was promised help to solve her childcare problems, but neither the cooperative nor the state gave her any assistance. Here again, the failure to receive care was attributed to the irresponsible exercise of power by state officials: "They kicked him out [...] They decided themselves whom to accept." Solving the issue of childcare further strengthened the bonds to the family and relations, including her own siblings.

Katalin narrates her experience of collectivization as an experience of subjugation. On the one hand, it involved subjugation to the cooperative as a production organization in which working conditions for women were so bad that many of them sustained lifelong injuries. The leadership cynically assumed that it was up to women to arrange for childcare, thus putting on their shoulders a double burden. On the other hand, subjugation was also articulated in the form of dependency on the state for the provision of care that it promised but failed to deliver. Katalin blames the state for its inability to provide social security to female workers who labored at the cooperative. She argues that her low pension was due to the mismanagement of her work record in the cooperative. Katalin portrays these shortcomings as arising out of the common concerns of her generation of women.

Experiences of subjugation preoccupy other female life stories in the sample describing collectivization, although the chosen type of agency varied along the parameters of acceptance, voicing, and exit (Asztalos Morell, 2009).

While Katalin's narrative critically reflects on the public forms of subjugation that women experienced during the early collectivization period, she recalls private relationships in a positive and idealized manner. The few positive memories of the collectivization period emphasize that the family and relatives were the only help to be had during the hardships caused by collectivization, which deprived not only Katalin and her husband, but also her husband's family at large, of resources. The family farm was the result of hard work by the whole family, and everyone felt deep solidarity with one another:

> They came with the (tractor) Zetor and packed everything up! They took... everything away from us! Can you imagine! My poor mother-in-law! They saved and scraped, oh, how they worked! And suffered! And everything was taken away! It was good we managed to buy them out, but still they felt sorry for us!

Despite the fact that Katalin's husband was employed outside the cooperative, she had to rely on his help to satisfy the collective's demand for labor. Similarly, following collectivization, the extended family was the only source of help with childcare. When the grandparents could not help, since they were also forced to work, the siblings (Katalin's ten-year-old sister and her husband's elder sister) pitched in. She attributes her ability to fulfill her maternal calling and perform her production duties to the help of her husband and her female kin. Thus collectivization reproduced women's dependency on a benevolent patriarch in the private sphere at the same time as it subordinated them to the emerging public patriarchal system of the cooperative. However, individual life conditions and choices differed. As some other life stories in the sample indicate, not all women had access to the assistance of a "benevolent husband," and some chose to exit the collective and its patriarchal division of labor, only to find themselves in other disadvantageous positions in the state socialist labor market (Asztalos Morell, 2009).

Katalin's narrative depicts her fate in a dualistic manner. On the one hand, she paints a picture of the agents of dictatorship carrying out collectivization without a human face. This was a victimizing process. On the other hand, she does not portray herself as a victim without agency. She first protests by voicing concerns. Later on, together with others, she comes to realize the meaninglessness of such voicing. Instead, she chooses obedience in order to avoid repercussions and seeks the support of her husband and family network. These allow her to realize a life with self-respect in which she focuses on her children's best interests as her major concern. Thus a dignified life is created outside what is offered by the collective. Self-sacrificing motherhood becomes Katalin's heroic protest against the inhumanity of early collectivization, a project that she could not perform without kinship solidarity. She narrates herself into the position of an agent by first voicing concerns against the state and later choosing a strategy of passivity. While her engagement in the cooperative inhibited her from realizing her own goals, she finds reinforcement of herself as a mother in her relations with her husband and relatives. These help her to give meaning to her life (a life as a self-sacrificing mother), and she portrays herself as having a fulfilling calling, despite (and in opposition to) the evils of collectivization.

Notes

1 See also Sen's (1985) dilemma of the benevolent dictator. For more on agency, see Asztalos Morell (2007).
2 This standpoint is inspired by oral history research (Hansson and Thor, 2006). Thompson pleads for a history from below. In Sweden, memory archives have a tradition both in ethnology (Löfgren, 1997) and in history writing, where they have been used to unravel the history of the working class (Isacson, 1996; Wikander, 1988).
3 This is inspired by the position evolved by Portelli (2004), who regards the accounts that workers gave of a murder not as sources for identification and justification of the actual event, but as expressions of their own identity formation: what did they find pride in, and what did they identify with? (Hansson and Thor, 2006).

References

Asztalos Morell, Ildikó. 1999. *Emancipation's Dead-End Roads? Studies in the Formation and Development of the Hungarian Mode for Agriculture and Gender (1956–1989)*. PhD diss., Uppsala University, Uppsala, Sweden.
———. 2007a. "Between Harmony and Conflicting Interests: Gendered Marital Negotiations in Hungarian Post-Socialist Farm Family Enterprises." *Journal of Comparative Family Studies* 37, no. 3: 435–458.
———. 2007b. "How to Combine Motherhood and Wage Labour: Hungarian Expert Perspectives during the 1960s." In *Gender, Equality and Difference dur-*

ing and after State Socialism, ed. Rebecca Kay, 41–62. Basingstoke, UK: Palgrave.

———. 2008. "Care Work in Hungarian Agrarian Entrepreneur Families during the Post-Socialist Transition." In *Gender Regimes, Citizen Participation and Rural Restructuring*, eds. Ildikó Asztalos Morell and Bettina Bock, 57–82. London: Elsevier.

———. 2009. "Self-Sacrificing Motherhood: Rhetoric and Agency in the Era of Hungarian Collectivization in Two Women's Life Histories." Paper presented at the Annual Convention of the American Association for the Advancement of Slavic Studies in Boston, November 12–15, 2009.

Björnberg, Ulla, and Anna-Karin Kollind. 2005. *Individualism and Families, Equality, Autonomy and Togetherness*. London: Routledge.

Bonnell, Victoria E. 1997. *Iconography of Power: Soviet Political Posters under Lenin and Stalin*. Berkeley: University of California Press.

Denisova, Liubov. 2010. *Rural Women in the Soviet Union and Post-Soviet Russia*. London: Routledge.

Eriksson, Kristina. 2003. *Manligt läkarskap, kvinnliga läkare och normala kvinnor: köns- och läkarskapande symbolik, metaforik och praktik* (Physicianship, female physicians and normal women: The symbolical, metaphorical and practical doing[s] of gender and physicians). PhD diss., Uppsala University, Uppsala, Sweden.

Farkas, Gy. 2003. "'Gyertek lányok traktorra!' Női traktorosok a gépállomáson és a propagandában" (Come, girls, on the tractor! Female tractor-drivers on machine stations and in propaganda). *Korall* 13, no. 9: 65–86.

Fodor, Éva. 2002. "Smiling Women and Fighting Men: The Gender of the Communist Subject in State Socialist Hungary." *Gender and Society* 16, no. 2: 240–263.

Glaser, Barney, and Anselm Strauss. 1967. *The Discovery of Grounded Theory: Strategies for Qualitative Research*. Hawthorne, NY: Aldine.

Goven, Joanna. 2002. "Gender and Modernism in a Stalinist State." *Social Politics* 9: 3–28.

Haney, Lynne Allison. 2002. *Inventing the Needy: Gender and the Politics of Welfare in Hungary*. Berkeley: University of California Press.

Hansson, Lars, and Malin Thor. 2006. *Muntlig historia* (Oral history). Lund, Sweden: Studentlitteratur.

Hobson, Barbara. 1990. "No Exit, No Voice: Women's Economic Dependency and the Welfare State." *Acta Sociologica* 33: 235–249.

Isacson, Maths. 1996. "Att bevara det industriella kulturarvet" (To preserve the cultural heritage of industrialism). *Arbetarhistoria* 20, no. 3: 38–40.

Juhász, P. 1976. *A mezőgazdasági termelőszövetkezetek dolgozóinak rétegződése munkahelycsoportok, származás és életút szerint* (The stratification of production co-operative workers according to working units, origin, and life path). Budapest: Szövetkezeti Kutatóintézet évkönyve.

Löfgren, Orvar. 1997. "Vi lever i historier" (We live in histories). In *Att gestalta historien* (Portraying history), eds. Jakob Christensson and Håkan Håkansson, 17–24. Lund, Sweden: Ugglan.

Melberg, Kjersti. 2005. "Family Farm Transactions in Norway: Unpaid Care across Three Farm Generations." *Journal of Comparative Family Studies* 36: 419–442.

Mella, O. 2007. "Grundad teori. En presentation" (Grounded theory. A presentation). Unpublished manuscript. Uppsala, Sweden: Department of Sociology, Uppsala University.

Öberg, Peter. 1997. *Livet som berättelse; om biografi och åldrande* (Life as narrative: On biography and aging). Uppsala, Sweden: Uppsala University.

Portelli, Alessandro. 2004. *The Order Has Been Carried Out: History, Memory, and Meaning of a Nazi Massacre in Rome.* New York: Palgrave.

Sen, Amartya. 1985. *Commodities and Capabilities.* Amsterdam: North-Holland.

Sireni, Maarit. 2008. "Agrarian Feminity in a State of Flux: Multiple Roles of Finnish Farm Women." In *Gender Regimes, Citizen Participation and Rural Restructuring*, eds. Ildikó Asztalos Morell and Bettina Bock, 33–55. London: Elsevier.

Skeggs, Beverly. 1997. *Formations of Class and Gender: Becoming Respectable.* London: Sage.

Szelényi, Ivan. 1988. *Socialist Entrepreneurs: Embourgeoisement in Rural Hungary.* Madison: University of Wisconsin.

Walby, Sylvia. 1997. *Gender Transformation.* London: Routledge.

———. 2007. "The Complexity of Theory, Systems Theory and Multiple Intersecting Social Inequalities." In *Philosophy of the Social Sciences* 37, no. 4: 449–470.

Waters, Elizabeth. 1991. "Female Form in Soviet Political Iconography." In *Russia's Women, Accommodation, Resistance, Transformation*, ed. Barbara E. Clements, Barbara A. Engel, and Christine D. Worobec, 225–242. Berkeley: University of California Press.

Wikander, Ulla. 1988. *Kvinnors och mäns arbeten: Gustavsberg 1880–1980: genusarbetsdelning och arbetets degradering vid en porslinsfabrik* (Women's and men's work: Gustavsberg 1880–1890; gender division of labor and the degradation of labor at a porcelain factory). Lund, Sweden: Studentlitteratur.

Viola, Lynne. 1986. "Bab'i Bunty and Peasant Women's Protest during Collectivization." *Russian Review* 45: 23–42.

Yuval-Davis, Nira. 2006. "Intersectionality and Feminist Politics." *European Journal of Women's Studies* 13, no. 3: 193–209.

CHAPTER 4

East German Women Going West: Family, Children, and Partners in Life-Experience Literature

CHRISTINE FARHAN

INTRODUCTION

"East German women are the losers of German unification" was a common slogan during the 1990s. This motto "conceals the fact that enormous and growing social differentiation exists among East German women" (Bütow, 1997; Dölling, 1998, p. 185). The idea behind the slogan was questioned by many publications, both scholarly and popular, that revealed that East German women showed strength in other ways. Using "a 'quiet' and individualized form of resistance, they retain with their 'own ideas' (*Eigensinn*), certain orientations of action and values against the constraints or pressures of the adopted West German structures which affect their everyday life" (Dölling, 1998, p. 187).

This chapter is interested in what memories were activated for self-representations that opposed the victims' discourse and presented different concepts of agency (compare the chapter by Asztalos Morell in this volume). Of concern is how former GDR (East German) family norms are handled and reacted to in this context. These include the role model of "working motherhood" (Kolinsky and Nickel, 2003, p. 20),[1] the rejected role model of the housewife, the officially declared accomplishment of gender equality, and the affirmative collective "we" against a pejorative "me."

The analysis is based on four books[2] containing former GDR women's life stories published during the transition period from 1990 to 2004. I approach these texts as literature, asking how authentic information—in this case interviews—is turned into stories that arrange memories and opinions to represent strength and agency in a certain discursive context. The texts are not based on scientific surveys[3] but are written for a broad audience of readers expecting both knowledge and entertainment. The books take quite different approaches to their subject. Often the editors' selection of women is coincidental and not motivated by concern for intersectional aspects such as generation, social-educational background, and place of residence, when such information is given at all. Certain social groups, such as women from the countryside and women with less education, are neglected. On the other hand, some groups, such as well-educated, middle-aged women often living in big cities and most often in Berlin, are highlighted. Some editors do not even account for their choice of interviewees; others do and are more eager to present a good mixture of ordinary and extraordinary biographies. Summing up the specifics of these texts, I would locate them somewhere between autobiography and sociological studies, between subjectivity and generalizations, between literature and non-fiction.[4] They reflect the enormous interest in the former GDR in the 1990s. Furthermore, during historical turning points, pure fiction often does not fully satisfy readers' needs. Claims for authentic narratives grow stronger, and literature is more easily exploited for political goals and agitation. Culture is used as a means of political combat. The promise of authenticity, genuineness, and objectiveness becomes more important and generates elements of excitement and entertainment. The subtitle of one book expresses that clearly: "Women Tell Real Life Stories"(*Frauen erzählen aus dem richtigen Leben*) (Rellin, 2004). Real life obviously has a great deal of aesthetic attraction to readers and evokes certain expectations.

Furthermore, the literary genre of life-experience literature had a certain historical context in the GDR. In the 1970s, when Maxie Wander published *Guten Morgen, du Schöne* (Good Morning, Beautiful) about women's everyday life in the GDR, her book was classified as rebellious (Mudry, 1991, p. 28) because it focused on the private sphere, an area that was not supposed to be a matter of public discourse in socialist society. In this respect Wander did not hew to socialist realism, the official theory of literature in the GDR, which focused on typical features in the construction of working-class heroes.

The texts analyzed in the present chapter have rebellious elements too, not so much in relation to the old system as in opposition to the negative consequences of the transition into a Western society. For a short time after the fall of the Wall, some GDR women fervently attempted to build a movement for women's liberation (Kahlau, 1990). But these efforts did not last long, and when they failed, writing life stories of various kinds became a kind of continuation of the feminist project by other means. By documenting their memories, these women enhanced female versions of truths in order to empower and to contradict a victimizing discourse.

The texts try to preserve the East German experience, because the "island called GDR does not exist any longer. [...] It exists only in our heads. And every day something else vanishes from my box called GDR" (Mudry, 1991, p. 106). Therefore it was so important for former GDR citizens to explain "correctly," to provide images of their own to counterbalance other text documents like newspapers that "can't give appropriate information about this period anymore" (Mudry, 1991, p. 110). Beyond these aspects we can learn a great deal about "social differentiation" among East German women by highlighting the micro-perspective of private spheres, including the family, and thereby correcting the macro-theoretical perspective of one homogeneous biography of "the" East German woman—governed from the top down and institutionalized (Dölling, 1998, pp. 36, 50).

By emphasizing their strength and the value of their own experience, the interviewed women reject and resist the role of victim. The very titles of the books give proof of that: "Without Us, No State" (*Ohne uns ist kein Staat zu machen*); "Strong Women Come from the East" (*Starke Frauen kommen aus dem Osten*); "The Silent Emancipation" (*Die stille Emanzipation*); "Of Course I Am a Woman from East Germany!" (*Klar bin ich eine Ost-Frau*). They are reactions to an oversimplifying discourse stigmatizing East German women as passive losers of unification and weak "mommies" (*Muttis*) who unquestioningly accepted the strong patriarchal state and the second shift at home as housewives and mothers.

> The end of the GDR has frequently been viewed as a negative turning point for East German women. They appeared to find themselves on the wrong side of developments, as "victims of modernization" or "losers of unification." Both images suggest that East German women remained passive and allowed events to take their course. (Kolinsky and Nickel, 2003, p. 13)

Seeing East German women as passive victims is far too one-dimensional. The stories reveal other aspects that make them appear instead as agents and creators of their own living conditions. All the books examined in the present study are intended to empower; they offer images of proud, self-confident, powerful, smart, ambitious, well-educated, and enterprising GDR women. I will discuss these texts with reference to five topics that are most frequently touched upon in the interviews: gainful employment and public commitment, children and family, gender identity, the relationship between man and woman, and the East-West clash.

Gainful Employment and Public Commitment

The women in these interviews take a mostly positive attitude towards gainful employment. Work is thought of as an important part of life and identity, mainly because it provides financial independence, professional pride, and social contacts. Women in the GDR enjoyed their salary and were conscious of their economic contribution to the household (chef, Berlin, 36).[5] For Kerstin work was a source of satisfaction; to her a person without work was worse off than a prisoner. In her opinion this was not necessarily due to the work itself but rather to her financial independence (author/nurse, Berlin, 34).

Money, though, was not all that counted. Work gave meaning to life and was a source of self-confidence (PhD in archeology, Berlin, 38). Women needed the feeling of success and social acceptance that they gained from working. They appreciated both stable routines (marketing worker, 34) and the possibilities for change: "I always love to start over again" (foster mother, 43). Colleagues were considered almost a substitute for the family: "You need contact with other people" (marketing worker, 34). "No matter what, I have to be among people" (farm worker, countryside). The workplace was called "a home" (skilled worker, 64), and not working meant not belonging anywhere (farm worker, countryside), something that could make a person feel isolated. Working alone at home was looked down upon because "you only work for yourself" (farm worker, countryside). Vivian (housewife, Leipzig, 27) compares housework to "working in flow production," which, though monotonous, sounds more attractive to her, because it allows her to be with other people. Just being a mother was to her a "one-track prospect," leading to a loss of self-confidence and the risk of "turning gray." Life as a housewife was and still is rejected as "dull and boring" because it left one feeling cut off, with no colleagues to talk to (farm worker, countryside). Johanna comments that her children and her tired husband do not satisfy her needs for communication (chef, Berlin, 36).

Though there were strict limits to freedom in the GDR, it was appreciated that women's lives were not reduced to matters of housework and what to wear. Instead they learned how "to make it on their own" (economist/politician, small town, 39). Work seemed to be a natural part of life, nothing you would question or reject. According to one farm worker: "At the age of 16, we left school, got educated, had to work, finished vocational training, went on working, grew into it, got married, still worked, got children, went on working" (farm worker, countryside). Because gainful employment for women was a social norm in the GDR, not working could be seen as an act of resistance. Thus an engineer explains her choice to be a housewife during the socialist period as her way of denying the state obedience (engineer, 44) by valuing time with her children more than work.

Contrary to official discourse, women did not seem persuaded that gender equality had been achieved in the GDR. On the contrary, they were quite aware of gender discrimination such as lower salaries and lesser responsibilities. Accordingly, it was more difficult for women to reach leading positions (skilled worker, 64). One woman tells about the disappointment she felt when she was employed in the GDR as a cleaner and kitchen assistant though she was a trained nurse (restaurant worker, Leipzig, 27). Some women even recall active rebellion against discrimination during the socialist period. When the boss wanted Greta to clean the windows, she simply refused: "That's not why I'm here" (marketing worker, 34).

Children and Family

Most of the women welcome the concept of working motherhood, meaning the successful combination of work, children, and family. That, however, does not prevent them from criticizing the way public day-care functioned in the GDR (songwriter, 45; linguist, 63; stylist, 37; deaconess assistant, 28; engineer, 44). Women seem to have accepted having the main responsibility for children and family in the GDR, but this came along with protests and feelings of ambiguity (sociologist, 45). Ruth says with pride that she was "the engineer of the family," though at the same time she feels that this role was forced upon her. While expressing great dissatisfaction, she says she was also happy to be with her child: "Every minute belonged to the boy" (farm supervisor, now editor, small town, 45; economist, 31). Johanna (chef, Berlin, 36) thinks mothers should stay at home at least until the child was three years old because these early years were "the best years." But she expects the same attitude from fathers and blames them for not showing sufficient interest in their children.

Though there are feelings of guilt for being at work, mothers are convinced that their children did not suffer. On the contrary, they grew into strong, self-confident individuals (restaurant owner, Berlin, 41; economist/politician, small town, 39). Another woman is eager to explain that she had no feelings of guilt at all, since she used the little time she had with her child effectively (marketing worker, 34). Gabi takes pride in being an Eastern woman, meaning that she has never been her child's slave and that there were always opportunities to be independent. She was taught to combine work, children, and household. She is determined always to work, even with a baby (hairdresser, Berlin, 31). Barbara points out that her children were born into her life and had to adjust to her lifestyle (songwriter, 45).

Day-care institutions are presented as an advantage in the GDR that is taken for granted in daily life. Liesbeth is convinced that she was able to give her children love and understanding even if she did not have much time to spend with them. She thinks the contact with other children in day-care institutions was good for her children's development (skilled worker, 64). Public day-care, though, was not only appreciated but also criticized for its lack of spontaneity and freedom (dancer, Berlin, 41; student of literature, Berlin, 29) and its ideological indoctrination (housewife, Leipzig, 27). Rules and routines were considered too strict, leading to distorted personalities without self-confidence (veterinarian, small town, 40).

The interviews show that even if mothers had hesitations about placing their small children in public institutions, most of them did so. However, quite a few women made their own choices. In Silvia's case, her mother helped take care of the children (office employee, Berlin, 45). Marion stayed at home with her son for three years. She wanted to be there for her child, and she enjoyed this period very much. Judith was not looking for a nursery since she preferred to stay at home with her child (stylist, 37), and when Christine was a little girl she appreciated having her mother at home. Referring to her own prejudice against nurseries, she had a lot of difficulty fitting into the role model of the GDR mother. In general she thinks that it is an important experience for a woman to have children and to monitor their development (engineer, 44). Alternative solutions such as keeping nannies or maids (dancer, Berlin, 41; scholar of Slavic studies, 39; linguist, 63), using grandmothers (dancer, Berlin, 41), or even taking sick leave (office employee, Berlin, 45) are mentioned. Erika proudly states that none of her children attended a nursery (linguist, 63). In order not to neglect her child, Elfriede chose to work in the evenings (restaurant worker, 74).

The desire for children is obvious, but so is the need to work and study (journalist, Leipzig, 33). One mother rejected the idea of being a housewife, but at the same time she wanted more time with her child (veterinarian, small town, 40). Many women experienced difficulties in combining motherhood with childrearing, but they were realistic in their assessment of the situation. Thus although they wanted to be with their children, they also worried about being isolated if they stayed at home (housewife, Leipzig, 27). In the GDR early childbirth was frequent and the social acceptance of illegitimate children fairly common. This fact is generally mentioned as something positive, but along with that there are also suspicions that the state simply needed a labor force and soldiers and thus exploited women as birth machines (office employee, Berlin, 45). Doris married in order to escape her parents' demands that she get a proper education. Then she had her first child because she was bored with her marriage. Otherwise she would probably have chosen to travel. But not even a child satisfied her in the long run, so she began to think about other alternatives (restaurant owner, Berlin, 41).

GENDER DIFFERENCES — A NONEXISTENT ISSUE

Gender equality is reflected upon in contradictory ways. Some women believe it was achieved in the GDR, while others think it needed to be discussed further. To the first group female identity is less important than being East German, an "Ossi" whose self-confidence needs no feminist support (office employee, 45; student/politician, 23). There is more identification with "the East" than with a specific sex: "I'm proud of us from the East" (economist/politician, small town, 39).

In the GDR the term feminism officially had pejorative connotations (singer/actor, 46). Gina remembers that gender-related questions were not discussed in the GDR during the early 1970s, when the women's movement started in the West. As Hildegard (sociologist, 45) points out, it was not accepted to study gender roles even on an academic level. Such studies were explicitly stigmatized as "bourgeois" sociology and thus in conflict with the official norm. Although Hildegard's academic career was cut short, her retirement allowed her to spend more time discussing gender-related questions, something that was possible only outside the system.

Another example is Brigitte, who considered the GDR too supportive of traditional gender roles in education. Thus in a trade union meeting she raised the question of traditional patterns of education, such as fostering a caring mentality in girls. This, Brigitte claims, was an extraordinary and brave thing to do. Referring to the 1968 students' movement in the West, when role models were fervently discussed and criticized, Brigitte noted in comparison that on the GDR's official agenda, the topic of gender remained nonexistent. When "bourgeois" behavior was changing in the West, she said, in the GDR it was carelessly handed down to the next generation (employees' representative, 53). But this was not accepted without questioning. Claudia got the idea at school to form a women's group, which was something crazy and completely unusual to do (restaurant worker, Leipzig, 27). In so doing, Silvia questioned the official norm that gender equality in the GDR was accomplished by turning women into breadwinners (office employee, Berlin, 45).

When the mother of one interviewee started her new career in the GDR, she felt discriminated against because of her sex, but she did not dare discuss it in public: "To say 'woman' was not permitted; it was not officially accepted" (student of literature, Berlin, 29). Only at home, in the private sphere of the family, did she dare joke about these matters. Salomea makes the same reflection. Only with her husband could she talk about the gender issues she would have liked to discuss in public. In her opinion the emancipation process in the GDR was "interrupted" when it was reduced to a question of mere economic independence. She felt psychologically abandoned. When she asked the leader of the government department Frau im Sozialismus ("woman in socialism") to put "gender" on the agenda, she was flatly refused: "We don't do that: it would lead to similar results as in the West, and that way we can't prove the superiority of socialism" (retired, Berlin, 58).

Together with other women, Petra (journalist, Leipzig, 33) prepared a series of lectures in the GDR based on women's special experiences. Only later did she learn about West German feminist groups and publications treating the same subjects. Despite the obstacles, feminist initiatives were taken sporadically in public, but for the most part the only space gender issues had was in the private sphere of the family and partner communication.

The Relationship between Man and Woman

Men and partners in marriage and relationships are given much space in the texts and are reflected upon in different ways. When the interviewed women talk about Eastern men in general, it is mainly in a positive manner. Katrin (economist, 31) is convinced that the GDR women had more power than men which made men more willing to take part in housework. Henni found that many Eastern men preferred an equal partner to a mere housewife (retired, Leipzig, 83). Other women felt more respected by men in the GDR (farm supervisor, now editor, small town, 45; dancer, 45), and Johanna believes that the GDR gave more power to women than to men (chef, Berlin, 36). Angelika gained her strength in life from her husband but also from the work collective. She was happy in her partnership, as her husband took care of all the housework and was one of "the two or three persons you need in life to carry on." She is convinced that many Eastern men are similar. When she was on the edge of a nervous breakdown, her husband shared the "baby year" (parental leave) with her and gave her the opportunity to study (economist/politician, small town, 39).

One woman (PhD in archeology, Berlin, 38) calls her husband the central person in her life, because he gives her support and protection. Another woman (entrepreneur, 44) says she needs love from her husband—but not at any cost, since she is the one used to breaking up. In an optimal partnership you can discuss important decisions in life, she says: "His opinion is not my decision, but I use his opinion as a basis for my decision" (Griebner and Kleint, 1995, p. 247). Breaking up from a partnership appears to have been rather easy, and several women changed partners because they were not getting sufficient support (dancer, 48). Together with her three daughters Karin left her husband after ten years of marriage because she was tired of his negative attitude towards her (foster mother, 43). Silvia (office employee, Berlin, 45) maintains that she does not need a man at all. If he does not help her out, she will leave him and look for someone better. With her current partner she has "a great division of labor."

Gina expects from her partner to have fun in bed, perfunctory sex turns her off (actor, Berlin, 41). Vivian, too, knows what she wants "in bed" (housewife, Leipzig, 27). If her husband tries to dominate her sexually, Johanna gets annoyed (chef, Berlin 36). She is quite conscious of the fact that she provides for the family as much as her husband does, which entitles her to demand his help around the house. In her opinion there was not a single family in the GDR in which men did not take part in family duties. Eastern men are "accustomed to working women" (economist/politician, 39).

Contrasting East and West

Though Katarina (ice dancer, 29) was prepared to change after unification, in her heart she has preserved a certain "Eastern mentality," which means she does not let efficiency and consumer demands take control of her life. She despises Western attitudes like "What's in it for me?" Gina (singer/actor, 46) remembered that the GDR stigmatized the concept of individualism, but now she has observed that the self and its competition with other selves are the most important perspectives in the unified German republic.

One woman (student/politician, 23) is worried about social insecurity and the risk of unemployment, the closing of day-care centers, and lower pensions. In the GDR, according to another interviewee, there was no preparation for unemployment, and the need to sell yourself makes her feel humiliated (restaurant worker, Leipzig, 27). Susanne (veterinarian, small town, 40) criticizes the new abortion law and finds it degrading that a woman is forced to explain why she wants an abortion. Susanne wants to feel free to make her decision. Another woman (office employee, 45) feels like a beggar; not having the legal right and yet not being punished for an abortion makes her feel "like a criminal."

Some of the informants associate the West with a certain lack of warmth in human relations (chef, Berlin, 36). Kiki (office employee, 45) thinks that there is a special feeling for the family in the East. Family orientation and solidarity are considered important East German values (student, 23). One informant (hairdresser, Berlin, 31) is proud of being an Eastern woman because they are able to combine work, children, and household and are more interested in politics and other important matters, while Western housewives only meet their neighbors during shopping trips.

Hanne (cultural manager, 28) found "less independence among young Western women" because they studied and expected their parents to pay, while their East German sisters went to work much earlier. One woman (employees' representative, 53) even comes to the conclusion that "Western people are too lazy to work." She finds it appalling when her child's day-care center demands documentation that the grandmother has a job and therefore cannot be asked to babysit. In the texts the Western housewife is often despised because she is willing to accept financial security through her husband in exchange for doing the work that needs to be done anyway, even if she has a paid job (dancer, Berlin, 41). Angelika (economist/politician, 39) criticizes the monotonous life of Western housewives, who have the same duties every day and just wait for their husbands to come home. Referring to the anti-housewife norm in the GDR, she says that housework should be done unquestioningly: "So I have been taught."

Kiki (office employee, 45) is annoyed when the day-care center advises her to take care of her daughter herself, as if criticizing her ambition to work. Although she loves to take care of her children, she needs to work in order to feel self-confident. Even if she "were a millionaire," she would not stay at home, because she needs confirmation through work and colleagues. She is convinced that in West Germany there is a widespread opinion that women should stay at home. Her decision to work has nothing to do with money. She links this to the identity of Eastern women: "We Eastern women grew up with the consciousness that we stand on our own two feet." Hanne (cultural manager, 28) believes that a woman in the West taking her three-year-old child to a day-care center is considered a *Rabenmutter,* a bad mother. In her opinion there was a different attitude in the GDR, because children were considered a normal part of life, even for single mothers.

According to Katrin (economist, 31), Western women have two options: taking care of the children at home or firmly deciding not to have children. Western men cannot accept strong women. Everything Katrin highly values in being a woman—being hardworking and insightful, with the ability to exceed one's limits—seems to have a negative effect on Western men.

Another woman used to feel accepted by men during the GDR era, but now she feels supervised (farm supervisor, now editor, small town, 45). Kiki (office employee, 45) appreciates the liberal concept of love in the GDR—the feeling that you are free to break up and move on to another relationship, since you are not tied to a partner economically. Frequently the interviewees define Eastern women as more emancipated than Western women (retired, Berlin, 58), and as such they felt more accepted "as women" in the GDR (chef, Berlin, 36).

Conclusion: Family—A Counterworld or Just a Loose Collective of Free Members?

Developments in one half of Germany were hardly possible to evaluate without references to the other, especially after unification. In their criticism of the West, the interviewees represent themselves as self-confident, empowered, and independent women, and thus they reflect a wide scale of different concepts of agency. We have to keep in mind, however, that due to the specific discursive context of the process of transition in the two halves of Germany, we must make do here with a limited selection of women's life stories. Less successful stories have probably been omitted. Furthermore, these women have chosen to portray their lives as successful, interpreting the past to gain advantage in the present. For the most part we meet the women that Kolinsky and Nickel call the "winners of unification," that is, "middle-aged women who were strongly career-orientated and keen to improve their qualifications and prospects already before the unification" (Kolinsky and Nickel, 2003, p. 16). Nevertheless, the findings provide interesting information about norms and values that were associated with the socialist state and are still alive. I present these findings below to provide a broader and deeper perspective.

The autobiographical material shows that the normative concept of working motherhood is internalized as self-evident and therefore not questioned. At the same time, the housewife concept is generally criticized because of its negative connotations. It is seen as a concept of privacy and isolation that excludes the woman from the group and its collective arrangements. Only through gainful employment can she count on social acceptance. Thus we see not only an affirmative "we" but also a pejorative "me" in the texts. They enhance the possibility for women to form public identities, gain acknowledgement, and thereby increase the self-confidence that they possessed in the GDR.

There are no signs in the texts indicating a desire to give up the future that work offers:

> The participation of women in the work force had been taken for granted in the GDR and has since become an intrinsic part of East German women's planning. Employment has lost none of its centrality. [...] East German women no longer want to live without the autonomy and the prestige that professional activity affords them. The biographical model of a housewife caring for her family is something an East German woman cannot imagine. (Uhlendorff, 2003, p. 225)

This attitude towards work corresponds to the official directive that "employment was hailed as a key sphere of social life" (Kolinsky and Nickel, 2003, p. 4).

As for the family, the situation looks more complex. Researchers insist that family privacy in the GDR was regarded as "politically undesirable" (Uhlendorff, 2003, p. 209), while the goal was to put the family at the same level as other social collectives like work and student and apartment groupings (cf. Zhidkova in this volume). Young children were integrated into socialist organizations as a possible substitute for family ties. But according to Uhlendorff, the state was not successful because East German families "vigorously defended their privacy" (ibid.). However, for women in this study, periods of stay-at-home motherhood involved depressing feelings of isolation, and they express a longing for social contact outside the family that was often realized in the work collective. In their comments, colleagues almost appear as a family substitute.

On the other hand, the analyzed texts also express a strong family orientation, which might confirm the thesis by Uhlendorff above. Most women consider a happy life to be defined by children, a good partnership at home, and a job. In the sphere of the family, the strong control of the state could be avoided, and delicate issues such as gender equality and role models could be discussed. This corresponds to "the very important role" that the family used to play in the GDR (Uhlendorff, 2003, p. 222). It was a kind of a "buffer between the state and the private sphere," a counterworld free of ideology and a space for private freedom not to be found anywhere else in society (Kolinsky and Nickel, 2003, p. 22). Scholars even speak of a stronger family orientation in the GDR than in West Germany. Surveys show that Eastern family bonds were and still are closer than in the West.[6]

But what kind of family concept is imagined? It is important to remember that the family in the GDR differed from the Western nuclear family.

One parent, generally the mother, and a child were enough to be called a "family:" "In East Germany [...] single motherhood had emerged as a new and distinctive form—a mother and her children constituting one household. There was no subtext of inferiority or deprivation" (ibid., p. 21). The state facilitated single motherhood and offered generous social support. Consequently, many East German single mothers chose to live without a partner and divorced their husbands.[7] The above-mentioned "family orientation" refers to a concept of family that differs greatly from the West German nuclear ideal type. It appears as a quite loose collective of free members, as opposed to a stable and unchangeable unit. Family arrangements often changed several times during a lifetime "[...] from two-parent families to single-parent to step-families. Thus nearly every second East German mother has lived as a single mother at least once, taking full responsibility for the care of the children" (Schuster and Traub, 2003, p. 167). Marriage did not necessarily last forever, and having children did not tie a woman to a partner for life.

This attitude is confirmed in the study. Women prefer to break up and live as single mothers rather than stay in boring relationships. Even though having a man is considered part of a successful life, the women are willing to accept the pain and burden from separation and divorce. Marriages and partnerships were deliberate and quite free of economic constraints. The decision to marry and to have a family was not difficult to make, as the consequences were relatively minor. Starting over, privately and professionally, was not a disaster, but a normal part of life. This might be the reason why social surveys find that partner relationships are closer (Uhlendorff, 2003, p. 209) in the East than in the West. If the relationship did not work out, the partners broke up and went on searching for new and better ones.

There is much evidence in the analyzed life stories of the importance of equal partnership, and many examples of husbands who were supportive both practically and mentally. Because of their economic and social independence, women had higher demands. Breaking up can consequently be interpreted as a subtle strategy of resistance to the double burden. Women chose their own life concepts regardless of partners and children. They did not feel trapped by their economic and parental involvement. The state gave them the opportunity to provide for themselves and their children. In this sense the strong state appears as a liberator—a chance to loosen traditional family concepts: "The extensive net of social policy measures and provisions to make it easier for women to combine employment and family duties [...] facilitated separation and divorce without risking poverty, homelessness or battles over custody" (Kolinsky and Nickel, 2003, p. 9).[8]

Men, on the contrary, lost quite a lot of power when deprived of their provider role. They were somewhat equal partners in the gender hierarchy, whereas the structures of society with a strong controlling state were patriarchal. This may explain why, when they met their Western sisters, many East German feminists found nothing wrong in fighting side by side with men, which gave them the reputation of being less emancipated "mommies."

However, in many stories women agreed with the official attitude that gender equality had been achieved and did not even see any need for a public gender discourse and feminist activities. Kolinsky and Nickel call this "the myth of their equal rights [that] had taken hold of women's minds to such an extent that the real patterns of gender discrimination and disadvantage did not merely hit women passively but were enforced by assumptions that all was well and nothing amiss" (2003, p. 6). Whether this was indeed a myth, or instead a feeling rooted in life experience, cannot be determined here.

The opposite attitude is also represented—an awareness of gender discrimination and strategies to establish a gender discourse, not only privately but in public as well. Thus the state did not succeed totally "in obscuring the fact that social policy [...] concentrated exclusively on combining employment and motherhood" (ibid.), as Kolinsky and Nickel put it. Several women put other important gender topics on the agenda—at least according to the stories examined here. These women knew that "the socialist formula of 'equal pay for equal work' [...] was never more than a hollow claim and an unmet promise" (ibid., p. 8).

According to the stories I have analyzed, attitudes towards children were not overly protective. In the self-representations there are only small signs of guilt and bad conscience. Many mothers do not regard themselves as irreplaceable for their children's happiness. Still, some of the interviewees reject the notion of a strong state taking over family duties. The combination of work and motherhood did not go well for all mothers, and many objected to small children going to nurseries. Alternative solutions were sought and found. Though many women in the autobiographical texts were demanding an equal partnership, mothers usually accepted that it was mainly their duty to care for the children and rarely discussed them as parental responsibilities. The traditional division of labor within the family still seemed intact. The burden of children and family was borne mainly by the mothers.[9]

Kolinsky and Nickel state that "the gender policies of the two German states cannot be understood without reference to one another." The manner in which these policies were implemented was quite negative, however, because "each gender regime tried to distance itself from that in the other Germany and purport to offer the better policy alternative" (Kolinsky and Nickel, 2003, p. 4). These attitudes persisted after unification and dominated the feminist discourse. The issue was discussed as a matter of modernization, asking which Germany offered the "right" path towards modernity, often in terms of a substandard East and a superior West, or conversely, "that GDR policies endowed East German women with a 'modernization bonus'" (ibid., p. 2).

More convincing in this discussion is Irene Dölling, who suggests two different concepts of modernization during transition in which different types of "modernization bonuses"[10] clashed with each other. Working motherhood was the social norm in the GDR and was supported by a state that offered independence by taking over different family duties, partially freeing women from housework and childrearing. In addition, however, the state institutionalized control and top-down governing of areas that traditionally belonged to the private sphere. Because of these and other measures, gender equality was officially declared to be accomplished, and the discourse about male and female behavior patterns in the private sphere was stifled and denounced. Here the Western modernization bonus made sense within the private sphere, aiming as it did to change traditional role models for relationships and family structures. The state, rather weak, stayed in the background and lent a helping hand when necessary. Fighting for gender equality meant first of all fighting against hierarchical structures between the sexes. The institutionalization of gender equality in terms of laws and regulations occurred rather late in West Germany and was not the first priority of West German feminist movements. The private sphere remained their main arena. These different approaches to gender equality led to countless emotional discussions between feminists from East and West Germany. It is clear from these discussions that the terms "modern" and "traditional" are unreliable and yet intimately related to the value systems of a specific societal context.

Unification did not happen on equal terms. One modernization concept, namely the one from the East, was suddenly outdated, whereas the Western concept predominated in the unified Germany. Kolinsky and Nickel's optimistic prediction that "East German women have opened a new chapter in gender relations that may lead to reinventing gender in Germany as a whole" (Kolinsky and Nickel, 2003, p. 23) apparently did not come true. Though they were " [...] offering their notion of dual identity, of working motherhood, as an alternative model for the future" (ibid., p. 25), they were not listened to but rather disqualified as victims and losers even by their feminist sisters. Analyzing tracks of empowerment as I have tried to do in this chapter, however, allows us to consider other possible conclusions. Working motherhood and the double burden of being breadwinners and "family engineers" may have better equipped women to adjust to new circumstances. Work experience and high education were combined with a great deal of social competence. This could be why there were so many examples of strong, successful East German women after unification.

NOTES

1 This term is used by Kolinsky and Nickel to denote a successful combination of family, children, and employment.
2 Two of the selected books (Fischer and Lux, 1990; Szepansky, 1995) attempt to present a broad spectrum of GDR women. They provide an average cross-section with respect to social background, age, place of residence, and profession. They present about fifteen life stories, each based on interviews. Fischer and Lux are both journalists, one from Austria and the other from the former GDR. They call their project a joint venture. Their intention is to give GDR women a voice because they count. For Szepansky it is important to point out the diversity of women's lives in order to counter stereotypical images. She has previously published a considerable number of women's life stories. The other two books (Griebner and Kleint, 1995; Rellin, 2004) take another approach to selecting women. They picked interesting and successful life stories, career women who turned the political transition to their own advantage. The volume includes thirteen portraits that mostly emphasize the women's leading positions in society and at work. Nothing is said about the background of the authors. Rellin's work comes rather late in this series. She wants to correct incorrect images and distortions of GDR women previously presented by the media (fourteen life stories based on informal conversations). Her intention is to promote the GDR woman as a new role model Western women can learn from, in other words, to find successful combinations of career, children, and family.
3 A similar approach was used earlier. Over a period of ten years Dodds (2003; see also Dodds and Allen-Thompson, 1994) conducted interviews with eighteen former GDR women on four separate occasions in order to study their response to unification and their different ways of adapting to altered living conditions. In a newspaper advertisement Dölling encouraged GDR citizens in autumn 1990 to write a diary for three months about their daily experiences of transition. About sixty people, fifty-five of them women, took part in the study, which resulted in a couple of articles (Dölling, 1992, 1998; Dölling and Dietzsch, 1996a, 1996b; Dölling et al., 1992).
4 "[...] zwischen Autobiographie und soziologischer Studie, Subjektivität und Pauschalität, Literatur und Non-Fiction" (Kraushaar, 2004, p. 98).

5 The books differ in the amount of information they provide about their interviewees. As this could be relevant to eventual conclusions, I include the information given about a person after the references in the following order: profession, place of residence (if known), and age. When there is no adequate term for the profession in question, the English translation gives at least a notion of what sort of work is involved. The references are to be found in the alphabetically arranged list of professions at the end of the chapter.

6 "All in all, 73 percent of the East Berliner grandparents, as opposed to 55 percent of the West Berliner grandparents, took care of their grandchildren [...] The East Berlin mothers and fathers described their marriages or partnerships as happier than parents living in West Berlin [...] The responses showed clearly that the women and men from East Berlin perceived themselves as being much closer to their partners than the couples from West Berlin. [...] East German women and men considered their partnership to be happier and more durable than West German couples. [...] West German adults felt lonelier than East German adults [...]" (Uhlendorff, 2003, p. 215–218).

7 "Single parenthood was a relatively common family form in the GDR. In 1991, shortly after the Wende, more than one in five families with children under 18 years of age was headed by only one parent. [...] In most cases—about 93 percent of these families—the mothers took the sole everyday responsibility for their children. [...] The main reason for single motherhood in the GDR was divorce. 49 percent of all single mothers were divorced in 1981 [...]. The GDR had a relatively high divorce rate in comparison to other nations, ranking fifth in the world [...] Another important aspect seemed to be the low marital age in the former GDR of just over 21 for women and under 24 for men. [...] two-thirds of all East German children below the age of 18 were affected by the divorce of their parents. [...] births out of wedlock: 1970: 13.3 percent; 1990: 35 percent" (Schuster and Traub, 2003, p. 154).

8 "It has been estimated that in the former GDR, the state bore between 75 and 80 percent of the cost of raising a child up to the age of 18. In the Federal Republic, the governmental contribution amounted to 25 percent or less [...]" (ibid., p. 161).

9 This perspective was supported by the state during the 1970s and 1980s, when a low birthrate demanded action, and "mommy" policies were introduced. These decades were preceded by other periods of family policies with differing role models. Scholars (Bütow, 1997; Gerhard, 1994; Merkel, 1994; Trappe, 1996) divide family policies in the GDR into three periods. Right after the war women were more or less compelled to join the workforce on a large scale. This was a "question of survival" (Trappe, 1996, p. 357) for society. The demand for labor was immense, not only because of war losses, but also because of emigration to West Germany before the Wall was built in 1961. "Equal pay for equal work" was promised in the Constitution of 1949 in order to integrate women into the workforce. In addition, household work and housewives were devalued, and those who did not have gainful employment were penalized or even criminalized. The "right to work" was also a strong obligation—even for women. Public

childcare was not available during this first period, but this issue was solved during the 1960s, when the need for skilled labor increased. Now women were given better access to qualified professions and higher positions through studies and vocational education. When decreasing fertility became evident in the 1970s, new measures were taken to facilitate the combination of work and family. "Mommy" policies—as they were called colloquially—were explicitly addressed to mothers, giving them several advantages in terms of time and money to care for children, such as paid leave after childbirth and for caring for sick children. This led to "one of the basic contradictions under state socialism [...] that women were defined as workers and mothers while there was no similar redefining of men's roles" (ibid., p. 358). Corresponding to the different availability of childcare in different periods, Trappe finds different concepts of working motherhood for different generations. While the older generation tended to sequence their roles in work and family by disrupting employment because of childbirth, the younger generation adjusted to another pattern in which childbearing and employment were practised at the same time (ibid., p. 358). Of course these different concepts were not strictly bound to any one generation, but coexisted throughout the history of the GDR. This variation is illustrated in this study by a wide range of concepts related to organization of work and motherhood (and parenthood) presented in the analyzed texts.

10 "DDR und BRD haben als gesellschaftliche Systeme unterschiedliche Modernisierungskonzepte verfolgt, die auch zur Herausbildung differenter 'Biografiemuster' [...] geführt haben. Mit der Vereinigungderbeiden Staateniste in Modernisierungskonzept hinfällige worden, und das andere wird in dieneuen Länder transferiert. Dabeitreffen in den Transformations prozessen Anforderungen und Erwartungen an Handlungs- und Persönlichkeitsstrukturen des 'siegreichen' Modernisierungs konzeptes auf Biografiemuster oder Selbstverständlichkeit enim biografischen Entwurf, die—teilweise zu mindest—'anders' modern sind. Die Ungleichzeitigkeiten von Modernisierungen haben in beiden Konzepten und entsprechenden Biografiemustern zu je spezifischen Figurationen von 'traditionalen' und 'modernen' Aspekten geführt" (Dölling and Dietzsch, 1996b, p. 19).

LIST OF PROFESSIONS WITH SOURCES

actor, Berlin, 41, in Fischer and Lux, pp. 100–110
author/nurse, Berlin, 34, in Griebner and Kleint, pp. 129–144
chef, Berlin, 36, in Fischer and Lux, pp. 111–124
cultural manager, 28, in Rellin, pp. 35–48
dancer, Berlin, 41, in Griebner and Kleint, pp. 145–162
dancer, 45, in Rellin, pp. 19–33
deaconess assistant, 28, in Szepansky, pp. 35–57
economist, 31, in Griebner and Kleint, pp. 91–127
economist/politician, small town, 39, in Griebner and Kleint, pp. 67–89

employees' representative, 53, in Rellin, pp. 85–101
engineer, 44, in Szepansky, pp. 254–273
entrepreneur, 44, in Griebner and Kleint, pp. 233–248
farm supervisor, now editor, small town, 45, in Griebner and Kleint, pp. 9–27
farm worker, countryside, in Fischer and Lux, pp. 174–184
foster mother, 43, in Rellin, pp. 103–121
hairdresser, Berlin, 31, in Griebner and Kleint, pp. 109–127
housewife, Leipzig, 27, in Fischer and Lux, pp. 165–173
ice dancer, 29, in Griebner and Kleint, pp. 49–65
journalist, Leipzig, 33, in Fischer and Lux, pp. 63–75
linguist, 63, in Szepansky, pp. 153–185
marketing worker, 34, in Rellin, pp. 49–62
office employee, Berlin, 45, in Fischer and Lux, pp. 31–41
office employee, 45, in Rellin, pp. 241–260
Ph.D. in archeology, Berlin, 38, in Griebner and Kleint, pp. 213–232
restaurant owner, Berlin, 41, in Griebner and Kleint, pp. 29–48
restaurant worker, Leipzig, 27, in Fischer and Lux, pp. 17–30
restaurant worker, 74, in Szepansky, pp. 79–89
retired, Berlin, 58, in Fischer and Lux, pp. 125–139
scholar of Slavic studies, 39, in Szepansky, pp. 141–152
singer/actor, 46, in Szepansky, pp. 283–305
skilled worker, 64, in Szepansky, pp. 126–140
sociologist, 45, in Szepansky, pp. 90–110
songwriter, 45, in Szepansky, pp. 58–78
student/politician, 23, in Rellin, pp. 261–78
student of literature, Berlin, 29, in Fischer and Lux, pp. 42–53
stylist, 37, in Szepansky, pp. 210–234
veterinarian, small town, 40, in Fischer and Lux, pp. 185–196

References

Bütow, Birgit. 1997. "EigenArtige Ostfrauen im Jahre 6 nach der Einheit—Bilanz und Perspektive der Forschung. Eine Skizze." In *Frauen nach 1989*, ed. Ilse Nagelschmidt, 34–54. Leipzig: Leipziger Universitäts-Verlag.
Dodds, Dinah. 2003. "Ten Years after the Wall: East German Women in Transition." *European Journal of Women's Studies* 10, no. 3: 261–276.
Dodds, Dinah, and Pam Allen-Thompson, eds. 1994. *The Wall in My Backyard: East German Women in Transition.* Amherst: University of Massachusetts Press.
Dölling, Irene. 1992. "'Man lebt jetzt regelrecht von Tag zu Tag, weil nichts mehr sicher ist.' Tagebücher als Dokumente eines gesellschaftlichen Umbruchs." *Journal für Soziologie,* no. 1: 103–111.
———. 1998. "Structure and Eigensinn: Transformation Processes and Continuities of East German Women." In *After the Wall: Eastern Germany since 1989*, ed. Patricia J. Smith, 183–201. Boulder, CO: Westview.

Dölling, Irene, and Ina Dietzsch. 1996a. "Das Eigene und das Fremde im Alltagsleben der Deutschen vor und nach der 'Vereinigung.'" *BIOS,* Opladen: 285–294.

———. 1996b. "Selbstverständlichkeiten im biographischen Konzept ostdeutscher Frauen. Ein Vergleich 1990–1994." *Berliner Debatte. Initial. Zeitschrift für sozialwissenschaftlichen Diskurs,* no. 2: 11–20.

Dölling, Irene, Adelheid Kuhlmey-Oehlert, and Gabriela Seibt, eds. 1992. *Unsere Haut. Tagebücher von Frauen aus dem Herbst 1990.* Berlin: Dietz Verlag Berlin.

Fischer, Erica, and Petra Lux. 1990. *Ohne uns ist kein Staat zu machen. DDR-Frauen nach der Wende.* Cologne: Kiepenheuer und Witsch.

Gerhard, Ute. 1994. "Die staatlich institutionalisierte 'Lösung' der Frauenfrage. Zur Geschichte der Geschlechterverhältnisse in der DDR." In *Sozialgeschichte der DDR,* eds. Hartmut Kaelble, Jürgen Kocka, and Hartmut Zwahr, 383–403. Stuttgart: J.G. Cotta.

Griebner, Angelika, and Scarlett Kleint. 1995. *Starke Frauen kommen aus dem Osten. 13 Frauen, über die man spricht, sprechen über sich selbst.* Berlin: Argon.

Kahlau, Cordula, ed. 1990. *Aufbruch! Frauenbewegung in der DDR. Dokumentation.* Munich: Frauenoffensive.

Kolinsky, Eva, and Maria Hildegard Nickel, eds. 2003. *Reinventing Gender: Women in Eastern Germany since Unification.* Portland, OR: Frank Cass Publishers.

Kraushaar, Tom, ed. 2004. *Die Zonenkinder und wir.* Reinbek bei Hamburg, Germany: Rowohlt.

Merkel, Ina. 1994. "Leitbilder und Lebensweisen von Frauen in der DDR." In *Sozialgeschichte der DDR,* eds. Hartmut Kaelble, Jürgen Kocka, and Hartmut Zwahr, 359–382. Stuttgart: J.G. Cotta.

Mudry, Anna, ed. 1991. *Gute Nacht, du Schöne. Autorinnen blicken zurück.* Frankfurt am Main: Luchterhand.

Rellin, Martina. 2004. *Klar bin ich eine Ost-Frau. Frauen erzählen aus dem richtigen Leben.* Berlin: Rowohlt.

Schuster, Beate, and Angelika Traub. 2003. "Single Mothers in East Germany." In *Reinventing Gender: Women in Eastern Germany since Unification,* eds. Eva Kolinsky and Maria Hildegard Nickel, 151–171. Portland, OR: Frank Cass Publishers.

Szepansky, Gerda. 1995. *Die stille Emanzipation. Frauen in der DDR.* Frankfurt am Main: Fischer Taschenbuch.

Trappe, Heike. 1996. "Work and Family in Women's Lives in the German Democratic Republic." *Work and Occupations* 23, no. 4: 354–377.

Uhlendorff, Harald. 2003. "Family and Family Orientation in East Germany." In *Reinventing Gender: Women in Eastern Germany since Unification,* eds. Eva Kolinsky and Maria Hildegard Nickel, 209–228. Portland, OR: Frank Cass Publishers.

Wander, Maxie. 1985. *Guten Morgen, du Schöne.* Darmstadt, Germany: Luchterhand (Orig. pub. 1977).

CHAPTER 5

Why Does Public Policy Implementation Fail? Lithuanian Office of State Benefits for Mothers of Large Families and Single Mothers, 1944–1956

DALIA LEINARTE

INTRODUCTION

The decree of the Presidium of the USSR Supreme Soviet "On Increasing Public Support to Pregnant Mothers, Mothers with Many Children, Single Mothers, Enhancing the Protection of Motherhood and Childhood, Proclaiming 'Heroine Mother' as the Title of Highest Distinction, and Establishing the Order of Maternal Glory and the Medal of Motherhood" was introduced on July 8, 1944. It aimed to encourage the growth of the birthrate and thus compensate for the huge loss of life incurred during World War II (Nakachi, 2006, pp. 40–68). Pronatalist politics was not a unique Soviet phenomenon in the postwar period, and such countries as France or Germany also took measures in order to compensate for their losses. However, the support of motherhood out of wedlock, along with stressing woman's role as worker, could be seen as rather specifically Soviet policy (Hoffmann, 2000). Although the birthrate in Russia had already been in decline before the war, it was nevertheless somewhat higher than in the newly incorporated Baltic states. According to Zakharov (2008, p. 955), in 1926 in Russia the total fertility rate (TFR) was 6.38. In 1923 in Lithuania it was 3.4. In 1936 the TFR dropped to 4.74 in Russia, in Lithuania in 1937 it decreased to 2.6, while in 1959 in Vilnius, the capital of Soviet Lithuania, the TFR was 1.8 (Stankuniene, 1989, p. 31). Thus the drafters of the new decree could reasonably expect the tradition of larger families to return, at least among Russian families. A financially supported pronatalistic policy would clearly produce the anticipated results in almost all countries. Yet as a measure for encouraging the birthrate to rise, this decree failed to meet expectations in the Soviet Union.

This chapter presents for the first time the process of the implementation of the decree in one of the Baltic republics—Soviet Lithuania. Introducing archival sources that have never been used before, the author analyzes the Office of State Benefits for Mothers of Large Families and Single Mothers (henceforth—the Office), which was directly responsible for the payment of benefits to single mothers and mothers of large families.

The chapter presents the main guidelines by which the Office worked, as well as the mechanism and process through which the benefits were handed out to these mothers. There is also a discussion of the reasons for the Office's inefficiency in Lithuania between 1944 and 1956. The hypothesis raised in the chapter is that for the most part, the new decree did not deliver the expected results and did not encourage a larger birthrate not only because society was not willing to accept the pronatalistic ideas behind it, but also because its administration was unsuccessful.

Main Work Objectives of the Office

One of the Office's most important initial tasks was to promote the decree of July 8 among the Lithuanian population. Since structurally the Office operated within the jurisdiction of the People's Commissariat of Finance of Soviet Lithuania, the latter sent it instructions. For instance, on October 8, 1945, Jonas Genys, vice-commissar of the People's Commissariat of Finance, warned the central administration of the Office about the lack of propaganda among mothers. According to him, staff at the branches waited until mothers found out about their rights and then sought support. Instead, Genys suggested making agreements with local newspapers in order to spread information about financial aid and awards for mothers.[1]

As a result, various measures were taken centrally and locally to popularize the decree. First of all, the Vilnius city branch suggested explaining its meaning and importance to the city district managers. They were given leaflets and flyers to be distributed among the citizens. Managers were also encouraged to publish articles in local newspapers and to involve trade unions in the popularization effort. Additionally, they were instructed to make a list of single mothers and mothers of large families that would help in identifying eligible mothers. It was also recommended that they distribute a leaflet to every militia commander in Vilnius in the hope that the commanders would pass on the information to their men. It was requested that leaflets and flyers be displayed in every maternity clinic, kindergarten, and hospital.[2]

Similarly, in 1946 the Šiauliai County branch expected assistance primarily from the local Women's Council. The branch suggested calling county-level Women's Council meetings with the purpose of presenting the decree to them.[3] Additional strict instructions came from the Prienai County branch in 1947. Executive committees of this county were obliged to make a list of all eligible mothers and to provide all single mothers and mothers of large families with the relevant information on benefits within a specified period from November 25 to December 20.[4]

The popularization of the decree of July 8 always remained on the agenda, and the Lithuanian SSR Ministry of Finance was obliged to report to the Presidium of the Supreme Soviet of the Lithuanian SSR on the results. Consequently, in 1946 Genys, then the vice-minister of the Lithuanian SSR Ministry of Finance, sent a report to Vincas Paleckis, chair of the Presidium of the Supreme Soviet of the Lithuanian SSR. In his report Genys emphasized that from July 8, 1944, to July 1, 1946, there were two radio announcements on the occasion of the one- and two-year anniversaries of the decree. Additionally, he pointed out eight articles in the republican press and six publications in local newspapers devoted to promotion of the decree. He also mentioned the decree in reports of meetings in plants and offices, in 5,000 leaflets and flyers disseminated all over the republic, and during awards ceremonies for mothers of large families.[5]

Composing term plans (*ketvirtiniai darbo planai*) every three months was another important task of the central administration and its branches in the provinces. Although the term plans differed slightly in every branch—much as they did in other workforce and industrial branches of the USSR—all of them were based on socialist planning. As a result, the number of mothers to be supported by the state was determined in advance, and the planners did not always know or take into account the actual number of allowance recipients. Thus the branch in Vilkaviškis County planned to pay allowances to 150 mothers and to award medals to 100 in the fourth term plan in 1946. This branch also planned fifteen face-to-face meetings with mothers in their homes. Additionally, there were weekly meetings planned to take place in a local birth clinic.[6] The branch in Šakiai County chose to focus on mothers' awards instead. The number of mothers to receive awards there was planned months in advance: forty in October and thirty in December.[7] The Office also made plans well in advance for the sums designated for allowances. In the third term plan of 1947, it allotted 500,000 rubles for mothers of large families and single mothers. In the term plans this money was divided on a monthly basis: 150,000 rubles in July, 150,000 in August, and 200,000 in September.[8] The Office also pledged to award medals and orders to ninety mothers.[9]

There is no doubt that planning far in advance seriously interfered with day-to-day tasks, because the fulfillment of the socialist plan demanded finding a certain number of single mothers and mothers with many children. The usual Soviet practice of falsification was not easy, for here it was a question of people rather than products. However, avoiding planning in terms of these "living" indicators was not an option: having reviewed the 1946 third term work plan for allowances paid out to the appropriate number of mothers, the USSR Ministry of Finance found no aberrations, only that the plan needed "socialist emulation and more rationalizing suggestions."[10]

As the workers at the Office outlined things such as transfers that had to be paid out, the number of allowance recipients and mothers to be honored, and the number of civil servants sent out on trips to spread propaganda, it was often difficult for them to implement plans that had been conceived far in advance. However, they soon learned the proper answers to any reproaches coming from Moscow. Once Kymantaitė, who headed the Office, received a memo from the USSR Ministry of Finance accusing her subordinates of wilfully skipping a trip to the city of Šiauliai and a planned lecture on mothers' rights. Kymantaitė, who could not make the inspector go to Šiauliai, explained that "Inspector Dobužinskas spent more time than had been planned in the town of Tauragė with his lecture" in order to provide a more detailed report.[11]

Beginning in 1947 planning became even more imperative. As a result, workers from the Office were forced to take special measures to ensure that the plans were implemented as intended. For example, civil servants from the Jurbarkas branch planned to check their files routinely to identify mothers who had given up receiving financial aid even though they were still eligible—so that they could be encouraged to continue with the formalities associated with receiving an allowance. Meanwhile, the workers of the Pagėgiai County branch planned to find thirty new eligible mothers every week so that they could fulfill the plan they had set out in advance.[12] As a consequence of such practices, data were falsified, and cases of allowances paid to dead or even nonexistent children multiplied.

Also beginning in 1947, much more attention in term of work plans was paid to awarding medals to mothers of large families. The stimulus was the subject of a report made by the chair of the Group for Registration of Award Winners at the Presidium of the Lithuanian SSR Supreme Soviet. The chair indicated that in Alytus, Biržai, Lazdijai, Trakai, Rokiškis, and Zarasai counties only 855 mothers had received awards during the years 1944–1947, or as many as in the cities of Klaipėda and Panevėžys combined. This report also mentioned that in the last fourteen months, only six eligible mothers had been identified in Alytus County. In addition, the Presidium of the Lithuanian SSR Supreme Soviet reproached county and district executive committees because they had neither identified mothers nor presented them with awards. As a result, the work of the Office received a negative evaluation.[13]

The main tasks of the Office also included training courses and meetings. The central administration would arrange several three- to five-day training courses annually for staff at the branches. As a rule, Kymantaitė invited senior inspectors from the branches to such gatherings, warning the participants beforehand that the meetings were compulsory. She also reminded the participants to bring their ration cards because they would "not be provided with food in Vilnius."[14]

During the period 1944–1952 there were no substantial changes in the agendas of such training courses. Since the central administrators returned repeatedly to the same questions during these courses, it can be assumed that the Office faced constant obstacles in implementing its goals. For example, the issue of popularizing the decree was permanently on the agenda during all the courses and other meetings. Constant attention was likewise paid to the composition of term work plans and to scrutiny of the mechanism for paying allowances, even though no changes in these procedures had been introduced since the establishment of the Office in 1944.[15] On the other hand, repetition of the agenda during courses may also have served as a simulated work process, a phenomenon that was very familiar under the socialist regime (cf. Kotkin's [1995] discussion of the meaninglessness of Soviet planning in all walks of Soviet life).

Awards for mothers of large families and other events worthy of celebration also took place during training courses and meetings at the central administration in Vilnius. For instance, on July 7–10, 1947, there was a celebration of the three-year anniversary of the July 8 decree. On this occasion speeches were delivered by Kymantaitė and Bašlakovas, the secretary of the party organization in the Ministry of Finance. In his speech Bašlakovas mostly focused on the importance of the anniversary. He also greeted all workers of the Office and expressed his wish that they would work "as well as did Comrade Kalininas, i.e. quickly, honestly, and without bureaucracy."[16]

From the very beginning, however, the Office was unable to arrange the work process smoothly. One reason for this was that the branches did not pay proper attention to the instructions of the center and sometimes even disregarded them. As a result, the branches often failed to compile the required lists of eligible mothers or send term work plans to the central administration on time. The branches almost never paid benefits regularly and did not keep mothers' files neatly or in good order. On the other hand, the branches were not satisfied with the requests and demands coming from the center. On some occasions the chairs of the branches disobeyed Kymantaitė's orders and even dared to lecture her. She responded to one such reprimand in a letter in July 1946: "I am returning your letter received on July 10 and registered as No. 1235, and I ask you not to send such nonsense in the future. You have no business instructing the chair of the central administration what to do. Instead you must submit a work plan for every term on time."[17]

DISTRIBUTION OF FINANCIAL AID: PRACTICE

Popularizing the decree, composing term plans, and arranging training courses and meetings required considerable work by the central administration and its provincial branches. However, the most important task of the Office was to distribute financial aid to single mothers and mothers of large families. The central administration instructed staff not to wait until mothers inquired about financial aid on their own initiative—provincial branch workers were themselves to compile lists of large families with many children and single mothers. Mothers were then urged to apply for allowances based on these lists. After receiving the mother's application, the staff would start a personal file for the mother that indicated the number and ages of children living with her (children who lived separately from the mother were not taken into consideration). The birth data of children had to be verified at the local registry office and militia. This kind of personal file had to be submitted to the county and city or rural district executive committee for approval (beginning in 1950, to the regional and district executive committee). After payment of the allowance was approved, the branch would note the amount of the allowance in the mother's personal file. When the mother actually received the money, she had to sign the payroll, which was kept in a safe place in every branch. A staff member had to ensure that both signatures of the beneficiary—the signature in the payroll and the signature in the personal file—were identical. The payment was made in one of two ways—either at the executive committee of the county (or region or district) or at the local savings bank.

However, this procedure, seemingly uncomplicated at first glance, was soon confounded by bureaucratic misunderstandings arising in the first stage of allowance payment—compilation of the lists of eligible mothers. On December 31, 1945, the chair of the Executive Committee Finance Division of Kėdainiai County, who was also serving as a chair of the Kėdainiai branch, complained in a letter to the central administration that he could not make lists of mothers because the rural district executive committees were not sending him the necessary data.[18] On December 20, 1945,

Sinaiskis, the deputy chair of the People's Commissariat of Finance of Soviet Lithuania, was insistently urging "the divisions of finance of all counties to submit information about eligible mothers who are not receiving any allowances. If submitted later than December 25, there will be strict punishment."[19] However, the reprimand was misunderstood.

The next year the branches flooded the central administration with lists of mothers of large families. These lists, however, were supposed to stay with the local departments of finance of the executive committees or in already established branches in the provinces, while all the central authorities requested were the number of mothers receiving the allowances and the number who were entitled to the allowance but had not yet received it. Meanwhile, after Sinaiskis's above-mentioned letter, the central administration started receiving long lists that included not only the names of mothers but also the names and birthdates of their children. These lists were sent back to the provinces with a note that the names of mothers were not needed centrally but only by local staff in order to organize payments properly.[20]

The payment of benefits was also disrupted by unnecessary bureaucratic requirements. The Soviet Lithuanian Ministry of Finance discovered that the Kupiškis County branch had started requiring mothers to submit documents, signed by an officer of the local militia, certifying that they were neither alcoholics nor promiscuous.[21] Mothers in Tauragė County had not only been asked to submit records testifying to their morality and behavior, but were also required to fill out extra forms created by the staff and submit a number of additional documents. Due to red tape, review of these mothers' applications took ten to twelve months instead of the official approval period of two weeks. Contrived application forms and additional documents were also requested in Vilkaviškis County.[22] In addition, during a large-scale audit in 1946 of the Tauragė, Švenčioniai, Utena, Prienai, Varėna, Kaišiadorys, Trakai, and Alytus county branches and the Tauragė, Švenčioniai, Utena, and Lazdijai savings banks, it was discovered that these branches did not have specimens of mothers' signatures. Moreover, the staff there did not require the registry offices to give notification of deceased children but trusted the mother to inform them herself. Such oversights in the procedure made it possible to continue paying allowances for deceased children.

There was also evidence that after the mothers received their allowances at the savings bank, they were forced to leave the money in the bank as a deposit or purchase bonds.[23] The savings bank in the town of Utena created artificial waiting lines to pressure applicants to pay bribes. The Lazdijai

County savings bank did not have lines, but it never had enough cash on hand, which delayed payment of allowances for several months.[24] The Kretinga, Utena, Trakai, and Zarasai savings banks were always short of money as well. Mothers who traveled as far as fifty to seventy kilometers therefore had to return home empty-handed. Savings banks in the above-mentioned counties also required mothers to buy bonds, or they would transfer the money to a savings account without permission and give the mother a savings bank card (the "little book," as women called it) instead of the actual money.[25] The Zarasai and Telšiai town militia would refuse to provide information about the number of children in families, which also slowed down receipt of the allowance.

It was not only bureaucracy, however, that obstructed allowance payments. Often the money was simply stolen or embezzled. Probably the easiest way to cheat was to receive payment for nonexistent or already deceased children. The 1949 inspection discovered that the staff of Kaunas County was concealing the fact of children's deaths and continuing to pay the allowance. Payments for these deceased children totaled 56,748 rubles. The inspection materials do not clarify whether the mothers were involved in the forgery and shared the money with the staff, or whether the staff found another way of pocketing the money. A check of the death certificates of children in 1944, 1945, and 1946 revealed that in October and November of 1948, allowances for children who had died several years earlier were still being allotted. The same Kaunas County branch also had cases in which mothers of children born during the interwar period received allowances.[26] For instance, the Alytus County branch staff accepted birth certificates on which the birthdates had obviously been altered.[27] In 1948 the Pagėgiai County savings bank would sometimes pay a mother without her signature or her personal mother's book, which meant that the money could have been paid to any woman.[28] On the other hand, some civil servants in the central administration were overly strict and unaccommodating. For instance, a Lazdijai County branch employee by the name of Giedraitis flatly refused to approve the benefits without the mothers' signatures, even though he knew that these women were illiterate. The materials of the inspection state that these women were not granted allowances.[29]

In 1947 a large-scale felony was revealed in the Šilutė County branch. In 1946–1947 the inspector-examiner and the chief accountant of the branch misappropriated 355,709 rubles from funds dedicated to the allowances. In this case, the money was pocketed in various ways, including payment for deceased and nonexistent children and fictitious mothers. The inspector-examiner and the chief accountant would mark a cross in place of the applicants' signatures. The audit determined that the money paid for the deceased children was shared with the mothers. As a matter of fact, this branch was undergoing a regular inspection at the time of the crime, and although the money had already been embezzled, the inspector did not notice anything suspicious. On the contrary, he described the inspector-examiner and the chief accountant as excellent workers. After the inspector left, the embezzlement continued for another six months. It was estimated that in the Šilutė County branch, allowances were stolen based on 392 fictitious mother files.[30]

Due to deliberate forgery and theft or incompetence, the branches of the Office constantly had to deal with financial problems caused by the overpayment or underpayment of allowances. On May 20, 1950, the Mažeikiai County branch overpaid a sum of 67,453 rubles.[31] In 1948 the Pagėgiai County branch overpaid 25,080 rubles. However, only a small part of the overpaid money was returned to the savings banks. In 1950 the Joniškis County branch overpaid 14,014 rubles, but only 2,520 rubles was returned to the bank.[32]

Confusion Concerning Single Mothers

There was one other factor that complicated the work of the central administration and its branches. Although the decree of July 8, 1944, provided allowances for single mothers, it unexpectedly turned out that the staff and even benefit recipients were unable to describe who exactly qualified as a "single mother." Inaccurate interpretation of the term created confusion and was one more reason why allowances were paid to those who did not deserve them or vice versa. The decree of July 8 was actually aiming at relationships as envisaged in the 1917 Soviet Family Law, according to which the Soviet state was supposed to provide support to mothers who raised their children alone or cohabitated without ever being officially married (on early Soviet family concepts, see Engel and Posadskaya-Vanderbeck, 1998; Goldman, 1993). In Russia single mothers had the same rights as other mothers, and unregistered common-law marriages were legally on a par with registered ones, until the new family legislation was adopted in 1936. However, this was not the case in Lithuania. In the nineteenth century, single mothers had no place in the Lithuanian community whatsoever, and national writers described bastards as "little rats" that would be better off dead. For the most part, illegitimate children were not cared for by their mother, other relatives, or the community in general. There is no doubt that single mothers were also stigmatized in Catholic and conservative prewar Lithuania and that a similar attitude was preserved after World War II. Accordingly, the only "single mother" Lithuanian society accepted was a married woman who had been abandoned by the child's father.

The Office's functionaries, let alone the average ethnic Lithuanian, were unable to grasp why an unmarried woman raising a "bastard" should be financially supported by the state. There was therefore very little chance that a larger group of single (never-married) mothers would actually be included in the quarterly plans of the Lithuanian Office in the first decade after World War II. According to statistics presented by the central administration in 1944, there were only six single mothers in all of Lithuania; in 1946 there were thirteen in Kaišiadoriai County.[33]

The staff of the branches would pay allowances (beginning with the first child) to women abandoned by their official husbands, while the decree did not provide for this possibility. Such facts were noticed by the numerous audits: of the Kėdainiai County branch on February 23, 1948, the Taurag savings bank on February 20, the Joniškis branch on November 21, 1950, and the Rokiškis branch on October 11, 1951.[34] The 1949 audit of the Pasvalys branch also stated that "single mothers continue to be paid the allowance even though the child's birth certificate indicates the father's name."[35] In the end, the frightened and confused staff stopped paying benefits altogether if the father's name was on the child's birth certificate. In such cases the term "single mother" was interpreted incorrectly not only by the staff of the central administration and its branches, but also by the auditors.

Subsequently the USSR Ministry of Finance issued a separate decree for Lithuania regarding who should be considered a "single mother." It revoked the central administration's resolution denying allowances to single mothers if the name of their child's father was on the birth certificate and specified the criteria for defining the target group. It disqualified abandoned but not officially divorced mothers and cohabiting parents in unregistered marriages who shared finances and jointly raised their child(ren).[36] Mothers in unregistered marriages were eligible for allowances, however, if finances were not shared and the cohabiting father did not help raise the children. Finally, benefits could be paid regardless of whether the child's father was recorded in the birth registry, but only if the marriage was unregistered and the couple did not cohabitate.

It was hard for Lithuanians to understand such labyrinthine interpersonal relationships. The central administration therefore prepared a leaflet defining the single mother for the staff to learn by heart. Apropos of this publication, the chair of the Biržai County branch wrote the Office: "We have repeatedly informed you that in our county we have only one mother whose child's birth certificate indicates the father's name, but who has never been in a registered marriage and does not live with the child's father and does not share household financial responsibilities with him. Grečkina Tatjana is such a single mother, and she is eligible for the allowance."[37]

As a matter of fact, the category of single and never-married women tended to grow annually in both Soviet Lithuania and Russia. According to Kymantaitė, the first chair of the Office, in 1945 1,232 single mothers received allowances. By the following year, 1946, that figure had increased to 5,873.[38] It is unclear whether the number of unmarried mothers was truly growing in Lithuania or whether Lithuanian citizens were gradually adjusting to the Soviet welfare system by changing their marriage status deliberately in order to qualify for the allowances. Another explanation may be that the increase in single mothers was directly related to the Lithuanian resistance movement. Thousands of young males left at this time for the forest to begin the struggle against the Soviet forces, which meant that their babies could only be registered as fatherless and the mothers as single. Answering these questions will require further research.

THE OVERALL RESULTS OF THE OFFICE'S ACTIVITY

The statistics presented by the Office and its branches were generally unreliable. As a result, there are discrepancies in the numbers of mothers who received benefits and/or were given awards. The chairs of local branches constantly complained that they had not been informed of the precise number of eligible mothers or of how much money had already been paid. In his letter to the central administration, for instance, the chair of the Department of Finance of the Executive Committee of Panevėžys County emphasized that there could be around 350 eligible mothers in the county. However, he warned, "this data is not reliable."[39] The number of beneficiaries was almost always falsified to satisfy the well-known Soviet requirement to fulfill term plans. As a result, overpayments were periodically discovered by the inspectors as money paid out to "dead souls." Nevertheless, the data presented for that same period of 1944–1946 by both Kymantaitė and Drobnys, commissar of the People's Commissariat of Finance of Soviet Lithuania, deserve attention as an illustration of the limits of Soviet-era statistics. As can be seen from these figures, the number of beneficiaries presented by Drobnys differs from what was indicated by Kymantaitė. In addition, the data received from the branches are also different and not much larger or much smaller than those from Drobnys or Kymantaitė. For example, the chair of the Panevėžys County branch reported around forty-four eligible mothers in 1945 and pointed out that this figure came from the local civil registry office. He explained to Kymantaitė: "We went to see these mothers in person in order to explain to them their rights to the benefits."[40] Yet Drobnys's data indicated 583 eligible mothers in the Panevėžys branch during the period from October 1944 to December 1, 1946.[41] Similarly, whereas the Kaunas County branch reported 3,129 mothers entitled to benefits in 1946,[42] between October 1944 and December 1, 1946, in Kaunas County Drobnys indicated only 947 eligible mothers of large families and single mothers combined.[43]

The number of eligible mothers was artificially increased not only to accommodate Soviet term plans, but also to facilitate theft and embezzlement. Artificially inflated numbers gave the Office staff the opportunity to skim benefits for themselves. Thus the statistics presented by the central administration on the sums of paid benefits in no way reflect how much actually went to single mothers and mothers of large families. It is important to stress that in different sources, the number of beneficiaries differed by dozens and, in some cases, even by hundreds. As a result, the data had to be corrected periodically. For instance, the chair of the Biržai County branch noted in a 1945 report: "We have registered 516 mothers of large families and single mothers so far. However, only 403 of them are eligible. The other 113 mothers are not entitled to receive benefits, because information on the number or age of their children is incomplete."[44]

DISBANDING THE OFFICE

Due to all the shortcomings in the activities of the Office, Kymantaitė was reprimanded by her superiors for unsatisfactory implementation of the decree of July 8. For instance, Gedvilas, commissar of the Council of the Lithuanian People's Commissariat, signed a report on April 13, 1945, addressing deficiencies in the Office's operation. He warned Kymantaitė to organize work at the Office more efficiently to provide for the timely payment of benefits. He also instructed her to ensure that workers at branches in the provinces compiling lists of eligible mothers demand full information from the militia on the number and age of children.[45] The Ministry of Finance of Soviet Lithuania was similarly dissatisfied with the activities of the Office. After the inspection of the Ukmergė County branch, Vice-Minister of Finance Genys concluded that the data in some 30 percent of mothers' files were incorrect. He also mentioned that written applications for financial aid were missing and that those that were included lacked signatures. In addition, he noted constant cash shortages in the local bank of Ukmergė County, which forced mothers to make multiple needless trips from the furthest reaches of the county, and that the personnel of the bank were known to be extremely rude with mothers. He also found out that the local newspaper and trade union of the county had never even heard of the decree of July 8.[46]

Similarly, the personnel at the Kėdainiai County branch did not know how much money eligible mothers were entitled to receive. As a result, in 1946 there were overpayments there totaling thousands of rubles that were never returned to the bank. Similarly, mothers remained uncompensated for unpaid benefits. Genys concluded that the chair of the Ukmergė County branch had not taken his duties seriously.[47] As a consequence, on July 25, 1947, Kymantaitė received an official reprimand from Drobnys at the Ministry of Finance of Soviet Lithuania.[48]

On May 10, 1950, the USSR Ministry of Finance issued a decree criticizing the Lithuanian Office for the confusion that caused benefits to be paid late or not at all. Another major case of embezzlement—this one at the Trakai County branch—led to even more negative reactions. As a consequence of all this, in 1950 Kymantaitė was removed as chair.[49]

Dismissing Kymantaitė did not improve the Office's performance, however. In December 1951 the new chair, Jurgaitytė, announced that on October 1 there were again large overpayments and underpayments. Unpaid benefits totaled 145,325 rubles.[50] As for overpayments, at the Šiauliai County branch, for instance, on January 1, 1952, the People's Court received evidence of the embezzlement of 109,380 rubles. There were also overpayments of 62,172.62 rubles that remained unmentioned. Besides these financial irregularities, the Šiauliai branch was guilty of other violations such as the dilatory processing of applications and failure to nominate mothers for awards. In 1951 the operation of the Lithuanian Office was again evaluated as unsatisfactory in a decree issued by Soviet Lithuanian Minister of Finance Zverev. Meanwhile, the central administration and its branches attempted to boost their image by focusing on the positive, in line with the spirit of socialist planning that only faintly reflected the actual allowance payment situation. For instance, a discussion of the performance of the Kaunas region branch noted achievements such as the following: "In the third quarter of 1951, ninety-five mothers were late in receiving their personal record books, while in the fourth quarter there were only seventy. It can be concluded that the tardy delivery of personal records decreased by more than 26 percent."[51]

Mothers were almost completely discouraged from applying for state financial aid by shortcomings in the performance of the local savings banks and branch offices that prevented them from receiving their rightful benefits. Thus many women traveled long distances in vain because the banks had insufficient cash on hand; in other cases the bank would refuse to give applicants cash and instead deposit the allowance in the mother's account or demand that she use the money to buy state bonds. Local offices often required that additional forms be completed or insisted that mothers prove their moral irreproachability. These difficulties were compounded by confusion over the definition of a single mother, a general lack of information, and numerous unconventional procedures. An audit of the Trakai County branch recommended compiling surveys of mothers who had not come forward to receive their allowances for over six months and that they be contacted personally in order to ascertain the reason why. Similarly, an audit of the Joniškis region also determined that twenty-seven eligible mothers had lost interest in the allowances and had not claimed their money for two to three years. In 1952 the staff of the Šiauliai regional branch also noticed that personal record books prepared for mothers were left lying in the drawers of the branch office because no one had come to collect them.[52]

On June 1, 1956, the Office was disbanded and its functions handed over to the LSSR Ministry of Social Security. The turmoil of the postwar period, an inability and unwillingness to work for the state, a form of state welfare for the family that was unfamiliar to Lithuanian society (as it was the first of its kind to be applied in the country), conservative Catholic Lithuanian family traditions, and the dishonesty of the Office staff rendered its work ineffective and were major factors in the failure of the new decree of July 8, 1944. The Lithuanian experience of application of the decree illustrates the significance of everyday family practices and traditional normativity as an important mechanism of the subversion of centrally designed family policy. In the case of the application of 1944 law in Lithuania, analyzed in this chapter, the policy that was centrally elaborated by the Soviet authorities and imposed on the population of the recently occupied Baltic countries subverted the initial concept of the law. Thus it led to results that were far different from those its authors intended.

NOTES

1 Paper of October 6, 1945, by Jonas Genys, vice-commissar of the People's Commissariat of Finance of Soviet Lithuania. Lithuanian Central State Archives (Futher-LCVA), f.R-164, op. 14, d. 1, l. 17.

2   Work plan of the Vilnius city branch of the Office, 1945. LCVA, f.R.-164, op. 14, d. 4. l. 6.
3   Work plan of the Šiauliai city branch of the Office regarding the popularization of the decree, 1946. LCVA, f.R.-164, op. 14, d. 4. l. 14.
4   Work plan of the Prienai city branch for the fourth quarter of 1947. LCVA, f.R.-164, op. 14, d. 7. l. 229.
5   Letter of Genys to Paleckis, September 20, 1946. LCVA, f.R.-164, op. 14, d. 5, l. 10.
6   Work plan of the Vilkaviškis County branch for the third quarter of 1946, October 5. LCVA, f.R.-164, op. 14, d. 4, l. 2.
7   Work plan of the Šakiai County branch for the fourth quarter of 1946. LCVA, f.R.-164, op. 14, d. 4, l. 8.
8   In December 1947 the Soviet government introduced a monetary reform that made it difficult to provide the size of average salary for that year as a comparison in order to understand the scale of these payments. According to USSR secret statistics, month salary was about 442 rubles in 1945 and 646 rubles in 1950 (Zubkova et al. 2003, pp. 501–502).
9   Work plan of the Office for the third quarter of 1947. LCVA, f.R.-164, op. 14, d. 7, l. 98.
10 A letter of the USSR Ministry of Finance. LCVA, f.R.-164, op. 14, d. 7. l. 42.
11 Kymantaitė's report on work plan of the fourth quarter of 1946. LCVA, f.R.-164, op. 14. d. 7, l. 33.
12 Work plan of the Jurbarkas County branch for the third quarter of 1948 and work plan of the Pagėgiai County branch for the fourth quarter of 1948. LCVA, f.R.-164, op. 14, d. 9, ll. 56, 133.
13 "On Awards to Mothers of Large Families." Presidium of the Lithuanian SSR Supreme Soviet, April 10, 1947. LCVA, f.R.-164, op. 14, d. 6, ll. 36–37.
14 Order of the Ministry of Finance of the Lithuanian SSR, November 14, 1946, LCVA, f.R.-164, op. 14, d. 3, l. 66.
15 Office seminar agenda, October 25, 1945. LCVA, f.R.-164, op. 14, d. 1, l. 22; Office seminar agenda, March 25–30, 1946. LCVA, f.R.-164, op. 14, d. 3, l. 18.
16 Office seminar agenda, July 7–10, 1947. LCVA, f.R.-164, op. 14, d. 6, l. 49.
17 Kymantaitė's report to the Pagėgiai County branch, July 1946, LCVA, f.R.-164, op. 14, d. 4, l. 15.
18 Letter from the chair of the Department of Finance of Kėdainiai County to the Office, December 31, 1945, LCVA, f.R.-164, op. 14, d. 2, l. 6.
19 Decree of the People's Commissar of Finance of Soviet Lithuania, December 20, 1945. LCVA, f.R.-164, op. 14, d. 2, l. 1.
20 Letter from the Office, 1946, LCVA, f.R.-164, op. 14, d. 2, l. 13.
21 Letter from V. Kuznecovas, deputy minister of finance of Soviet Lithuania, October 6, 1950. LCVA, f.R.-164, op. 14, d. 16, l. 32.
22 On the audit of the Tauragė, Švenčioniai, Utena, Prienai, Varėna, Kaišiadorys, Trakai and Alytus County branches and the Tauragė, Švenčioniai, Utena and Lazdijai savings banks, December 30, 1946, LCVA, f.R.-164, op. 14, d. 3, l. 71; Genys's report on the audit of the Biržai, Marijampolė and Vilkaviškis County branches, May 30, 1946, LCVA, f.R.-164, op. 14, d. 3, l. 38.

23 Op.cit., ll. 71–72.
24 Op. cit. ll. 72–73.
25 Report by Kymantaitė, chair of the Office, and Drobnys to the Central Committee of the Lithuanian Communist Party (b), July 6, 1946, LCVA, f.R.-164, op. 14, d. 5, l. 5.
26 Kaunas County branch audit material, January 29, 1949, LCVA, f.R.-164, op. 14, d. 12, l. 3.
27 Alytus County branch audit material, October 20, 1949, LCVA, f.R.-164, op. 14, d. 12, l. 43.
28 Pagėgiai County branch audit material, February 20, 1948, LCVA, f.R.-164, op. 14, d. 1, l. 4.
29 Decree of the Minister of Finance of Soviet Lithuania on the performance of the Lazdijai County branch, June 28, 1950, LCVA, f.R.-164, op. 14, d. 15, l. 38.
30 Decree issued by A. Sinaiskis, acting minister of finance of Soviet Lithuania, regarding the Šilutė County branch's performance, October 24, 1947, ll. 92–93; decree issued by Drobnys regarding the Šilutė County branch's performance, l. 103; resolution issued by M. Gedvilas, chair of the Ministers' Council of Soviet Lithuania, regarding the Šilutė County branch's performance, December 31, 1947, l. 112. LCVA, f.R.-164, op. 14, d. 6.
31 Mažeikiai County branch audit material, May 20, 1950, LCVA, f.R.-164, op. 14, d. 16, l. 77.
32 Pagėgiai County branch audit material, February 20, 1948, LCVA, f.R.-164, op. 14, d. 11, l. 8; report of the Joniškis County branch, May 24, 1950, LCVA, f.R.-164, op. 14, d. 16, l. 47.
33 Report by a chair of the Department of Welfare of the Executive Committee of the Kaišiadorys County for the third quarter of 1946, LCVA, f.R.-164, op. 14, d. 7, l. 84.
34 Kėdainiai County branch's audit results, February 23, 1948, LCVA, f.R.-164, op. 14, d. 11, l. 11; Tauragė County savings bank audit results, February 20, 1948, op.cit, l. 6; decree issued by the minister of finance of Soviet Lithuania regarding the Joniškis regional branch's work performance, November 21, 1950, LCVA, f.R.-164, op. 14, d. 15, l. 66; on the Šiauliai regional branch's work performance, October 11, 1951, LCVA, f.R.-164, op. 14, d. 20, ll. 59–60.
35 Pasvalys branch audit results, June 3, 1949, LCVA, f.R.-164, op. 14, d. 12, l. 24.
36 Ministry of Finance of the USSR Decree on the work performance of the Lithuanian Office. 1950 (no exact date given). LCVA, Ap. 14, B.15, l.16–23.
37 Letter from the chair of the Biržai County branch to the Office, June 3, 1950, LCVA, f.R – 164, Op. 14, d. 16, l. 42.
38 Statistics presented by the Office to the Women's Department of the Central Committee of the Lithuanian Communist Party, February 15, 1947. LCVA, f.R - 164, Op. 14, d. 8, l. 3.
39 Letter of the chair of the Department of Finance at the Executive Committee of Panevėžys County, 1945. LCVA, f.R.-164, op. 14, d. 2, l. 19.
40 Report by a chair of the Department of Welfare of the Executive Committee of Panevėžys city, 1945, LCVA, f.R.-164, op. 14, d. 2, l. 18.

41 Report by Drobnys, commissar of the People's Commissariat of Finance of Soviet Lithuania, to Sniečkus, the first secretary of the Lithuanian Communist Party, February 1, 1947. LCVA, f.R.-164, op. 14, d. 5, l. 1.
42 Report by a chair of the Kaunas County branch, 1946, LCVA, f.R.-164, op. 14, d. 2, l. 4.
43 Report by Drobnys, commissar of the People's Commissariat of Finance of Soviet Lithuania, to Sniečkus, first secretary of the Lithuanian Communist Party, February 1, 1947. LCVA, f.R.-164, op. 14, d. 5, l. 1.
44 Report of the Department of Finance of Biržai County, December 22, 1945, LCVA, f.R.-164, op. 14, d. 2, l. 2.
45 Draft of decree of the Council of the People's Commissariat regarding the work of the Lithuanian Office, April 13, 1945, LCVA, f.R.-164, op. 14, d. 1, l.l. 5-6.
46 Genys's report regarding the work of the Ukmergė County branch, November 14, 1946, LCVA, f.R.-164, Ap. 14, B. 3, L. 66-67.
47 Genys's report regarding the work of the Kėdainiai County branch, April 10, 1946, LCVA, f.R.-164, op. 14, d. 6. l. 22.
48 Decree issued by minister of finance of Soviet Lithuania A. Drobnys regarding the work of the Office, September 7, 1947, LCVA, f.R.-164, op. 14, d. 6, l. 75.
49 Decree of the Minister of Finance of the USSR, May 10, 1950, LCVA, f.R.-164, op. 14, d. 15, ll. 26–27. Of course, the Soviet leadership could have dismissed M. Kymantaitė for political or other reasons. Arguing against such a version of events, however, is the fact that the Office itself was shut down soon after and its functions passed on to another structure. It is also important to note that in the first years after the war, Lithuanians who opposed occupation by the Soviet regime did not engage in passive resistance but joined an armed struggle. The only Lithuanians who collaborated with the Soviet leadership in 1944 were those who believed in the Soviet system or had consciously decided to support it for practical reasons. In addition, until anti-Soviet resistance in Lithuania was neutralized, the initial targets of the resistance were the first Soviet civil servants and, as such, they were treated particularly harshly.
50 Letter from Drobnys regarding the performance of the Office, December 27, 1951, LCVA, f.R.-164, op. 14, d. 20, l. 20.
51 Letter of a chair of the Department of Finance of the Executive Committee of the Šiauliai region regarding the work performance of the Šiauliai branch, January 26, 1952, LCVA, f.R.-164, op. 14, d. 20, l. 15, 2; Decree no. 84 issued by A. Zverev, USSR minister of finance, January 18, 1951, l. 121; a letter of a chair of the Department of Finance of the Executive Committee of the Kaunas Region regarding the work performance of the Kaunas branch, February 18, 1952, l. 5.
52 From materials of the Trakai County branch, October 14, 1949, LCVA, f.R.-164, op. 14, d. 14, l. 21; materials of audit by the Ministry of Finance of Soviet Lithuania of the Joniškis regional branch, November 21, 1950, LCVA, f.R.-164, op. 14, d. 15, l. 67; a letter of a chair of the Department of Finance of the Executive Committee of the Šiauliai region, March 6, 1952, LCVA, f.R.-164, op. 14, d. 20, l. 14.

References

Engel, Barbara A., and Anastasia Posadskaya-Vanderbeck, eds. 1998. *A Revolution of Their Own: Voices of Women in Soviet History*. Boulder, CO: Westview.
Goldman, Wendy Z. 1993. *Women, the State and Revolution: Soviet Family Policy and Social Life, 1917–1936*. Cambridge: Cambridge University Press.
Hoffmann, David. 2000. "Mothers in the Motherland: Stalinist Pronatalism in its Pan-European Context." *Journal of Social History* 34, no. 1: 35–54.
Kotkin, Stephen. 1995. *Magnetic Mountain: Stalinism as a Civilization*. Berkeley, CA: University of California Press.
Nakachi, Mie. 2006. "N.S. Khrushchev and the 1944 Soviet Family Law: Politics, Reproduction, and Language." *East European Politics and Societies* 20, no. 1: 40–68.
Stankuniene, Vlada. 1989. *Demograficheskoe razvitie Litvy: retrospektiva, sovremennye problemy, sravnitel'nyi analiz* (The demographic evolution of Lithuania: Retrospective, problems, comparative analysis). Vilnius, Lithuania: Institut ekonomiki Akademii Nauk Litovskoi SSR.
Zakharov, Sergei. 2008. "Russian Federation: From the First to the Second Demographic Transition." *Demographic Research* 19, no. 24: 907–972.
Zubkova, Elena, L.P. Kosheleva, G.A. Kuznetsova, A.I. Miniuk, and L.A. Rogovaia, eds. 2003. *Sovetskaia zhizn'. 1945–1953 gg.* (Soviet life. 1945–1953). Moscow: ROSSPEN.

CHAPTER 6

The Latvian Family Experience with Sovietization 1945–1990

Maija Runcis

Introduction

According to Soviet propaganda, the care of children and mothers and families was always one of the most important tasks of the Soviet state.[1] As we know from previous research on Soviet family and gender politics, the Soviet state challenged existing "traditional" gender norms. The official explanation of this policy was that it liberated women from patriarchal oppression, but in practice it was reduced to the regulation of motherhood and the stimulation of women's involvement in productive work. Mothers, especially working mothers, were idealized as rhetorical heroines. At the same time, the propaganda construction of masculinity was almost untouched. The proletarian man was "muscular," "productive," "combative," and "heroic" (Goven, 2002, p. 7). The Communist Party struggled to find a way to integrate women into the proletarian vision of equality between men and women, and the way to do it was through work, which also impacted family life.

The entry of women into the workforce was "inextricably associated" with their liberation from traditional patriarchal family roles (ibid.). Women became more socially and economically independent from men, which in turn reduced men's authority in the family, since they could no longer be the only breadwinner and the unconditional head of the household. This kind of politicization of motherhood neglected the role of the father and his traditional power within the family by handing it to the state (Bureychak, 2010). Soviet propaganda differentiated women from men by stressing women's identity both as mothers and working heroes, while fathers were made almost invisible. In reality women ended up with the double burden of work outside the home combined with uncompensated domestic labor and responsibility for child raising (Lapidus, 2003).

In this chapter I explore how Soviet normative policies concerning gender and family applied to Latvian citizens under Soviet rule. Using archival documents, magazines, and life stories, I am looking at discourses of Sovietization in order to gain insight into everyday family life and women's strategies within the family. My research question to the sources is the following: How did women meet the challenges in the new family ideology, and how did they experience the societal changes affecting their lives?

These questions are important, since Latvia was occupied and the communist government did not have much legitimacy within society. However, Sovietization in postwar Latvia sought to replace Latvian "bourgeois" society with the proletarian state.[2] Nationalism became a crime against Soviet ideology, and "nationalists" were declared to be "enemies of the people" (Bureychak, 2010; see also Weiner, 1999). To Latvians, who had experienced national independence for only two decades, this was hard to accept.

Latvia in between Foreign Powers and Independence

In the following short exposition, I will try to give a picture of the Latvian struggle for independence and the political and social "map" before World War II. Throughout modern history, Latvia has been populated by large ethnic minority groups, such as the Baltic Germans until 1940 and Russians from the tsarist era to the present. It was governed by an upper class of the old Baltic Germans, which left no room for the emergence of an individual Latvian upper class. As Latvia's landowning class, the Baltic Germans remained extremely influential until the end of the nineteenth century (Plakans, 1995, p. 189). The end of the nineteenth century marks the beginning of a very rapid modernization of the entire region. This development changed the situation and gave the Latvian inhabitants new possibilities to get a better education and raise their social status.

Latvia got its independence after the destruction of World War I, the 1917 revolution and the Latvian War of Independence, which lasted from 1918 to 1920. The manors, possessions, and power of the Baltic Germans and Russians were swept away, and the land was distributed to Latvian farmers (Balodis, 1990, p. 197). Independent Latvia was ruled first as a democracy and after 1934 as a nationalist dictatorship, when the leader of the Farmers Party, Karlis Ulmanis, launched a coup d'état, and all socialist parties and extreme right-wing organizations were forbidden (ibid., p. 200). In 1940 the Soviet Red Army entered Latvia and declared it a republic of the Soviet Union. Shortly thereafter Nazis invaded and occupied the country from 1941 to 1944. Soviet rule was re-established in October 1944, accompanied by industrialization and collectivization and the nationalization of the public sphere (Shabalov, 2010, p. 5). During the interwar period Latvia started to build its own social welfare system with certain implications for gender divisions. Normally, however, gender is largely invisible in welfare policy documents.

Latvian family patterns (before Sovietization in 1940) followed the Western European nuclear family model, with late marriages and thus relatively few children per family (Katus et al., 2008). Social welfare was administered by non-state organizations but was supported by the state. Health insurance was compulsory for all workers and farmers and included their families. Maternity leave for working mothers was paid four weeks before delivery and eight weeks after. The system of social and health insurance (pensions, maternal leave, health insurance) was quite well-developed for those who were employed (Balodis, 1990, p. 209). In 1938 the Latvian state used 13.1 percent of the state budget for social insurance. The average in Europe was 9.3 percent. As in several other Western European countries, such as Sweden, citizens not connected with a workplace were not included in the social system. Still, married women and mothers were generally housewives, who depended on male breadwinners or charity for their sustenance.

During the period from 1939 to 1959, the population decreased by more than a half-million (Latvijas vestures institutas apgads, 2001, p.13). Due to substantial male losses during World War II, the female-to-male ratio among people aged 30–34 was 1,427 per thousand, and among those aged 35–39 it was 1,597 per thousand (Eglitis, 2010, p. 161). More than 250,000 refugees left Latvia, and kulaks, "enemies of the people," and "fascists" were continuously deported up until 1959. Repressions and deportations separated many families. As a result many Latvian women were left alone with the household and children and were forced to take more responsibility, which put their independence and autonomy in a new perspective.

Other issues that confronted many Latvian families during the Soviet occupation were problems in acquiring basic necessities such as housing, heating, and food, and difficulties in reuniting with family members due to repression and deportation. Characterizing the social climate during those years, Latvian researcher on gender history Vita Zelce writes: "The social consciousness was imbued with a hatred of war and politics, with suspicions against ideological games and any calls to sacrifice oneself on the altar of an idea or of the state" (Zelce, 2006).

The Beginning of Sovietization

Immediately upon establishing Soviet rule in Latvia in 1940, the authorities began constructing and disseminating a historical narrative for the Latvians, portraying them as both inherently revolutionary and as longstanding friends of the Russians. The narrative used both class-based and national interpretations in an effort to legitimize the Soviet regime and to play down inherited tensions between class and nation (Shabalov, 2010, p. 3).

In Soviet Latvian propaganda from 1940 on, the Latvian family model was called "the bourgeois family," in contrast to the socialist family, which was the Soviet ideal. The Soviet socialist family discourse underscored the significant change that was to occur in relation to the former Latvian bourgeois family model from the old capitalist family system, where family members were said to be economically dependent on each other, to a modern socialist family model with mutually economically independent members. The Soviet social policy that was introduced in Latvia after its annexation was considered an obvious advantage of socialist society. The Soviet authorities proclaimed the goal of improving the living conditions of the industrial proletariat and underprivileged groups in general as a matter of social justice. The first step in introducing a new power and social system was taken in 1940 by establishing the People's Commissariat (that is, the ministry) of Social Security. The next step was to concentrate all social welfare in organizations controlled by the state. Responsibility for welfare was divided among the People's Commissariat of Social Security, state-controlled trade unions, and local authorities (executive committees of districts and cities). Deputies and reliable party members were sent from other parts of the Soviet Union to help the Latvian Communist Party implement the new social system. According to central Soviet authorities in Moscow, the Latvian officials in the local executive committees lacked the background knowledge and qualifications necessary to implement the Soviet political and social system. Thus these bodies were headed mostly by Russian communists and backed up by instructors from Moscow (Bleiere, 2008).

The Sovietization of Latvian society involved major societal and organizational change. In every region, municipality, and city an executive committee was inaugurated. These committees consisted of Russian-speaking party members and trade union leaders (Berklavs, 1998, p. 90). They administered houses and apartment buildings and thereby controlled the tenants. In Riga, where immigration from other parts of Latvia and other

Soviet republics created a housing shortage, four square meters became the legal minimum for each lodger. Tenants in these houses shared common spaces such as the kitchen, bath, toilet, and corridor. Large private apartments were expropriated and divided up into what came to be called communal apartments. Space restrictions made family privacy almost impossible, and living conditions were not very convenient for families with children at home.

The Ministry of Social Security was established with the aim of "reorganizing Latvian bourgeois social welfare," which it set about implementing after the war.[3] One important task was to support and educate trade unions in how to organize social welfare and special work for needy target groups. The way to do this was to provide all inhabitants, including needy persons and invalids, with productive work (Samsons, 1955, p. 581). Trade unions and executive committees were also given the power to decide who was in need of social support. The Ministry of Finance disbursed government allowances to invalids, pensioners, pregnant women, mothers with many children, and single mothers. Although Latvia was incorporated into the Soviet economic system, it took some time for the society to adjust to the standards of state provision of the welfare already established in the older Soviet republics.

Sovietization was implemented under strict and centralized ideological control, which presupposed the cutting off of any cultural contacts that Latvians had from before the Soviet occupation. Among the three Baltic states, Latvia was the only one without any influences from the "outside" during the Soviet period. Estonia had a "window" to the West through Finnish television and some cultural contacts with Central Europe and Sweden, while Lithuania was involved in the Catholic resistance against Soviet ideology alongside its larger neighbor Poland (Mertelsmann as quoted in Clemens, 2003). Latvia shared its borders with Estonia in the north, Lithuania in the south, and Russia in the east. As a result of this lack of information, Latvians were kept almost completely uninformed about changes in gender roles that took place in much of Western Europe in the 1970s. According to Shabalov (2010), the interwar period was widely remembered by Latvians, and this "memory of the non-Soviet regime affected the way Latvians responded to Sovietization, ideology and the official historical narrative" (ibid., p. 5).

THE SOVIET FAMILY IDEAL

In contrast to the prewar Latvian social welfare system, which covered only workers and farmers and their families, the first Soviet family edict (1944) included single mothers and mothers with more than three children in the category of those entitled to social support. With the 1944 family edict the Soviet Latvian state took on the responsibility for the social protection of a selected group of mothers and children, which was to "guarantee the all-round physical and mental development of the new generation and children" (Samsons, 1956). Prospective mothers and young mothers were to be guaranteed health and work protection. The goal of the communist state and family policy was said to give women "real possibilities to combine upbringing and care for the children with productive work and social life" (ibid.). The edict proclaimed a break with past family traditions, women's subordination, and gender and social relations; it sought to undermine the Latvian "bourgeois" family and promote the socialist family. The daily newspaper *Cina* (The Struggle) wrote that the ideal Soviet Latvian woman needed to be an active participant in the communist state and lifestyle. Thus Soviet propaganda in Latvia did not differ from that of other regions. According to Ashwin, "women should be liberated from the patriarchal family and transferred from private dependence on men to the 'protection' of the Soviet state" (Ashwin, 2000, p. 10).

Thus pregnant women, single mothers, and mothers with many children were entitled to material support from the Soviet state, and the state did not expect much in return. All they had to do was to prove the age and number of children who lived at home (Family Law of the Latvian SSR, Akts no. 67/1956: 308–309). By contrast, unmarried and single citizens without any children and families with only one child had to pay special taxes. These taxes could be interpreted as punishing citizens who did not fulfill the demands of the state. This punitive taxation was intended to get people to have more children. Thus the edict used carrots and sticks in an attempt to regulate reproductive behavior in the name of the Soviet state in order to raise the birthrate. It is nevertheless difficult to determine how much these policies influenced Latvians' everyday reproductive and sexual behavior.

The discourses concerning the Sovietization of Latvian family life are visible in women's magazines and the newspapers. In these publications officials and professionals instructed people how to achieve the socialist goal of becoming a good working mother who was free from the ideals of the bourgeois family (see, for example, *Darba Sieviete* [Working Woman], *Padomju Latvijas Sieviet* [Soviet Latvian Woman], and the daily newspaper *Cina* [The Struggle] 1/9 1946, 1954 nos. 7–12).

DATA AND METHODOLOGY

On a private level, family life differed from the way it was presented in magazines. In order to study how Latvian women dealt with Sovietization, I present life stories told by Latvian women from different generations and time periods. These interviews are a part of a collection of thirty-six life stories in which women talk about their relations to men, sexuality, family, and gender roles. The interviews were made in 1990–1991 by specialists of the Latvian Oral History Center (the LNOH),[4] and the women were between twenty-seven and sixty years old. The transcriptions include indications concerning sights, laughter, coughing, and other emotional sounds in the voices, all of which brings the narratives closer to the interpreter.

I have chosen three life stories from the collection that reflect the understanding of experiences of everyday family life as well as ways of dealing with the Soviet system during different time periods. Their experiences are embedded in the context of the tragic events of the 1940s and 1950s; of the critical turn in 1955, when the repressed began to return home from Siberia; and the period from the 1960s to the 1980s, which is considered peaceful and stable.

I structure my analysis using Albert O. Hirschman's concepts of *exit*, *voice*, and *loyalty* (1970; see also Runcis, 2007). The concept of "exit" represents a withdrawal from a relationship, for instance, to Soviet ideology, to the state or to the nation (the Latvian nation). "Voice" is interpreted as an attempt to repair or improve the relationship through communication of a complaint or proposal for change. Members of a family, workplace/trade union, society, a nation, or any other form of human grouping can choose two possible responses when they perceive that the group or organization is demonstrating a decrease in quality or benefit to the member. They can exit (withdraw from the relationship), or they can voice (complain). For example, using family privacy as a shelter from the Sovietization process could be interpreted as a form of exit. Complaining in letters to the authorities or the newspapers could be interpreted as both voice and loyalty. It was voice because of the real complaint and discontent; it was loyalty because the complaint could be interpreted as an adaptation to the Soviet system, in which inhabitants were encouraged to write letters (see Carlbäck in this volume).

As stated above, political repression was part of the Sovietization process. With this in mind, it is important to note the two most frequent responses to it: emigration and protest. The exit does not necessarily have to be physical; it can also be mental or emotional (Hirschman, 1970). In Soviet Latvia the majority of the population could not physically exit the country, but they did not want to participate in the ideological Soviet system either. In these cases citizens could be said to exit from civic or political participation, as they were neither loyal to the party nor willing to voice their dissatisfaction, because doing so could lead to various kinds of punishment, imprisonment, or deportation. Finally, there is the concept of loyalty, which in my research could be interpreted as adaptation to the Soviet system or sympathizing with Soviet ideology.

WOMEN'S STRATEGIES

The first life story is told by Aina, a married woman with one child; she was born in Riga in 1931. The second woman, Maija, is divorced and lives in Riga with her daughter. Maija was born in 1939. The third and last woman, KZ, wants to be anonymous. KZ is married and lives with her husband and four children in Aluksne. KZ was born in 1963 in Aluksne. The interviews with Aina and KZ were conducted in Latvia in early January 1990, and the interview with Maija is from June 1991. Two native Latvians conducted all three interviews at a time when the Soviet system was collapsing and the future was quite uncertain.[5] In this situation the narrators could position themselves as both a part of the recently lost Soviet system and a part of the old Latvian traditions. In any case, they could not predict what life in an independent Latvia would be like, but they were free to tell their life stories from a new position they had never had before. My presentation concentrates on aspects of childhood, gender roles, housing, and work.

Memories of childhood and life in the parental home
Aina tells her life story with intensity, talking a lot, remembering both happiness and sorrow in her childhood. Talking about her family, two sisters and her mother and father, she remembers that her youngest sister, Ruta, born in autumn 1940, had to be baptized quickly in spring 1941, because "you never know what would happen in the future" (during those turbulent times) and before the Soviet rules changed this Latvian Christian custom.

Her childhood before the occupation is very vivid and pleasant in her memory. Her mother was a housewife, and her father was a bus driver who was shot by the Soviet Army in June 1941, when Aina was ten years old. They lived in a small apartment in the same house as her grandmother, who was working and who had her own flat (one room and a kitchen). Aina is very proud of her family and of her mother, who did all the housework. Aina describes her upbringing as strict and very traditionally Latvian.[6] Consequently, she was shocked by the first attempt to Sovietize Latvia in 1940–1941. She describes the Soviet system in very negative terms as loud and noisy (with marching music and speeches) and with red flags and paintings of Stalin hanging on the walls. Already as a child (Aina was in third grade at the time of the first occupation) she felt repulsed by the Soviet (Red)[7] Army. When the Germans invaded Latvia in 1941, Aina seems to have been quite satisfied with the situation in school, for everything turned back and was "as usual," the way it was before the Red Army came. Aina describes herself as someone from a family where education was highly valued: when her father died, her mother "fulfilled his wishes" and sent the daughters to high school. At that time (before the Soviet education system) they had to pay for school, but Aina got it for free because of her good grades.

Aina's narrative about her childhood contains many small details that are intended to indicate her resistance to the Soviet system and the Red Army. Examples of resistance include stressing her Latvian identity (the baptizing of her sister) and depicting the Soviet system as a deviation from Latvian culture (loud and noisy, a bit vulgar). Her childhood is marked by war traumas; she emphasizes family bonds as her shelter against Sovietization.

Maija tells her life story, sometimes laughing, sometimes with irony and at a distance from herself. She is fifty-one years old, and Latvia has just gained independence for the second time in history. At the time of the interview, Maija was active in the Latvian People's Front (*Tautas fronte*), the party that initiated the political movement against Soviet rule. When Maija was only six months old, the Red Army invaded Riga. She tells about her family being "thrown out" of their apartment: "[...] and then we moved to the countryside, and stayed there for a while." In autumn 1941, when the Germans invaded Latvia, the family moved back to Riga. They had a two-room flat with a big kitchen and bath. Her father was a driver, and her mother was a hairdresser. Maija's little brother was born in 1944, and from then until 1953 her mother stayed at home as a housewife. Her father worked hard and was seldom at home. Maija says that her mother and father were Latvian nationalists, which meant a strict upbringing: "My parents wanted me and my brother to be honest, obedient and correct; we were forbidden to tell lies." When, without asking her parents, she took part in the communist children's organization Octobreni,[8] her father got very angry and physically punished her. She was eight years old then and unhappy not to be able to participate with other children. But after that punishment she never tried to join any communist organizations. She says with a laugh: "Father's hard punishment kept me out of the party for the rest of my life."

Maija says that her parents hated the Soviets because they deported and executed some relatives, thus diminishing and dividing her mother's family. This seems to have made the family more nationalistic. She tells how they tried to keep their Latvian identity by celebrating Christmas and New Year's Eve, Easter and midsummer in the traditional Latvian way and by going to church, which she found very boring. Also, she remembers birthday celebrations and other family festivals as typical Latvian traditions, with twist buns and gifts.

Based on Maija's story, we see that Soviet occupation influenced everyday life in her family and had an impact on gender roles. Asked about the family budget and who was responsible for it, Maija answers that her father earned and distributed the money, but they did not have enough because "after the war father liked to drink, and then the money was finished. Before that, he never drank, but after [...] But then my mother took all the responsibility for the family." They never had enough money for the family expenses and had to live on preserved mushrooms, potatoes, vegetables, and dairy products. Finally, Maija's mother went back to work as a hairdresser—Maija's father died of cancer when she was nineteen years old and her brother was fourteen.

Thus in her narrative Maija chooses to present her childhood as viewed by her parents; she tries to understand their difficulties and sorrows, which had a sad effect on her own life. The story shows that the family got no help from the state—no day-care for the children and no allowances—nor did they ask for any. Instead the family chose to exit from the entire Soviet system. This excluded Maija from socialist society and made her unable to decide on her own whether to participate in communist activities. The tight family bonds and strict upbringing restricted her childhood in many ways. Her narrative could be interpreted as loyalty to the traditional Latvian family—but without happiness—and voice against the Soviet system that ruined her childhood and family life. Family privacy, in her case, not only became a shelter against Sovietization, but also built a wall against Soviet Latvian society.

The way KZ tells her story differs very much from Aina's and Maija's. Her account is very simple and terse, and she answers the interviewer's questions with just a few words. She was twenty-seven when she told her story on January 10, 1990. When she was six, her mother worked as a farmhand and milkmaid, and her father was a tractor driver. Her parents worked hard, and KZ and her younger brother were helping them even before they began school; they continued to do so throughout their childhood. According to KZ the family had no access to childcare or nursery school. The children were alone at home when the parents were at work; sometimes KZ's mother took KZ with her. Furthermore, the children had to do a lot of work at home. KZ did all the cooking while her brother carried water and chopped firewood. Still, like her brother, KZ had the possibility of attending music school. However, she says, there was not enough time for her to do her homework, and she did not like the school. Her father was a drunkard; he was hardly ever at home and she was left alone. KZ talks about her childhood with a tone of sorrow.

The family lived in one part of a house with a small garden. When the interviewer asks KZ about the family budget and who was responsible for it, she answers with bitterness: "At that time it was like this—my father used his salary for booze and drinking, and my mother received a salary from the farm, and with this money she raised us, bought food, and covered living expenses." As in KZ's case, the mother fulfilled a double role—caring for her children and providing for her family.

Describing her childhood in Soviet Latvia, KZ implies that the gender roles children were taught in school were inappropriate. With a quiet laugh she says that she learned to sing and how to handle and drive a tractor but nothing about needlework. She also says she had trouble learning Russian and did not want to study it. As a child and teenager, KZ was a member of the Pioneers[9] and Communist Youth League, but the activities in these organizations were nothing special, just the usual youth activities, she says: "they were just ordinary organizations—just names—nothing special."

KZ's narrative about her childhood in the mid-1960s is full of references to hard work and sorrows. The Soviet system had then been in place for twenty years. The changes in agriculture during this period had been huge; the forced collectivization that accompanied Sovietization impoverished Latvia's economy and made life hard for many farm workers. KZ's parents did not get any support from the state or the municipality; there was no day-care center or nursery for her and her brother. Her mother had complete responsibility for the children, the family budget, and the household, while the father was a worthless drunkard. Still, it is difficult to find expressions of resistance in KZ's narrative. Her unwillingness to study Russian could be interpreted as arising from difficulties in learning the language or boredom with the way it was taught. Furthermore, the sorrow in her story could be interpreted as neither resistance nor loyalty.

Work, housing, and marriage
When Aina finished high school, all education was free, and Aina went on to teachers' training college. For a short period between 1950 and 1952, she worked as a teacher in a small town outside of Riga. She got a small one-room flat from the executive committee, which distributed municipal housing, and she was satisfied. Later she moved back to Riga and got a new job at a radio factory. This job she liked, she says, because all of the employees were Latvians, which was quite unusual at that time. There she met her husband in 1956, and six months later they got married. Aina remarks that they married only a half-year after they had met and registered their marriage only with the public record office. Thus, contrary to Latvian traditions, she remarks, they did not have a church wedding. However, her mother and grandmother persuaded her to go to a priest to be married in a Latvian Christian ceremony, and so they did on November 18, the anniversary of Latvia's independence. They celebrated with a traditional Latvian wedding party for three days.

When Aina married, she and her husband moved into her grandmother's flat, and the grandmother moved in with Aina's mother. Although housing regulations allowed only four square meters per person, Aina's grandmother had sixteen square meters.[10] According to Aina, this move was a conscious choice because they wanted to prevent "Russians" from moving in. In her story Aina also stated that after the birth of her son (in 1960), Aina stayed home for three years at her husband's insistence (before the birth she had a heart operation). Finally, after staying home for three years as a housewife, she attempted to put her child in a nursery school, but her son could not get used to it, and a few months later it was her mother who began taking care of him. Again Aina stresses the problems with organization and distribution of housing and childcare, a system that was imposed on the Latvian population by the authoritarian Soviet state. Later on, Aina and her family got another apartment. The story of how they acquired it shows that Aina knew how to take advantage of the Soviet system to benefit herself and her family. She got a doctor's certificate that she could use in order to get a better flat, and she applied to the trade union for a new one. She tells: "From early on, it was very difficult since immigrants from other Soviet republics were prioritized. So I didn't succeed." But later a colleague advised her to complain to the daily newspaper *Cina*: "You have to show that you have the right to a new flat because of your heart disease," her colleague said to her. Aina wrote a letter to the newspaper and explained her situation in detail. She says she did not stress in her letter that she really needed a flat, but she underlined that she wanted some help and advice from the newspaper about how to get her rights from the trade union.

Aina's standard of living rose during the Soviet period. She also knew how to utilize the Soviet system to secure childcare and health insurance for her family. Indeed, she had a lot of strategies for getting what she wanted. Still, she is eager to stress her Latvian identity (for example, when she tells about her humble letter to the newspaper), and she distances herself from Russians and Russian behavior as she understands it. Thus she hardly could be seen as loyal to the Soviet system.

In her story Maija devotes a great deal of time to her romantic and sexual relationships with men. Because of her parents' strict morals, she had to hide a relationship she had with a man when she was sixteen. She also had to be careful with her relationship with her future husband when she was eighteen because her mother complained about it. She talks about him with an ironic laugh: "the first love, the first man, but we married." They had a church wedding after the registration, not because of religion but because Maija was used to celebrating all Latvian traditional festivals in church. This was a time "when no one had church weddings. I had a long white dress with a veil. Mother, of course, was the one who arranged everything." The couple lived with Maija's mother in a two-room flat. A year later (in 1960) they had a daughter, but family life was far from happy: "By then everything had already gone bad in our private life. My husband was like this—I really don't know how to say—he didn't like to work, but he liked to drink. When I married, I thought that love would last forever and change everything."

Right after their child was born, her husband was called up for military service and was away for three years. During this period Maija was trained as a dental technician, and her mother took care of Maija's daughter. Maija got a job as a dental technician in Jurmala, outside Riga, and by that time her daughter was attending a day-care center that was quite far from home. When her husband came back home from the military, they moved to his parents' home, because Maija wanted to get away from her own mother. However, her family life did not improve, and Maija divorced her husband two years later, moving back in with her mother. In order to provide for her family, she worked illegally at night (helping at a dentist clinic), for which she was paid in "black money" to supplement her meager official salary. This was the only way to earn money during the Soviet era, Maija says. She was also tired because of her responsibility to support the family financially and because of her extra work. Unlike Aina, Maija is bitter about her marriage and her family life, especially about having to live with her own mother.

KZ's story of her family life is also told in a rather gloomy way. She got married in 1984 when she was twenty-one years old and pregnant. She married a twenty-two-year-old driver. Her parents and mother-in-law were not happy about the marriage. The couple did not have their own flat, so they lived together with KZ's parents in a three-room flat. By the age of twenty-seven, KZ had four children, and by 1990, eight people shared one flat. Unlike Maija, KZ describes her husband as very helpful. He was helpful with the children, and they shared the responsibility for family duties and expenses. However, since they had a lot of housework to do and they had to care for their children and their own parents, they did not have much time for pleasure together.

In her narrative, KZ appears to be ashamed of her living conditions. She deplores the fact that she and her family are still living in the same flat as her parents and that she is dependent on her husband and her mother. When the interviewer asks KZ what in her life she is most proud of, she answers in her typical brief way: "Proud? I suppose that I don't have anything to be proud of." KZ ends her narrative very pessimistically, saying that nothing will change in her future, "everything will be as usual."

Gender roles
As for gender roles, the three narrators indicate that Sovietization negatively influenced how power was distributed between men and women in the family. In her narrative Aina emphasizes Latvian traditions and morality, and she is proud of the traditional gender roles in her family. She talks about herself as an independent woman, but she is not sure if this is a good quality, because it could mean a loss of femininity. She defines femininity as gentle caretaking, with no resistance to men and husbands. However, in Soviet Latvia, families were quite often headed by mothers. Mothers were forced to become independent because they had sole responsibility for the household and the children's education while having to earn a living at the same time. When the interviewer asks Aina about this, she replies: "Maybe it is good to be independent, because [...] And such, how to say, such real femininity—that is possibly or maybe a Western style, in the Western world where a woman is a woman [...] From my point of view this is what women

are lacking here, because just think—this life, our burden, how we got here by force, how we had to raise our children, wait in lines [...] We were forced to survive under such circumstances [...] And if I had been soft and gentle, I am not sure, for God's sake, whether I would have survived."

Aina emphasizes that the Soviet system took femininity away from her because she had to work doubly hard, and she had no more energy to put on makeup or get a hairdo. She complains that under the Soviet rule women had to be like "half-men," and children had to stay in kindergarten. "Who will then raise the children—other people, not the family?" With this statement Aina once again blames the Soviet system for the hardships her family experienced.

Maija seems rather confused about gender roles. Although she met her future husband when she was only eighteen years old, men are almost invisible in Maija's life story. When the interviewer asks, "What is a good man to you?" Maija answers with suspicion: "A good man? [...] I don't want a man supporting me financially and giving me a lot of gifts, because I am not used to it. As all women do, of course, I like it when a man pays attention to me." And when asked, "What is a good woman?" Maija says with a laugh: "A good woman—what does that mean? Difficult to answer—maybe a good human being." Later, Maija returns to her negative experience of family life, which she associates with the Soviet period: "In the future—in independent Latvia [...] women should not be like me, maybe not so masculine as I am. You see, I have to carry everything on my own shoulders. Our women have always done men's work, even in 'normal' average families. They earned more, they worked harder—so it has been. Men are no longer the masters of the family. We women were the heads of the family; it is the same now. That is a big mistake."

KZ connects family problems with men's drinking: "It's such a misery, which in many families brings a lot of tragedies." To some extent she blames the heavy drinking on the Sovietization of agriculture, hard work, a lack of social welfare, and the cheap booze. She does not talk about herself in terms of "female" or "male" work or gender equality. This seems unimportant to her, and her narrative contains many references to predestination and women's destiny.

With respect to gender roles, we can note that Aina, and to some extent Maija, prefer an old traditional division between the sexes. Both Maija and KZ blame the Soviet system and the Sovietization of society for the hard work required from both sexes and the drinking, which they say made men worthless at caretaking and taking responsibility for the family and forced women to work even harder. Thus the Soviet system could not provide gender equality. It is striking that the men and fathers are invisible in family life, even if both Aina and KZ are satisfied with their husbands. The life stories support the conclusion drawn by Tatyana Bureychak concerning Ukrainian society: men's loss of power in the private sphere usually resulted in negative reactions in the form of tyranny, aggressiveness, alcoholism, escape from responsibility, and infantilization (Bureychak, 2010). However, it is interesting that the argument that the Soviet system was too empowering towards women is rarely to be found in today's anti-feminist discourse in post-Soviet countries.

Conclusions

In this article I explored the Sovietization of Latvian society with respect to the everyday life of families and to gender roles. World War II and the Soviet occupation thoroughly changed Latvian society and the population in many ways. The Russian language became predominant within state authorities and local executive committees. Sovietization was connected with repressions against Latvian nationalist groups, who were accused of being German collaborators, kulaks, and "enemies of the people." The new social system was organized through workplaces and trade unions. The family as an institution was seen as suspicious by part of the state, and relatively few families—those of single mothers and mothers with more than three children—received any economic support. Soviet propaganda constructed new ideal gender roles—the independent working mother and the productive masculine man that together were to build a new communist society.

Analysis of the life stories demonstrates how Sovietization was met with negative sentiments and resistance in everyday life. Family privacy is presented in the stories as a shelter against Sovietization. In some families this shelter isolated the children from Soviet ideology and society by preventing them from taking part in youth activities and organizations. The traditional Latvian lifestyle is shown as idealized and constructed as something religious and very Christian—as far away as possible from communist ideology. The ideal Latvian woman is constructed in the life stories as the opposite of the hardworking mother. A "real" Latvian woman should be feminine and gentle toward her husband and children, which according to the life stories was not possible during the Soviet period in Latvia. This construction of a feminine woman, however, was more akin to the feminine ideal characteristic of postwar Western Europe than the prewar and Soviet-era reality of Latvian women.

The three different life stories show the different strategies for demonstrating their relationship to the Soviet system. Aina, who was sixty years old when she told her life story in 1990, was proud of her Latvian identity and her struggle to keep it despite Sovietization, but she also showed in her narrative how she used the Soviet social system as a benefit for her and her family. She seemed to be quite satisfied with her family life and work during Soviet times.

Since the family bonds were kept tight during her childhood, in order to protect her from Soviet influence, Maija's experience is an unhappy one, unlike Aina's. And even if Maija was later integrated in the Soviet system of social welfare and employment, she remained distrustful towards the regime and strove to be a "real" Latvian. When she told her story, Latvia had won independence and Maija was an activist in the People's Front. In telling her story, she chooses to stress that Soviet rule was most to blame for her negative life experiences. As for the last narrator, KZ, she hardly indicates any resistance at all in her story, but the mood of her narrative itself could be interpreted as exit. She did not want to be a part of life in Soviet society.

The narratives show that the family was an important arena for Sovietization. In some cases the family became a prison, "locking in" the Latvian traditions. In other cases—in the name of "doing your best for your family"—Latvian women started interacting with the system.

Notes

1 This was stated in "The USSR Family Law Decree of July 8, 1944, on Increasing Public Support to Pregnant Mothers, Mothers with Many Children, Single Mothers, Enhancing the Protection of Motherhood and Childhood, Proclaiming 'Heroine Mother' as the Title of Highest Distinction, and Establishing the Order of Maternal Glory and the Medal of Motherhood" (Schlesinger, 1949, pp. 367–390).
2 Examples of "Sovietization" include the mass transfer of Soviet cadres to ensure the replacement of the elites; the nationalization of industry, trade, and banks and their integration into the centrally planned Soviet economy, and also a land reform with the distribution of expropriated land holdings and the collectivization of agriculture.
3 LPSR Socialas nodrosinasanasministrijasvesturiskaizzina, August 26, 1949. After 1940 the ministry was named the People's Commissariat of Social Security.
4 The primary goal of the LNOH is to document as many accounts as possible of the everyday life of Latvia's inhabitants during the complex and shifting circum-

stances of the twentieth century. This is being done by recording events from the point of view of the participants themselves. Over the past fifteen years a considerable archive of life stories has been created. The LNOH archives consist of interviews recorded by LNOH project researchers and trained volunteers during expeditions throughout Latvia and also of collections of memoirs submitted by other Latvian scholars (Bela, 2008, pp. 88–91).
5 Anita Timans Kalns and Mara Zirnite conducted the interviews with the aim of collecting women's narratives from the Soviet era.
6 When the interviewer asks her about the Latvian tradition and what it means to her, she talks about "Latvian mentality, religiosity, and morality."
7 In the following I will use "Red Army" since this was the conventional name used for the Soviet Army. It was officially renamed the "Soviet Army" in 1946.
8 Named after the October Revolution, this was a kind of scouting organization under the aegis of the Communist Party for the smallest children.
9 This was a kind of scouting organization under the aegis of the Communist Party for children ten to fifteen years old.
10 When the Soviet Army occupied Latvia, Aina's grandmother moved in with an uncle, who died shortly before Aina got married.

References

Ashwin, Sarah, eds. 2000. *Gender, State and Society in Soviet and Post-Soviet Russia*. London: Routledge.

Balodis, Agnis. 1990. *Lettlands och det lettiska folkets historia* (The history of Latvia and the Latvian people). Stockholm: Lettiska nationella fonden.

Bela, Baiba. 2008. "Poliphony of Latvian Identity: The Latvian Community in Sweden." *Humanities and Social Sciences: Latvia* 2, no. 55: 39–60.

Berklavs, Eduards. 1998. *Zinat un neaizmirst* (To know and not forget). Riga, Latvia: Preses nams.

Bleiere, Daina. 2008. *Latvija Otraja Pasaules Kara* (Latvia during World War II). Riga, Latvia: Jumava.

Bureychak, Tetyana. 2010. "Men's Issues in Ukraine: Soviet and Post-Soviet Experience." In *Gender, Politics and Society in Ukraine*, eds. Hankivsky, O., and A. Salnykova. Toronto: Toronto University Press.

Clemens, Walter. 2003. "Comparative Repression and Comparative Resistance: What Explains Survival?" *Nationalism and Ethnic Politics* 9, no. 3: 74–101.

Eglitis, Daina. 2010. "Cultures of Gender and the Changing Latvian Family in Early Post-Communism." *Journal of Baltic Studies* 41: 151–176.

Goven, Joanna. 2002. "Gender and Modernism in a Stalinist State." *Social Politics* 9: 3–28.

Hirschman, Albert O. 1970. *Exit, Voice, and Loyalty: Responses to Decline in Firms, Organizations, and States*. Cambridge, MA: Harvard University Press.

Katus, Kalev, Asta Poldma, and Allan Puur. 2008. "Work-Family Orientation and Female Labour Market Participation." *European Studies in Population* 16, no. 1: 319–343.
Lapidus, Gail Warshofsky. 2003. "Women in Soviet Society: Equality, Development, and Social Change." In *Stalinism: The Essential Readings*, ed. David Hoffman. Malden, MA: Blackwell Publishing.
Latvijas vestures institutas apgads. 2001. *Latvija padomju rezima vara 1945–1989. Dokumenta krajums* (The Soviet regime in Latvia 1945–1989. Printed documents). Riga: University of Latvia.
Plakans, Andrejs. 1995. *The Latvians: A Short History*. Stanford: Hoover Institution Press.
Runcis, Maija. 2007. *Makten över barnen: [tvångsomhändertagande av barn i Sverige 1928–1968]* (Power over children [forced custody of children in Sweden 1928–1968]). Stockholm: Atlas.
Samsons, V., ed. 1955. *Latvijas PSR Maza Enceklopedija* (Small encyclopedia of the Latvian SSR). Riga, Latvia: Zinatne.
———, ed. 1956. *Latvijas PSR Maza Enceklopedija* (Small encyclopedia of the Latvian SSR). Riga, Latvia: Zinatne.
Schlesinger, Rudolf. 1949. *The Family in the USSR: Documents and Readings*. London and New York: Routledge.
Shabalov, Anna. 2010. *Long Road in the Dunes: Latvia and the Soviet Historical Narrative*. Saarbrücken: VDM Verlag Dr. Müller.
Weiner, Amir. 1999. "Nature, Nurture, and Memory in a Socialist Utopia: Delineating the Soviet Socio-Ethnic Body in the Age of Socialism." *American Historical Review* 104, no. 4: 1114–1155.
Zelce, Vita. 2006. "The First Contract Between the Stalin's Regime and Latvian Women: 1945." *Ennen ja Nyt* 3, no. 4, http://www.ennenjanyt.net/2006_3/zelce.pdf (accessed October 12, 2011).

PART II

1990s–2000s
SOCIAL TRANSFORMATION
IN THE MIRROR OF
FAMILY LIFE

CHAPTER 7

"Two Children Puts You in the Zone of Social Misery:" Childbearing and Risk Perception among Russian Women

ANNA ROTKIRCH AND KATJA KESSELI

INTRODUCTION

In most EU member states and other industrialized countries, people are having fewer children and becoming parents later in life than previous generations did. On average, women are in their late twenties, and men a couple years older, when they have their first child. This trend has stimulated much research and debate focused on explaining the postponement of first births (Billari et al., 2006; Sobotka, 2004). However, there is another, distinct social path to low fertility, where parenthood arrives early in the life course while the second child is postponed or is never born. Not enough attention has been paid to Eastern European countries such as Russia and Ukraine, which "have achieved very low fertility through the postponement of second and higher-order births while maintaining a relatively early and universal pattern of first births" (Perelli-Harris, 2006, p. 729). The aim of this chapter is to discuss "postponement Russian style" by studying women's incentives and hesitations related to having a second child.[1]

For over a century, Russians have formed families at a younger age than other European nations. At the same time, the average number of children a woman had fell rapidly from almost ten in the late nineteenth century to less than two in the late twentieth century. Childlessness has remained rare in Russia. The one-child family became increasingly common, however, although most people prefer to have at least two children of their own. Today having only one child is especially typical for highly educated women, ethnic Russians, and women living in urban areas (Zakharov, 2008). This makes St. Petersburg—Russia's second-largest city, with a highly educated, mainly ethnic-Russian population—a suitable case for studying the underpinnings of the single-child family.

This chapter first discusses the two-child norm and the actual numbers and timing of children among St. Petersburg women. We then present the main reasons for hesitating to have a second child based on in-depth interviews. These reasons relate to economic concerns, health, and personal and social independence.

Research Materials and Methods

In 2004 the Reproductive Health and Fertility Patterns (REEFR) research consortium, directed by Professor Elina Hemminki, collected qualitative and statistical materials on women's fertility behavior in St. Petersburg. Both the in-depth interviews and the survey materials are available for researchers upon request. First, we collected seventy-two in-depth interviews on domestic life, reproductive decisions, and sexuality. The collection was organized by the Centre for Independent Social Research under the direction of Professor Elena Zdravomyslova from the European University of St. Petersburg. Interview topics covered wage work and domestic work, family life, reproductive health, fertility intentions, and childcare arrangements. A majority of respondents were middle-class women, although poor working women, the upper classes, and men were also represented. We interviewed forty-five respondents aged 24–42 years (born 1962–1980). Fifteen were career-oriented single women with and without children, fifteen women and one man were living in a dual-earner relationship with small children, and fourteen were housewives with small children. We also interviewed ten nannies and nine cleaners aged 22–61 years and conducted four expert interviews. The respondents were recruited through acquaintances, the networks of the respondents, and through Internet advertisements. In-depth interviews were given a thematic analysis.[2]

Second, we conducted a representative survey of women's reproductive health and fertility intentions in St. Petersburg in 2004. The survey studied women in their reproductive years (18–44 years old, born between 1959 and 1985) with a target sample of 2,500 and response rate of 67 percent, final sample N=1147. Study participants were randomly chosen from the catchment areas of three clinics from two St. Petersburg city districts, Krasnogvardejskii and Primorskii. Both districts have a socially diversified population, although more workers live in Krasnogvardejskii, while more middle-class people and businesspeople live in Primorskii. We generalize these two areas here to represent St. Petersburg as a whole. Study participants were primarily encouraged to visit a women's clinic to answer the survey questions. In some cases, women were provided with the questionnaire at their homes (for more detail, see Kesseli et al., 2005). The survey data was analyzed with cross-tabulations and logistic regressions.

Third, we collected register data on births in St. Petersburg. Data by birth order and age of mother were obtained from St. Petersburg demographic statistics (Petrostat, 2004). Age structures for the female population were obtained from the Institute of Urban Planning in St. Petersburg (courtesy of Semyon Sivanshinsky).

THE SOLID TWO-CHILD NORM

As outlined above, our seventy-two in-depth interviews were conducted with St. Petersburg women from various social classes and life situations. The oldest respondent entered adulthood just before Soviet perestroika in the mid-1980s, while the youngest came of age during the turbulent first decade of post-socialism in Russia. Notwithstanding these differences, most respondents declared without any particular reflection their ideal number of children to be two, or in rare cases, three.

> Without a doubt, I want two children. Having just one seems somehow incomplete, and it's very sad to be the only child in a family. (30-year-old professional woman, no children)

> Two... when there are three children, it's just unrealistic. (30-year-old housewife, two children)

> We always wanted two children with two years between them. Well, we wanted two children, a boy and a girl. (35-year-old housewife, two children)

The three quotations above came from educated, well-to-do women. But the two-child norm was also reflected, although less rigidly, among working-class respondents. For them as well, the zone of childbearing expectations appeared to lie in the region of two or, at most, three children:

> Generally I would have wanted more [than two] children, but the way the situation has developed in our country made me simply afraid of making more children—I wouldn't have been able to raise them. I can't even provide these two with everything I would like to, so if... But if suddenly... [refers to an accidental pregnancy], God forbid, but then yes, probably, there would be three. (46-year-old uneducated woman, working as a nanny and housekeeper for a rich family)

Only a few respondents defended having more than two children.

> I think that two children is a must. Three is, in principle, normal. (32-year-old professional woman, one child)

> The thing is that we had three in our family, me and my brothers—and my husband, they had five, so for us, three children, for us it is totally normal. (41-year-old mother of three children born from two unions, has worked in kindergartens)

The respondent quoted last stresses that having several children is "totally normal" for her and her husband. It is, however, clearly a choice that has to be justified and defended among friends. As the same mother noted:

> My girlfriends were saying things like: what do you need this for? You have a son and a daughter, what more do you need? What for? I said, what else is there to do? We all started laughing. (41-year-old mother of three)

Ideals of having more than two children were rare and typically reported indirectly, by referring to the opinion of other family members. For example, the husband of one respondent was said to "like to be with children. In his fantasies, he is the head of the family [laughs], the head of a large and happy family."

While two children is the ideal and sometimes a "must," having three children is for most respondents "many," if not "too many." People in St. Petersburg typically associated having three children with wayward and irresponsible parents.

> In our conditions families with many children are, as a rule, poor families.

> If you can't look after your children, then you shouldn't have them; you lack money, you lack this and that.

> Three—it's just unreal.

> I consider many children a very positive thing, if it does not include living off others, as it usually does.

This strong two-child ideal was also visible in our survey results. The ideal number of children in a family in general was, on average, 2.3 among women in St. Petersburg (see Table 1). A clear majority, more than two out of every three women, said two children was the ideal number in a family.

Every fourth woman thought three children was the best number. One child was seen as the ideal number in a family by only 3 percent of the respondents.

TABLE 1. *The ideal number of children in a family in general and in the family of the respondent, from a survey of 18-to-44-year-old women in St. Petersburg in 2004*

Desired number of children	18–24 years		25–34 years		35–44 years		Total, 18–44 years	
	In general	For oneself	In general	For oneself	In general	For oneself	In general	For oneself
0	–	0	–	0.6	–	0.4	–	0.3
1	1.8	22.8	2.5	24.6	3.6	18.7	2.9	21.8
2	76.3	63.5	66.9	57.5	63.0	55.5	68.0	58.4
3	19.0	8.8	28.3	11.0	28.3	14.7	25.5	11.9
4 or more	2.6	1.5	1.7	1.7	2.2	2.2	2.2	1.8
No answer	0.3	3.5	0.6	4.5	2.9	8.5	1.4	5.8
Average	2.2	1.9	2.3	1.9	2.3	2.1	2.3	2.0
N	341	330	352	337	436	411	1132	1081

Source: Kesseli et. al., 2005, pp. 63–65.

As in other low-fertility societies, the declared ideal number of children in general exceeds the number that respondents judge is ideal in their own lives. Every fifth respondent saw one child as the ideal number for herself. However, childlessness was an extremely rare choice. Not a single woman among the 18-to-34-year-old respondents wished to have no children at all.

A clear majority, 58 percent, regarded two children as a personal ideal. The youngest women most clearly favored two children, while older age groups voiced more support for other family sizes, including the single-child family. This may reflect a generational difference in attitudes. Two or even three children are lately emerging as signs of wealth and family success in Russia, and it is possible that the youngest respondents were more open than the older ones toward having several children. It may also be that older women who have already stopped their childbearing adjusted their personal ideals to match their actual number of children. Among all respondents, 12 percent thought three children would be the ideal number of children in their own lives. Interestingly, when the question concerned four or more children, very few respondents—around two percent—supported the idea of so many children in general, and the same small percentage wanted that many children for themselves.

"Dva luchshe" — Policies Countering the Single-child Trend

The strong ideal of a two-child family rooted itself in Soviet Russia in the 1960s. During this period Soviet Russia's total fertility rates for the first time fell below the hypothetical replacement level of 2.1 children per woman. According to the leading scholar on Russian fertility, Sergei Zakharov (2008, p. 914), young postwar couples clearly sought "to fulfill this ideal model of a two-child family with great consistency," and this marked the end of the first Russian demographic transition from large to small families.[3]

The drop in fertility raised concern among Soviet politicians. Several campaigns aimed to counter the spread of the single-child family. While one in ten women in Russia born in the beginning of the century gave birth to one child only, more than one in three women born in the 1960s had only one child (Ivanov et al., 2006). Thus a propaganda poster from 1968 declared that *Odin rebenok—khorosho, dva—luchshe!* (One child is good, two is better!). The first of the two pictures on this poster showed two parents kissing a single, screaming child. The next picture showed two happy parents being kissed by their two devoted children, apparently a boy and a girl.

In lamenting the single child, Soviet propaganda resonated with popular ideals, although it did not stop fertility rates from falling. Soviet propaganda also praised mothers in families with many children (*mnogodetnye sem'i*), where "many" was defined as either three, five, or more, depending on the context. However, such family sizes were not perceived as a realistic goal and had little effect on people's reproductive behavior. Interestingly, Zakharov (2008, pp. 912–915) claims that the ideal of a three- or four-child family "evidently did not exist historically as a mass social norm, neither in traditional society nor in the course of the demographic transition, nor even more so after the transition" in the postwar period.

The ideal of the two-child family also rooted itself among members of the Soviet medical profession. One woman we interviewed, a mother of three, recalled how her gynecologist had suggested sterilization as a method of family planning after the birth of her second child in 1993. The thought that she and her husband might like to have more children than two had evidently not crossed this doctor's mind.

Early First Births

While Russian women's childbearing ideals today are not very high, actual birth rates are even lower (Bodrova, 2002). At the beginning of this century, the total fertility rate for St. Petersburg averaged 1.2 children per woman (Rotkirch and Kesseli, 2009; 2010). True, fertility rates are recovering, but for the whole country the actual fertility rate is expected to be a maximum of 1.6 children among women who are now in their reproductive years (Zakharov, 2008, p. 948).

Until recently, Russians have also become parents at comparatively young ages. For several centuries, Russia and other Eastern European countries have had earlier family formation than Western Europe (Fahey and Spéder, 2004; Therborn, 2004). Even as women's education grew higher during late socialism, women did not postpone childbearing; on the contrary, people became parents at slightly younger ages on average. Motherhood was highly valued, and relatively few people remained childless.

Russian fertility behavior, even in the last few years, can thus be characterized as universal and early (Kesseli, 2007/08). The mean age of a Russian woman at the birth of her first child was 23 in 1980 and younger than that in the 1990s, reaching 24 years only in the last decade. Zakharov (2007) ironically calls this the "golden age" of Russian matrimonial relations, a time characterized by early marriages lacking family planning skills, the low use of adequate contraception, and the high importance placed on marriage and motherhood (see also Zakharov, 2008; Perelli-Harris, 2005).

Structural reasons also contribute to the tradition of early births. Russians finish their professional education earlier than people in many Western countries do, and their traditional reliance on grandparents' help may lead them to favor having children while the older generations are not too old to provide care and assistance. Perelli-Harris (2005, p. 68) also perceptively notes that while Western women postpone childbearing until their financial situation is more stable, in Eastern Europe many women living through the transitional economies of the 1980s and 1990s could not be sure that the economic situation would improve later. This interpretation would be in line with evidence from several other countries indicating that in situations of long-term insecurity and risk, women opt for earlier rather than later reproduction (Nettle, 2011). While there are signs that Russians as well are postponing their first births until they are older, the pattern of early fertility continues to differ greatly from most other European countries.[4]

Figure 1 shows at which ages St. Petersburg women give birth to their first, second, and third child. In Figure 1a, we see that until 2003, most women had their first child when they were 20–24 years old. There was also a growing trend of becoming a mother at 25–29 years. Compared to the 1990s, there was a slight increase in women having their first child in their early thirties. There are thus signs of the so-called second demographic transition related to a postponement of first births. However, very few first children were born to mothers older than that.

In St. Petersburg the second child was typically born to women in their late twenties (Figure 1b). We see how this event became rarer from 1989 to 2003. The number of 25-to-29-year-old women who had a second child fell from 4 percent to about 2 percent in that age group. Finally, Figure 1c shows the very low occurrence of three children in all age groups. Social policy studies indicate that these families are also usually very poor and in need of considerable social assistance (Bezrukova, 2007).

FIGURE 1a–c. *Age- and parity-specific fertility rates in St. Petersburg, 1/1000 women in each age group*

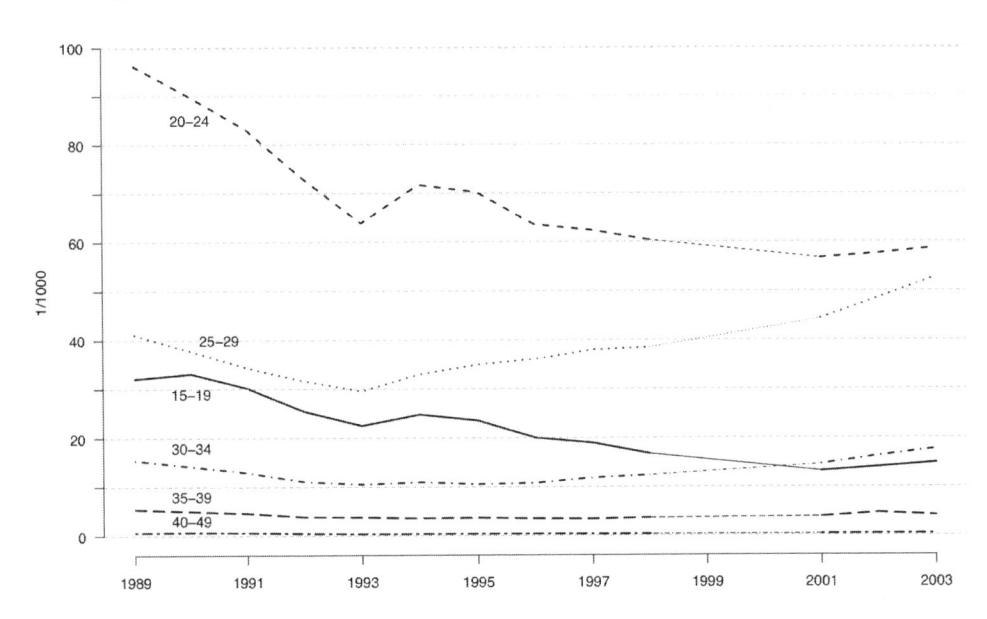

a: Age of women at the birth of their first child

b: Age of women at the birth of their second child

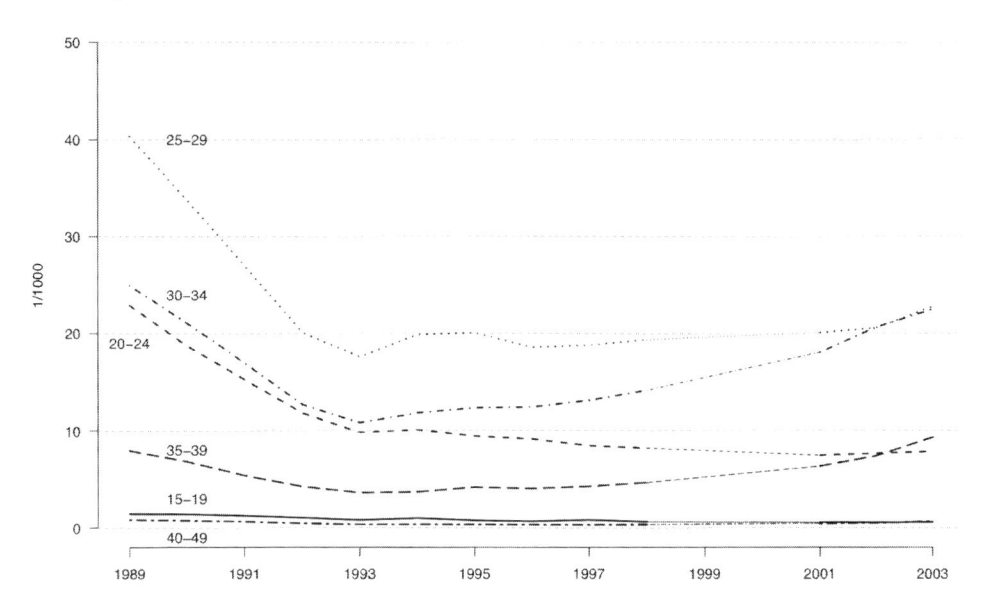

c: Age of women at the birth of their third child

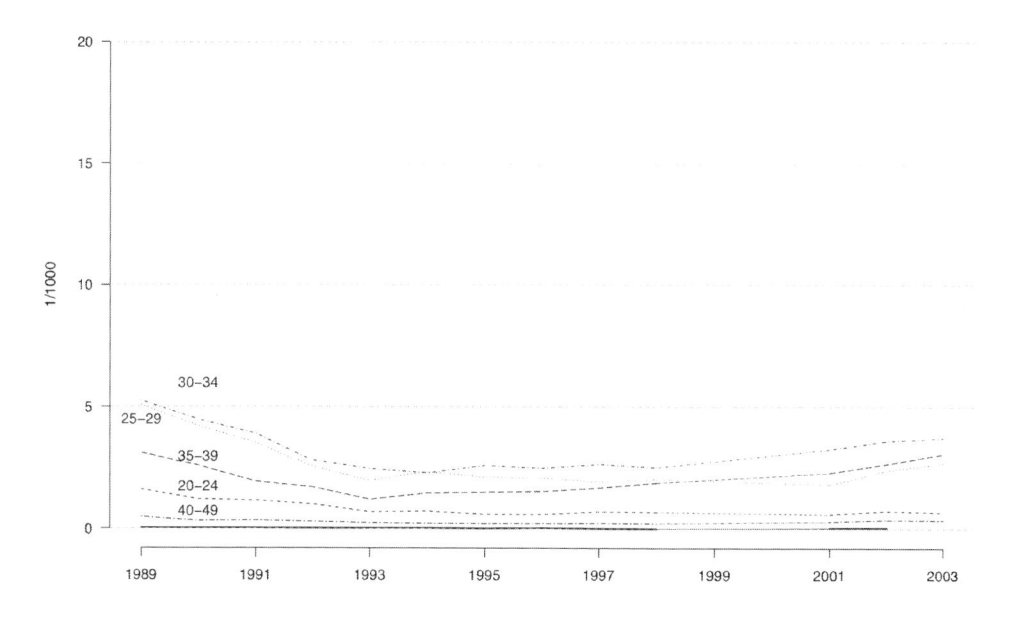

Sources: Kesseli's calculations based on data specified in research materials and methods.

The Second Child — A Careful Decision

In today's St. Petersburg, access to contraceptives has improved since Soviet times (Perelman and McKee, 2009; Regushevskaya et al., 2009). But once a couple moves in together, pregnancy is often seen as a possible and desirable event (Meilakhs, 2009). Indeed, our respondents often laughed at the question of planning when discussing their first child. Becoming a parent for the first time was seen as something that "just happened" (Rotkirch and Kesseli, 2009, 2010).

What about a possible second child? According to survey results, nearly 35 percent of women with one child was planning to have a second child (Table 2). The highest probability of planning for another child was among 25-to-29-year-old mothers, who also most often end up giving birth to second children (Figure 1b above).

TABLE 2. *Number of children in relation to childbearing intentions, 24-to-39-year-old women in St. Petersburg in 2004, N=800*

No. of children	Childbearing intentions Does not intend or is not sure	Intends to have another child	Sum	N
0	25.7	74.3	100	397
1	65.3	34.7	100	300
2	91.1	8.9	100	90
3+	84.6	15.4	100	13
Average/Sum	48.9	51.1	100	800

Source: Ikonen (2009).

Unlike the first child, a second child was not typically described as a romantic and quasi-automatic event in our in-depth interviews. Indeed, the arguments for having or not having the second child were dramatically different from those regarding the first. In deciding whether to have another child, women considered three main types of reasons: economic arguments, the question of health, and their personal degree of independence. Let us look at these more closely.

When analyzing the arguments presented by women themselves, one should keep in mind the gap between declared intentions and actual behavior. Childbearing intentions may change over time: children are often planned "one at a time" or not planned at all. A respondent who says she wants one more child may not succeed or may change her mind, or may indeed have a second child and then also a third. The motivations a respondent ascribes to her reproductive choices may also differ depending both on whom she is talking to and from which life situation she judges her earlier actions and future plans.

Economic reasons for postponing the second child
When the interviewer asked whether economic considerations were involved when having the first child, the answer could be simple: "There weren't any." However, in our in-depth interviews there was no such answer regarding the second child.

> If the first child was really the fruit of love, it was all, all done for love. ... The second child ... well, it is reasonable and it ought to be done, but first you have to manage to do everything. When that time arrives, I don't know. (24-year-old mother with two-year-old child)

Obviously, having a spouse or a suitable partner was often a requirement for having the next child. If the husband was around, he tended to support the idea of a second child—reluctant males were not mentioned in these interviews.

Some respondents said that they could choose to have a second child even without a stable partner if they "really" wanted more children. Thus the presence of a committed spouse was not necessarily the main criterion. For instance, the potential father was not even mentioned (albeit not directly asked about, either) in the following quote by a divorced woman:

> "And have you thought about another child? You're still so young."
> "Of course, of course I've thought about it but... right now it is just such a catastrophe, what should I do, how will I have the time with everything, a-ah... I don't know yet how that would all happen."
> (24-year-old economist, single mother of a six-year-old child)

One respondent, a 25-year-old married woman with one child, summarized the gap between ideals and behavior as follows: "Theoretically I'm ready for it, but in practice not at all."

Respondents also mentioned the need to move to a bigger apartment or to finish ongoing household repairs as reasons for postponing the second child. Thus at least on the level of conscious and articulated childbearing intentions, socioeconomic factors played a crucial role in the decision to have more than one child. Middle-class respondents often wanted to acquire a higher and more stable social and economic status before having more children. One respondent, an economist herself, succinctly formulated this constellation, referring to the poverty of families with small children:

> Because at the moment, our zone of social misery is simply families with two children. That's a fact. That means that you can fall directly from the middle classes to the very lowest class just because you had two more children. (32-year-old economist, mother of a three-year-old)

In logistic regression analysis of the survey data, a better economic position proved to have some, albeit not a sizable, effect on fertility intentions. Respondents who had more living space and those who very seldom had problems in paying their bills were more often planning to have a second child (Ikonen, 2008; see also Maleva and Siniavskaia, 2007).

Health concerns
As a second reason for hesitating to have a second child, several respondents expressed fears of childbirth and the effects of their first pregnancy and delivery on their own health. This is an interesting finding, considering that our respondents mainly belonged to the middle and upper-middle classes and were generally healthy, active, and resourceful women whom one would not normally expect to have high health risks.

> "Wouldn't you like to have a second child?"
> "I would, if it would kind of appear by itself..."
> "Ah... how do you mean, by itself?"
> "Well, I really don't want to give birth. To me it was extremely unpleasant to have a baby."
> "Was your labor painful?"
> "Yes, horrible. A nightmare. I wouldn't wish it on anyone."
> (30-year-old mother, gave birth at 23 years old in 1997)

Fears of delivery are common in many countries. As Russian women give birth younger than many other Europeans, they often have physiologically easier births. However, the general situation of reproductive health and health services is far from ideal in Russia, and there is a widespread distrust of health-care providers (Belozerova, 2002; Zdravomyslova and Temkina, 2009).

Some respondents discussed at length the need to improve their general health before even attempting the next pregnancy.

> "Are you planning to have a second child?"
> "I am! I'm going to have a second little child!"
> "When are you planning it?"
> "I'm planning to give birth all the time. I'm planning to, but my health doesn't really permit it yet. [With the first child] I didn't feel well at all. It was a difficult pregnancy and a rather difficult delivery. Although that child is now grown, I still bear the consequences. And I just feel very uncertain because I would like to bring up a healthy child. Therefore I'm trying to improve my own health a little, have a little bit of rest and gather my strength."
> (25-year-old woman, mother of a four-year-old child)

The quotation above showed a concern for both the mother's and the child's health and a wish to minimize risks by making the "right" preparations. The following respondent resolved her health problems and successfully had a second child, but only after long-term preparations and arrangements.

> We'd planned the second child for one to three years. So for three years prior to that month, I was doing different kinds of purifications. I mean all those things: the stomach, the kidneys, and the liver... With the first I had problems with constant diathesis and other things. I didn't want to have that with the second... And made big efforts with my health, I lost weight. That is, I was already focused and preparing. (Born in 1968, had children in 1990 and 1998)

Interestingly, some St. Petersburg doctors advocate a similar view, according to which pregnancy planning includes medical tests and health examinations (Larivaara, 2011). There seems to be a clear discrepancy between the spontaneous, often unplanned majority of (first) births and the massive and medicalized planning advocated by some professionals and lay people alike.

Maternal independence and strength
Apart from economic and health concerns, St. Petersburg women also often expressed doubts about their own psychological and personal strength in relation to a possible second child. In particular, educated women who had

stopped working voiced this kind of uncertainty. Taking care of the first-born, they felt, had already created a major disruption in their intellectual and social life. Such respondents had "sat at home enough" and deplored that their "brains were going sour." One woman felt that several years had been lost:

> Of course I would like my child to grow up a little bit faster [smiling], to become more independent, so I could go out to work [laughs]. Yes. Because seven years have been wiped out of my life [laughs]. Simply wiped out with black ink. (38-year-old housewife)

Another remarked:

> It's perfectly possible to stay home with the child until he goes to school, send him off to school, then have a second child and again sit at home with him until school, and so on. But that's not my way. I get irritated all the time. I want to rely on myself. I need to have a little control over myself. Therefore, when three years had already passed, and with a higher education—that does leave a certain mark; with time you come to feel that your brain is going sour. After three years it really does go sour. I didn't want that. I really wanted to go to work. (28-year-old biologist and mother of one, married)

The need to "rely on myself" and "have a little control over myself," as in the latter quotation above, appeared to be a crucial factor for many mothers of one child. The traditionally low level of childcare provided by Russian fathers and the quasi-automatic way a mother gets full-time custody in case of divorce contribute to this emphasis on the woman's own strength and resources. As Zhanna Kravchenko (2008) has argued in her comparison of Russian and Swedish family policies, the lower involvement of men in household chores and childcare in Russia compared with Sweden is due both to the prevailing gender ideology and policies and to prevailing attitudes. Many Russian women feel that they can do things more effectively and reliably themselves.

However, roughly every second St. Petersburg mother did plan to have two or even three children (Table 2 above). In the in-depth interviews, these choices were often explained by positive examples from their own family and the family of their husband.

Well, additionally I am accustomed to the fact that in all our families there were no less than two children. Two, three children, four. Therefore, I naturally aim for a minimum of two children in the family. (30-year-old woman without children)

In a previous study, subjective well-being and social entrepreneurship was related to having a second child (Golovlianitsina, 2007; Perelli-Harris, 2006). Our respondents' emphasis on their personal characteristics and social situation appear to be in line with this finding. Having a second child was connected with strong coping skills and an ability to "count exclusively on my own strength."

Conclusion

The majority of mothers in contemporary St. Petersburg have one child only. Both in Soviet times and in contemporary Russia, becoming a mother has been an integral part of Russian female identity, a final step to socially prescribed adulthood and womanhood. In addition to socioeconomic and life course factors, this cultural ideal partly explains why Russian women still enter parenthood earlier than in many other European countries.

However, having many children is not part of normative Russian femininity. The two-child norm that rooted itself in the 1960s remains the ideal family size among young women as well. In our survey from two St. Petersburg city districts in 2004, three out of four 18-to-24-year-old women said two children in a family was their general ideal, and almost two out of three women held this to be their personal ideal as well. But whereas the first child is often perceived as a self-evident part of the life course of Russian women, the second child is subject to careful timing and planning. Reproductive decision-making in St. Petersburg is thus typically focused on a possible second child and not, for instance, on the first or the third child.

Our in-depth interviews showed how for many women, the second child is theoretically welcome at some stage, but first "everything else" has to be in order. This kind of delay and planning is often behind the postponement of first births in contemporary Western Europe. Decision-making regarding a second child in Russia thus resembles the process in many other European countries. St. Petersburg women typically have their second child when they are in their late twenties. In this age group only a few percent considered one child to be the ideal number for a family in general, while a much bigger proportion—one woman out of four—regarded one child as the ideal number for themselves.

A sensible aim for family-friendly policies is—within reasonable limits—to support people in having as few or as many children as they wish to have. In this regard Russia's current situation appears promising. At first glance, at least, it should be relatively easy to encourage people who are already parents to have the second child they long for. President Vladimir Putin's family policy as first presented at the State of the Nation Address in 2006 introduced economic measures calculated precisely to stimulate the birth of the second child (Kuz'mina, 2007; Rotkirch et al., 2007). The president's focus thus appears to have been in tune with the doubts and hesitations among ordinary people described in this chapter.

Younger women favored families with more than one child to a greater extent than older women did. Along with the postponement effect due to rising ages at first birth, this positive attitude may be one factor contributing to the slight recovery of fertility rates that is now taking place in Russia. Nevertheless, economic, health, and social concerns complicate people's implementation of their fertility ideals and intentions, and respondents outline clear obstacles to having second and third children.

Based on our results, two policy aspects can be stressed. First, health-related concerns even among healthy and resourceful women underline the need for improving reproductive health services, especially related to the psychological and physical experiences of the first birth (Belozerova, 2002; Larivaara, 2011; Zdravomyslova and Temkina, 2009). Second, women's concerns about the effects of an additional child on their economic status and personal independence indicate that many perceive the daily hassles of motherhood as too exhausting. Taking into account the high demands of the contemporary Russian labor market, this is especially true of highly educated women. Both official ideology and lay values still assume almost exclusive female decision-making in child-bearing and -rearing (Kravchenko, 2008; Rotkirch et al., 2007). More shared parenthood, with fathers who are more practically involved, would alleviate the exhaustion and the isolation experienced by many mothers. Family-friendly social policies should ensure reasonable working hours. Parental leaves and sick leaves should be followed in all areas of working life. As many middle-class women spend several years away from the labor market taking care of their children, policies could also aim at supporting more flexible combinations of wage work and childcare.

Only rarely did female interview respondents explicitly discuss their partners when presenting reasons to have or not to have more children. The father of the existing first child or the potential second child was almost invisible in women's deliberations concerning more children. This may stem from the absence of direct questions concerning partners in most interviews. However, the fact that they did not include their partners spontaneously is interesting in itself. A husband or partner was mentioned as a romantic partner in raising the first child and as a socioeconomic guarantor in raising the second, but his wishes, attitudes, and practical support in childcare are not something these respondents elaborated on. We were left with the impression that many women guarded themselves against possible social, economic, and family crises and wanted to be sure they could manage as single parents or as sole providers. This impression would merit further study by specifically asking about marital relations and also interviewing men.

Notes

1 The research is part of the REFER reproductive-health and fertility-research consortium financed by the Academy of Finland, nos. 208186 and 208180. Parts of this article have previously appeared in Russian (Rotkirch and Kesseli, 2009).
2 This corpus of interviews is analyzed in the Russian anthology *Novyi byt* (Zdravomyslova et al., 2009).
3 Russia's population stopped replacing itself as early as the 1930s. The average number of children who survived until the age of 20 fell below 2.1 for women born in 1906–1910, dropped to 1.75 for women born in 1916–1920, almost reached 2 for women born in 1931–1935 and is today around 1.50 (Zakharov, 2008, p. 959).
4 By comparison, among the children of women born in 1960–1961 in the Nordic countries, 30–40 percent were born to mothers younger than 26 years old. In Russia the same figure was 70 percent, and in many countries of the former Eastern bloc it was even higher (Zakharov, 2008, p. 965).

References

Belozerova, Yulia. 2002. "Praktiki beremennoi zhenshchiny: lichnyi opyt" (Practices of a pregnant woman: Personal experience). In *V poiskakh seksualnosti* (In search of sexuality), eds. Elena Zdravomyslova and Anna Temkina, 338–365. St. Petersburg: Dmitrii Bulanin.

Bezrukova, Olga. 2007. *Sem'ia v Sankt-Peterburge: Sostoianie i perspektivy sotsial'noi raboty (po rezul'tatam sotsiologicheskogo issledovaniia)* (Family in St. Petersburg: The state and prospects of social work [on the findings of a sociological research project]). St. Petersburg: St. Petersburg State University.

Billari, Francesco C., Aart C. Liefbroer, and Dimiter Philipov. 2006. The Postponement of Childbearing in Europe: Driving Forces and Implications. Vienna Yearbook of Population Research 2006, 1–18. Vienna: Austrian Academy of Sciences.

Bodrova, Valentina. 2002. "Skol'ko detei hotiat imet' rossiiane?" (How many children do Russians want?) *Demoscope-Weekly,* 81–82, www.demoscope.ru/weekly/2002/081/tema01.php (accessed July 9, 2011).

Fahey, Tony, and Zsolt Spéder. 2004. *Fertility and Family Issues in an Enlarged Europe.* Dublin: European Foundation for the Improvement of Living and Working Conditions, www.eurofound.europa.eu/pubdocs/2003/115/en/1/ef03115en.pdf (accessed July 9, 2011).

Golovlianitsina, Ekaterina. 2007. "Rol' sotsial'no-psikhologicheskikh faktorov v reproduktivnykh namereniiakh" (The role of socio-psychological factors of reproductive intentions). In *Roditeli i deti, muzhchiny i zhenshchiny v sem'e i obshchestve* (Parents and children, men and women in family and society), eds. Tatiana Maleva and Oksana Siniavskaia, 217–250. Moscow: NISP.

Ikonen, Sanna. 2008. *Lastenhankinta-aikomukset Pietarissa* (Child-bearing intentions in St. Petersburg). Helsinki: Department of Sociology, University of Helsinki.

Ivanov, Sergei, Anatolii Vishnevskii, and Sergei Zakharov. 2006. "Population Policy in Russia." In *Demography: Analysis and Synthesis,* eds. Graziella Caselli, Gillaume Wunsch, and Jacques Wallin, 407–433. New York: Academic Press.

Kesseli, Katja. 2007/08. "First Birth in Russia: Everyone Does It—Young." *Finnish Yearbook of Population Research* 43: 41–62.

Kesseli, Katja, Elena Regushevskaya, Tatyana Dubikaytis, Svetlana Kirichenko, Anna Rotkirch, Elina Haavio-Mannila, Olga Kuznetsova, Elina Hemminki, and the REFER group. 2005. *Reproductive Health and Fertility in St. Petersburg: Report on a Survey of 18–44 Year Old Women in 2004.* Helsinki: University of Helsinki, Department of Sociology, http://www.stakes.fi/verkkojulkaisut/muut/WomenSurveyStP04_english.pdf (accessed July 9, 2011).

Kravchenko, Zhanna. 2008. *Family (versus) Policy: Combining Work and Care in Russia and Sweden.* Stockholm: Acta Universitatis Stockholmiensis.

Kuz'mina, Natalia. 2007. *Materinskii (semeinyi) kapital. Prakticheskoe posobie* (Maternal [family] capital: A practical guide). Moscow: Knorus.

Larivaara, Meri. 2011. "A Planned Baby Is a Rarity: Monitoring and Planning Pregnancy in Russia." *Health Care for Women International* 32, no. 6: 515–537.

Maleva, Tatiana, and Oksana Siniavskaia. 2007. "Sotsial'no-ekonomicheskie faktory rozhdaemosti v Rossii: empiricheskie izmereniia i vyzovy sotsial'noi politike"

(Socioeconomic factors of the birth rate in Russia: Empirical dimension and the challenges to social policy). In *Roditeli i deti, muzhchiny i zhenshchiny v sem'e i obshchestve* (Parents and children, men and women in family and society), eds. Tatiana Maleva and Oksana Siniavskaia, 171–216. Moscow: NISP.

Meilakhs, Nastya. 2009. "Neslyshnye peregovory: vybor sposoba predokhraneniia i otnoshenii mezhdu partnerami" (Silent negotiations: Choosing contraception and relations between partners). In *Novyi byt v sovremennoi Rossii: gendernye issledovaniia povsednevnosti* (The new way of life in contemporary Russia: Gender studies of the everyday), eds. Elena Zdravomyslova, Anna Rotkirch, and Anna Temkina, 356–372. St. Petersburg: EUSPb.

Nettle, David. 2011. "Flexibility in Reproductive Timing in Humans: Integrating Ultimate and Proximate Explanations." *Philosophical Transactions of the Royal Society* 366, no. 1563: 357–365.

Perelli-Harris, Brienna. 2005. "The Path to Lowest-Low Fertility in Ukraine." *Population Studies* 59, no. 1: 55–70.

———. 2006. "The Influence of Informal Work and Subjective Well-Being on Childbearing in Post-Soviet Russia." *Population and Development Review* 32, no. 4: 729–753.

Perelman, Francesca, and Martin McKee. 2009. "Trends in Family Planning in Russia, 1994–2003." *Perspectives on Sexual and Reproductive Health* 41, no. 1: 40–50.

Petrostat. 2004. *Osnovnye pokazateli demograficheskikh processov v Sankt-Peterburge i Leningradskoi oblasti, 1990–2004* (Basic indicators of demographic processes in St. Petersburg and Leningrad oblast, 1990–2004). St. Petersburg: Petrostat.

Regushevskaya, Elena, Tatyana Dubikaytis, Jouko Nikula, Olga Kuznetsova, and Elina Hemminki. 2009. "Contraceptive Use and Abortion Among Women of Reproductive Age in St. Petersburg, Russia." *Perspectives on Sexual and Reproductive Health* 41, no. 1: 51–58.

Rotkirch, Anna, and Katja Kesseli. 2009. "Detorozhdenie i ego mesto v zhiznennom tsikle peterburgskikh zhenshchin" (Childbirth and its place in the life course of St. Petersburg women). In *Novyi byt v sovremennoi Rossii: gendernye issledovaniia povsednevnosti* (The new way of life in contemporary Russia: Gender studies of the everyday), eds. Elena Zdravomyslova, Anna Rotkirch, and Anna Temkina, 426–455. St. Petersburg: EUSPb.

———. 2010. "'The First Child is the Fruit of Love:' On the Russian Tradition of Early First Births." In *Witnessing Change in Contemporary Russia*, eds. Tomi Huttunen and Mikko Ylikangas, 201–220. Helsinki: Kikimora.

Rotkirch, Anna, Anna Temkina, and Elena Zdravomyslova. 2007. "Who Helps the Degraded Housewife? Comments on Vladimir Putin's Demographic Speech." *European Journal of Women's Studies* 14: 349–357.

Sobotka, Tomás. 2004. *Postponement of Childbearing and Low Fertility in Europe*. Amsterdam: Dutch University Press.

Therborn, Göran. 2004. *Between Sex and Power: Family in the World, 1990–2000*. London: Routledge.

Zakharov, Sergei. 2007. "Transformatsiia brachno-partnerskikh otnoshenii v Rossii: 'zolotoi vek' traditsionnogo braka blizitsia k zakatu?" (The transformation of marital partner relationships in Russia: Is the "golden age" of the traditional marriage nearing its end?) In *Roditeli i deti, muzhchiny i zhenshchiny v sem'e i obshchestve* (Parents and children, men and women in family and society), eds. Tatiana Maleva and Oksana Siniavskaia, 75–126. Moscow: NISP.

———. 2008. "Russian Federation: From the First to the Second Demographic Transition." *Demographic Research* 19, no. 24: 907–972.

Zdravomyslova, Elena, and Anna Temkina. 2009. "'Vracham ia ne doveriaiu, no…' Preodolenie nedoveriia k reproduktivnoi meditsine" (I don't trust doctors, but… Overcoming the mistrust of reproductive medicine). In *Zdorov'e i doverie. Gendernyi podkhod k reproduktivnoi meditsine* (Health and trust: A gender approach to reproductive medicine), eds. Elena Zdravomyslova and Anna Temkina, 179–210. St. Petersburg: European University of St. Petersburg Press.

Zdravomyslova, Elena, Anna Rotkirch, and Anna Temkina, eds. 2009. *Novyi byt v sovremennoi Rossii: gendernye issledovaniia povsednevnosti* (The new way of life in contemporary Russia: Gender studies of the everyday). St. Petersburg: EUSPb.

CHAPTER 8

"Supporting Genuine Development of the Child:" Public Childcare Centers versus Family in Post-Soviet Russia

YULIA GRADSKOVA

INTRODUCTION[1]

Researchers of Russian history and society have conventionally looked upon the Soviet politics of public childcare primarily from the perspective of the state's need for female employment, while the role of preschool centers is seen as a substitute for the lack of maternal care (Chernova, 2008; Kravchenko, 2008; Kurganov, 1968; Saxonberg and Sirovatka, 2007; Teplova, 2007). The assumption that children were collectivized and deprived of maternal love during communism was probably one of the most influential arguments of anti-Soviet and anti-communist propaganda. However, recent studies of Soviet social and gender politics show that nurseries and kindergartens were seen by parents, and particularly by women, as an important social institution that helped them in their everyday parenting (Engel, 2004, p. 227; Kelly, 2007; Teplova, 2007, p. 285; Zhuravlev and Mukhin, 2004). Furthermore, studies of Soviet social politics show that in practice, during prolonged periods of hunger, wars, and crisis, preschool centers and other forms of institutionalized childcare and education often protected children from social abandonment and various kinds of abuse (Bendina, 2007; Kelly, 2007, pp. 348–349; Krinko et al., 2008). Indeed, the contradictory relationship between Soviet preschool centers and the well-being of the child (*blago rebenka*) was noted by Catriona Kelly in her recent profound study on Soviet childhood: "Some children were miserable at nursery schools; but others were considerably more miserable at home" (Kelly, 2007, p. 420).

Perestroika in the late 1980s, and even more so the liberal reforms in Russia after 1991, opened the way for public discussions about the need for a change in balance between the state and the family with respect to various social and economic matters. The Russian state started to view the family as an important source of welfare for its members, allowing it to withdraw from many of its previous responsibilities in guaranteeing social welfare. During the 1990s the number of kindergartens and particularly nurseries was drastically reduced.[2] However, at the beginning of the following decade, about 40 percent of all preschool children still continued to attend public preschool centers (Seliverstova, 2005, p. 96; Teplova, 2007).

This chapter explores how the role of preschool centers was viewed in the life of children and their families in the post-socialist transformation period in Russia. Did the concepts of "the well-being of the child" and "the genuine development of the child" with respect to public care and education change during these years? If so, in what ways? What responsibilities do parents have according to preschool teachers? What kind of help can parents expect from the preschool center? How do parents perceive the preschool center and its ability to support the development of the child?

The chapter is based on two kinds of materials. The first is the magazine *Doshkol'noe vospitanie* (Preschool Education), established in 1928, (designated *DV* below) and some other pedagogical texts. *DV* is the leading magazine on preschool education; its articles are written mainly by educators and experts—heads of preschool centers and instructors and administrators of local educational departments, as well as scholars in education or psychology, many of whom have a PhD degree. In 1989 *DV* had a circulation of 983,000 copies; in 1995 it was 112,891 copies, and in 2007 it was 44,500. However, despite this decline in circulation, caused by economic crises and the collapse of the Soviet Union, the magazine has largely preserved its leading role in the field of preschool education. Throughout its existence, it has published materials intended for use in the everyday work of the preschool centers. These include scenarios for celebrating holidays such as New Year's Eve, educational programs, legal documents having to do with children and education, information about new models of toys and furniture to be used in the centers, and recommendations for how to teach children about nature and music. At the same time, the magazine is also directed at parents.

The second source for my study consists of Internet sites with forum discussions on how to be a mother and how to bring up children.[3] I have chosen three thematic websites—materinstvo.ru, mamka.ru, and nanya.ru—since they all include topics on kindergartens and childcare. Although topics for discussion in the forums are different, I pay attention only to discussion topics that are common to all three of them. Furthermore, they are all open-access forums that do not require registration just to read the materials, while it is also easy and free of charge to register in order to take part in the discussions.[4] In my examination of Internet entries, I follow Norman Denzin's approach to cybertext discourse, which presupposes a deep reading of particular texts and takes into account that "it is a mistake to read cyberwriting as if it would reflect a direct connection to the conscious meaning and intentions of the writer" (Denzin, 1999, p. 112). Thus I see the entries of the forums not simply as expressions of the sender's opinion, but also as opinions that have been influenced by norms established by the particular cybercommunity.

CHILDCARE IN SOVIET AND POST-SOVIET RUSSIA—POLITICS, STRUCTURES, AND PROBLEMS

Throughout the postwar period the Soviet state was concerned about decreasing birth rates. However, a more public airing of the problem started only in the 1970s, and serious political measures were not undertaken until the early 1980s. One such measure was a gradual increase in the number of days for maternity leave. Furthermore, maternity leave gradually became better-paid and was made more accessible to a growing number of categories of women.[5] However, unlike many Eastern European countries such as Hungary or Czechoslovakia, maternity leave was always insufficiently compensated.[6] Furthermore, until the late 1980s women were expected to work in the socialist economy, while their children were expected to attend public childcare institutions.

The post-1991 Russian state developed policies that partly continued Soviet ones. Thus in 1995 maternity leave was extended from 120 to 140 days. On the other hand, the new policies sought to increase the number of mothers who took care of their children at home, at least until the children turned three years old. Beginning in 1992 a woman with children below the age of three could not be dismissed or refused work. At the same time, the context of this protective legislation regarding motherhood was entirely different from Soviet times. In the public discourse the Soviet regime was now accused of having deprived women of their "natural" role of homemaker. Accordingly, raising children at home was presented as the most legitimate occupation for women (Gradskova, 1997; Zhurzhenko, 2004). However, although the ideological pressure on women to work outside the home was removed, many families could not survive without dual incomes in a market economy marked by economic instability. Thus women frequently had to find additional work or become self-employed in order to preserve the family's living standard (Sätre, 2007). At the same time, recent sociological research shows that many women wanted to continue working (Ashwin, 2006, p. 44). On the other hand, a new Family Code was passed in 1995 that sought to increase gender equality with respect to childcare. The code introduced the notion of "individuals with parental obligations;" both parents, as well as other relatives, were eligible to take parental leave after 140 days of maternity leave. Still, the law does not seem to have achieved its goals. On the contrary, welfare measures such as prolonged parental leave—encouraging the caregiver to withdraw from the labor market—combined with a conservative interpretation of gender roles contributed to a neofamilialist rather than a "gender equality" model. Consequently, women continued to be seen as primary caregivers and secondary workers (Teplova, 2007).

Before 1991, at the beginning of the reform period, the main type of public preschool center was the "nursery-kindergarten" (*iasli-sad*), which was established in the late 1950s. Children attended nursery-kindergarten from around one up to seven years of age. The institutions were supervised by the Ministry of Education. Nursery-kindergartens and kindergartens (for children aged three to seven) were usually referred to as institutions of "preschool education and care." By 1991 about 70 percent of the preschool centers were financed by various enterprises and only about 30 percent by local public budgets (Sobkin and Pisarskii, 1998, p. 76). A problem throughout the Soviet period was that the preschool centers lacked qualified staff. However, the level of qualification gradually increased, and by the mid-1990s about 70 percent of the preschool teachers had a midlevel professional education (ibid., p.76).

During the 1990s major changes took place in the structure and financing of the preschool centers. First, all preschool centers were simply called kindergartens, since the nurseries as a special institution for small children were by now considered unnecessary (Postanovlenie..., 2002). Furthermore, the kindergartens were defined as "educational institutions" intended mainly for children over three (Ministerstvo obrazovaniia..., 2001). Second, as a result of the economic reforms, most of the kindergartens previously financed by enterprises ceased to exist. Instead, municipal kindergartens financed from local budgets became the most common form of preschool centers.

In Soviet as well as in post-Soviet times, parents were obliged to pay fees to the preschool centers. Soviet legislation, however, reduced fees for some categories of parents. Thus a 1944 edict on family and marriage stated that single mothers and mothers of more than three children needed to pay only half the fee. In 1974 the reduced fee was also granted to low-income families. Later, the following categories were included: families with disabled children (1979), divorced parents whose partner did not pay alimony (1985), and families with a widowed parent (1986). Finally, in 2007 the categories with reduced fees were extended to families in which the parents were students (Pravitel'stvo Moskvy, 2007). However, due to corruption and the low number of kindergartens in the post-Soviet period, measures designed to provide wider access to preschool education were mostly nullified. This is something that I return to in the second part of my chapter.

The number of preschool centers and children in the system grew constantly over the years in the USSR. In the mid-1980s roughly 65 percent of all children from one to six years old attended preschool centers (Sobkin and Pisarskii, 1998, p. 75). However, due to a shortage of places and to personal preferences, between 1960 and 1991, many working mothers left their children with grandparents, other relatives, or neighbors (Gradskova, 2007, pp. 212–222; Kelly, 2007, p. 349). In the mid-1980s about 1.7 million applications to preschool centers in the USSR were turned down due to lack of places (Medvedeva, 1990, p. 3). Since the drastic reduction of preschool centers in the 1990s, the shortage of places in the childcare system has been a constant problem. According to data of the Institute of Social and Gender Policy in Moscow, in 2006–2007 the lack of childcare places in some cities of the Russian Federation resulted in several collective actions by parents demanding that the state increase the number of preschool centers. Consequently, from 2007 on, several regional authorities were forced to pay compensation to parents who were not able to find a place in preschool centers for their children aged one-and-a-half to three years.[7]

After this overview of the general situation with preschool centers in Soviet and post-Soviet Russia, I now move on to a closer analysis of how the Russian magazine *Doshkol'noe vospitanie* viewed the role of the preschool center and the family, respectively, in the upbringing of children.

REPRESENTATIONS OF PRESCHOOL CHILDCARE
AND EDUCATION AFTER 1991

After the collapse of the Soviet Union, the Russian preschool centers had to find a new system of norms and orientations that differed from the Soviet system. The sources of the new ideals were numerous and contradictory, ranging from "Western" psychology to international declarations on children's rights, from reborn religious sentiments to images of Russian history. In this new situation the role of the teacher became less clear, and simultaneously the social benefit of the preschool center itself was called into question. Most of the materials of the magazine asserted that in post-Soviet Russia, children under three belonged mainly to the home space and the care of their mothers. Nevertheless, the well-being of the child and its genuine development (*podlinnoe razvitie*) after three most frequently was presented as a result of cooperation between parents and teachers. Consequently, "parents and teachers should join efforts to guarantee that the child gets protection, emotional comfort, and an interesting and meaningful life in the kindergarten as well as at home" (Doronova et al., 2001, p. 5).

According to sociologist Olga Shevchenko, however, the search for new ideas and regulations took place in a situation marked by feelings of insecurity and evaluated by many Russian citizens as a "permanent crisis" (Shevchenko, 2009). Still, the pedagogical publications rarely brought up the dramatic reductions of childcare facilities or the changes in the financial and structural system of preschool education. One of the most important exceptions is a 1995 interview with Rina Sterkina, head of the Department of Preschool Education within the Russian Ministry of Education. Sterkina referred to changes in the financial and organizational system of preschool education (Sterkina, 1995, pp. 3–9). *DV* also paid little attention to the negative aspects of social changes, such as poverty or racism. Social problems seem to have become generally invisible for post-Soviet education; in cases when they were noticed, they were presented mainly as problems of individual families and parents.

Thus *DV* rarely commented on the problem of the decreasing number of preschool centers. The first note of difficulties within the sphere of preschool education came in mid-2006, when President Putin was reported to be taking measures to create more centers with better quality. Only then did the journal begin to enlighten its readers about the dimension of the change that had taken place in preschool education, noting that during the last fifteen years the number of preschool centers in Russia had fallen by half (Dneprov, 2006). Soon other articles on the same topic followed: "The Russian Constitution states that all citizens have the right to the services of preschool education. Thus the main aim of the state in the sphere of preschool education to guarantee every child accessibility has still not been fully realized" (Kalinina, 2006). Finally, one article from 2007 promised that the lines for placing children in preschool education centers would be shortened throughout the country, and that in some regions like Moscow, Mordovia, Volgograd, and Belgorod, the waiting lists would even disappear by 2010 (Tret'iak, 2007).

Basically, however, instead of writing about structural and social problems of childcare, *DV* elected to boost the importance of freedom for educational ideas by presenting a variety of programs for educators to choose from, including "Development," which was aimed at developing the intellectual activity of small children, and "Rainbow," which focused on the emotional well-being and harmonic development of the child. Some of the programs—particularly Rainbow—considered one of their main goals to be better communication between children, parents, and teachers (Doronova, 2004). Several programs were designed to develop a love of nature and addressed environmental issues. Programs with an international profile were designed specifically for post-socialist countries. To mention one example, in 1995 a project supported by George Soros's Open Society Foundation and developed by Georgetown University was introduced in a few kindergartens in Moscow and the Samara region. It was described as different from all other programs in Russia in that it could be easily modified according to the aspirations of the children, teachers, and parents (Mikhailenko, 1995). All of the programs aspired to replace the standardized Russian "Program of Education and Upbringing in Kindergarten," which had continued virtually unchanged since 1985. However, according to sociological studies from the year 2000, 75 percent of the kindergartens have continued to use exactly this standardized program (Sobkin and Marich, 2000, p. 57).

Many publications and programs strongly emphasize the protection of children's rights; the UN declaration on the issue appeared for the first time in 1986 in new textbooks on child psychology (*Doshkol'noe vospitanie*, 1986). More and more frequently, the child was presented as a person with certain rights whose genuine development demanded a certain respect for his or her personality: "nobody can force children to eat or to do anything, nobody can prevent them from going to the toilet or make them stay in their chairs or stand in the corner as punishment" (*Doshkol'noe vospitanie*, 1993). In 2002 *DV* published an article about a special help center, Ozon, which was started by several Russian and international organizations to protect children against cruelty and violence. The article mentioned that in 1999 the children's hotline received a special award from the Open Society Foundation for its work (Safronova, 2002).

Furthermore, the 1970s-era psychological perspective employed to analyze "childhood" and "child education" not only persists but has contributed to the creation of a mass profession (psychologists) in the sphere of education. In the late 1980s psychologists started to work on an experimental basis in kindergartens (Veresov, 1995); starting in the late 1990s, every kindergarten was supposed to have at least a part-time psychologist (Tepliuk, 2006). The number of articles in the magazine written by professional psychologists also grew, and in 2006 *DV* even introduced a special section called "A Psychologist's Advice."

Thus the pedagogical publications of the post-Soviet period represent a mixture of pedagogical and social ideas and demonstrate the confusion that the experts on preschool upbringing have to live with, given Russia's new economic and social conditions. Furthermore, the search for the best pedagogical solutions seems to be seriously hampered by a lack of adequate attention to the new situation that families and children encounter, which includes growing social and economic inequality and difficulties with access to public childcare.

A New Image of the Parent

Changes in the way parents are represented in Russian society in the early 1990s are reflected in *Doshkol'noe vospitanie*. An important change can be detected in the depiction of parents' responsibilities for their children. Actually, the balance between preschool centers and parents has shifted. Thus according to the "guidelines for preschool education," the family provides what no institution can give the child, which is the intimate and personal connection, the unity between the child and its own people (Kutuzova, 1993, p. 58). Many programs welcomed the participation of parents in organizing the everyday life of kindergartens, stressing that parents should be partners. As was the case before the 1990s, cooperation with parents was seen as particularly important during the child's first days and months in the preschool center. Thus referring to "The Scientific Institute for Education and Upbringing," in 1993 the magazine published a five-step program for collaboration with parents. "When meeting parents for the first time, the teacher should show respect and subtlety and only in the second step of the communication bring up 'problems' connected with the child". And this should be done in a "careful" manner. A further development of this program presupposes the establishment of agreed-upon demands on the individual child and the development of collaboration. Also, the teacher is not to claim omnipotence and assert that there have been no problems, but on the contrary is advised to express her doubts about things and ask for advice from the parents (ibid.). Vera Aliamovskaia, a preschool teacher from Nizhnii Novgorod, went even further in her book *Nursery is a Serious Thing*. She advocated that the parents perform yearly evaluations of the teachers and that special curatorial practices be established vis-à-vis families with a child about to start nursery (Aliamovskaia, 1999, pp. 10–13).

The new equal relationships between parents and preschool teachers do not seem to have been that easy to build up, however, particularly considering that in the early 1990s both families and kindergartens experienced economic uncertainty due to high inflation, unemployment, and general instability. Not surprisingly, some of the articles from these years depict the parents' attitude as more negative than in the Soviet period. Thus one article quotes a teacher complaining that, compared to a few years earlier, the situation had deteriorated: "It is impossible to have a word with the mothers, since as soon as I open my mouth a flood of words come from them ... You can't imagine how they have changed; they don't seem to care at all for their own children!" (Markusha, 1993, p. 60).

At the same time, ideas about parenting started to be picked up from different and often contradictory sources. For example, in 1993 the magazine published articles with contradicting messages: one article advocated that parents read both *Domostroi*[8] and the second article contained the well-known American psychologist Virginia Satir's advice to parents to respect the individuality of their child (Evstratova, 1993; Satir, 1993). Furthermore, parents were urged to encourage their children to participate in various activities organized by the kindergarten, ranging from the conventional commemoration of Victory Day (Chechel'nitskaia and Potapenkova, 1995), with its Soviet-era origins, to the celebration of Easter. With regard to the latter, the magazine suggests that both an Orthodox priest and the parents participate (Vlasova, 1995).

As the economic situation gradually improved in the first few years of the twenty-first century, educational experts and preschool teachers were again called upon to influence the supervision of children's well-being in families. More and more often, families were classified as being "at risk" with respect to the well-being of their children. Tatiana Doronova, a well-known pedagogue and the author of a popular program for kindergartens, recommends that the staff identify parents belonging to risk groups and pay them more attention (Doronova et al., 2001). One cannot avoid the suspicion, however, that such labeling could easily contribute to stigmatizing children.

Thus sometimes quite contradictory recommendations were given due to the fact that interpretations of how a good parent should act became more and more diverse. However, publications from the early 1990s indicate that in the economic and socially unstable position in which many parents found themselves, they simply did not pay much attention to the new educational demands from preschool centers. Nevertheless, *Doshkol'noe vospitanie* and other publications on education from the 1990s and even more from subsequent years continued to view their readers as teachers and parents interested in enhancing their pedagogical skills.

CYBERTALK ON CHILDREN, CHILDHOOD,
AND EDUCATION

I now go on to analyze a very different source of information, namely Internet forums. Unlike *Doshkol'noe vospitanie*, in which the discourses emanate from experts in the field, the main participants on the Internet forums are parents who view their parental role as crucial and thus could be called "involved parents" (Forsberg, 2009). It should be stressed that the gender-neutral term "parents" that is frequently used in the educational publications is not appropriate in an analysis of the Internet forums, since there the participants almost exclusively identify themselves as "mothers" and refer to other participants as "girls" and "moms." Furthermore, "I" is replaced by a symbiotic "we." Thus mother and child are presented as inseparable. For example, people typically write "we started kindergarten" (instead of "my child started kindergarten") or "we were sick" (instead of "my child was sick").

The mothers' cybertalk touches on various topics related to children, childcare, and education. Here we find an atmosphere of sisterhood, where the participants feel close to one another in their search for the best for their child. The centrality of the children is strongly felt in the way texts and pictures are composed. Funny pictures give an idea of the age of the child, photos are displayed where the children are "cute" and "handsome," and the emotions of the mothers are often central to the arguments. Thus they cry when they have to leave the child at kindergarten, they do not sleep when the child has problems, or they get very annoyed by the smallest sign of bad treatment from the teacher. Sometimes participants express strong disagreement with other participants, sometimes swear words are used, and occasionally the participants are superstitious.[9] All these means of expression, including the mother's showing her own vulnerability, contribute to a construction of the child as central in the life of the mother, thus confirming her "normal motherhood."

Sociological data collected by Vladimir Sobkin and Ekaterina Marich show that one of the main arguments for why children should attend preschool centers is that they need to develop communication skills and to be prepared for school (Sobkin and Marich, 2002, pp. 123–133). Preschool centers as important agents of early socialization also figure in the discussions in the Internet forums. Still, most of the participants seem to devote at least some time to the question of whether their child should indeed attend kindergarten and if so, from what age. The website nanya.ru is strongly opposed to public childcare: "You should not take your child to kindergarten." In mamka.ru and materinstvo.ru, the topic is brought up differently, the norm being that public childcare is simply something parents use: Thus there are threads like "Starting Kindergarten," "Continuing to Attend Kindergarten," or "How to Adapt to Nursery?" while the thread "How Come Parental Leave Is Only a Year and a Half, while Kindergarten Only Accepts Children of Two Years of Age and up?" suggests a much stronger degree of acceptance.

Following Denzin, I differentiate between the "self" and the "self communicated in written form" under the influence of the cybercommunity norms and rules (Denzin, 1999, pp. 113–114). In my analysis I pay attention to what forum participants treat as obvious and how they relate their own opinions to the "obvious." A close reading of the forum entries suggests that according to implicit cyber normativity, the mother is expected to be the main caregiver. Thus when some participants feel the need to apologize for not corresponding to "normal" patterns of family and maternity, they are assuming that a good mother stays at home with her child until it is time for kindergarten, something that could be decided only according to the need of the child itself. This need is most frequently defined as the need for interaction with other children. Thus a participant from the Moscow region wrote: "I would not bring my child to kindergarten when she is only two, and I really hope that I will not have such an urgent need ... But when she is four I will be happy to do so."[10] Another participant asked, how could someone possibly leave their one-and-a-half-year-old child in kindergarten? She understands that there might be economic motives, but she still says that the child's physical and psychological health must be the first priority.[11] However, some participants made no apologies for tending to their own professional and educational needs:

> I am in my final year of studies, and I work as well. The father of the child is also a student who works at the same time. So we wouldn't survive without nursery! Grandmother is getting very tired looking after our daughter, and I can't drop my classes any longer. I don't want to leave her with someone else, but what can I do?[12]

One of the discussions on materinstvo.ru started after the site published an article by Olga Khvorova entitled "There Is No Such Thing as a Child Not Fit for Kindergarten."[13] The author insisted on the importance of kindergarten because of its age-appropriate educational programs and schedules and because it allowed for ample interaction with other children. However, the author also cited psychologists' recommendations in advising parents not to bring children to kindergarten until the age of two. The participants of the forum had different reactions to the article. Some supported the argument that kindergarten was important for children's development and stressed the need to develop communication skills, as well as the need for a qualified staff. Others disagreed with Khvorova, insisting on keeping the child at home for a longer period. Kindergarten was "very convenient for the mothers," since at home "you have to do something with your child all the time and it takes all your time and energy, so when you bring your child to the kindergarten you feel relieved."[14] Thus here we sense that mothers who put their children in kindergarten are being blamed somehow for not fulfilling the requirements of normative motherhood.

Some of the discussions help us understand why preschool centers are frequently viewed negatively. Parents tend to see kindergarten as a place that endangers the health of the child, particularly if the child is not appropriately "prepared." In this case "preparation" primarily means tempering (*zakalivanie*)—something, by the way, that teachers widely advised during Soviet times. Sports activities are also part of the preparation. Sometimes "preparing" the child means treating him or her with medications. Some participants complained that in spite of the different preparations and preventions they undertook, they were still constantly forced to stay home with their sick children.[15] Yet other parents were more afraid of fights between children or bad treatment by the staff. This argument was frequently supported by their own negative memories of Soviet preschool centers.[16] According to the participants of the various Internet forums, access to kindergarten was far from unproblematic; as a matter of fact, in most cases it was really difficult. And the problem, as some participants put it, was not really a question of quality, but simply the dire shortage of public kindergartens.

According to various entries the waiting line for a place in kindergarten was sometimes as long as three years. Thus one participant from the city of Togliatti claimed that there you had to apply for a place as soon as the child was born.[17] Actually, the way the problem of access to public day-care centers is described reminds us very much of practices during Soviet times (Ledeneva, 1998). Informal payment and services rendered to kindergartens seem to be legitimized through the notion of "help." So how is "help" being requested and what role does it play in the relationship between teachers and families? Many participants wrote that they filled in documents promising "help from a voluntary sponsor," which in practice meant making a deposit in the kindergarten's bank account.[18] In other cases money was simply handed over to the kindergarten director in person. Alternatively, the parents had to offer the kindergarten certain services—help repairing the buildings, buying new furniture, or doing some gardening. The sums and forms of services seem to vary not only from one region to another, but also between different kindergartens in the same city. For example, one participant from Perm wrote that in order to avoid a long wait, parents were required to pay 30,000 rubles for a place in suburban areas and 50,000–100,000 rubles for a kindergarten in the center of the city.[19] The initial sum for a place in a Moscow kindergarten was indicated by some forum participants to be 12,000–60,000 rubles. In the city of Ufa, the sum was 20,000 rubles; in Yekaterinburg it was 30,000 rubles ("it is cheaper to become a university student," one participant commented).[20] In Krasnodar it was U.S. $100–400 (3,000–12,000 rubles).[21] After having waited in line, parents were still expected to "help" buy pots, paint fences, and fix windows or other things. In a few cases "help" also meant that mothers were expected to work as teachers at the kindergartens in which they wanted to place their children.[22]

After the child has been admitted to kindergarten, parents and teachers are supposed to cooperate in order to make the transition from home to the preschool institution as smooth as possible. In the forum discussions, parents see their own roles in different ways. When speaking to their child about kindergarten, they try to stress the positive sides, and when speaking to the teachers they discuss the behavior, appearance, and development of the child. Finally, they continue to "help" by offering the kindergarten money and services. These topics are discussed by parents in several forums on materinstvo.ru and mamka.ru.

In my view, the complex relationship between parents and teachers is most clearly represented in the thread dealing with the activities of the parents' committee at the preschool center. Parents' committees were born during the Soviet era and were connected with the idea of collective upbringing. While in the 1920s and 1930s parents—mostly mothers—were expected to take part in cooking for the children and cleaning the kindergarten, later on, beginning in the 1950s, parents' committees were supposed to help organize parties and excursions and acquire goods in short supply ranging from toys to building materials.

Judging from one discussion about parents' committees, this institution continues to be an important mediator between parents and preschool centers. The discussion was triggered when a participant from Kostroma asked for advice on whether to participate in such a committee.[23] The answers show that most participants in the discussion agreed on the importance of the committees in helping the kindergartens. The following were considered the most important activities: providing goods and services such as furniture and toys, repair work, and presenting the staff and the children with gifts on various holidays such as New Year's, Women's Day, and birthdays. Such activities could provoke many conflicts, and the cybertalk on these problems offered the participants some orientation and gave them some feeling of support and solidarity.

Some entries show that these committees were sometimes also perceived as independent organizations of parents siding with the children and families in conflicts with the staff. Thus one entry from Moscow tells us about a mother's achievement:

> When there is a conflict, I myself can call for a meeting with the parents and deliver an ultimatum to the staff. I succeeded in eliminating the established system of closing at 5 p.m. Now the kindergarten is open until 7 p.m., and I think this is how it should be.[24]

Thus according to the forum discussions, kindergarten basically continues to be part of a "normal" childhood. In spite of very diverse expectations with regard to educational and communication skills, kindergartens continue to be important for parents. Still, cybertexts indicate that most parents who discuss childcare via the Internet are concerned about the shortage of preschool centers and the quality of care that their children get there.

Conclusion

My analysis of the magazine *Doshkol'noe vospitanie* and other texts on education demonstrates changes in the way concepts such as the "wellbeing of the child" and "the genuine development of the child" were mainly interpreted. Some publications insist on taking the perspective of children's rights, including freedom from abuse and violence and the need to pay attention to the emotional needs of the child. Furthermore, there is an emphasis on the need to shift responsibility from the state to parents; specifically, the care of children under three is viewed as an almost exclusively parental concern. Thus the authoritative position of the preschool teacher vis-à-vis both the child and the parents has been weakened. However, some previous interpretations of childhood and parenthood persist and are even reinforced in the educational texts published since 1991, particularly the view of the mother (in contrast to the father) as the main caregiver and the importance placed on the role of the preschool centers in guiding parents with respect to upbringing.

At the same time, the articles published in *Doshkol'noe vospitanie* frequently contradict one another, a fact that leaves room for many doubts with respect to the depth and character of changes in everyday childcare practices. The same goes for the lack of flexibility in applying new concepts to specific situations in the everyday life of individual kindergartens that have children and parents with particular needs and interests. That is probably the reason why the Internet forum participants—predominantly mothers, most of whom consider preschool centers to be important for their children's well-being and development—do not really discuss the benefits or shortcomings of different educational programs. They are focused mostly on the practical aspects of communication with the kindergarten staff and on the physical and emotional well-being of their children there. The forums reveal several aspects of preschool center practices that are not visible in educational publications. These include the established normativity of informal favors, the worries of many mothers that the kindergartens do not pay due attention to their children's individual needs, and, of course, the serious problem parents face in finding childcare facilities. Women participate in these forums with the aim of guaranteeing the "genuine development" of their children. However, the forums can also be seen both as a source of information and advice and as a source of emotional support and a way for mothers to confirm their roles of "involved parents" taking an interest in current changes in the preschool system.

Notes

1 Parts of this article have appeared in Yulia Gradskova, "Kogda otdavat' rebenka v detskii sad i platit' li vospitateliu? Roditel'stvo, gender i uchrezhdenia doshkol'nogo vospitaniia v internet-forumakh." (2010) *Laboratorium* 3: 44–57.
2 According to Teplova, several factors contributed to this, including the inability of the enterprises to serve as micro-welfare states during privatization and the instability that the neoliberal reforms created. Furthermore, there was reduced demand for labor, the widespread practice of multiple and informal employment, and finally the diffusion of ideas about bringing women "back home." In the latter case the diminishing fertility rate was an influential factor for policymakers and society in general (Teplova, 2007, pp. 290–291).
3 For more extensive studies on Internet-forum discussions of childcare, see Gradskova (2010).

4   The process of registration normally requires the name, city, and region (or country) of the user, as well as the year of birth of both the user and her children. The user must also provide a photograph, and she can also submit additional information about her interests, profession, and date of marriage.
5   Parental leave was introduced as early as the 1960s, but initially it was unpaid and thus only guaranteed the mother the right to keep her job during parental leave.
6   In 1982, 112 days of partly paid parental leave were added (up to one year). In 1989 the leave was extended to three years, of which one-and-a-half years were to be paid. However, the money was minimal and did not correspond to the rate of inflation. According to Teplova's calculation, a mother caring for her child at home received about U.S. $ 17 per month. At the time, the poverty line in Russia was around U.S. $ 200 (Teplova, 2007, pp. 297, 313).
7   For more detail on compensations from regional authorities, as well as parents' attitude toward childcare in various regions of the Russian Federation, see the online materials of the Institute of Social and Gender Policies (Institut... 2007).
8   A sixteenth-century household manual with advice on social behavior.
9   For example, they write "TTT" when they fear that they might "damage" something good by naming it.
10 Moscow region, July 8, 2008.
11 City not stated, July 8, 2008.
12 Mother of an eleven-month-old child, Moscow, August 2, 2007.
13 "Not fit for kindergarten" (*nesadovskii rebenok*) is a term frequently used by administrators and doctors in kindergartens describing children who in some way lag behind in individual development or have some sort of health problem (Khvorova, 2007).
14 Sevastopol (Ukraine), September 4, 2008.
15 Moscow, May 22, 2008.
16 See a thread from October 16, 2008: http://forum.forumok.ru/index.php?showtopic=27810 (accessed October 22, 2008).
17 Togliatti, August 3, 2007.
18 Moscow, September 18, 2006.
19 Perm, February 6, 2006.
20 Ekaterinburg, August 8, 2006.
21 Krasnodar, September 25, 2005.
22 Moscow, October 27, 2004.
23 Kostroma, October 17, 2005.
24 Moscow, October 17, 2005.

REFERENCES

Aliamovskaia, V. 1999. *Yasli—eto ser'ezno* (Nursery is a serious thing). Moscow: Linka-Press.
Ashwin, Sarah, ed. 2006. *Adapting to Russia's New Labour Market: Gender and Employment Behaviour*. London and New York: Routledge.
Bendina, Olga. 2007. "Chem rebiat branit' i bit', luchshe knizhku im kupit'!" (Instead of scolding and beating your kids, buy them some books!) In *Sovetskaia sotsialnaia politika 1920-kh-1930kh godov: ideologiia i povsednevnost'* (Soviet social policy of the 1920s and 1930s: ideology and everyday life), eds. Elena Iarskaia-Smirnova and Pavel Romanov, 392–413. Moscow: Variant.
Chechel'nitskaia, S., and T. Potapenkova. 1995. "Slavsia, Den Pobedy!" (Glory to the Victory Day!) *Doshkol'noe vospitanie* 4: 114–126.
Chernova, Zhanna. 2008. *Semeinaia politika v Evrope i v Rossii: gendernyi analiz* (Family policy in Europe and Russia: Gender analysis). St. Petersburg: Norma.
Denzin, Norman. 1999. "Cybertalk and the Method of Instances." In *Doing Internet Research*, ed. Steve Jones, 107–125. Thousand Oaks, CA, and London: Sage.
Dneprov, Eduard. 2006. "[Vstupitelnaia stat'ia, bez nazvaniia]" (Introduction, untitled). *Doshkol'noe vospitanie* 6: 1.
Doronova, T.N. 2004. "Vzaimodeistvie doshkol'nogo uchrezhdeniia s roditeliami" (The interaction between preschool institutions and parents). *Doshkol'noe vospitanie* 1: 60–68.
Doronova, T.N., E.V. Solov'eva, A.E. Zhichkina, and S.I. Musienko. 2001. *Doshkol'nye uchrezhdenia i sem'ia—edinoe prostransvo detskogo razvitiia* (Preschool institutions and the family: The common space of child development). Moscow: Linka-Press.
Doshkol'noe vospitanie.1986. "Novyi uchebnik po detskoi psikhologii" (A new textbook on child psychology). 9: 65–66. [Announcement of a new publication.]
———.1993. "Pochta odnogo dnia" (One day's mail). 3: 67–70. [Review of readers' letters.]
Engel, Barbara. 2004. *Women in Russia, 1700–2000*. Cambridge: Cambridge University Press.
Evstratova, L. 1993. "Narodnoe nasledie" (The legacy of the people). *Doshkol'noe vospitanie* 5: 72–73.
Forsberg, L. 2009. "Managing Time and Childcare in Dual-Earner Families: Unforeseen Consequences of Household Strategies." *Acta Sociologica* 52, no. 2: 162–175.
Gradskova, Youlia. 1997. "Novaia ideologiia sem'i i ee osobennosti v Rossii" (The new ideology of the family and its peculiarities in Russia). *Obshchestvennye nauki i sovremennost'* 2: 181–185.
———. 2007. *Soviet People with Female Bodies: Performing Beauty and Maternity in Soviet Russia in the Mid 1930–1960s*. Stockholm: Acta Universitatis Stockholmiensis.
———. 2010. "Kogda otdavat' rebenka v detskii sad i platit' li vospitateliu? Roditel'stvo, gender i uchrezhdenia doshkol'nogo vospitaniia v internet-forumakh"

(When should children be put in nursery school, and should the staff be paid? Parenthood, gender, and institutions of preschool upbringing in Internet forums). *Laboratorium* 3: 44–57.

Institut sotsial'noi i gendernoi politiki (Institute of social and gender policies). 2007. "Dostupnost' detskikh sadov—regional'nyi opyt" (Accessibility of kindergartens—a regional experience), http://www.genderpolicy.ru/265 (accessed May 14, 2009).

Kalinina, I.I. 2006. "Problemy i perspektivy razvitiia doshkol'nogo obrazovaniia v Rossiskoi Federatsii" (Problems and prospects of the development of preschool education in the Russian Federation). *Doshkol'noe vospitanie* 9: 3–5.

Kelly, Catriona. 2007. *Children's World: Growing Up in Russia, 1890–1991*. New Haven, CT: Yale University Press.

Khvorova, Olga. 2007. "Net takogo poniatiia—nedetsadovskii rebenok" (There is no such thing as a child not fit for kindergarten). *Materinstvo*, http://www.materinstvo.ru/art/1962/ (accessed July 12, 2011).

Kravchenko, Zhanna. 2008. *Family (versus) Policy: Combining Work and Care in Russia and Sweden*. Stockholm: Acta Universitatis Stockholmiensis.

Krinko, Evgenii, Tatiana Khlynina, and Ilona Yurchuk. 2008. "Na grani vyzhivania: detskie doma Kubani v 1941–1945 gody" (On the borderline of survival: Children's homes in the Kuban, 1941–1945). In *Sovetskaia sotsialnaia politika: stseny i deistvuyushchie litsa, 1941–1985* (Soviet social policy: Scenes and actors, 1941–1985), eds. Elena Iarskaia-Smirnova and Pavel Romanov, 2: 35–59. Moscow: Variant.

Kurganov, I.A. 1968. *Zhenshchiny i kommunizm* (Women and communism). New York.

Kutuzova, I. 1993. "Dialog s sem'ei" (Dialogue with the family). *Doshkol'noe vospitanie* 1: 58–59.

Ledeneva, Alena. *Russia's Economy of Favors: Blat, Networking and Informal Exchange*. Cambridge: Cambridge University Press, 1998.

Markusha, Anatolii. 1993. "Nachnu s IRP" (I'll begin with parents' letters). *Doshkol'noe vospitanie* 6: 55–62.

Medvedeva, G.S. 1990. "Sotsial'naia pomoshch' gosudarstva v vospitanii detei v detskikh uchrezhdeniiakh" (State social support in the upbringing of children in children's institutions). In *Trud, sem'ia, byt sovetskoi zhenshchiny* (The work, family and daily life of the Soviet woman), ed. Svetlana Polenina, 339–355. Moscow: Yuridicheskaia literatura.

Mikhailenko, N. 1995. "Rebionok v detskom sadu" (The child in kindergarten). *Doshkol'noe vospitanie* 8: 4–8.

Ministerstvo obrazovaniia Rossiiskoi Federatsii (Ministry of Education of the Russian Feneration). 2001. "Tipovoe polozhenie ob obrazovatel'nom uchrezhdenii dlia detei doshkol'nogo i mladshego shkol'nogo vozrasta, 1997." (Standard statute on the educational institution for children of preschool and early school age, 1997). In *Doshkol'noe obrazovanie v Rossii v dokumentakh i materialakh* (Preschool education in Russia in documents and materials), 48–56. Moscow: Ministerstvo obrazovaniia Rossiiskoi Federatsii.

Postanovlenie Pravitel'stva Rossiiskoi Federatsii (Decree of the government of the Russian Federation). 2002. "Ob utverzhdenii tipovogo polozheniia o doshkol'nom obrazovatel'nom uchrezhdenii ot 01.07.1995" (On the approval of standard regulations for institutions of preschool education, July 1, 1995). In *Doshkol'noe obrazovanie v Rossii v dokumentakh i materialakh* (Preschool education in Russia in documents and materials), 7–15. Moscow: Ministerstvo obrazovaniia Rossiiskoi Federatsii.

Pravitel'stvo Moskvy (Government of Moscow). 2007. *Vmeste s Moskvoi—druzhnoi sem'ei: sotsial'naia podderzhka semei s det'mi v gorode Moskve* (Together with Moscow, a happy family: Social support of families with children in Moscow). Moscow: Krug zhizni.

Safronova, N. 2002. "Tsentr 'Ozon' i ego deiatel'nost'" (The "Ozon" Center and its activities). *Doshkol'noe vospitanie* 1: 40–44.

Satir, Virginia. 1993. "Pravila, po kotorym vy zhivete" (The rules you live by). *Doshkol'noe vospitanie* 5: 76–78.

Saxonberg, Steven, and Tomas Sirovatka. 2007. "The Re-Familisation of the Czech Family Policy and Its Causes." *International Review of Sociology* 17, no. 2: 319–341.

Seliverstova, I.V. 2005. "Dostupnost' doshkol'nogo obrazovaniia: vliianie territorial'nogo faktora" (Accessibility of preschool education: the influence of the territorial factor). *Sotsiologicheskie issledovaniia* 2: 95–104.

Shevchenko, Olga. *Crisis and the Everyday in Postsocialist Moscow.* Bloomington: Indiana University Press, 2009.

Sobkin, Vladimir, and E.M. Marich. 2000. *Vospitatel' detskogo sada: zhiznennye tsennosti i professional'nye orientatsii* (The kindergarten teacher: Life values and professional orientation). Moscow: TsSO RAO.

———. 2002. *Sotsiologiia semeinogo vospitaniia. Doshkol'nyi vozrast* (Sociology of family upbringing: Preschool age). Moscow: TsSO RAO.

Sobkin, Vladimir, and Petr Pisarskii. 1998. *Tipy regional'nykh obrazovatel'nykh situatsii v Rossikoi Federatsii* (Types of regional educational situations in the Russian Federation). Moscow: TsSO RAO.

Sterkina, R.V. 1995. "Ia prodolzhaiu byt' optimistom" (I continue to be an optimist). *Doshkol'noe vospitanie* 1: 3–9.

Sätre, Ann-Mari. 2007. *Vild kapitalism och gammal byråkrati. Om småföretagare i Ryssland* (Wild capitalism and old bureaucracy: On small entrepreneurs in Russia). Stockholm: Premiss förlag.

Tepliuk, L. 2006. "Ulybka malysha v period adaptatsii" (The infant's smile in the adaptation period). *Doshkol'noe vospitanie* 4: 46–49.

Teplova, Tatyana. 2007. "Welfare State Transformation, Childcare, and Women's Work in Russia." *Social Politics: International Studies in Gender, State and Society* 14, no. 3: 284–322.

Tret'iak, N. 2007. "Metodicheskie rekomendatsii po priniatiiu mer po razvitiiu doshkol'nogo obrazovaniia v 2007–2010 gg." (Methodological recommendations for the implementation of measures for the development of preschool education in 2007–2010). *Doshkol'noe vospitanie* 11: 6–13.

Veresov, N. 1995. "Den' dlinoiu v god" (A year-long day). *Doshkol'noe vospitanie* 3: 7–16.

Vlasova, N. 1995. "Prazdnik prazdnikov" (The holiday of holidays). *Doshkol'noe vospitanie* 3: 123–125.

Zhuravlev, Sergei, and Mikhail Mukhin. 2004. *Krepost' sotsializma: povsednevnost' i motivatsiia truda na sovetskom predpriiatii, 1928–1938 gg.* (Socialism's fortress: everydayness and work motivation in the Soviet enterprise, 1928–1938). Moscow: ROSSPEN.

Zhurzhenko, Tatiana. 2004. "Staraia ideologiia novoi sem'i: demograficheskii natsionalizm Rossii i Ukrainy" (Old ideology of the new family: Demographic nationalism in Russia and Ukraine). In *Semeinye uzy: modeli dlia sborki (Family Bonds: Models to Assemble)*, ed. Sergei Oushakine, 268–296. Moscow: Novoe Literaturnoe Obozrenie.

ONLINE SOURCES

Forum.Nanya. In *Nanya.ru Internet portal dlia roditelei* (Nanny.Internet portal for parents), http://forum.nanya.ru/ (accessed fall 2008).

Konferentsiia Materinstvo. In *Materinstvo.ru*, http://forum.materinstvo.ru/ (accessed fall 2008).

Forum.Forumok. In *Mamka.ru (Forum.Forumok.ru)*, http://forum.forumok.ru/ (accessed fall 2008).

CHAPTER 9

Everyday Continuity and Change: Family and Family Policy in Russia

ZHANNA KRAVCHENKO

INTRODUCTION

Social development in Russia in recent decades has been characterized by a complex and often contradictory constellation of traditional and modern elements of family life (Zdravomyslova, 2002). Public response to family change in the form of social policy has been contradictory as well. On the one hand, family policy inherited many legal and practical instruments from the Soviet period, which ensured some continuity in policy design. On the other hand, it has been reconsidered, redefined, and transformed. In the 1990s and the decade after, many national studies (see, for example, Antonov and Borisov, 1990; Darmodekhin, 2001; Lovtsova, 2003) were dedicated to formulating a normative foundation for implementing family policy—ideas about what *should* be done in order to sustain "a *healthy, wealthy,* and *law-abiding* family" (Klimantova, 2002, p. 13; emphasis added).

The research on the relationship between institutionalized policies and family patterns tells us that "the governments do a lot [according to their ideas of the desired results for families] and want to do much more to support families with children" (Abrahamson et al., 2005, p. 210). It is commonly expected that such measures will be gratefully received by the target groups and incorporated into their practices. However, if it is assumed that the family is not merely a passive target of public policy and that individuals (groups) take responsibility for their own well-being, it is only logical to suggest that a policy can have varying effects that have not necessarily been anticipated by policymakers.

This chapter first discusses the theoretical opportunities that the analysis of everyday life provides for understanding social policy. It then highlights how the transformation of family policy in one particular national context (the Russian Federation) suffers from data shortage, and it goes on to make a case for applying an everyday life perspective that has already produced an insightful body of research on social change in the country. Data analysis follows with a focus on daily routines developed by working parents and their reflections on the appropriate division of responsibilities and the role of policies in the process of reconciliation. I argue that family interactions at the individual level embrace the structural opportunities embedded in the design of family policy, translate the established hierarchical principles of gender organization in society, and at the same time create room for maneuvering and sustaining practices that are efficient for families depending on their individual circumstances.

SOCIAL POLICY AND THE THEORY OF THE EVERYDAY

There are several axioms in classic social policy analysis. First, welfare policy is conceptualized in terms of interaction between the market and the state aimed at the (re)distribution of resources via the cash nexus and authoritative redistribution (Esping-Andersen, 1990). Second, redistribution effects vary between countries, but redistribution is generally aimed at decreasing the inequalities in the living standards (re)produced by the market (Korpi and Palme, 1998). And third, the opportunities for organizing the redistribution are structured by the system of economic and political relationships in a particular national context (O'Connor and Olsen, 1998). The most common criticism of this classical approach is presented by feminist scholars, who emphasize that the conventionally accepted postulates outlined here are rooted in the experiences of men. As a result, primarily by upholding the patriarchal division between the public and private spheres and by binding the entitlement to social rights to participation in the labor market (Sainsbury, 1996), they fail to reveal some of the mechanisms that in fact sustain inequalities.

A considerable amount of research has emphasized the role of female employment and social rights (e.g., Hobson, 1990, 2000; Lewis, 1992; Orloff, 1993; Sainsbury, 1996). But more importantly, it has revealed that the welfare system can mirror and regulate gender relations in a rather explicit way before, during, and beyond employment. With regard to the latter aspect, it is important to note that, although women's position as workers is important for how they realize their social rights, their role as potential caregivers (mothers) is also built into social policy design, even though not all women necessarily experience it (Daly and Lewis, 2000; Leira, 1992). Crompton (1999) and Pfau-Effinger (2004) introduce one more dimension to the discussion about the gendered division of labor in society, namely men's involvement in work and care. All these studies develop the notion that there are multiple dimensions in gender relations that can both exist in various constellations and change over time. The realm of everyday particularities has been largely overlooked in the analysis of gender and social policy, which still operates with aggregated generalizations and strives for high-level synthesis (which is most vividly illustrated by the proliferation in welfare-state typologies).

When social policy is constructed, the indicators that control its efficiency and quality are embedded in its design. If the measures include financial transfers, the way to evaluate the results is to collect the data on the number of recipients, the levels of provision in comparison to some standard indicator (average salary, for instance), or their effect on alleviating poverty. If the measures include social services, the coverage/take-up rates are often used in the analysis of their results. At a more general level, employment rates, income levels, and inequality indices combined with various attitudinal measurements are common tools in research on social policy. A more individual-based approach has recently emerged and focuses on the complex part of social reality that does not present itself as self-evident and transparent—for instance, discourses and power relations that are formed in the process of realization of certain practices related to social policies (e.g., Forsberg, 2009; Gerhard et al., 2005; Kröger and Sipilä, 2005).

Viewing social policy in the context of everyday life is not common in contemporary research. This is partly due to the fact that "everydayness" is a rather elusive object of inquiry. Definitions of the everyday vary with the subject of research. Some theories link the concept with the daily habits and routines of domesticity, while others examine publicly displayed accounts of everyday, more dynamic and diverse behavior (Schor, 1992). The operationalization of everyday life is much more problematic than the operationalization of social policy indicators (Shevchenko, 2009). Besides the methodological "ooziness" of everyday life as a concept (Kelly, 2002), the challenge is to link theories that exist at different ontological levels, given that policy analysis is structure-oriented and everyday analysis is focused on the individual. As Ahrne (1981) argues, everyday reality and structural reality are two different parts of societal reality: the former is the complexity of various contents created by each and every individual, while the latter is the abstract connection between many different everyday realities. Ideas about the essence of the relationship between the everyday and structural reality vary greatly, ranging from the "mechanical" view, which makes the former directly determined by the latter (through the mediation of ideology, market production, or symbolic means of exchange), to the dialectical approach, which emphasizes the complexity of the process of creating the meaning and practice of the everyday through interaction with the everyday realities of others and their physical, social, cultural, and ideological contexts.

Individual knowledge about everyday reality is very subjective, as is knowledge about the structural factors that mediate human interaction and create "objectified" social reality. Nevertheless, it does reflect aspects of social reality that are relevant for each particular individual. This selective view of social reality in the individual's everyday life is of the highest importance for the (re)production of social structure and can be seen as one of the targets of various forms of intervention, including social policy. The latter, from this point of view, would be considered an attempt to regulate the individual's relationship with the social and physical environment through the redistribution of resources, and as one of the nodal points where such a relationship reveals itself in a clear way. An analysis of social policy from the point of view of how it is being incorporated into everyday reality, therefore, can provide an account of a policy's efficiency that is otherwise overlooked in a more aggregated analysis.

The choice of family policy (in particular, childcare services and financial benefits and privileges, which specifically target working parents) for the analysis of interplay between social policy and everyday life is motivated by the fact that these policies attempt to regulate the "collision" between two spheres of social and everyday reality that are often theorized as separate—the public domain of waged work and the private domain of unpaid care. The set of routines within the former is traditionally associated with men, and the daily habits of the latter are assigned to women (Schor, 1992). However, men and women are present in both realms, and the development of family policy in contemporary industrialized countries can be seen as an attempt to overcome the asymmetrical division of labor between the sexes. By looking at how family policy is incorporated into the everyday lives of men and women, we can explore an alternative account of the functioning and effects of family policy, move beyond the officially assigned expectations and generalizations, and reveal differences and commonalities in the experiences of families that previously remained hidden and unproblematized. In the following section I briefly touch upon the recent trends in the development of Russian family policy and some earlier research on everyday life in Russia.

Russian Family Policy and Everyday Life

As in many other European countries, the Russian family exhibits a trend toward "thinner (with fewer siblings), more often de-institutionalized (non-marital), non-co-resident families" (Hantrais, 2006, p. 12). The traditional life-cycle model of a commitment to a lifelong marriage followed by having children is giving way to more complex family and life-cycle patterns. Behind the statistical data usually discussed with regard to the demographic crisis in Russia (see, for example, the chapters by Rotkirch and Saarinen in this volume) are men and women who have been marrying and having fewer children and at older ages, cohabiting and divorcing more than ever before, and who are faced with huge demands from work and family life. Census indicators are widely used by social scientists and policy-makers to raise concerns about the consequences that the "shrinking" of the family may have for the overall reproduction and socialization of the population in the long run, and to argue for certain policy solutions. The outlined demographic transition takes place in an explicitly defined institutional framework of public policies that aims at regulating the conditions of a family's well-being. During the period of socioeconomic and political reforms, the country has suffered serious economic problems that have led to low living standards and the risk of unemployment and increased the costs of welfare for both individuals and households. Privatization has brought more diversity in social security and services. Different parts of family policy were changed in different ways during the period in question, which makes it difficult to identify a unified direction to the reforms. Overall changes do not seem very drastic. On the contrary, a continuation of the explicit (late-)Soviet pronatalist, formally institutionalized, and centrally administered principles can be tracked in the present policy design.

The childcare service organization was an integrated part of the old Soviet system of education, which had its own national curriculum and strove for universal coverage. Despite early advancements in education, the shortage of childcare facilities was a problem during the period of Soviet rule, and the problem only intensified during the 1990s (Teplova, 2007). The network of public preschool facilities was reduced by approximately 4–5 percent, and the number of children in them shrank by 1.8 million from 1994 to 2002 (Statistika Rossiiskogo obrazovaniia, 2006). These are, however, official statistics. Teplova (2007, p. 292) reveals a far more drastic drop in the number of available places in childcare (from 87,900 in 1990 to 53,300 in 2000) and enrolled children (by 50 percent) based on Goskomstat and survey data. The system of financial means-tested benefits was devised in Russia in the early 1990s. Currently the available benefits include: 1) universally available lump-sum benefits at birth; 2) monthly benefits during parental leave during the first 1.5 years; and 3) means-tested child allowances for families with children 1.5–16 years old (for more details on the procedures of applying for the means-tested allowance, see Iarskaya-Smirnova and Romanov's chapter in this volume). The period of parental leave is earning-related and lasts for seventy weeks (with a flat-rate benefit for previously unemployed/uninsured individuals) and an optional seventy-eight unpaid weeks. The minimum benefit for the insured is 40 percent of income during the previous twelve months (for a more detailed overview, see Ovcharova and Pishniak, 2007).

Any structural analysis of Russian family policy often faces one common problem—the lack of comprehensive aggregate data on coverage rates for benefits, enrollment rates for childcare services, or take-up rates for parental leave. The design of the official statistics obscures whether any families eligible for services and benefits are left out due to the non-transparent process of target-based provision (see chapter by Iarskaya-Smirnova and Romanov in this volume). As in the example above, evaluations of childcare restructuring by different public agencies and independent experts vary considerably. There are no official data on take-up rates; however, survey analysis indicates that the average length of maternity leave is 15.5 months out of the available 18, and it is reduced with each subsequent child (Arkhangel'skii et al., 2005). Savinskaya (2008) also shows that women most often return to work when the child is at the age of 31–36 months (30 percent), 19–24 months (17.6 percent), or 0–5 months (17.5 percent). The variation depends greatly on the professional status of women and the availability of childcare.[1] One finding is that there is no scientific or public problematization of the fact that although it is available to both men and women, parental leave is being used only by the latter.[2]

The formal structure of family policy arrangements suggests that public policy in Russia strives to produce the dual-earner family model (Crompton, 1999), promoting female employment by providing substantial financial assistance and services. With regard to care, formal attributes such as the availability of parental leave to both parents and substantial public investment in care outside the home suggest that the care model is somewhat fragmented, with elements of dual/state/female care provision in no clear pattern. Analysis at this level of generalization suffers from the poor quality or absence of data and makes it difficult to determine the trajectory and scope of the changes that have taken place. By looking at what sense people make of the available facilities and transfers and whether they take them into account when making their decisions about work and care, we might better understand the relationship between the structural conditions of reconciliation and everyday practices and thus shed some light on the effectiveness of the policies.

Several empirical studies on various aspects of everyday practice in contemporary Russia have been conducted by national and international groups of researchers. One of the classical works in this field, by Boym (1994), reveals that the traditional opposition between public and private is less relevant for Russian cultural history: the private sphere was never fully cultivated. Pre-revolutionary intellectuals were willing to "sacrifice private concerns for the good of a larger community-in-the-making," denying the private sphere as merely irrelevant. Meanwhile, Bolsheviks proclaimed private life to be of communal importance, and by doing so made it an object of public penetration and ideological prescription (Kiaer and Naiman, 2006, p. 9). Nevertheless, the analysis of everyday life provides an understanding of various aspects of social reality in contemporary Russia. For instance, analysis of the organization of life in communal apartments (Boym, 1994) reveals how cultural history and modernity are internalized into domestic ideas of privacy and the common good. An examination of gender identities and strategies of reproductive behavior (Zdravomyslova et al., 2009) provides insights into social stratification and the commercialization of domesticity. And a study of food consumption and taste preferences (Caldwell, 2009) can illustrate ideas about health and well-being, social change, and globalization. The research also shows that throughout the hardships brought on by the collapse of the system in the early 1990s, people were able to organize their private life and achieve some sense of normality and stability (Shevchenko, 2009). It is especially noteworthy that the increased importance of domesticity in this process of making sense of social reality was accompanied by an increased sense of autonomy from the (dis)order of public institutions.

The question is how the family would react to increased pressure by the state as it attempts to solve the demographic crisis. As they make concrete decisions related to their private preferences, individuals are more likely to take into account their own needs and preferences than they are to consider the demographic problems of the country (cf. Ahrne 1981, p. 83). However, do they incorporate existing structural opportunities as they satisfy their own needs, and what are the factors that allow them to do so effectively?

DATA AND METHODOLOGY

Operationalizing everyday life includes the individual's activities, the meaning that these activities have in people's eyes and in a larger social context, and the role that they play in the reproduction of habitual patterns and in their selective reinterpretation in response to novel social conditions (Shevchenko, 2009, p. 5). For the purpose of this study, the actual content of the relevant activities was not established a priori. However, the general direction of the activities was defined as the reconciliation of work and care. The logic behind such an interpretation comes from the phenomenological tradition in everyday sociology that is concerned with the intention of an action carried out "in order to" [reach some goal] instead of "because" [of some reason] (cf. Ahrne, 1981, p. 50).

The empirical data stem from face-to-face interviews with nine women and two men conducted in spring 2007 in St. Petersburg.[3] The study was initially designed as part of a PhD dissertation project; hence the selection criteria and instruments were shaped by an earlier analysis of policy framework and large-scale survey data (for more detail, see Kravchenko, 2008). The choice of the parameters was based on knowledge of the main target groups of family policy as it was formulated in official documents that are not subjected to frequent revisions. The criteria for selecting the respondents included the following: 1) they had to have children aged between five and fifteen (so that information could be collected about all the available family policy mechanisms, as different benefits are directed to children of different ages); 2) both partners (or the lone parent, in the case of one-parent households) had to have been active in the labor market both before and after the birth of the children. The main rationale for the second condition was the need to exclude those families that had chosen to withdraw from the labor market as a solution to their role conflict. Although the experiences of such family units would also be of interest for family policy studies in relation, for example, to the development of new policy initiatives, in this particular project they were not examined. All interviews were conducted in St. Petersburg for the sake of convenience. Although the study is not representative with regard to sampling, I hope that it will be of value in suggesting a new analytical approach useful for an understanding of social policy development and realization in other structural and national contexts.

Early in the fieldwork, an open-answer question-guide was used that was eventually transformed into a mind-map summarizing the main topics for conversation (see Table 1). The conversations were constructed around the typical, "normal" routines of organizing work and care and atypical, "emergency" situations. The aim of this division was to capture and formulate the habitual organization of life and determine what situations required a reconfiguration of resources and how durable the routines were in general. Those events that called the existing order into question usually actualized and revealed the interplay between policies and practices more clearly than those that arose in "ordinary" settings.

TABLE 1. *Interview topics: synchronization of everyday routines*

I. General introduction	Household routines	Working routines		
II. Daily	Morning ↓ waking up, meals, emergency situations	Afternoon private and public arrangements ↓ getting there and home, meals, costs, duration	Evening a) after-school activities ↓ getting there and home, meals, costs, duration	b) after-work activities ↓ free time without children	Night ↓ going to bed, staying outside home (location, duration)
III. Weekly	Working schedules	School schedules	Weekend activities		
IV. Yearly	School breaks	Family vacations	Parental leave arrangements	Sick leave arrangements	

EVERYDAY FAMILY PRACTICES IN FOCUS

The fieldwork took place in the spring of 2007, when a new national reform was launched under the slogan of boosting fertility rates and increasing the well-being of families with children. The reform included an increased and earning-related differentiation of parental leave payments, an increase in compensation for the health-care costs related to childbirth and expanded subsidies for multiple births (known as "maternal capital"). This reform was the first explicit attempt in post-socialist Russia to formulate gender/family-related politics as a legislative expression of the dominant official ideology that advocates traditional family values but at the same time expresses support for female wage-work (Rotkirch et al., 2007). Although this political initiative was not preceded by public hearings or debates, it received a great deal of attention from the media, politicians, and experts. Consequently, I expected my interviewees to be well-informed about the content of the reform and able to reflect on whether it would have any direct consequences for their lives. But more importantly, I assumed that the wide media exposure had, in general, prepared them to consider the issue of balancing work and family. Each and every narrative provided an account of a complex constellation of circumstances that enabled families to reconcile seemingly incompatible demands of family obligations and labor market responsibilities, together with a somewhat skeptical attitude toward official propaganda and a commitment to mobilize necessary resources at any moment.

Public policy enters the private domain
The reconciliation of family and work life is a dynamic process that reflects a turning point in a family's life cycle. For working parents, such critical moments occur first when the child is born, later when the primary caregiver (the mother) returns to the labor force and the child enters a childcare institution (these events do not necessarily coincide), and once again when the child is enrolled in a school. Each of these situations requires major reassessment of established routines and the creation of new ones, including new "backup" arrangements for new emergency situations. Family policy by definition serves as a form of mediation between the private and public spheres (Repo, 2004) that aims to reduce role conflict while engaging the family in a network of interrelated public organizations that create a normative and physical framework for family practices. Profound as the idea behind it may be, for many families public support in the form of family policy serves as only one of the resources that make reconciliation possible, and it is often a secondary one.

Parental leave is chronologically the first policy measure that is available to employed individuals with children. It is also the most generous privilege in terms of duration and compensation level, and it is accompanied by the right to a shorter working day/week, flexible hours, and extra vacation days. As was mentioned before, no data is available by which to measure the extent to which this social right is used by eligible parents. Among my respondents there was nevertheless an almost unanimous sense that taking full advantage of parental leave entailed sacrificing other opportunities and suffering the inevitable penalties that come with a long career break:

> [...] nobody wants a woman with a technical education [...] I have two technical degrees. I don't know anything else. And even [what I know] I'm starting to forget already. You see, computers change quickly. I can work as a programmer, but I am a technician. It's what's inside the machine that I know. After all these years at home, the hardware has changed. So if I open the computer now, I don't know if I'll understand what I see. (IT specialist, 28 years old)

There is no general agreement in the research community as to whether the design of parental/maternity leave is necessarily damaging to women's position in the labor force. On one hand, the evidence suggests that the availability of job security regulation of this kind strengthens women's attachment to the labor market (Gornick et al., 1997). On the other hand, a long-term absence limits career opportunities and job retention (Mandel and Semyonov, 2005; 2006). Gerber and Perelli-Harris (2009) confirm that the maternity leave provisions in Russia supported women's access to employment and protected them from layoffs during the most difficult times of the recession. However, as my interviews revealed, loss of qualification during the leave or negative attitudes from employers, who view mothers as unreliable workers, often coerce them into precarious job patterns, thereby damaging their careers and social security in the long run.

Unlike payment during parental leave, which is considered to be a significant substitute[4] for the loss of income, neither the flat-rate benefit nor childcare allowance, which is available after the child reaches 1.5 years of age, was counted on in family budgets. As a result, it was completely absent from the talks about family practices. Formal childcare, on the other hand, was seen as highly important for creating successful reconciliation practices as working arrangements. In fact, parents need to find a routine that allows them to synchronize leaving children at a childcare center or with a babysitter before going to work and picking them up after the workday is over. Two major obstacles to creating a sustainable practice can appear—the working hours of different organizations do not always coincide with the timetable of childcare facilities, and the shortage of vacancies at childcare centers can make it virtually impossible to use formal care. During the Soviet period, these problems were solved more easily because childcare was often attached to enterprises, whose work schedules were synchronized and suited to the working hours of parents, and early childcare coverage was much more extensive. Today the second problem is sometimes easier to solve than the first one.

Many childcare facilities practice subtle extortion to compensate for underfunding and the underdevelopment of social infrastructure:

> You go and write an [enrollment] application. They say: "No vacant places." Well, then you pay. And write a statement that this money is a charitable contribution, so that you can't go [to the authorities] and complain. A vacant place appears immediately.
> (Nurse, currently working in sales, 35 years old)

The fact that enrollment in a childcare facility has become a source of illegal profit-making is not surprising in a society with a rather high degree of corruption at all levels. As Gradskova shows in this volume, the problem is widespread on the ourskirts of densely populated metropolitan areas such as St. Petersburg, where the shortage of facilities/places is most common in fast-growing residential areas because the construction of childcare facilities lags behind housing construction. Bribery has become so routine that it is now accepted as almost a norm:

> As usual, parents channel the information [...] Parents are sharing the information concerning which kindergarten is best. Our pediatrician told me which kindergarten is the best one. I even got information at work. [...] Then I needed to apply. I found a person who knew where to call and who recommended me.
> (University lecturer, 35 years old)

The choice of childcare facility is certainly an important event for any family with children of preschool age. In the experience of some of my informants, the process of finding a place often involves the personal stories of other people—not only relatives directly concerned with the well-being of a particular child, but with colleagues, neighbors, and brief acquaintances. The relevant information includes the range and quality of services provided in the facility, but also the number of extracurricular activities (especially if they involve additional payments) and most importantly, the habits of the administration staff concerning working hours, hygienic practices, and extortion routines.

The problem of discrepancies between the work schedules of different organizations can be solved by informal agreements with co-workers and employers. Successful reconciliation arrangements are often based on an "understanding" reached with the management and on colleagues' and parents' skills in negotiating more flexible working hours or leaves of absence in case of need. Such informal or latent work arrangements may be instrumental in "synchronizing" different spheres of individuals' activity. At the same time, they may impact very negatively on the work situation of individuals with family obligations. Each situation that requires negotiation may result in parents failing to reach an agreement with the employer, even if such an agreement lies within the legally prescribed range of rights. Whatever the regulations prescribed in formal legislative acts, many informants reported irreconcilable opposition from their employers to fulfilling their obligations:

It was a war [at work]. The head of the department was like an exploiter, as if it was a private clinic. [...] I never even took sick leave! (Nurse, currently working in sales, 35 years old)

As Zaslavskaia (2002) notes, formal legal norms do not necessarily translate into actual administrative practice in the Russian context. Ignoring and violating the existence of privileges related to working parents, as in the above example, can be seen as one of the adaptation strategies developed by both private and public organizations during the turbulent economic transformation. In Soviet times, returning to the same workplace after a leave of absence of any length or kind was guaranteed not simply by law but by the structure of the relationship between the main employer (the state) and the employees, which aimed to reduce the mobility of the labor force (Kapeliushnikov, 2002). With the development of market-oriented labor relationships, however, these regulations became an obstacle. Many employers choose informal mechanisms of regulation such as emotional pressure or even illegal threats of layoffs (Polenina, 2000) to force parents to choose work obligations over those of the family.

"Balancing" and "reconciling" means making choices and sorting priorities. Parents have to make adjustments in their working arrangements to meet the organizational rhythm of the public childcare facilities and prepare for inevitable periods of absence from work. They also have to accept the consequences of missing out on time with their children. In the process of creating a sustainable balance, the family's internal resources play the most important role.

Family "power resources"
The complex set of routines related to reconciling work and family life is often perceived as rather fragile—small interruptions and changes in circumstances may threaten the whole construction. Although arrangements are often formed spontaneously, they are more stable than they may seem at first sight and involve several options, including informal intra-familial and informal work-related networks and formal policy measures. Managing performance in all spheres is often compared by working parents to existence in parallel realities that need to be planned and "shuffled" to create effective solutions. The main theme of the stories I was introduced to was about the intensity of family life, a complex set of interdependences between different generations, attempts to break free from close kin networks, and the inability to succeed without them.

The economic recession of the 1990s, together with increased housing problems, created the so-called "anti-nuclearization" of the Russian family (Prokof'eva, 2007) by forcing relatives to reside with members of the extended family or at least to consider the (dis)advantages of distances between them. Such arrangements are especially vital for the families of single or young and newly married mothers. The mechanisms of mutual assistance include joint budgeting, care provision, and in-kind help. Some of the services are exchanged regularly, such as providing informal childcare, working at garden plots, and taking children out on weekends. At other times, families are used as the most reliable resource when individuals find themselves in problematic life situations caused by unemployment, bankruptcy, or homelessness. Such needs sometimes transcend spatial distances:

> [My] mother came [from another city] when there was a fire [at the shop] this year. She came to help with the children. I had exams at that time [at the institute]... Everything at the same time—she spent her vacation here, a whole month.
> (Nurse, currently working in sales, 35 years old)

The involvement of grandmothers in early childcare and education is one of the strongest cultural traditions not related to the issue of availability of childcare (Semenova, 1996; Visson, 2004). As one of the interviewees expressed it: "I think this is our Russian [phenomenon...] If I was raised by my grandmother, then my children will be raised by their grandmother" (crane operator, 37 years old). This account referred to a common pattern of care-giving that was established partially due to early female retirement age and necessary because of the rigid employment practices discussed above. The importance of extended networks becomes much more evident in the narratives of families who do not have them. As reported by a widowed mother of a school-age girl who needs a daily ride to school on the other side of the city:

> I am not allowed to get sick, I have absolutely no right to get sick! [...] I live, as many Russians [do], hoping for the best. We'll figure it out when it comes, when it strikes. As a last resort, I will ask someone for help, but everyone is working, too.
> (University lecturer, 35 years old)

The fear of not being able to perform a necessary daily routine and having no one to rely on for help if it is needed gives rise to an overwhelming sense of anxiety. A similar frustration is often reported when referring to interruptions in everyday patterns due to unforeseen changes in work schedules or rather predictable but nevertheless unavoidable school breaks that do not coincide with parents' vacations:

> Oh, it's horrible… because the child stays all alone [at home] and you feel guilty. So—here—yes […,] you try to find some time and on Saturdays and Sundays, if possible, let him choose whatever he wants to do, and you agree to everything. Just to compensate for the fact that he's been sitting all alone for a whole week. (Nurse, 34 years old)

In some two-parent households, the lack of extended family members to whom some family-related responsibilities could be delegated calls for more equality in the division of these responsibilities between the spouses.

> We were talking just yesterday [and I said], "You're working, I'm working, we share all the housework equally."
> (Cook and entrepreneur, 32 years old)

Such a point of view is rare among families who enjoy generous support from grandparents:

> When Arisha was little, we got a lot of help from my mother-in-law and her sister, my husband's aunt. I had two whole days off per week. My mother-in-law and Aunt Nina came, went for a walk [with the baby], took care of her. I had some rest; I could go wherever I wanted. All the time. (IT specialist, 28 years old)

The "double burden," a notion that has become a commonplace to describe the dual obligations of work and care assigned to women by Soviet and post-Soviet policies, is amplified: a woman living in a conjugal relationship is more likely to share the care-related or household workload with female members of her extended family than she is with her male partner. Men are gradually given some care responsibilities such as school-related activities or physical training when children grow older, but domestic chores remain excluded from their role as a caregiver:

> […] it is more interesting for him with Masha, she is older, she needs guidance, and I do the rest. Shopping for groceries… bags. […] I think we each get [to do] what we do best. My parents lived this way

too [...] and they have lived together their whole lives. But there were times... when Masha was little and there was no car... I had Masha in my hands, bags in my teeth, pushing the stroller... (Narcologist, 36 years old)

The most obvious conclusion to be drawn from an analysis of the unequal distribution of work and care in the household is that the discrepancy arises from differences in attitudes and socially assigned role expectations. Structural opportunities, however, whether they are viewed as the determinants or the consequences of socially constructed meanings, cannot be isolated from the discussion. Men and women mobilize resources that are available to them in the process of caregiving.

In a situation where flexible arrangements with the employer are sometimes hard to achieve, assistance from the male partner is limited and extended family networks are weak, negotiating with coworkers the hours of work and even the days of the week on which work is possible (the latter is typical for people working in shifts) is done more willingly and usually with more success. Sometimes practices of mutual support even transcend the formal agreements of working routines and draw colleagues into private, almost family-like relationships:

I have worked at the same place for many years already; everyone is very understanding [...] One-third of my colleagues are my friends, and we've been friends for years. So I guess I could say that we were all bringing up my son together [...] I had some complications after giving birth, and they were all by my side. (Nurse, 35 years old)

Such intense relationships can be developed with other categories of people, such as neighbors. This demands a great deal of investment in time and effort outside the family, but it is preferred to less-close networks of people or care services provided on a market basis, even though the latter is becoming more widespread (Zdravomyslova, 2008).

I started this section by referring to the policy reform that took place right before my fieldwork began. Its main shortcoming was not so much the controversial set of measures it proposed as the very formulation of the problem that it was supposed to solve. Rotkirch et al. (2007) have analyzed President Putin's address to the State Duma in 2006, which outlined the reform for the first time and contained the most fundamental points in the new family policy ideology and practice. The authors emphasize that the issue of low fertility in the current political discourse was seen as a result of decreased economic well-being and that the solution to this problem would therefore require a return to the gender contract of working mothers that was dominant in the Soviet period, and without reconsidering the role of men as possible care-providers. The speech and the subsequent legislative act make the unequal distribution of paid and unpaid work seem natural and unquestionable.

In the analysis of everyday reconciliation routines, we have to consider two major problems that families face and which go beyond the issue of financial resources. These include the inability to rely upon the existing employment legislation and public provision for childcare organization, as well as a culturally accepted pattern of unequally distributed care responsibilities. While the former is a traditional subject of government policies, the latter is not officially problematized, although it can also be addressed by means of public intervention. It can be done, for instance, through the introduction of quotas into parental leave regulations, which would encourage men to use legislative provisions as a starting point in assuming a larger share of care work.[5] In the discussion above I have been able to relate the daily problems of working people to previously explored problems having to do with the malfunctioning labor market and public administration system, as well as traditional aspects of the gender contract. The findings are not new in themselves, but they have not previously been linked together into a framework that shapes strategies for reconciling work and care.

Conclusion

The conventional approach to the study of social policy treats the family as an object of intervention, "as basically reacting to changes in the macrostructure of society" (Fisher and Khotin, 1977, p. 368). Thus many scholars turn their attention to the study of the institutional framework and aggregate-level statistics in an effort to understand the transformation that the family is undergoing. Such a perspective hinders the theoretical conceptualization of the family as an active agent of welfare production and distribution rather than simply as a mediator between the state and the individual. This chapter has explored the opportunities provided by everyday theory for the analysis of one segment of social policy, namely provisions aimed at facilitating the combination of work and care. The analysis has revealed that a simplified and ideal-typical version of family life as regards work and care is used as a background for public provisions: partners are expected to be employed full-time, to have access to social insurance that covers any potential breaks in paid work arising from certain family-related situations, and to have access to public/private childcare facilities that operate during the parents' working hours.

The policies translate a normative version of how family life should be organized in time and space but fail to ensure the realization of their own regulations. When combining work and care, families incorporate the policy support available to them in different—often spontaneous—ways, complementing them with other resources and sometimes even diverging from the "paths" shaped by the policy framework. The policies are incorporated in different ways, depending not only on family needs but also on opportunities shaped by work regulations and the specifics in the functioning of other public organizations. Families' daily routines are forcefully structured by work and school schedules, mealtimes and bedtimes, housework allocation and employment arrangements, summer vacations and sick leaves. Social relations partly shape everydayness, for the expectations and actions of others organize and determine family routines. The life of the family becomes "a world, the social character of which arises in the constant ongoing intercoordination of actual activities" (Smith, 2002, p. 278). One distinct feature of the interaction between the state and the family in Russia becomes apparent here: the family has more flexible mechanisms to adjust to changes in its environment and to incorporate or isolate them than the policy has to adjust to the changes and needs of the family.

Notes

1 Both studies were limited to specific regions—Novgorodskaia Oblast (Arkhangel'skii et al., 2005) and Moscow (Savinskaya, 2008).
2 For example, in Savinskaya (2008), the research group formulates the problem of work and care reconciliation as a problem of *women* and not *parents*.
3 Seven of the respondents were either married or cohabiting without civic registration, and four were raising their children alone. There were seventeen children in all; more specifically, four families had one child, five families had two, and one family had three. Four of the respondents had a higher education (at least a bachelor's) degree, while the other seven had professional training. Two of these were in the process of obtaining a diploma at the time of the interview. The underrepresentation of the male perspective on reconciliation practices and the norms that surround them is one of the limitations of this study.
4 For more on the impact of cash benefits to families with children on poverty rates in Russia, see Kravchenko (2009).
5 Legally established periods of parental leave that are to be used by fathers and cannot be transferred to mothers are already being implemented in several

European countries, such as Sweden (two months), Iceland (three months), Norway (six weeks), and Denmark and Slovenia (two weeks) (Kvande, 2007; Wall, 2007).

REFERENCES

Abrahamson, Peter, Thomas P. Boje, and Bent Greve. 2005. *Welfare and Families in Europe.* Aldershot, UK: Ashgate.
Ahrne, Göran. 1981. *Vardagsverklighet och struktur* (Everyday reality and structure). Gothenburg, Sweden: Korpen.
Antonov, Anatolii, and Vladimir Borisov. 1990. *Krizis sem'i i puti ego preodoleniia* (The crisis of the family and how to resolve it). Moscow: Institut sociologii AN SSSR.
Arkhangel'skii, V., V. Elizarov, N. Zvereva, and L. Ivanova. 2005. *Demograficheskoe povedenie i ego determinatsiia (po resul'tatam sotsiologo-demograficheskogo issledovaniia v Novgorodskoi oblasti)* (Demographic behavior and how it is determined [based on a sociological-demographic research project in Novgorod oblast']). Moscow: TEIS.
Boym, Svetlana. 1994. *Common Places: Mythologies of Everyday Life in Russia.* Cambridge, MA: Harvard University Press.
Caldwell, Melissa L., ed. 2009. *Food and Everyday Life in the Postsocialist World.* Bloomington: Indiana University Press.
Crompton, Rosemary, ed. 1999. *Restructuring Gender Relations and Employment: The Decline of the Male Breadwinner.* Oxford: Oxford University Press.
Daly, Mary, and Jane Lewis. 2000. "The Concept of Social Care and the Analysis of Contemporary Welfare States." *British Journal of Sociology* 51, no. 2: 281–298.
Darmodekhin, S. 2001. *Sem'ia i gosudarstvo* (The family and the state). Moscow: NII Sem'i.
Esping-Andersen, Gösta. 1990. *The Three Worlds of Welfare Capitalism.* Princeton, NJ: Princeton University Press.
Fisher, Wesley A., and Leonid Khotin. 1977. "Soviet Family Research." *Journal of Marriage and Family* 39, no. 2: 365–374.
Forsberg, Lucas. 2009. "Managing Time and Childcare in Dual-Earner Families: Unforeseen Consequences of Household Strategies." *Acta Sociologica* 52, no. 2: 162–175.
Gerber, Theodor P., and Brienna Perelli-Harris. 2009. *Maternity Leave in Turbulent Times: Effects on Labour Market Transitions and Fertility in Russia, 1985–2000.* MPIDR Working Papers WP 2009–028.
Gerhard, Ute, Trudie Knijn, and Anja Weckwert, eds. 2005. *Working Mothers in Europe: A Comparison of Policies and Practices.* Cheltenham, UK: Edward Elgar.
Gornick, Janet, Marcia Meyers, and Katherin Ross. 1997. "Supporting the Employment of Mothers: Policy Variation Across Fourteen Welfare States." *Journal of European Social Policy* 7, no. 1: 45–70.

Hantrais, Linda. 2006. "Living as a Family in Europe." In *Policy Implications of Changing Family Formation: Study Prepared for the European Population Conference 2005*, eds. Linda Hantrais, Dimiter Philipov, and Francesco C. Billari, 11–18. Population Studies, no. 49, Strasbourg: Council of Europe Publishing.

Hobson, Barbara. 1990. "No Exit, No Voice: Women's Economic Dependency and the Welfare State." *Acta Sociologica* 33: 325–249.

———. 2000. "Economic Citizenship: Reflections through the European Union Policy Mirror." In *Gender and Citizenship in Transition*, ed. Barbara Hobson, 84–117. London: Macmillan.

Kapeliushnikov, Rostislav. 2002. "Rossiiskaia model' rynka truda" (The Russian model of the labor market). In *Kuda idet Rossiia? Formal'nye instituty i real'nye praktiki* (Whither Russia? Formal institutions and actual practices), ed. Tatiana Zaslavskaia, 127–136. Moscow: Moskovskaia Vysshaia Shkola Sotsial'nykh i Ekonomicheskikh Nauk.

Kelly, Catriona. 2002. "Ordinary Life in Extraordinary Times: Chronicles of the Quotidian in Russia and the Soviet Union." *Kritika: Explorations in Russian and Eurasian History* 3, no. 4: 631–651.

Kiaer, Christina, and Eric Naiman, eds. 2006. *Everyday Life in Early Soviet Russia: Taking the Revolution Inside*. Bloomington: Indiana University Press.

Klimantova, Galina. 2002. "Gosudarstvennaia semeinaia politika—vazhneishaia politicheskaia strategiia sovremennoi Rossii" (State family policy—the most important political strategy of contemporary Russia). In *Sem'ia: XXI vek. Problemy formirovaniia regional'noi semeinoi politiki (iz opyta raboty Tomskoi oblasti)* (The family: The 21st century; Problems in shaping regional family policy), ed. Galina Klimantova, 12–16. Moscow: Sovet Federatsii Federal'nogo Sobraniia Rossiiskoi Federatsii.

Korpi, Walter, and Joakim Palme. 1998. "The Paradox of Redistribution and Strategies of Equality: Welfare State Institutions, Inequality and Poverty in the Western Countries." *American Sociological Review* 63: 661–687.

Kravchenko, Zhanna. 2008. *Family (versus) Policy: Combining Work and Care in Russia and Sweden*. Stockholm: Acta Universitatis Stockholmiensis.

———. 2009. "On Public Support for Working Parents in Russia." In *Poverty and Social Policy Research in Central and Eastern Europe*, ed. Jolanta Aidukaite, 99–114. New York: NOVA Science Publishers.

Kröger, Teppo, and Jorma Sipilä, eds. 2005. *Overstretched: European Families up against the Demands of Work and Care*. Oxford: Blackwell.

Kvande, Elin. 2007. "Leave Policy and Social Inequality: The Case of Norway." In *International Review of Leave Policies and Related Research 2007*, eds. Karin Wall and Peter Moss, 19–24. London: BERR.

Leira, Arnlaug. 1992. *Welfare States and Working Mothers*. Cambridge: Cambridge University Press.

Lewis, Jane. 1992. "Gender and the Development of Welfare Regimes." *Journal of European Social Policy* 2, no. 3: 159–173.

Lovtsova, N. 2003. "Zdorovaia, blagopoluchnaia sem'ia—opora gosudarstva? Gendernyi analiz semeinoi sotsial'noi politiki" (Are the health and well-being of the family a support for the state? A gender analysis of family social policy). *Journal of Social Policy Studies* 1, nos. 3–4: 323–39.

Mandel, Hadas, and Moshe Semyonov. 2005. "Family Policies, Wage Structures, and Gender Gaps: Sources of Earnings Inequality in 20 Countries." *American Sociological Review* 70, no. 6: 949–967.

———. 2006. "A Welfare State Paradox: State Interventions and Women's Employment Opportunities in 22 Countries." *American Journal of Sociology* 111, no. 6: 1910–1949.

O'Connor, Julia, and Gregg M. Olsen, eds. 1998. *Power Resource Theory and the Welfare State: A Critical Approach*. Toronto: University of Toronto.

Orloff, Ann S. 1993. "Gender and the Social Rights of Citizenship: The Comparative Analysis of Gender Relations and Welfare States." *American Sociological Review* 58: 303–328.

Pfau-Effinger, Birgit. 2004. *Development of Culture, Welfare States and Women's Employment in Europe*. Aldershot, UK, and Burlington, VT: Ashgate.

Polenina, Svetlana. 2000. *Prava zhenshchin v sisteme prav cheloveka: mezhdunarodnyi i natsional'nyi aspekty* (Women's rights in the human rights system: International and national aspects). Moscow: Institut Gosudarstva i Prava RAN.

Prokof'eva, Lidia. 2007. "Domokhoziaistvo i sem'ia: osobennosti struktury naseleniia" (The household and the family: Features of population structure). *SPERO* 6: 57–68.

Repo, Katja. 2004. "Combining Work and Family in Two Welfare State Contexts: A Discourse Analytical Perspective." *Social Policy and Administration* 38, no. 6: 622–639.

Rotkirch, Anna, Anna Temkina, and Elena Zdravomyslova. 2007. "Who Helps the Degraded Housewife? Comments on Vladimir Putin's Demographic Speech." *European Journal of Women's Studies* 14: 349–357.

Sainsbury, Diane. 1996. *Gender, Equality and Welfare States*. Cambridge: Cambridge University Press.

Savinskaia, O., ed. 2008. *Rabota i sem'ia v zhizni zhenshchin s det'mi-doshkol'nikami: opyt goroda Moskvy* (Work and family in the life of mothers of preschool-age children). Moscow: Variant.

Schor, Naomi. 1992. "Feminist and Gender Studies." In *Introduction to Scholarship in Modern Languages and Literatures*, ed. Joseph Gibaldi, 262–287. New York.

Semenova, V. 1996. "Babushki: Semeinye i sotsial'nye funktsii praroditel'skogo pokoleniia" (Family and social functions of the grandparent generation). In *Sud'by liudei: Rossia XX vek. Biografii semei kak ob"ekt sotsiologicheskogo issledovaniia* (People's fates: Twentieth-century Russia; Family biography as the subject of sociological research), eds. V. Semenova and E. Fateeva, 326–354. Moscow: Institut Sotsiologii RAN.

Shevchenko, Olga. 2009. *Crisis and the Everyday in Postsocialist Moscow*. Bloomington, IN: Indiana University Press.

Smith, Dorothy E. 2002. "A Feminist Methodology." In *The Everyday Life Reader*, ed. Ben Highmore, 271–281. London: Routledge. (Orig. pub. 1987.)

Teplova, Tatyana. 2007. "Welfare State Transformation, Childcare, and Women's Work in Russia." *Social Politics: International Studies in Gender, State and Society* 14, no. 3: 284–322.

Visson, L. 2004. "Uroki vospitaniia Vani Smita: deti v rossiisko-amerikanskikh sem'iakh" (Parenting Vanya Smith: Children in Russian-American families). In *Semeinye uzy: modeli dlia sborki,* (Family Bonds: Models to Assemble) ed. Sergei Oushakine, 2: 9–31. Moscow: Novoe Literaturoe Obozrenie.

Wall, Karin. 2007. "Leave Policy Models and the Articulation of Work and Family in Europe: A Comparative Perspective." In *International Review of Leave Policies and Related Research 2007*, eds. Karin Wall and Peter Moss, 25–43. London: BERR.

Zaslavskaia, Tatiana. 2002. "O sotsial'nykh faktorakh raskhozhdeniia formal'no-pravovykh norm i real'nykh praktik" (On social factors in the discrepancy between formal legal norms and actual practices). In *Kuda idet Rossiia? Formal'nye instituty i real'nye praktiki* (Whither Russia? Formal institutions and actual practices), ed. Tatiana Zaslavskaia, 11–21. Moscow: Moskovskaia Vysshaia Shkola Sotsial'nykh i Ekonomicheskikh Nauk.

Zdravomyslova, Elena. 2008. "Niani: kommertsializatsiia zaboty i izmeneniia gendernogo kontrakta (Nannies: The commercialization of care and change of the gender contract)." In *Social'naia politika v sovremennoi Rossii: reformy i povsednevnost'* (Social policy and contemporary Russia: Reforms and the everyday), eds. Pavel Romanov and Elena Iarskaia-Smirnova, 320–348. Moscow: CSPGI Variant.

Zdravomyslova, Elena, Anna Rotkirch, and Anna Temkina, eds. 2009. *Novyi byt v sovremennoi Rossii: gendernye issledovaniia povsednevnosti* (The new way of life in contemporary Russia: Gender studies of the everyday). St. Petersburg: EUSPb.

Zdravomyslova, Olga. 2002. "Rossiiskaia sem'ia v 90-e gody: Zhiznennye strategii muzhchin i zhenshchin" (The Russian family in the '90s: Life strategies of men and women). In *Gendernyi kaleidoskop. Kurs lektsii* (The gender kaleidoscope. Lectures), ed. Marina Malysheva, 473–489. Moscow: Academia.

CHAPTER 10

Single Mothers—Clients or Citizens?
Social Work with Poor Families in Russia

ELENA IARSKAIA-SMIRNOVA AND PAVEL ROMANOV

INTRODUCTION

As the standard of living decreased during market reforms in Russia, the pressure on the social welfare system increased considerably. Due to the costliness and ineffectiveness of universalistic approaches, means-tested schemes became the dominant form of social support. That has led to a decrease in the number of groups eligible for welfare, and to the introduction of monetary benefits instead of social services and privileges (such as free public transport and reduced fees for communal services). The process of social policy liberalization in contemporary Russia is characterized by this shift to a market welfare system and the use of means-testing in the distribution of welfare and social support. The system of means-tested assistance (*adresnaia pomoshch'*) now depends, more than before, on social workers to determine the degree of need (*nuzhdaemost'*—neediness)[1] and reliability of the clients' applications. The procedures and techniques for checking "neediness" are not fully defined; nor are they or the legal status of such procedures clearly described. Thus this process was given to executors guided in this area by everyday life definitions, stereotypes, and informal organizational norms within the welfare services. Although means-tested assistance was supposed to increase the effectiveness of the social welfare system, it nevertheless has negative effects on the most vulnerable parts of the population, especially women with small children.

In the contemporary theory of social welfare, the concept of citizenship as formulated by T.H. Marshall (1998) is one of the key theoretical tools used to explore the distribution of rights and responsibilities among different groups in a society. In recent decades feminist scholars have provided an understanding of how various groups of a population (depending on their gender, race, and other categorical attributes) are included in or excluded from various spheres of social life (Bussemaker and van Kersbergen, 1994; Lister, 1997; Okin, 1992; Walby, 1994). They also emphasize that there is a direct connection between the discourses and practices of state welfare policies with respect to various population groups and how these groups perform their role as citizens (Lessa, 2006). In this chapter we aim to examine the discourses created and reproduced through the interaction between single mothers and representatives of social services. In the process of interaction, clients tend to have similar perceptions of their social rights (opportunities and limitations), while social workers arrive at an understanding of the essence of the problems their clients experience and the criteria for inclusion into the client category.

The analysis is based on twenty-six interviews with single mothers and six interviews with social workers conducted in 2001–2003, and six interviews with single mothers and three with social workers conducted in 2006 in the Saratov region in Russia,[2] as well as official documents and the publications of other researchers. In our interviews with mothers, we focused on the issues of familial well-being and interactions with social services, while social workers were asked to discuss their experiences with clients.

A short overview of statistics and social policy terminology prefaces a discussion of how mother-headed families and state social policy interrelate and affect each other. The subsequent sections contain analysis of the interviews with single mothers who, as the heads of low-income households, interact with the social service system. The analysis demonstrates that single mothers are frustrated by inadequate assistance and the impossibility of improving their life situations. The discussion goes on to show that social workers, who are used to interpreting complex issues in the life situations of single mothers as individual psychological peculiarities, tend to blame the victim, thus ignoring important social conditions and imposing on women a responsibility for problems that are societal in origin.

One-parent Families in the Rhetoric and Practice of State Social Policy

The number of women who are raising their children without a spouse or a partner is increasing worldwide. The same process has been observed in recent decades in Russia, where the number of one-parent families has been steadily rising. By 1989 every seventh child under eighteen years old was living in a one-parent family (Brui, 1998, p. 73). Thirty years ago the proportion of out-of-wedlock births was hardly more than 10 percent, while by 2006, according to official statistics, the number of such births was 29–30 percent (UNDP, 2009, p. 47; see also Vishnevskii and Bobylev, 2009). In 1979 the proportion of one-parent families was 14.74 percent (Breeva, 1999, p. 103), while according to the census data, between 1989 and 2002 the ratio of one-parent families increased from 15.2 percent to 21.7 percent (Ovcharova et al., 2007).

In the lexicon of Russian officials, social workers, journalists, and teachers, the widespread expression "an incomplete family" reflects a vision of the nuclear family unit (mother–father–child/children) as the "complete," "normal," "full" family structure. It needs to be stressed that in a legal sense the term "single mother" in Russia refers only to women who have borne children out of wedlock. Such a status entitles a woman to some additional benefits from the regional government, which makes the single mother's income dependent on the region's economic wealth. The benefit is usually insignificant. For instance, as of January 1, 2008, in Saratov Oblast, the basic monthly child allowance for families with a per capita income below the subsistence minimum was 225 rubles (U.S. $ 8.8) and 450 rubles (U.S. $ 17.5) for a single mother, while the subsistence minimum was 4,125 rubles for an adult and 3,988 rubles for a child (U.S. $ 160.5 and U.S. $ 155.2 correspondingly).[3]

If a woman has been married or the fatherhood was recorded according to special procedures in a court or registry office (*Semeinyi kodeks...*, 1995, art. 48, 49), she is entitled to alimony, which is seen as an alternative to a state benefit. In a wider societal sense, single mothers are those who raise their children without a spouse, including those women who are divorced or widowed. As a rule, all such families are called "incomplete" (*nepolnye*) or "mother-headed families" (*materinskie*). Low-income "incomplete" families are entitled to receive support and services at local agencies. In the present chapter, the term "single mother" includes all households with a woman as a solo parent.

The needs of low-income families in the Soviet Union were recognized in 1974 when target monetary allowances were introduced. In the 1980s the state's concern about the well-being of children in one-parent families was reflected in the establishment of some modest measures for their support, including some small monetary benefits and privileged access to childcare services. On the whole, the Soviet approach encouraged economic equality and gave women raising their children alone a degree of independence. However, the implementation of Soviet welfare policies worked against their intended purpose. Financial support provided to single mothers could not significantly improve their living standard and contributed to their stigmatization by separating them into a special group of the needy.

In the early 1990s both the level of real wages and the capability of households and individuals to cover their expenses seriously declined (Ovcharova and Prokof'eva, 2002), and the development of the labor market was rather unfavorable for women (UNICEF, 1999). All this has played a major role in worsening the life situation of the majority of one-parent families. The decrease in the state social-protection programs, the lack of accessible childcare services, the shortage of options in the labor market, and gender inequality in career opportunities have put single mothers at a high risk of poverty. As a result, single-mother households came to have among the lowest economic status of any households in Russia (Lokshin et al., 2000; Ovcharova, 2008).

Three main factors hinder the full realization of the social rights of single mothers and limit their capacity to remain relatively autonomous economic actors and sustain an acceptable standard of living for them and their children. These factors are 1) limited access to the labor market and a low level of work performance due to the high pressure of combining waged work and childcare; 2) an inadequate level of support from registered fathers (alimony); and 3) a low level of state support and public transfers for the families of single mothers (Lokshin et al., 2000). Due to the decrease of public assistance during the economic reforms in Russia, single mothers have faced a higher risk of poverty and have therefore preferred to live with other adults or relatives.

According to the 2002 census, the majority of children under eighteen years old live in families with both parents (73 percent) and have at least one sibling (52 percent). Half of the rest of the children live in "incomplete" families with one parent, while the others live in households of a complex structure (Prokof'eva, 2007, p. 261). This means that every second single mother in Russia lives with her parents, adult siblings, or other adult relatives (Lokshin et al., 2000). The statistics show that in the 1990s and for a few years thereafter, the proportion of nuclear families in the population structure decreased from 80 percent to 70.8 percent (Prokof'eva, 2007, p. 261). In 2002 monoparental families comprised more than 25 percent of all families and 30 percent of families with children under eighteen (mostly headed by mothers). Quite often such families are parts of another household, as they live with relatives (41.9 percent). This is especially true of families with children under eighteen (53 percent) (ibid., p. 259). Although such a strategy has a range of advantages, it certainly results in a lack of autonomy and privacy.

The most recent changes in the structure of child allowance included an increase in the size of transfers, the introduction of a means-tested model of assistance and special support to children of single parents, and the stimulation of fertility rates by means of large lump sums for bearing children. However, if we take into account the existing budgetary restraints, the present situation is far from optimal. As the data show (Ovcharova, 2008;

Ovcharova and Prokof'eva, 2002), the welfare programs are inadequate to deal with the enormous poverty in Russia. Single mothers receive less public assistance than ever, while fathers often ignore their responsibilities with impunity. Almost 40 percent of single-mother families in Russia were below the poverty line in 1996, and this proportion continues to grow (Luniakova, 2001, p. 95). By the end of 2006, the poverty level in Russia was 12.8 percent, while the poverty risk for families with small children is two times higher (Ovcharova et al., 2007). According to the Generations and Gender Survey data, in 2007 "incomplete families" with children comprised 18.3 percent of all families with children, including 2.7 percent of families with one parent who is not working, 4.6 percent of families with one parent who is working for a wage below the subsistence minimum, and 5.7 percent of families with one parent who is working but earning below the subsistence minimum for one adult and one child (Burdiak et al., 2009, p. 148). The parental leave and income replacement have increased significantly in recent years and are now tied to previous incomes.[4] At the same time, the monthly child allowance available to low-income families has not been reconsidered and still provides no more than four percent of the subsistence minimum for a child. Therefore, if a woman fails to find a well-paid job with a wage above the subsistence minimum by the time her child is 1.5 years old, the life situation in such a family, especially a single-parent family, will be quite poor (Ovcharova et al., 2007).

The academic discourses on single mothers in various research areas have an impact on the political agenda. Works devoted to the financial circumstances of one-parent families are written from a neutral perspective (Kalabikhina, 2002, pp. 96–97; Ovcharova and Prokof'eva, 2002; Ustinova, 1992), while publications on upbringing contain moralizing, shaming, and blaming that serves to stigmatize single mothers and their children (Dement'eva, 2001, pp. 108–109). In the 1990s and a few years thereafter, several researchers problematized state policy toward one-parent families in Russia. They looked at discourses created through official documents and practices from the point of view of human rights and studied the diversity of life strategies of single mothers (Baskakova, 1998; Karimova, 2007; Kiblitskaia, 1999; Liborakina, 1999; Luniakova, 1998, 2002, 2004; Malysheva, 2001, pp. 325–326). Demographical data on the rapid increase of the single-parent population in Russia are sometimes overdramatized, which contributes to widespread societal concern about the crisis of the traditional nuclear family as a social institution and constructs a general image of mother-headed families as deficient, pathological, and a source of social problems. Moral arguments have tended to stigmatize single parents by stressing their economic dependency as evidence of their inferiority (see the criticism of such approaches in Iarskaia-Smirnova, 1998; Iarskaia-Smirnova and Romanov, 2007, 2008).

In his 2006 presidential address, Vladimir Putin declared 2008 the Year of the Family in Russia, thus launching an extensive propaganda campaign. Numerous actions, celebrations, special days, and other symbolic activities have been arranged to highlight the pronatalist mission of the new family policy. Most recent publications that critically examine the new social policy initiatives (Chernova, 2008; Gurko, 2008; Maleva and Siniavskaia, 2007; Ovcharova et al., 2007; UNDP, 2009) conclude that the rhetoric of official documents dealing with the position of the family and children in many respects presumes the normality of the nuclear family unit. From the official viewpoint, single mothers continue to be rather "problematic" citizens.

Single Mothers: The Discourse of "Unworthy" Citizens

Formal procedures: preconditions for exclusion
The social welfare sector in Russia covers a variety of agencies that provide direct care and support to service users according to Federal Law No. 195-FZ (1995). The main component of family and child services is work with families, which encompasses family care centers, rehabilitation facilities for children with disabilities and children from families at risk, part-time day-care facilities, and nursing homes for mentally disabled children. The clients of the social services are predominantly women and include mothers of many children (*mnogodetnye materi*[5]), mothers of children with disabilities, and single mothers. Agencies such as departments of social security, centers for social services, departments (or centers) for the assistance of family, women and children, and family centers provide clients with various services, including means-tested assistance in kind, home care, psychosocial and social-medical care, and vouchers for free meals.

According to Decree N 60-P, issued by the Saratov Oblast Government on June 1, 2001 (Postanovlenie..., 2001), the criteria of eligibility for means-tested assistance are based on a combination of the following conditions: evidence-based confirmation of per capita income below the subsistence minimum; the absence of potential sources of income such as a mortgage, savings, or a plot of land; and a difficult life situation. The neediness of a family is to be identified in every individual case by the local social security agency.

In Russia the monthly base rate of aid per child is 6.4 percent of the minimum wage (as of March 2007) and less than 0.6 percent of the average monthly wage (UNDP, 2008, p. 56). According to the "Concept of Means-Tested Assistance for the Population of Saratov Oblast," "the neediness of a family and an individual living alone is defined by the social protection agencies at the place of residence in accordance with the Federal Law on State Social Assistance" (Kontseptsiia razvitiia sistemy adresnoi sotsial'noi pomoshchi naseleniiu Saratovskoi oblasti, 2002). The social protection agencies have the right to check the accuracy of the information presented to them by any means that are not in contradiction with the legislation of the Russian Federation (Smirnov and Kolosnitsyn). As a consequence, the principles of means-tested assistance have introduced ambivalence into the professional identity of social workers: "But I feel hurt by this means-tested assistance" (Social worker, Krasnoarmeisk, 2002).

Until 1999, child allowances were officially allocated according to the universal principle, but in 1999 federal law introduced a means test. The right to receive a monthly child benefit was assigned to one of the parents in families whose income per capita was below the subsistence minimum. The idea of improved targeting was based on the assumption that "because they are spread over a large number of people, many of them not poor, average benefits are often very small. For example, basic child allowances range from only 70 to 105 rubles a month (U.S. $ 2.7–U.S. $ 4.1), which is not enough to have a significant impact on poverty" (World Bank, June 2007, p. 20). Child allowances were financed from the federal budget in 2001–2004, but the regions could use their own budgets to allocate child allowances more broadly. Since the introduction of Federal Law No. 122-FZ (2004), the size, rules of allocation, and transfers of child allowance have become the responsibility of the regional budgets.

While a great deal of social assistance in the country is still not targeted specifically at the poor, Russia has been developing targeted social assistance in three areas: child allowances, housing and utility allowances, and regional programs for the poor (ibid.). Targeted or means-tested assistance (*adresnaia pomoshch*) is a kind of service conducted under the jurisdiction of the regions of the Russian Federation. The value of monetary and in-kind assistance varies according to the size of budget allocation in the given territory. Regional and municipal legislation typically lists the categories of clients eligible for such a service (usually including low-income families), the types of assistance, and the documents to be submitted to prove eligibility. In addition to these documents, living conditions are assessed and documented by the agency. Apart from this kind of service, regular benefits are provided on a universal basis and include non-recurrent transfers after the birth of a child, monthly transfers during maternity leave, and monthly child allowances up to eighteen months. The service users consider the most important benefit to be childcare, followed by child allowances and support to help the family get started after childbirth. Other targeted kinds of support are ranked lower (Trygged, 2009, p. 208).

The impact of the policy change from universal to means-tested child allowances on targeting efficiency and poverty reduction is not clear. Analysis (Gassmann and Notten, 2006, pp. 26–27) has shown that targeting is not perfect, that there are errors of exclusion, and that the very modest size of the benefits decreases their impact on the poorest households, in which children are disproportionately more numerous. A number of problems have been identified related to the design of targeted or means-tested "assistance programs, the measurement and verification of income, and insufficient cooperation among government bodies in sharing information" (World Bank, June 2007).

This model requires but does not have proper methods for income monitoring, which leads to significant errors of inclusion (entitling those who are not poor to a benefit) and errors of exclusion (refusing to entitle those who are poor). Women with small children must collect many documents[6] to establish their right to social assistance—to claim the benefits to which they have been guaranteed by the state, and which they often perceive as inadequate: "What can I buy with a hundred rubles, tell me? Nothing. Maybe two pairs of socks, which we will wear out in two months" (single mother Tatiana, Saratov 2002).[7] For rural inhabitants the procedure of registering for such an allowance is too expensive because they have to travel to a bigger town to access a welfare agency, and the ticket sometimes costs more than the allowance itself.

Schools in rural areas usually have their own garden plots, but these are not enough to provide meals to all children, in fact not even those legally entitled to be exempted from fees:

> I am [entitled to it] as a single mother, my girl should get meals for free there. But here [at school] I'm supposed to give them food, fifty rubles per month [...] They have no finances [and tell us]—pay, that's all! And if there is no money—they stop feeding [the child]. I say: wait, I'll get a salary, I'll get a children's [allowance] and I'll pay! Not at all—the month ends, and the child doesn't get any food! (Single mother Maria, Lysye Gory, Saratov Oblast, 2006)

The state and local governments attempt to alleviate poverty by paying needy families a small benefit, but such assistance does little when a household budget cannot cope with the cost of living:

> [...] they are far below the poverty line, they live in misery and nobody is going to help them. [They] just give them one thousand rubles per year, that's all.[8] Some children cannot even go to school because they have nothing to wear, let alone textbooks, notebooks, etc. (Social worker, Lysie Gory, Saratov Oblast, 2006)

For some single mothers, cheap assistance in kind seems to be another instrument of deprivation and social inequality. These feelings are usually connected to discussions about unequal access to certain resources among clients of different status—mothers of many children and single mothers:

> There was help, once or twice, perhaps. It looked funny—a kilo of flour not of the best quality, a kilo of macaroni—all of this we can afford ourselves. My child never has fruit, but they bring us the same groceries that we buy ourselves—the cheapest, the worst. I know they provide help for children with disabilities, for families of many children, while single mothers are forgotten. (Single mother Natalia, Krasnoarmeisk, Saratov Oblast, 2002)

In the quote above, the client compares her situation with that of other groups of "needy" people. Such a presumption—that some important resources are in the hands of the less worthy—is a traditional theme in narratives of social services clients. Inequality of status, doubtful and nontransparent criteria for division into worthy and unworthy—all of this raises inner conflicts and feelings of being outcasts. This is how the inspection procedures and size of the benefits are subjectively perceived by the clients, who in turn tend to look upon social workers and welfare organizations as alien forces. As Peter Blau (1960, p. 348) indicates in his study of a public welfare agency in a big American city, the clients were in dire need, since the assistance allowance, originally set low, never caught up with inflation. Needless to say, those who function as monitoring agents also feel alienated from the clients. Blau has shown that the new case worker was typically very sympathetic toward clients but that an internalization of bureaucratic constraints could limit the service. Lynne Haney (2000) has shown in her research on welfare restructuring in Hungary that the shift from the socialist-era universalist welfare regime to the (neo-)liberal regime of poverty regulation has meant that all needs are now conceived of only in material terms, and social support has been reduced to poverty relief. New surveillance techniques and disciplinary welfare practices have been introduced, and social workers strive to increase the distance between them and their clients.

Structural limitations and direct discrimination
Lack of awareness is one of the common problems reported by the informants. It is related to a wide range of issues, from not knowing their rights to a lack of information concerning the existing services, certain benefits, and resources. Such a situation is most characteristic of small towns and rural areas, where formal networks are limited and informal networks are sometimes weak or have dissolved. Although the proportion of single-parent households in rural areas is lower than in urban areas, such households experience much higher levels of poverty. As earlier research has shown, in rural areas job opportunities are limited for women who are single mothers (see Golubeva, 2007; Urbanskaia, 2004). These limitations are the combined effect of structural problems in the rural labor market (remote areas, poor transportation, low wages, few job options, low territorial mobility, the seasonal nature of work), the traditional limitations on "women's work" available there, and difficulties caused by the monoparental status of the household. All this increases the social isolation and deprivation of single mothers. As Iaroshenko (2004) has noted, monoparental families in rural areas are the most frequent users of public services because it is difficult for them to combine paid and unpaid work. The means of public assistance cannot compensate for their low incomes and help them overcome poverty.

The share of public and private transfers into the family budget is much higher for households with a single mother than for an average Russian household. In those where a single mother lives with her parents, the share of income from pensions is higher than the share of income from wages. At the same time, for single-parent households with children, the share of income from benefits is almost seven times lower than from wages (Lokshin et al., 2000). The meaning of all these statistical calculations is captured in a comment by one of our respondents in 2003: "Do you call seventy rubles a [sufficient] benefit? [laughing]" (single mother Marina, Balashov, Saratov Oblast, 2003).[9]

Due to the limitations outlined above, some of the informants living in small towns do not enter the field of social support. The role of a client is unacceptable to them not because they are able to manage on their own, but because the system does not have any significant effect on their lives.

When asked whether the Center of Social Services provides her with any help, one of our informants said: "I do not even know where it is located" (single mother Marina, Balashov, Saratov Oblast, 2003).

There are more working women among single mothers than among married women with children. In 1996, 81 percent of single mothers living with children were employed, compared with 71 percent of mothers in nuclear families (Lokshin et al., 2000). Our research supports data collected by Kiblitskaia (1999), who has shown that many single mothers face discrimination and violations of their rights in the area of employment, and humiliation and open rudeness in their interaction with officials. Our respondents also reported that they often encountered undisguised hostility or ultimate indifference from the bureaucratic structures:

> Some time ago I was registered at the employment office. I remember it very well, I was coming to a job interview, and as soon they learned that I had two children, they immediately rejected me. For instance, in PTU [vocational school] No. 15 they said that when my children get sick, I will go on sick leave, and that is unprofitable for them. I said, "Well, write that and make it official—that you reject me for that reason." They did not put it in writing. I tried to work at the market as a shop assistant. But if I work the whole day, my kids are abandoned. (Single mother Liubov, Balashov, Saratov Oblast, 2003)

A similarly desperate situation may occur when single mothers attempt to enroll their children in childcare. For example, Irina, whose only source of income is a child allowance, reported that she was planning to get a job to improve her financial situation. However, the issue of employment was related to the need to place her three-and-a-half-year-old child in a kindergarten. Although single mothers have priority in getting a place that is supposed to be given to them free of charge, Irina was unable to resolve this issue on her own or through the authorities.

Combining paid work and the care of their children is one of the most crucial issues for single mothers. The work biographies of women reflect the cycles in their children's upbringing—the loss of a job or leaving university coincides for many with the birth of a child, while getting another job or moving from one workplace to another occurs as children grow up, enter kindergarten, school, and college. Single mothers lack support in the home, so such cycles have an especially powerful influence on their biographies.

Some women hope to improve their life situation as their children grow up:

Maybe some day [my life] will change. These [kids] will grow up and go to kindergarten. Mom will go to work, then the children will go to school, and Mom will also work.
(Single mother Irina, Krasnoarmeisk, Saratov Oblast, 2002)

Older children in the family increase the probability that their single parents will be able to live more independently. According to census data, the proportion of nuclear monoparental families increases as the children grow up: 74 percent of monoparental families with children older than eighteen years do not include grandparents in the same household—this is close to the average number of nuclear families in Russia (Prokof'eva, 2007, p. 261). The oldest children can contribute to the household budget by taking paid jobs and caring for younger siblings in the family.

The ability of women to be independent economic subjects determines the degree to which they are able to enjoy their social rights. The status of single mothers, in their relations with the state and state services, is predominantly that of clients. The procedures of applying for state support, the structural conditions of the labor market, and the level of services and benefits foster the idea that single mothers are not "worthy" full citizens entitled to the same social rights as members of a "normal" nuclear family.

Social Workers: "The Smell of Poverty" Discourse

Formal procedures: who is poor?
An important aspect of social work on poverty is the conceptual space in which the clients' problems are formulated. Single mothers from small towns have clearly defined themselves in interviews: "'Poor' is not a word. Now the word is 'paupers' (*nishchie*)" (single mother Natalia, Krasnoarmeisk, Saratov Oblast, 2002). In the Russian context, the word *nishchie* is traditionally associated with beggars. In everyday life this word is used to express extreme need and deprivation. In our interviews, social workers admit that the incomes of those who come to the agency are "below the poverty line, and they are paupers rather than merely poor" (social worker, Krasnoarmeisk, Saratov Oblast, 2002). Another term, "people with limited resources" (*maloobespechennye*), is used in welfare agencies instead.

Besides lower incomes and the disadvantages of the labor market, living conditions in small towns present additional challenges. Many houses are not equipped with central heating, and the water supply and plumbing system are in very poor condition. According to the survey data, the living space (in square meters per person) for more than one-third of families with children is below established norms and does not provide what can be considered a reasonable comfort level (Ovcharova et al., 2007). The decrease in production and the economic crisis have led to a significant pauperization of the population and the appearance of the so-called "new poor" (teachers, medical professionals, social workers) in both large cities and regional towns.

Social workers often live in conditions of poverty similar to those of their clients: "Our flat is not that different from this one" (social worker, Saratov, 2002). As a result, the decision about who is or is not "needy" is based on the subjective judgment of a person who lacks perspective. Social service workers earn about 60 percent of the minimum subsistence level,

> [a salary] equivalent in size to a social benefit, which has contributed to the creation—alongside the traditional poor (the disabled, pensioners, families with many children, and single-parent families)—of an additional category that is characteristic in particular of Russia— the "working poor," meaning employed persons whose earnings do not provide a minimum subsistence level. (Chekorina, 2002, p. 172)

This fact points up a new dimension in the relationship between clients and social workers, who are predominantly women. The marginalization of social-services employees negatively impacts the quality of their work. On the one hand, social workers accept the introduction of the means-tested assistance scheme, which gives them more power in terms of control over who receives the benefits and other forms of social assistance. On the other hand, deciding who is truly worthy of aid has proven to be very difficult. The social worker perceives him/herself as an agent of state bureaucratic control, which conflicts with the humanitarian purpose of social services:

> And here you are really facing a dilemma—we provide them with help, but [they] will drink this money up, and the child will get nothing anyway. But when you visit them for an inspection and look into their eyes—it is hard.
> (Social worker, Krasnoarmeisk, Saratov Oblast, 2002)

Social workers measure poverty by various means, including inspections of housing according to the government decree mentioned above (Postanovlenie..., 2001). In order to cope with uncertainty in their everyday routine, social workers develop a discourse of poverty based on available professional concepts, common-sense values, and emotions. In interviews these codes of poverty are related to an evaluation of external characteristics of well-being that is usually done through comparison with the social worker's own conditions. According to a social worker in Krasnoarmeisk, the living conditions in such houses are hard, but comparable to those of social workers, who also receive a very small salary. The emotional encounter with poverty deeply affects social workers:

> At first, I would just come home and say, God, how well we live here, my house is strong enough, although our flat is very small and many people live here, but I told myself, how happy I am living here! And now, I've been working for two years and still cannot adjust to the appearance [of poverty]... Recently, ten days ago, I was shocked by a family—migrants moved in, two boys, a girl and a baby—four [kids]. Mother was at work, they were heating a stove. [There was a lot of] smoke—as when wood doesn't burn well, such smoke and stench. There was a table—a box crudely cobbled together out of planks—and one bed—a frame without a mattress just covered with a torn rug. They are all sitting on this bed. The majority [of our clients] live like that. (Social worker, Krasnoarmeisk, Saratov Oblast, 2002)

In one case there was a similar emotional response in a little old wooden house with low ceilings and poor furniture consisting of a table, a bed, and a very old sofa "on which I was afraid to sit" (social worker, Krasnoarmeisk, Saratov Oblast, 2002). In another case it was an apartment undergoing major repair that was not going to be completed because the owner did not have enough money: "The repair work has been going on for several years now—bare, ugly walls, the bathroom is awful, of course" (social worker, Krasnoarmeisk, Saratov Oblast, 2002). In another there was a "dark and narrow entrance hall" in a "typical old 'Khrushchev house'[10] that had not been repaired since it was built" (social worker, Saratov, 2003).

In yet another case the definitive trait was a specific smell of poverty and old things:

> It smelled there. Yes, that is perhaps what made the most powerful impression, you know what I mean? Well, it was how it smells in houses full of a lot of old things—a special smell, not that it was bad, but such a smell, rather specific. In general, it smelled old, because of the lack of ventilation, perhaps. And as for the furniture, my impres-

sion was that it was all placed here long ago and never moved since then, as though it was not 2001 but rather 1980 or even earlier. That's the kind of furniture they had there. (Social worker, Saratov, 2003)

The untidiness of the dwelling plays an important role in descriptions and evaluations that later are extended to the appearance of the women clients: they all "looked gray," except for one, who "more or less takes care of herself."

Analyzing their remarks about poverty, we saw that these external signs of neglect influence the social worker's conclusion: "we at once see a person who cares and another who neglects herself [...] even rarely washes her face, it seems" (social worker, Krasnoarmeisk, Saratov Oblast, 2002). Our informants seemed to find special words to describe single mothers who keep up a neat appearance and elicit sympathy: "Not just clean but rather neat, well-groomed poverty" (social worker, Saratov, 2003). Social workers, who are authorized by the system of means-tested assistance to determine "neediness," construct their own "tacit knowledge" about poverty out of the repertoire of images from their own life experience.

Subjective categorizations
The relationships that single mothers and other categories of clients have with employees of social services and employment services and educational institutions are built upon a complex ideology in which the state and the providing agency play an important role. Thus the specific (self-)definitions of people as clients have certain consequences both for individual biographies and on a structural scale. The reaction of service users towards the activity of the social work agency results in a classification of clients as "thankful" or "unthankful:"

> There was one woman with three children, an incomplete family. When we came to her for an inspection and later brought food to her—when you see her eyes, you understand, yes, we are useful, people need us. And sometimes it happens that [clients] come and are rude, but you smile in return, because otherwise the director will accuse you of being impolite.
> (Social worker, Krasnoarmeisk, Saratov Oblast, 2002)

> We are helping one woman, she is a teacher, [has] an incomplete family—her husband died long ago—well, they live so-so—and when provided with assistance, she feels ashamed, because she works. [...] And

she was so thankful—frankly speaking, it was pleasant. She was provided that help because it really went to the right place.
(Social worker, Krasnoarmeisk, Saratov Oblast, 2002)

Such a form of "moral knowledge" could be seen as serving to justify professional practice, and it shapes the service providers' everyday definition of social work. Poverty as explained by social workers places single mothers as social service clients into a separate group burdened with specific problems. In social service there is no attempt to analyze the causes of poverty:

The social worker just puts it down as a fact and thinks, "What can I do? For instance, do we have spaghetti today? Yes. We'll give you some. All right, are you registered in [the division of] urgent social assistance—no? Well, we'll do that." But why [the person] is poor, what are the reasons—no leg, no arm, mentally deficient, why or how—[I] never heard social workers or clients talking about it, about poverty in general. (Social worker, Saratov, 2003)

By saving resources, government ideologies create a gap between clients and social workers, which may explain why clients view practitioners not as sources of help but as obstacles that must be overcome to get required services (Dominelli, 2004). Social welfare administration in Russia was inherited from the Soviet regime, with its central planning and rigid system of social security based in public institutions. The general modernization of the system of social welfare in Russia is an ongoing process nowadays, and it has had a contradictory effect on social work ideology. Rather than following the paternalist scheme of thought and action, social workers are gradually acquiring new knowledge and skills to effect social change in a democratic egalitarian way. Each successfully completed case—helping the client to find a job, to accumulate resources and networks—generates a more positive attitude towards the agency and the workers. It is important for the government, non-governmental organizations, and the academic community to focus more on critical issues in social welfare, the development of conflict resolution skills, and the development of social services research. Democratic egalitarian and non-discriminatory ideology is required in social services as well as in social work training (Iarskaia-Smirnova, 2011).

Social work that is reduced to checking neediness or to material assistance to the poor cannot be an effective means of solving the economic problems of single mothers, and it does not remove the symbolic boundaries that exclude them from the category of "normal families." Many of our social worker informants understand this. Describing the strategies of social work with clients, one informant emphasized the need to avoid complex issues when diagnosing and dealing with problems. Social service employees "prefer not to dig too deep, because they are afraid they might dig up something they think they might not be able to solve. Usually they do something but not all they could; they do the minimum possible" (social worker, Saratov, 2003). This reluctance is related primarily to the limited resources and possibilities available to social workers and agencies. It also reflects the lack of competence among social workers who have no professional training and are not confident in their ability to analyze and treat a problem correctly.

A client's problems might stem from beliefs in traditional gender roles and traditional family definitions, which presume that women are unequal and subordinate. Because they often subscribe to such definitions, however, models of social work practice aggravate the condition of women. Moreover, not only in the mass media but even in social-work textbooks, single mothers are often portrayed as immoral or unfortunate and considered dangerous to their own children and to society as a whole (Iarskaia-Smirnova and Romanov, 2008). Furthermore, instead of bringing women with similar experiences together, which could provide group support, practitioners try to solve the problems of each woman separately. Dividing the poor into deserving and undeserving has proved to be a useful means for scientifically rationalizing resource allocation.

Conclusion

Although single mothers in many countries of the world share the same problems, due to variations in social welfare systems and models of social policy and social work practice, the position of this social group differs from one nation to another. In Russia the families of single mothers confront some of the same transitional-society problems as several other population groups, including insufficient social assistance resources, a low level of state support, and the collapse of many social networks. At the same time, single mothers must deal with the additional negative factors of social isolation and stigmatization, relegation to the less prestigious sector of the labor market, and treatment as clients whose "neediness" is subject to scrutiny.

Our research sheds light on the role of state policies in forming the patterns of family structure and providing opportunities for a decent level of life. Whether single mothers secure their rights as citizens depends on how "friendly" the state is toward women in general and female-headed families in particular, as indicated by a widely developed network of public services, the availability of childcare, and opportunities for paid work. It is important for women to be able to choose either to provide care themselves or to delegate it to public services.

The experiences of social workers and their clients demonstrate that single mothers are stigmatized as clients whose claims to social rights may be invalidated by professional experts. As a result, because social work is trapped in existing stereotypes, rules of justification, and patterns of behavior, it helps sustain inequality in society. The discourses examined in the practice of social work with single mothers reflect the fact that some categories of people are perceived as "worthy" of social rights, while others are not. This idea is being internalized and legitimized by both sides of the social worker-client relationship.

The growing level of poverty among single parents in Russia, together with additional indicators of the decreasing quality of life in their families, shows how important it is to tackle this problem immediately at the political level by reconsidering the forms and procedures of social assistance. It is also necessary to improve single mothers' ability to (re-) enter the labor market and to guarantee them non-discrimination in recruitment and career opportunities.

Notes

1. The new term "neediness" (*nuzhdaemost'*) was invented in the late 1990s to convey the status of a person in need subject to regular checking before being entitled to a benefit or in-kind assistance.
2. Part of this research was conducted within an international project led by Rolv Lyngstad, University of Bodö, Norway (see Lyngstad et al., 2004).
3. The size of payments is calculated based on the currency rate in November, 2011.
4. Beginning on January 1, 2007, the child allowance is calculated as 40 percent of the average salary for the last twelve months prior to maternity leave but not less than 1,500 rubles per month for the first child, 3,000 rubles for the second (this minimum is also provided for a non-working woman). The maximum sum for such an allowance is fixed as 6,000 rubles (U.S. $ 1 = 26.5 rubles in January 2007).
5. In contemporary Russia, as in the USSR, families with three and more children are classified in the special category "families with many children." They are

entitled to a number of services and privileges not available to other categories of families.
6 Birth certificate, income certificates for all household members, certificate of place of residence, divorce (or death of spouse) certificate, medical certificate (in the case of a child's disability), and inspection report.
7 According to Law No. 134-3CO of Saratov Oblast of August 1, 2007, effective January 1, 2008, the monthly allowance for children in Saratov Oblast was increased from 100 to 225 rubles. A single mother receives twice as much (U.S. $ 1 = 24.5 rubles on January 10, 2008).
8 The citizens of Saratov are eligible for this transfer once a year if they find themselves in an extremely difficult situation. If the statement by a special commission determines that the applicant and family members do not demonstrate the initiative to provide for the family and that they lead "a parasitic way of life," material assistance is denied.
9 Seventy rubles in 2003 (equivalent to U.S. $ 2.50) was a universal child benefit. A single mother receives twice as much.
10 A "Khrushchev house" is an apartment house built during the period of Khrushchev's housing policy; it is usually a five-story building with small apartments.

References

Baskakova, Marina. 1998. "Problemy i prava rabotnikov s semeinymi obiazannostiami" (Problems and rights of employees with familial responsibilities). In *Prava zhenshchin v Rossii: issledovanie real'noi praktiki ikh sobliudenia i massovogo soznania (po resul'tatam anketnogo oprosa)* (Women's rights in Russia: A study of their observance and mass consciousness [based on a survey]), ed. N.A. Kochneva, 235–258. Moscow: MCGS, Institute of Socioeconomic Problems.
Blau, Peter M. 1960. "Orientation toward Clients in a Public Welfare Agency." *Administrative Science Quarterly* 5, no. 3: 341–361.
Breeva, Elena. 1999. *Deti v sovremennom obshchestve* (Children in modern society). Moscow: Editorial URSS.
Brui, B. 1998. "Vliianie sotsial'nykh i mediko-demograficheskikh faktorov na uroven' rozhdaemosti v Rossii" (The influence of social and medico-demographic factors on the birth rate in Russia). *Voprosy statistiki* 1: 72–74.
Burdiak, Aleksandra, Irina Korchagina, Lilia Ovcharova, Lidia Prokof'eva, and Oksana Siniavskaia. 2009. "Novye mery semeinoi politiki i ikh vliianie na material'no-imushchestvennoe polozhenie semei s det'mi" (New measures of family policy and their effects on the material status of families with children). In *Sem'ia v tsentre sotsial'no-demograficheskoi politiki* (Family at the center of social-demographic policy), ed. Oksana Siniavskaia, 127–160. Moscow: NISP.
Bussemaker, Jet, and Kees van Kersbergen. 1994. "Gender and Welfare States: Some Theoretical Reflections." In *Gendering Welfare States*, ed. Diane Sainsbury, 8–25. London: Sage.

Chekorina, Natal'ia. 2002. "Zhenshchiny i sotsial'naia politika v usloviiakh rynochnogo reformirovaniia" (Women and social policy under market reforms). In *Gender i ekonomika: mirovoi opyt i expertiza rossiiskoi praktiki* (Gender and economics: world experience and an assessment of Russian practice), ed. Elena Mezentseva, 249–274. Moscow: Russkaia Panorama.

Chernova, Zhanna. 2008. *Semeinaia politika v Evrope i v Rossii: gendernyi analiz* (Family policy in Europe and Russia: gender analysis). St. Petersburg: Norma.

Dement'eva, Izabella. 2001. "Negativnye faktory vospitaniia detei v nepolnoi sem'e" (Negative factors of bringing up children in incomplete families). *Sotsiologicheskie issledovaniia* 11: 108–113.

Dominelli, Lena. 2004. *Social Work: Theory and Practice for a Changing Profession.* Cambridge: Polity Press.

Federal'nyi Zakon No. 195-FZ (Federal Law No. 195-FZ). 1995. "Ob osnovakh sotsial'nogo obsluzhivaniia naseleniia v Rossiiskoi Federatsii" (On the basis of social service provision for the population of the Russian Federation), December 10, 1995.

Federal'nyi Zakon No. 122-FZ (Federal Law No. 122-FZ). 2004. "O vnesenii izmenenii v zakonodatel'nye akty Rossiiskoi Federatsii [...]" (On introducing amendments into legislative acts of the Russian Federation [...]), August 22, 2004.

Gassmann, Franziska, and Geranda Notten. 2006. "Size Matters: Targeting Efficiency and Poverty Reduction Effects of Means-Tested and Universal Child Benefits in Russia." *Global Action on Aging,* www.globalaging.org/elderrights/world/russia.pdf (accessed April 24, 2011).

Golubeva, Lidia. 2007. "Osobennosti zhenskogo truda v sel'sko-khoziaistvennom proizvodstve" (Peculiarities of female labor in agricultural production). *Vestnik Tambovskogo universiteta* 5: 296–299.

Gurko, Tatiana. 2008. "Alimenty: factor kachestvennogo i kolichestvennogo vosproizvodstva naseleniia" (Alimony: a factor of the qualitative and quantitative reproduction of the population). *Sotsiologicheskie issledovaniia* 9, no. 110– 120.

Haney, Lynne. 2000. "Global Discourses of Need: Mythologizing and Pathologizing Welfare in Hungary." In *Global Ethnography: Forces, Connections and Imaginations in a Postmodern World,* ed. Michael Burawoy, 48–73. Berkeley: University of California Press.

Iaroshenko, Svetlana. 2004. "Bednost' nezavisimosti" (The poverty of independence). *Sotsiologicheskie issledovaniia* 7: 71–83.

Iarskaia-Smirnova, Elena. 1998. "Problematizatsiia sem'i v sotsiologii" (Problematization of the family in sociology). *Rubezh* 12: 71–87.

———. 2011. "Professional Ideologies in Russian Social Work: Challenges from Inside and Outside." In *Social Work Education in Countries of the East: Issues and Challenges,* ed. Stanley Selwyn. Hauppauge, NY: Nova Science Publishers.

Iarskaia-Smirnova, Elena, and Pavel Romanov. 2007. "Gender in Russian Textbooks on Social Policy and Social Work, 1997–2004." In *Weibliche und mannliche Entwurfe des Sozialen,* eds. Elke Kruse and Evelyn Tegeler, 215–227. Opladen, Germany, and Farmington Hills, MI: Verlag Barbara Budrich.

———. 2008. "Gendering Social Work in Russia: Towards Anti-Discriminatory Practices." *Equal Opportunities* 27, no. 1: 64–76.

Kalabikhina, Irina. 2002. "Teoreticheskie napravleniia gendernogo analiza domokhozaistva i nekotorye voprosy sotsial'noi politiki" (Theoretical perspectives of gender analysis of the household and some issues of social policy). In *Gender i ekonomika: mirovoi opyt i expertiza rossiiskoi praktiki* (Gender and economics: World experience and expertise of Russian practice), ed. Elena Mezentseva, 88–105. Moscow: Russkaia Panorama.

Karimova, Zilia. 2007. "Zhiznennye tsennosti odinokikh materei" (Life values of single mothers). *Sotsiologicheskie issledovaniia* 6: 131–134.

Kiblitskaia, Marina. 1999. *Ispovedi odinokikh materei* (Confessions of single mothers). Moscow: Eslan.

Kontseptsiia razvitiia sistemy adresnoi sotsial'noi pomoshchi naseleniiu Saratovskoi oblasti (Concept of the development of the system of means-tested assistance to the population of Saratov Oblast). 2002. Saratov.

Lessa, Iara. 2006. "Discursive Struggles within Social Welfare: Restaging Teen Motherhood." *British Journal of Social Work* 36, no. 2: 283–298.

Liborakina, Marina. 1999. *Zhenshchiny i privatizatsiia* (Women and privatization). Moscow: Fond "Institut Ekonomiki Goroda."

Lister, Ruth. 1997. *Citizenship: Feminist Perspectives*. Basingstoke, UK: Macmillan.

Lokshin, Michael, Barry Popkin, and Kathleen M. Harris. 2000. "Single Mothers in Russia: Household Strategies for Coping with Poverty." *World Bank Policy Research Working Paper*, no. 2300, http://papers.ssrn.com/sol3/papers.cfm?abstract_id=629150 (accessed June 8, 2011).

Luniakova, Larisa, 1998. "Materinskie sem'i: sobliudenie prav i garantii (na primere g. Rybinska)" (Mother-headed families: observance of rights and guarantees [the case of the city of Rybinsk]). In *Prava zhenshchin v Rossii: issledovanie real'noi praktiki ikh sobludenia i massovogo soznania (po resul'tatam anketnogo oprosa)* (Women's rights in Russia: a study of their observance and mass consciousness [based on a survey]), ed. N.A. Kochneva, 259–284. Moscow: MCGS, Institut sotsial'no-ekonomicheskikh problem, Vol. 1.

———. 2001. "O sovremennom urovne zhizni semei odinokikh materei" (On the contemporary living standard of single-mother families). *Sotsiologicheskie issledovaniia* 8: 86–87.

———. 2002. "Uroven' zhizni i material'naia podderzhka gosudarstvom nepolnykh semei" (Living standard and material support of incomplete families by the state) In *Rossia: 10 let reform. Sotsial'no-demograficheskaia situatsiia* (Russia: 10 years of reforms. Social-demographic situation), ed. Natalia Rimashevskaia, Moscow: ISEPN.

———. 2004. "Chem muzhika kormit', luchshe rebenka vospityvat' odnoi: sotsial'nyi portret materinskikh semei" (Why should you feed a man, it's better to raise a child by yourself: A social portrait of mother-headed families). In *Semeinye uzy: modeli dlia sborki,* (Family Bonds: Models to Assemble) ed. Sergei Oushakine, 2: 60–82. Moscow: NLO.

Lyngstad, Rolv, Gunn Strand Hutchinson, Lisbet Lund, and Siv Oltedal, eds. 2004. *Single Mothers, Poverty and Social Work: Case Studies from Norway, Australia, Canada, Russia and USA*. Bodoe, Norway: Hoegskolen i Bodoe.

Maleva, Tatiana, and Oksana Siniavskaia, eds. 2007. *Roditeli i deti, muzhchiny i zhenshchiny v sem'e i obshchestve* (Parents and children, men and women in family and society). Moscow: NISP.

Malysheva, Marina. 2001. *Sovremennyi patriarkhat. Sotzial'no-ekonomicheskie esse* (Modern patriarchy. Social-economic essays). Moscow: Academia.

Marshall, Thomas H. 1998. "Citizenship and Social Class." In *The Citizenship Debates: A Reader*, ed. Gershon Shafir, 93–111. Minneapolis: University of Minnesota Press.

Okin, Susan M. 1992. "Women, Equality, and Citizenship." *Queen's Quart. Kingston* 1, no. 90: 56–71.

Ovcharova, Lilia. 2008. "Bednost' i ekonomicheskii rost v Rossii" (Poverty and economic growth in Russia). *Journal of Social Policy Studies* 6, no. 5: 439–456.

Ovcharova, Lilia, Alina Pishniak, and Daria Popova. 2007. "Novye mery podderzhki materinstva i detstva: stimulirovanie rozhdaemosti ili rost urovnia zhizni semei s det'mi?" (New measures in support of maternity and childhood: stimulation of the birth rate or growth in the living standard of families with children?) *SPERO* 6: 5–30.

Ovcharova, Lilia, and Lidia Prokof'eva. 2002. "Sotsial'no-economicheskie faktory feminizatsii bednosti v Rossii" (Socioeconomic factors of the feminization of poverty in Russia). In *Ekonomika i sotsialnaia politika: gendernoe izmerenie* (Economy and social policy: The gender dimension), ed. Marina Malysheva, 36–63. Moscow: Academia.

Postanovlenie Pravitel'stva Saratovskoi oblasti (Decree of the Saratov Oblast Government), June 1, 2001, No. 60-P "O kontseptsii razvitiia sistemy adresnoi sotsial'noi pomoshchi naseleniiu Saratovskoi oblasti" (On the concept of the development of the system of means-tested assistance to the population of Saratov Oblast). 2001, http://www.social.saratov.gov.ru/laws/detail.php?SECTION_ID=25&ELEMENT_ID=789 (accessed June 8, 2011).

Prokof'eva, Lidia. 2007. "Domokhoziaistvo i sem'ia: osobennosti struktury naseleniia Rossii" (Household and family: specificity of population structure of Russia). In *Roditeli i deti, muzhchiny i zhenshchiny v sem'e i obshchestve* (Parents and children, men and women in family and society), eds. Tatiana Maleva and Oksana Siniavskaia. Moscow: NISP.

Semeinyi Kodeks Rossiiskoi Federatsii (Family Code of the Russian Federation). 1995.

Smirnov, Sergei, and Igor Kolosnitsyn. 2000. "Sotsial'nye obiazatel'stva gosudarstva: sokrashchenie ili restrukturizatsiia?" (Social obligations of the state: Reduction or restructuring?) *Mir Rossii* 1, 139–181.

The World Bank. 2007. "Developing Targeted Social Assistance in Russia." *Russian Economic Report* 14, http://siteresources.worldbank.org/INTRUSSIANFEDERATION/Resources/RER14_eng_p3.pdf (accessed April 24, 2011) (June 2007).

Trygged, Sven. 2009. "Social Work with Vulnerable Families and Children in 11 Russian Regions." *European Journal of Social Work* 12, no. 2: 201–220.

UNDP. 2008. *Demographic Policy in Russia: From Reflection to Action*. Moscow: United Nations Development Programme.

———. 2009. *Doklad o razvitii chelovecheskogo potentsiala v Rossiiskoi Federatsii, 2008. Rossia pered litsom demograficheskikh vyzovov* (Report on human development in the Russian Federation, 2008. Russia faces demographic challenges). Moscow: United Nations Development Programme.

UNICEF. 1999. *Zhenshchiny v perekhodnyi period. Regional'nyi monitoringovyi doklad No. 6*. (Women in transition. Regional monitoring report N.6). Florence: UNICEF.

Urbanskaia, G. 2004. "Sotsial'no-demograficheskaia situatsiia na sele" (Social-demographic situation in rural areas). *Ekonomika sel'skogo khoziaistva* 2: 432.

Ustinova, Mara. 1992. "One-Parent Families in the USSR: Ethnoregional Specificity." In *One-Parent Families*, ed. Ulla Björnberg, 7–11. Amsterdam: SISWO Publication.

Walby, Sylvia. 1994. "Is Citizenship Gendered?" *Sociology* 28, no. 2: 379–395.

Vishnevskii, Anatolii, and Sergei Bobylev, eds. 2009. *Russia Facing Demographic Challenges: National Human Development Report; Russian Federation 2008*. Moscow: United Nations Development Programme.

CHAPTER 11

Welfare Crisis and Crisis Centers in Russia Today

AINO SAARINEN[1]

INTRODUCTION

The "shock therapy" implemented in Russia in the early 1990s and the economic decline of the late 1990s led to a tenfold increase in poverty at the same time as social rights as a whole were badly eroded. Women in particular—both as paid employees and recipients of various benefits and services—suffered from the disintegration of the state welfare system (UNICEF, 1999, pp. 1–21). Today there is at last some good news about Russia. By the mid-1990s, the UNDP Human Development Report (HDR) ranked Russia seventy-second among the countries of "medium human development." In 2007 it ranked sixty-seventh and was in the top category, which, for instance, includes all the EU-15 countries and a few post-socialist countries such as the Baltic states (UNDP, 1990, p. 127; 1998, p. 127; 2007/08, p. 229).

The HDR has been published annually since 1990 and uses a set of indexes that capture several aspects of welfare development, including gender equality. These indexes are the human development index (HDI), the gender-related development index (GDI), and the gender empowerment index (GEM).[2] The first two indexes suggest that women are doing as well (or badly) as men: the absolute GDI value (0.801) is at the same level as the HDI value (0.802) (UNDP, 2007/08, p. 331). When measuring women's parliamentary representation, the GEM scored Russia well below the median of the EU-15 states (8 percent versus 27 percent) and placed the country 144th out of 172 states around the world (UNDP, 2006a, pp. 367–370). The global UNDP team (Human Development Reports) stressed that the indicators do not capture many important dimensions of discrimination, such as private childcare provision and violence against women (Saarinen, 2007, p. 280; UNDP, 2006a). This brings up the question of whether such aggregated measures are properly scaled and unbiased, which opens up an opportunity for further, more qualitative analysis of welfare policies in Russia.

During the two terms of Vladimir Putin's presidency (2000–2004 and 2004–2008), several social policy reforms and reallocations of resources took place, including salary increases for public employees and the abolishment of arrears in payments. In 2008, when Dmitry Medvedev took office, the government assured the people that an increasing share of the Federal Stability Funds, which are derived from the oil and energy surplus, would be used for pensions (President of Russia, 2008). Both changes benefit women, who constitute the majority of public employees and retired people (see World Bank, 2003, pp. 65–68). Presently, about 10 percent of the Russian federal revenues are directed to the National Priority Programs (President of Russia, 2006), which, according to Cook (2011) and Kulmala (2008), will benefit a large portion of the population in the future. The question addressed by this chapter is whether these changes indicate a move toward social justice and gender equality.

Recent analyses suggest that the policies of the first decade of the twenty-first century were characterized by a shift back toward statism (Cook, 2007). The state has become more interventionist and taken more responsibility for the welfare of the population. This development, along with continuing policies of state paternalism, does not benefit women. It is therefore the task of this chapter to turn to the years 2000–2009 to analyze the instruments for federal policy-making: how welfare crises are defined and especially how the much-discussed mortality crisis related to men is approached and how it is intertwined with the fertility crisis related to women. More specifically, in the search for any real solutions to the demographic crisis, the whole problematic of both reproduction and gendered violence must be included in order to redefine welfare and stress the importance of personal integrity and sexual-reproductive issues. All these issues relate to the institution of the family, which has never been questioned with respect to gender equality—either in the Soviet Union or in today's Russia—by seriously challenging men's private power and privileges.

In this context, the aforementioned indexes, which were reanalyzed in Russia and "adapted" to local conditions (The Millennium Report [UNDP, 2005b, p. 19], the Equality Report [UNDP, 2005a, p. 6], and the National Projects Report [UNDP, 2006b, p. 2]), as well as the Replies to the UN (United Nations, 2004) on gender policies in the same years, illustrate the sort of values, principles, and prioritizations that lay embedded in the policy instruments as the statist approach was being re-established. As a contrast, I include materials produced by transnational civil society in order to concentrate on the most deprioritized issue, violence against women (VAW). The situation of civic actors, especially the NGO crisis centers for women, is of special relevance to the discussion. A crisis center survey carried out within the project "Welfare, Gender and Agency in Russia in the 2000s" (WGA) (Johnson and Saarinen, 2011) in 2008–2009 confirms the restatism thesis. Finally, this chapter contributes to analyses of Russian democracy and the role of the interventionist state. In the present analysis the family plays a key role.

Sources, Method, and Issues

To analyze the transition expressly with respect to gender and women, it is vital to focus on socioeconomic, sexual-reproductive, and bodily problems related to personal integrity; many of them are centered on the family. For this analysis I adopted the periodization of the welfare policy development suggested by Cook (2007, pp. 24–28), in which socioeconomic and political components are interdependent. According to Cook, the first or "non-negotiated" phase spanned the early 1990s, when women were formally granted access to power but in practice were excluded from it. It was followed by the "contested phase" in the mid- to late 1990s; in those years, women also entered the national scene, at least marginally. This was symbolically reflected in the existence of a women's coalition called the Women of Russia. The third phase, the first few years after 2000, entitled "negotiated within the elites," is again characterized by a lack of influence from below and the marginalization of women politicians. In brief, as can be noted also in the Russian women scholars' 2003 report to the World Bank (World Bank, 2003, pp. 1–4, 94–105), the trends since the early 1990s have been hard for women in particular. It is worth recalling that the political order in Russia is a somewhat peculiar form of liberal democracy that took shape after the year 2000. This "super-presidential model" (Meleschevich, 2007, p. 146), as it is called, allows no room for real parliamentary influence or for mobilization from below. In this context, the central planning and implementation mechanisms are of more interest than those in Western democracies.

A collection of UN-related materials provides sources for cross-reading and frame-centered discourse analysis (Bacchi, 2005), which introduces the angle of agency. This type of institutionalized discourse analysis is not a new version of content analysis or any purely constructionist approach. It asks other kinds of questions arising directly from the intersections of knowledge production and institutional power. These questions inquire as to the sources, the purpose, and the authors of these documents; the institutional positions from which they have been written; and the intended users of the information and analyses.

Questions on the nature and causes of the welfare problem and how it is to be solved relate to both the normative and policy levels, where practice-oriented programs and resource allocation are also highly relevant.

To begin with the links between power and knowledge production, the first set of documents consists of documents outlined directly in relation to the UN Millennium Development Goals (MDGs) and formed through the triad of goal, target, and indicator/s, all for internal Russian use. The Millennium Report (UNDP, 2005b) is structured around all eight MDGs, whereas the parallel Equality Report (UNDP, 2005a) stresses selected issues such as the labor market, time distribution, education, poverty, health, political representation, and finally, regional dimensions. In this constellation the gender problematic is a special issue in two ways: as a chapter of the main report and as a separate report. Both teams of analysts are formally UNDP-related and institutionally independent from the government. At the same time, because they have "liaised closely with the state representatives" and have links to various bodies for strategic planning (UNDP, 2005b, pp. 2–4), they have "upward" connections that make them part of the elite dynamics. The reports therefore include brief comments from both individual experts and federal ministries, as well as citations of presidential addresses and speeches. The National Projects Report (UNDP, 2006b) from the Institute for Complex Strategic Studies (ICSS) is also relevant because it was prepared at the request of the local UN office but combines the global MDGs with shorter-term national planning and budgeting.[3] Lastly, according to the acknowledgements in the Millennium Report (UNDP, 2005b, pp. 2–4) and the Equality Report (UNDP, 2005a, pp. 1–2), both were finalized under the supervision of a male scholar, whereas women produced primary material and probably wrote some of the sections. In the National Projects Report (UNDP, 2006b, p. 2), which does not reflect the issue of gender equality except when discussing demographic rates, women are the main authors but worked under male leadership. In addition to these sources, the presidential addresses of the period (cf. President of Russia, May 10, 2006; November 5, 2008) are of interest, as they link the reports to legislation, policies, and resource allocation.

The second set of documents consists of federal reports written outwards and upwards to multi-level governance bodies and deals specifically with gender and equality. The Replies to the UN (United Nations, 2004) with regard to the UN women's conference in Beijing in 1995 and the continuation session in New York in 2000 on the implementation of UN resolutions is not signed by any individual. However, as it comes from the Ministry of Health and Social Development, one can assume that some high-level women professionals have been involved.[4] The dialogue between the UN and Russia would, as such, be of more interest because the Convention on the Elimination of all Forms of Discrimination against Women (CEDAW) has, since its founding in 1979, been the principal instrument for monitoring the implementation of UN norms and policies in the member countries (American Bar Association, 2006, p. 7).

The third set of documents is the Open Society Institute (OSI) Report from 2007. It was formally drafted from the outside and from a transnational civic perspective. However, the OSI, which is affiliated to the Soros Foundation, has promoted research and civic institutions in Russia and Eastern Europe and grounds its analyses on knowledge and insights from insider informants. The title of the report is a challenge: *Violence against Women: Does the Government Care in Russia?* (OSI, 2007). As such, it is a part of the Institute's global monitoring of the results of UN actions against violations of women's human rights. Most of the contributors and persons named as sources are Russian women working in research and in the crisis center movement, which is in this case coordinated by ANNA, the National Center for the Prevention of Violence (ibid., p. 10, footnotes).

Not surprisingly, different types of reports give different answers as to the nature of the welfare crises in Russia today, and consequently they approach the gender and family problematic in different, even contradictory, ways. In these three institutional contexts, the outlined problems and issues are partly separate, partly parallel and overlapping and even conflicting; in addition to contradictions between them, there are also internal tensions and inconsistencies. Framing and reframing bring up different problematics in relation to the MDGs. The three issues to be discussed here from the gender perspective—the demographic crisis, the reproductive crisis, and the crisis of violence against women—are of course linked to what policies and actual reforms have or have not been carried out. The discussion concludes with an analysis of the equality and anti-VAW policies from above and the situation of the autonomous crisis center movement below, based on the first results of the WGA survey. This is essential, because in the first decade of the 2000s there was a turn for the worse for these civic actors. Simultaneously, it was during these years that public crisis centers came to the fore.

THE "MORTALITY CRISIS" AND THE "FERTILITY CRISIS"

This section examines how the main welfare problem is discussed in the selected documents. The dominant discourses deal with depopulation connected with the mortality crisis among working-age men, which is unique both in the Soviet Russian historical context and in international comparative terms. The life expectancy of men has declined to a low of 58 years, a level typical of many developing countries. But the demographic drop is not stopping: from 143 million in 2006, the population might decrease to some 100 million in the 2050s (UNDP, 2006b, p. 20). In the Millennium Report (UNDP, 2005b, p. 74) the situation is characterized as "crude" and "catastrophic," whereas the Equality Report (UNDP, 2005a, pp. 26–28) speaks neutrally of "extra-high mortality." In the words of one representative of the highest level of power, the situation is "critical" (President of Russia, 2006).

As for the solutions to this prioritized welfare problem, behavioral and socioeconomic factors are often cited to explain why, during the transition, the decline in life expectancy for men has been much sharper than that for women. Interestingly, one of the explanations deals with the family and claims that in these hard times men have found it stressful to be "breadwinners" (Lane, 2007, pp. 60–66; UNDP, 2005a; b). Irrespective of this, the two mainstream reports—the Millennium and National Projects Reports—do not mention in this context the gender contract, which since Soviet times has offered men privileges in working life and released them from "private" responsibilities. Instead, they turn to women and bring up a dual problem that can be called a fertility crisis. They admit that the rapidly declining birth rate in the 1990s started to rise in the following decade. At the same time, they hardly notice that the figures in Russia are not significantly lower than in many EU-15 countries (UNDP, 2007/08, pp. 191–194). Increasing the birth rate is particularly stressed in the National Projects Report (UNDP, 2006b, p. 21), which even outlines a new National Project for stimulating it.

The materials in the first set are relatively consistent and unanimous on the importance of the demographic crisis. One of the most-discussed policy instruments initiated with regard to the outlined problem is best known as the "maternity capital" reform. It was first mentioned in the presidential address to the State Duma in spring 2006 and came into force in 2007. "Maternity capital" encouraged women to give birth to a second and even a third child by providing families with a substantial financial incentive (Federal'nyi Zakon No. 256-FZ 2006). In essence this reform, which concentrates on pregnancy, birth, and the post-natal period, was not intended to be women-friendly, but, as Rotkirch et al. (2007) note, was meant to serve state, national, and family-centered purposes. The majority of the capital is reserved for the child; actually, it is apparently needed to pay for many services such as advanced education and housing that in Soviet times were free or low-cost (see Cook, 2007, pp. 33–37). The smaller part is for the woman herself, but only in the future, as an investment in her pension fund; to view it critically, it compensates for a loss to mothers caused by the pension reform in the first years after 2000.[5]

The absence of interest in gender issues becomes more evident when we take a closer look at the maternal mortality problem, which is one of the main issues in the UN-MDGs. It is well-known that in the USSR, abortion was used as the main means of contraception (for more see Engel, 2004). The Millennium Report (UNDP, 2005b, pp. 84–85) reveals that at one point there were two abortions for every birth. But the present situation is far from satisfactory. The Report emphasizes that maternal deaths have been decreasing and mentions some measures implemented within the national health programs from the 1990s on. However, the number of legal and illegal abortions and, consequently, the number of women dying of abortion is still so high that the analysts have problems comparing Russia's maternal mortality with that of the EU-15 countries. To correct the figures, they exclude deaths caused by abortions.

Here there is reason to pay serious attention to the conclusion presented in the Millennium Report (UNDP, 2005b, p. 88). The analysts recognize that Russia is so far behind in diminishing pre- and post-natal maternal mortality that deaths would have to be reduced by 75 percent to reach the MDG in question. Irrespective of this, they state that "the effect on life expectancy of achieving [the goal] would be felt only by women, whose life expectancy is already 13 years greater" and recommend that scarce resources be directed toward preventing "adult mortality" (ibid.)—in other words, male mortality. In sum, this contradicts making the stimulation of the birth rate a national priority. It should also be mentioned that in its health section, the Equality Report (UNDP, 2005a, pp. 26–28) concentrates on death rates and does not even mention sexual-reproductive issues. These, of course, would be essential in view of Russian women's notorious double or triple burden, since they have to do with the equalization of rights and obligations within the family.

The "Reproductive Crisis"

In their analysis of the presidential address, Rotkirch et al. (2007) note that the recent demographic policies encourage women to return to the labor market one-and-a-half years after giving birth, which suggests that the mother-worker contract is still in place. In this context, policy measures aimed at providing women with the opportunity to reconcile waged work and care deserve special attention within the present discussion.

One of the policy initiatives included support for families by offering a replacement of childcare costs. Compensation for the second child amounts to 50 percent, and for the third child 70 percent, of the costs. This is not to be belittled, because during the first period of transition, when the public network of kindergartens had crumbled, many impoverished families and single mothers could not afford to pay for kindergarten (World Bank, 2003, p. 67). However, it is not clear what is happening to restore the kindergarten network as a whole as a major welfare service. It is not discussed in the first set of documents in any length and is not given any importance in the address either.

The only document that takes up the issue of childcare provision is the National Projects Report (UNDP, 2006b, pp. 22–23), which estimates that shortage at close to one million places. The report also refers to a "lively discussion" on the address and therefore advocates a "comprehensive approach" to both empowering women and stimulating the birth rate but does not offer any concrete proposals. Critical analysis of the relationship between women and men in the private sphere and promotion of what often is called social fatherhood are not pursued any further, here or at the presidential level. Sharing childcare and household chores are, however, mentioned both in the Millennium Report (UNDP, 2005b, p. 66) and the Equality Report (UNDP, 2005a, p. 20) in references to problems labeled "traditional gender roles" and "time distribution," respectively. The Replies to the UN (United Nations, 2004, pp. 20–21) confirm that the government aims to involve men and boys and that changes have already been made in the labor and family codes to encourage "young fathers" to take their share of "maternal obligations." In practice, this entitles a father to take parental leave (Trudovoi Kodeks..., 2001), but only some 2 to 3 percent of men have done so (World Bank, 2003, p. 60).[6]

In sum, when giving birth to the second or the third child, women may have to stay at home for several years, meaning that following the federal policy might become a trap. All in all, the early years of the twenty-first century did witness a few developments that could be called pro-woman. But with regard to gender, the key question is whether problems are solved at *the expense of* women versus *for* and *with* them and, moreover, whether men are also involved. From the perspective of women's welfare rights and their civic obligations (see Lister, 1997, pp. 15–28), therefore, the situation should more properly be analyzed as a reproductive crisis rather than as a mere fertility or birth rate crisis. Framing the problem in such a manner would also be in accordance with the UN-MDGs, in which reducing child and maternal mortality is always linked to overall gender equality (UNDP, 2000)[7]. In summary, none of the Russian reports or documents takes the decisive step of speaking out about both public care and men's involvement in the private domain; that is, nothing is said about changing the gendered structures within the family. From another angle, some observers have concluded that mid-1990s feminist discourses stressing the gender order as a whole and dealing with the crisis of masculinity and the deconstruction of bipolar gender identities were and are too advanced for Russia (Rotkirch et al., 2007; World Bank, 2003, pp. 59–63; Zdravomyslova, 1996).

THE "VIOLENCE AGAINST WOMEN" CRISIS AS A DISTORTED ISSUE

Without any doubt, the issue of violence against women (VAW) is topical in Russia and in need of attention in regard to the UN-MDGs and human rights, resolutions that have been ratified by Russia. Internal inconsistencies and contradictions between the Russian documents are especially striking with regard to this issue, in which combating domestic violence is of key importance. It is particularly difficult to make visible and quantify domestic violence in its various direct and indirect and psychological and physical forms (European Commission, 2009, pp. 62–75). There is, however, one indicator that is relatively reliable, namely the number of women killed by males close to them. The domestic-violence death toll—some 14,000 women annually—was brought up by the Russian women's crisis center movement even before the Beijing conference (RACCW, 1995) and was confirmed by the state's reports to the CEDAW committee and other multilateral bodies after the late 1990s (American Bar Association, 2006, p. 91; OSI, 2007, p. 50). In demographic terms, this figure is marginal, but as numerous Russian women scholars have been repeating for years (Pashina, 2004), in terms of human rights and gender ethics, it signifies a crisis of violence against women in Russia.

Despite all the evidence, the Millennium Report analysts seem to ignore and reframe the issue of domestic violence against women. They entitle the section dealing with the topic "Gender Aspects of Violence" and discuss the mortality crisis of working-age men by making use of the International Crime Victim Survey (ICVS), which claims that Russian men are exposed to physical violence more often than Russian women. In other words, the focus is mainly on violence between men. At the same time, although the Report (UNDP, 2005b, p. 67) states that over 90 percent of victims of domestic violence are women, it does not reflect on the phenomenon or bring up the aforementioned figure concerning women. It does mention creating "effective mechanisms" to combat VAW, but only in the appendix and on the last page in a list of objectives for empowering women (ibid., pp. 71–73, 185). The analysis and the appendix read as if they are from different texts. Even the only specified anti-VAW target—zero rapes by 2015—is arbitrary.

The Equality Report (UNDP, 2005a, pp. 28–30) does point to gender, but it is confusing in other ways. It presents more detailed information on everyday violence and criticizes conceptions of the private nature of VAW and the delay in legislative reforms demanded by the UN. Irrespective of this, the section on the issue is also entitled "Gender Aspects of Violence," and the discussion does not challenge the views outlined by the mainstream team. Interestingly, this kind of male-centered framing is absent in the second set of documents. The Replies to the UN (United Nations, 2004, pp. 15–20) also clearly state that violence against women is extensive, but it is silent about the most brutal evidence of VAW, namely the number of domestic deaths. Lastly, it goes without saying that at the presidential level VAW is a non-issue: it is included neither in the 2006 presidential address (President of Russia, 2006), which focused on the importance of family, nor in any other address before or since.

In sum, if all the basic forms of violence are incorporated into the UN human rights regime, the situation in Russia looks very gloomy from the perspective of women. Ultimately, if gendered violence[8] were to be included in the UNDP gender-related welfare index, the GDI value would fall, particularly in countries like Russia. As for combating VAW, the distortion allows Russia to leave women unprotected; in this respect it is far behind the EU-15 countries (European Commission, 2009, pp. 65–72). Self-evidently, ignoring domestic violence is harmful to familial well-being, to say the least.

The State of Pro-equality and Anti-VAW Policies: The "Declarative" Problematic

In many ways the Millennium Report gives the impression that men's problems are highlighted, and that women's problems are, if not excluded, then at least undervalued in the name of making a version adapted to Russia. To some extent this applies also to the Equality Report. The section on poverty is especially illustrative in this regard, as the issue of poverty is directly related to women's opportunities for reproductive choices and to combating VAW at the personal level. The Millennium Report (UNDP, 2005b, pp. 30–45) does not even mention the feminization of poverty, an issue that would open a critical gender perspective on the Russian transition. The Equality Report (UNDP, 2005a, pp. 22, 39), on the other hand, speaks about the feminization of poverty and problematizes the high proportion of single mothers and women pensioners among the poor. In brief, women pay a high price for unequal family relationships that affect their position in the labor market even in their late years and as widows. Empowering women in and through politics is an urgent issue in Russia.

Interestingly, in the end all Russian documents (except the National Projects Report) approach the problem of women's political disempowerment. A few times it is concluded that in the 1990s work for equality consisted more of rhetoric than of action and lacked budget funding, and that in the subsequent decade it became even worse, as the federal agency for equality was dissolved. When evaluating the state policy, the Millennium Report (UNDP, 2005b, pp. 59–60) claims that now "the state has given up both declarations and actions" and has dropped gender issues.

Box 3.4, "Official View of Gender Issues in the Russian Federation" (UNDP, 2005b, p. 72), attached to the Report, tells another story. Not surprisingly, it is in harmony with the second set of documents. The Replies to the UN (United Nations, 2004) is internally relatively coherent, but as a whole the document is a mixture of criticism from women's perspectives and political proclamations. In many ways it is a confirmation of the declarative nature of high-level gender policies and as such is a continuation of the Soviet heritage. According to this document, the National Action Plans for 1997–2000 and 2001–2005 (cf. Ministerstvo truda..., 2002; Postanovlenie..., 1996) have been adopted, all along the lines of the Beijing women's conference, and legislative changes are underway to make VAW a "serious domestic crime" and a "criminally punishable act" (United Nations, 2004, pp. 17–19). Some policy measures are also listed, such as improving statistics on violence and activities in regions and localities. But a cross-reading of all Russian reports results in confusion about the state policy-making process, whether there exists any valid gender strategy, and what is happening to the anti-VAW norms and policies, not to mention funding.

The third set of documents, the contribution by transnational civic actors, is of special value because many of the contributors work inside Russia. The Open Society Institute presents *Violence against Women: Does the Government Care in Russia?* within the UN Human Rights Frame. The report is directed to both Russian and UN officials, specifically the

CEDAW, as well as to the Council of Europe (CoE), which Russia joined in 1996. The OSI Report (2007, pp. 11–14) claims that Russia experiences a high level of domestic violence, particularly murders of women, and it also highlights the number of women killed by persons close to them. As for the political situation, the report concludes that there is no federal policy framework for gender equality or combating VAW. Furthermore, the major legislative changes required by the UN and the CoE have not been carried out, as domestic violence is still not defined in the Criminal Code and, consequently, is not subject to public prosecution. Some other reforms, for instance, on harassment, have not been carried out either. In addition, there are no guidelines for interpreting the (present) Code regulations in practice; no monitoring of the state of affairs; no action plan in the long, medium, or short term; and no budgeting through national programs. Finally, the Report states that there are hardly any services for victims, the training of authorities, or public information and awareness-raising, let alone research and statistics. In sum, the pictures provided by official and NGO experts contradict each other. Moreover, while making numerous declarations of intent, none of the Russian reports assures the reader that the gender problematic will, in some continual and coherent way, be included into the decision-making process regarding equality and anti-VAW measures.

Autonomous Crisis Centers on the Decrease, Public Centers on the Increase

None of the documents discussed in this chapter refers to evidence of the low representation on women at the policy-making level (GEM values) in Russia in the recent decades. This is especially problematic in view of the recently evolving state-centered order. As long as the state is becoming more active and women remain as excluded from federal power as they are today, there is little prospect of real change. Women-friendly progress, especially in combating VAW, must clearly be sought within the policy-making process and through democracy at the grassroots level. As is reflected in all the documents analyzed here, the history of grassroots organizations dealing with VAW has been turbulent in the last twenty years.

The first centers were founded in Moscow and St. Petersburg in the early 1990s, and the Russian Association for Crisis Centers for Women (RACCW) already existed prior to the Beijing conference. Soon the movement spread out to the regions. For instance, the Nordic-Russian "Network for Crisis Centres in the Barents Region" (NCRB) was built in the late

1990s (Saarinen et al., 2003). The movement started by providing services to women victims of male violence and carrying out political campaigns by contesting the state authorities in ways that were not customary in the USSR or Russia (see Cook and Vinogradova, 2006). It put the VAW issue on the public agenda and initiated a reform of the Criminal Code that was not subsequently realized (Johnson, 2006; Johnson and Saarinen, 2011; RACCW, 1995). The progress of the movement was in line with the overall institutionalization in civil society (Brygalina and Temkina, 2004).

But the optimism faded away just a few years later. On the one hand, transnational aid started decreasing due to agenda changes in the multilateral bodies (Johnson, 2009; Saarinen, 2006). On the other hand, pressure from the national authorities started increasing. The NGO Act came into force (Federal'nyi Zakon No. 18-FZ, 2006), which strictly regulated the registration, budgeting, and reporting of NGOs and opened the way for state control of their activities (Kamhi, 2006). Combined, these trends pushed to the margins of the political arena those who mobilized for feminist and democratic aims.

A reading of the first sets of documents might make a positive impression. According to the Millennium Report (UNDP, 2005b, pp. 174–184) as well as the National Projects Report (UNDP, 2006b, pp. 24–27), collaboration between the state and NGOs is crucial for the implementation of the UN-MDGs. The National Projects Report presents an institutionalized structure for the collaboration between state and civil society. As for the VAW issues specifically, in the Replies to the UN (United Nations, 2004, p. 18), the federal authorities declare that the state is working in close collaboration with relevant NGOs by organizing seminars and roundtables. Contrary to this, the OSI Report (2007, p. 32) says that the NGOs are not integrated into preparation, decision-making, implementation, or evaluation.

The OSI Report, however, overlooks one important policy instrument—1999 Decree No. 32 of the Ministry of Labor and Social Development on the Organization of State Institution "Complex Center for Social Services" (Postanovlenie..., 1999). The number of public centers or crisis departments affiliated with these multi-functional state, regional, or municipal social units has been growing in recent years, and at least in northwestern Russia, many of them have been very successful (Jäppinen, 2009; Kulmala, 2008). For example, in St. Petersburg, sixteen out of the eighteen city districts have now founded a crisis department.

In sum, these trends testify to a recasting of the political constellation between civic actors and the state. The shift toward statism leads to a partial reframing of the issue in favor of familialist or one-sided "women's rights" views, to the detriment of feminist, gender-centered views (Liapounova and Dracheva, 2004; Pashina, 2004; Saarinen et al., 2003). While the practices may vary inside the centers and among individual co-workers (Jäppinen, 2011), it is worth noting that certain types of activities receive public support from the federal, regional, and local authorities. In this respect the address of the new president (President of Russia, 2008), which stressed the importance of NGOs working for social and health issues in close collaboration with local authorities, is a mixed message: it mentions collaboration and co-operation, not political confrontation, let alone feminist views. It goes without saying that the family is not discussed from any critical perspective.

Conclusion

So what does the latest phase of transition look like from the perspective of women's rights, the issues of bodily and sexual-reproductive integrity, gender, and agency? Are there prospects for increased social justice, gender equality, and political inclusion—and changing the family as an institution characterized by male privileges and domination? It is worth noting that the aforementioned Decree No. 32 (Postanovlenie..., 1999), which incorporates "women-friendly" elements and mentions VAW, is from the "contested" liberalization period (Cook, 2007, pp. 99–144), when the crisis center movement was getting stronger and women had a voice in the Duma. The present shift toward statism does not offer similar opportunities for women's agency at the federal level; at the same time, the confrontational grassroots organizations in civil society are fewer and disempowered.

The institutionally sensitive discourse/frame analysis of the Millennium Reports confirms this conclusion. The lack of coherence, continuity, and institutional stabilization in the pro-equality and anti-VAW policies becomes evident from a cross-reading of the Russian documents and evaluations from outside established politics and abroad. The controversies in and between the documents suggest what might be termed "triple talk." The mainstream reports may perhaps contain conscious attempts to misuse the Millennium process for nationally framed demographic purposes at the expense of women's reproductive rights and the right to safety and personal integrity. But even the Equality Report, which discusses women's and gender issues, becomes distorted when it adapts the frame entitled "Gender Aspects of Violence." The Replies to the UN are internally most consistent, in that they do not repeat the distortions and stress the reproductive problems and anti-VAW aims, but they do not have much political credibility. The OSI Report must be acknowledged for its gender perspective and systematic follow-up of the state of affairs in Russia. But it has bypassed relevant developments and ignores the new role of the state. From another angle, the contradictions between the documents of the second and third sets are proof of essential problems stemming from the absence of contacts or collaboration between civil society and those wielding power. In Russia, the boomerang strategy (Keck and Sikkink, 1998) is not working as planned: the state and the autonomous Russian and transnational crisis center and women's movements are quite distant from each other.

A remark by the team of Russian women scholars (World Bank, 2003, p. 8) is still valid: the main approach at the national level is declarative and frames the problems at best as women's problems rather than as gender problems. In the first decade of the twenty-first century, the demographic crisis that stresses the problem of male mortality and, by problematizing the fertility crisis, makes women into instruments of the state, was constructed under the leadership of men and within a masculist framework. For the state, this is a short-sighted strategy. Until there is a focus on the reproductive crisis as a whole, it will not be possible to increase birth rates. Lastly, referring to the violence-against-women crisis, abused women hardly make happy mothers to second and third children, even if given the possibility to combine work and motherhood. In sum, transformation of the family as a key social institution is a *sine qua non* precondition for solving the welfare crises in Russia.

On the other hand, as Kulmala (2008, 2011) claims, with respect to state-civil society relations, a more women-friendly society might be evolving at the regional and local levels. The WGA project[9] has taken the challenge by adding "Case St. Petersburg" to its agenda to explore these trends by concentrating on the new public crisis centers in its work in 2011–2012.

NOTES

1 My warmest thanks to Irina Dracheva for collaboration in regard to the Russian materials. The editors deserve special thanks for their numerous comments and suggestions on improving this chapter.
2 The HDI consists of indicators on life expectancy, education, and income. The GDI concentrates on the same variables as the HDI but has a special focus on gender differences with regard to living standards. The GEM captures women's participation in political decision-making, their access to professional opportunities, and their earning power (UNDP, 1995, p. 72). In general, Russia's HDI

has been on the same level as the GDI index, but the GEM is much lower than the GDI. Globally, the HDR materials have been used for determining the UN Millennium Development Goals (UNDP, 2000) by 2015. One of them is promotion of gender equality, while the others deal with poverty, education, mortality of mothers and of children, HIV/AIDS, the environment, and grassroots participation in global development. In brief, the MDGs are to uphold "the principles of human dignity, equality and equity" at the global level and within regions and countries. In the midst of the post-socialist turmoil, they help divide the transition into different subperiods both from the perspective of the population at large and the vulnerable sections of it, such as women.

3 On the links between the elites, politics, and planning, see Cook (2007, pp. 141–192) and Lane (2007).
4 On women in leading positions in the ministry in 2004–2005, see http://www.minzdravsoc.ru/.
5 According to Cook (2007, p. 172), women do not earn any pension from parental leave. This does not come up in the address.
6 It is worthnoting that the documents concentrate on "complete" families. Single-parent families that in the Millennium Report (UNDP, 2005b, p. 35) and the Equality Report (UNDP, 2005a, p. 23) are called "less than two parents" or "incomplete" families are not on these agendas, although their problems have multiplied in every possible way during the transition (World Bank, 2003, pp. 65–68).
7 In developing countries, gender equality is of course linked to reducing the birth rate.
8 Pre- and post-natal maternal deaths, as well as "murders" of women, are of course included in the life expectancy of women in Russia, but the figures are of the variable rather than analytic type.
9 The crisis center team consists of Irina Dracheva, Janet Elise Johnson, Olga Liapounova, and Aino Saarinen.

References

American Bar Association. 2006. *CEDAW Assessment Tool Report for the Russian Federation: Central European and Eurasian Law Initiative.* CEELI. Promoting the Rule of Law, http://www.abanet.org/rol/publications/russia-cedaw-eng.pdf (accessed June 24, 2011).

Bacchi, Carol. 2005. "Discourse, Discourse, Everywhere: Subject 'Agency' in Feminist Discourse Methodology." *Nordic Journal of Women's Studies* 13, no. 3: 198–209.

Brygalina, Julia, and Anna Temkina. 2004. "The Development of Feminist Organisations in St. Petersburg 1985–2003." In *Between Sociology and History: Essays on Microhistory, Collective Action and Nation-Building*, eds. Anna-Maria

Castren, Markku Lonkila, and Matti Peltonen, 207–226. Helsinki: Finnish Literature Society.
Cook, Linda J. 2007. *Postcommunist Welfare States: Reform Politics in Russia and Eastern Europe.* Ithaca, NY: Cornell University Press.
———. 2011. "Russia's Welfare Regime: The Shift Toward Statism." In *Gazing at Welfare, Gender and Agency in Post-Socialist Europe,* eds. Maija Jäppinen, Meri Kulmala, and Aino Saarinen, 14–35. Newcastle upon Tyne, UK: Cambridge Scholars Publishers.
Cook, Linda J., and Elena Vinogradova. 2006. "NGOs and Social Policy in Russia's Regions." *Problems of Post-Communism* 53, no. 5: 28–41.
Engel, Barbara. 2004. *Women in Russia, 1700–2000.* Cambridge: Cambridge University Press.
European Commission. 2009. *Beijing+15: The Platform for Action and the European Union.* Report from the Swedish Presidency of the Council of the European Union, http://www.se2009.eu/polopoly_fs/1.22825!menu/standard/file/Beijing_low_link.pdf (accessed June 24, 2011).
Federal'nyi Zakon No. 18-FZ (Federal Law No. 18-FZ). 2006. *O vnesenii izmenenii v nekotorye zakonodatel'nye akty* (On introducing amendments into certain legislative acts of the Russian Federation), January 10, 2006.
Federal'nyi Zakon No. 256-FZ (Federal Law No. 256-FZ). 2006. *O dopolnitel'nykh merakh gosudarstvennoi podderzhki semei, imeiushchikh detei* (On additional measures of state support for families with children), December 29, 2006.
Johnson, Janet. 2009. *Gender Violence in Russia: The Politics of Feminist Intervention.* Bloomington: Indiana University Press.
Johnson, Janet Elise. 2006. "Public-Private Permutations: Domestic Violence Crisis Centres." In *Russian Civil Society: A Critical Assessment,* eds. Alfred B. Evans, Jr., Laura A. Henry, and Lisa McIntosh Sundstrom, 266–283. New York: M.E. Sharpe.
Johnson, Janet Elise, and Aino Saarinen. 2011. "Assessing Civil Society in Putin's Russia: The Plight of Women's Crisis Centers." *Communist and Post-Communist Studies* 44, no. 1: 41–52.
Jäppinen, Maija. 2009. *Perheväkivaltatyön menetystarina Sortavalassa. Arviointi Solidaarisuuden ja Sortavalan kaupungin toteuttamista lähiyhteistyöhankkeista vuosina 2004–2008* (Combating domestic violence: A success story in Sortavala; A review of the cross-border project between the [Finnish] Solidarity Foundation and the [Russian Karelian] Sortavala Municipality in 2004–2008). International Solidarity Foundation, http://www.solidaarisuus.fi/@Bin/119303/Evaluaatio%20Sortavalan%20hankkeista.pdf (accessed June 24, 2011).
———. 2011. "Tensions Between Familialism and Feminism: A Case Study of Domestic Violence Frameworks in a Crisis Centre in Central Russia." In *Gazing at Welfare, Gender and Agency in Post-Socialist Europe,* eds. Maija Jäppinen, Meri Kulmala, and Aino Saarinen, 125–144. Newcastle upon Tyne, UK: Cambridge Scholars Publishers.

Kamhi, Alison. 2006. "The Russian NGO Law: Potential Conflicts with International, National and Foreign Legislation." *The International Journal of Not-for-Profit Law* 9, no. 1, http://www.icnl.org/KNOWLEDGE/IJNL/vol9iss1/art_6.htm (accessed June 24, 2011).

Keck, Margaret E., and Kathryn Sikkink. 1998. *Activists Beyond Borders: Advocacy Networks in International Politics*. Ithaca, NY: Cornell University Press.

Kulmala, Meri. 2008. "Kansalaisyhteiskunta ja valtio Venäjän Karjalassa" (Civil society and state in Russian Karelia). *Futura* 2: 43 60.

———. 2011. "Rethinking State-Society Boundaries: The Case of a Municipal Social Service Center in Sortavala, Russian Karelia." In *Gazing at Welfare, Gender and Agency in Post-Socialist Europe*, eds. Maija Jäppinen, Meri Kulmala, and Aino Saarinen, 170–198. Newcastle upon Tyne, UK: Cambridge Scholars Publishers.

Lane, David. 2007. "Two Outcomes of Transformation." In *The Transformation of State Socialism: System Change, Capitalism or Something Else?* ed. David Lane, 1–33. Basingstoke, UK, and New York: Palgrave MacMillan.

Liapounova, Olga, and Irina Dracheva. 2004. "Crisis Centres for Women in North West Russia: Ideology, Management and Practice." In *Crisis Centres and Violence against Women: Dialogue in the Barents Region*, eds. Aino Saarinen and Elaine Carey-Belangér, 39–68. Femina Borealis, vol. 9; Gender Research: Methodology and Practice, vol. 7. Pomor State University. Oulu, Finland: Oulu University Press.

Lister, Ruth. 1997. *Citizenship: Feminist Perspectives*. Basingstoke, UK: Macmillan.

Meleschevich, Andrey. 2007. *Party Systems in Post-Soviet Countries: A Comparative Study of Political Institutionalization in the Baltic States, Russia, and Ukraine*. New York and Basingstoke, UK: Palgrave Macmillan.

Ministerstvo truda i sotsial'nogo razvitiia (Ministry of Labor and Social Development). 2002. *Natsional'nyi plan deistvii po uluchsheniiu polozheniia zhenshchin v Rossiiskoi Federatsii i povysheniiu ikh roli v obshchestve na 2001–2005 gody* (National action plan to improve women's position in the Russian Federation and to advance their role in society in 2001–2005), http://www.owl.ru/content/docs/rus/p11731.shtml (accessed June 28, 2011).

OSI. 2007. *Violence against Women: Does the Government Care in Russia? Network Women's Program Violence against Women (VAW) Monitoring Program*. Open Society Institute, http://stopvaw2.extranet.urbanplanet.com/sites/3f6d15f4-c12d-4515-8544-26b7a3a5a41e/uploads/Russia_2.pdf (accessed November 2, 2009).

Pashina, Albina. 2004. "The Crisis Centre Movement in Russia: Characteristics, Successes and Problems." In *Crisis Centres and Violence against Women: Dialogue in the Barents Region*, eds. Aino Saarinen and Carey-Bélanger, Elaine, 19–38. Femina Borealis, vol. 9; Gender Research: Methodology and Practice, vol. 7. Oulu, Finland: Oulu University Press.

Postanovlenie Ministerstva truda i sotsial'nogo razvitiia Rossiiskoi Federatsii (Decree of the Ministry of Labor and Social Development of the Russian Federation), July 27, 1999, No. 32. "Ob utverzhdenii metodicheskikh rekomendatsii po organizatsii deiatel'nosti gosudarstvennogo (munitsipal'nogo) uchrezhdeniia 'Kompleksnyi tsentr sotsial'nogo obsluzhivaniia naseleniia'" (On the approval of methodological recommendations for the organization of the activities of the state [municipal] Comprehensive Social Services Center), http://www.humanities.edu.ru/db/msg/61253 (accessed June 28, 2011).

Postanovlenie Pravitel'stva Rossiiskoi Federatsii (Decree of the Government of the Russian Federation), August 29, 1996, no. 1032. "Natsional'nyi plan deistvii po uluchsheniiu polozheniia zhenschin v Rossiiskoi Federatsii i povysheniiu ikh roli v obshchestve do 2000 goda" (National action plan to improve women's position in the Russian Federation and to advance their role in society before 2000), http://www.businesspravo.ru/Docum/DocumShow_DocumID_48953.html (accessed June 28, 2011).

President of Russia. 2006. *Annual Address to the Federal Assembly*. Marble Hall, the Kremlin, Moscow, http://archive.kremlin.ru/eng/speeches/2006/05/10/1823_type70029type82912_105566.shtml (accessed April 8, 2011); May 10, 2006.

———. 2008. *Annual Address to the Federal Assembly*. Grand Kremlin Palace, Moscow, http://archive.kremlin.ru/eng/speeches/2008/11/05/2144_type70029type82917type127286_208836.shtml (accessed April 8, 2011); November 5, 2008.

RACCW. 1995. *Russian Association for Crisis Centres for Women: Violence Against Women in Russia. Research, Education and Advocacy Project*. A Report of the Non-Governmental Meeting. United Nations Conference in Beijing, China.

Rotkirch, Anna, Anna Temkina, and Elena Zdravomyslova. 2007. "Who Helps the Degraded Housewife? Comments on Vladimir Putin's Demographic Speech." *European Journal of Women's Studies* 14: 349–357.

Saarinen, Aino. 2006. "Naisten kriisikeskukset Venäjällä: selviytymiskamppailuja ulkoisen 'demokratia-avun' ja sisäisen 'demokratiavajeen' välissä" (Women's crisis centres in Russia—struggle for survival between the external "democracy assistance" and internal "democracy deficit"). In *Katse Venäjään—suomalaisen Venäjätutkimuksen antologia* (Gazing at Russia: The anthology of Finnish studies of Russia), ed. Jouko Nikula, 266–288. Helsinki: Aleksanteri-sarja.

———. 2007. "Idäntutkimuksen ongelmia—sukupuoli" (Problems in research of Eastern Europe). *Idäntutkimus* 14, no. 1: 82–84.

Saarinen, Aino, Olga Liapounova, and Irina Dracheva. 2003. *NCRB: A Network for Crisis Centres for Women in the Barents Region; Report on the Nordic-Russian Development Project 1999–2002*. Vol. 5, *Gender Research: Methodology and Practice*. Centre for Women's Studies and Gender Research. Arkhangelsk, Russia: Pomor State University.

Trudovoi Kodeks Rossiiskoi Federatsii (Labor Code of the Russian Federation). 2001. Enforced by Federal Law No. 197-FZ, http://www.consultant.ru/popular/tkrf/ (accessed June 28, 2011).

UNDP. 1990. *Global Human Development Report: Concept and Measurement of Human Development*. United Nations Development Programme, http://hdr.undp.org/xmlsearch/reportSearch?y=1990&c=g&t=*&lang=en&k=& orderby=year (accessed June 28, 2011).

———. 1998. *Global Human Development Report. Consumption for Human Development.* United Nations Development Programme, http://hdr.undp.org/xmlsearch/reportSearch?y=1998&c=g&t=*&lang=en&k=& orderby=year (accessed June 28, 2011).

———. 2000. *Millennium Development Goals.* United Nations Development Programme, http://www.undp.org/mdg/basics.shtml (accessed June 28, 2011).

———. 2005a. *Gender Equality and Extension of Women Rights in Russia in the Context of UN the Millennium Development Goals.* United Nations Development Programme, http://www.undp.ru/Gender_MDG_eng.pdf (accessed June 28, 2011).

———. 2005b. *National Human Development Report. Russia in 2015: Development Goals and Policy Priorities.* United Nations Development Programme, http://hdr.undp.org/en/reports/national/europethecis/russia/Russian_Federation _2005_en.pdf (accessed June 28, 2011).

———. 2006a. *Global Human Development Report. Beyond Scarcity: Power, Poverty and the Global Water Crisis.* United Nations Development Programme, http://hdr.undp.org/xmlsearch/reportSearch?y=2006&c=g&t=*&lang=en&k=& orderby=year (accessed June 28, 2011).

———. 2006b. *The Millennium Development Goals and Russia's National Projects: Strategic Choices.* Institute for Complex Strategic Studies. Moscow, 2006, http://www.undp.ru/download.phtml?$481 (accessed June 28, 2011).

———. 2007/08. *Global Human Development Report. Fighting Climate Change: Human Solidarity in a Divided World.* United Nations Development Programme, http://hdr.undp.org/xmlsearch/reportSearch?y=2007&c=g&t=*&lang=en&k=& orderby=year (accessed June 28, 2011).

UNICEF. 1999. *Zhenshchiny v perekhodnyi period. Regiona'lnyi monitoringovyi doklad No. 6.* (Women in transition. Regional monitoring report N.6). Florence: UNICEF.

United Nations. 2004. *Russian Federation: Replies to the Questionnaire of the United Nations Secretariat on the Implementation of the Beijing Platform for Action Adopted by the Fourth World Conference on the Status of Women (Beijing, 1995) and the Final Documents of the 23rd Special Session of the United Nations General Assembly (New York, 2000)*, www.un.org/womenwatch/.../responses/RUSSIAN-FEDERATION-English.pdf (accessed June 28, 2011).

World Bank. 2003. *Gender Profile of the Russian Federation (Based on Domestic Publications, 1993–2003).* World Bank Document, November 2003, www-wds.worldbank.org/.../393330RU0Gender0profile01PUBLIC1.pdf (accessed June 24, 2011).

Zdravomyslova, Elena. 1996. "Problems in Becoming a Housewife." In *Women's Voices in Russia Today*, eds. Anna Rotkirch and Elina Haavio-Mannila, 33–48. Aldershot, UK: Dartmouth.

CHAPTER 12

Marriage and Divorce Law in Russia and the Baltic States: Overview of Recent Changes

OLGA A. KHAZOVA

INTRODUCTION

One of the immediate results of the 1991 collapse of the Soviet Union and the formation of the new independent states was significant law reform in these countries. Family law reform was an integral part of this revision. It had to be adapted to the new social and economic realities, which were accompanied by tremendous political change. New legislation on marriage and the family was enacted both in Russia and the Baltic states. In Russia it took the form of the Family Code adopted in 1995. In the Baltic states, new family law provisions were incorporated into the Civil Codes: the Civil Law of Latvia of 1992[1] (Part One on Family Law), the Civil Code of Lithuania of 2000 (Book Three on Family Law), and the Family Law Act of Estonia of 2009,[2] which was included as a separate book in the Civil Code.

The former Soviet republics did not have much freedom in designing their own family laws. In accordance with the Edict (*Ukaz*) of the Presidium of the Supreme Soviet of the USSR of November 6, 1940, the Codes of the Russian Federation (RSFSR[3]) were temporarily applied in Latvia, Lithuania, and Estonia, thereby abolishing legislation that was in force in these countries before their annexation by the Soviet Union. Later, in 1969–1970, after the 1968 Fundamentals of Legislation of the USSR and Soviet Republics on Marriage and the Family (the "Fundamentals") were enacted, all the Soviet republics, including the Baltic Soviet republics, adopted their own marriage and family codes on the basis of the family law provisions stipulated in the "Fundamentals." However, there was not much difference among the codes of the Soviet republics. All were essentially the same, as they were based on the "Fundamentals" and had the RSFSR family law as a common—in fact, compulsory—model. It is not surprising, therefore, that after these countries became independent and were released from the pressure of the Soviet state, a completely different picture of family law emerged. Family law in post-Soviet Europe is currently a mixed bag of new and old laws and rules.

What were the main ideas that legal drafters might have had in mind as they worked on the new post-Soviet family laws? They were probably driven by three considerations, although in the Baltic countries and in Russia these considerations became apparent to different degrees. One of them, as far as the Baltic countries were concerned, was to reject the old Soviet legislation regardless of its value, since it had been brought to the Baltics by force along with the Soviet regime. Apart from that, many of the Soviet family law rules were indeed outdated and did not correspond to the new order that was established in these countries after the Soviet Union ceased to exist. This was especially true of property and financial relations between spouses, both in existing marriages and after divorce (for more detail, see Khazova, 2009).

Another idea that naturally guided the legal drafters in the Baltic countries was to consider—where reasonable—restoring the family law or some of the legal concepts that were in force before annexation. A good example is Latvia, which re-enacted the Civil Law of 1937, the drafting of which "was guided by the latest trends in the civil law of the time in continental Europe."[4] In Estonia the restoration of some of the concepts and ideas of the draft Civil Code of 1940 has been widely discussed in connection with the "next round" revision of the family law (Kullerkupp, 2001b, pp. 79. 82).

A third motivation was to follow recent European trends of family law. In this regard, many of the French, Dutch, German, Italian, Swedish, and even English family law provisions served as models. For instance, the initial draft of the provisions on the cohabitation of unmarried persons in the Lithuanian Civil Code followed Swedish legislation on cohabitation (Keserauskas, 2004, p. 332).[5] For the Baltic countries, which planned to join the European Union, conformity with EU law was of particular importance. One of the main concerns in the area of family law was connected with human rights and child-protection issues, where the discrepancy between the former Soviet legal provisions and European standards was the most obvious.[6] As for Russia, I venture to assume that if Russia had joined the Council of Europe by the time the draft Family Code had been worked out, the influence of European law on Russian family law would have been more profound, and many of the code's provisions would have been more in line with European trends.[7]

The present chapter is based on comparative legal analysis of post-Soviet European legislation on marriage and the family and aims to identify the main innovations brought about by the reforms, the main differences between the national laws, and, if possible, the main trends in the development of national family laws (see, for instance, Khazova, 2007). In this regard, the Baltic countries are unique in the post-Soviet space, as their family-law reforms show the most significant departure from the Soviet family-law model. The goal of the chapter is to analyze the changes that were made to the family law of Russia and the Baltic countries after the breakdown of the USSR in two main family-law institutions: marriage and divorce, as these are the areas where this departure is the most obvious. Because analyzing legal issues in these spheres in a broad historical, social, demographic, and economic context is beyond the scope of the present format, I have chosen to focus on recent changes in the legal regulation of marriage and divorce with some limited comparisons across space and time that I consider to be necessary. The structure of the paper reflects its main goal: one part of it is dedicated to marriage law and the other to divorce law.

Marriage Law

Latvian, Lithuanian, and Estonian laws have restored the religious form of marriage. From the legal point of view, it is not mandatory, nor does it replace the civil (secular) marriage that existed before the enactment of new legislation. The religious form is an alternative to civil marriage performed by a government official. The restoration of the religious form of marriage seems to be a natural reaction to the suppression of the church under the Soviet regime, where the mandatory civil form of marriage "was associated with the militant atheism of the Soviet domination" (Antokolskaia, 2006, p. 302). This new freedom gave the citizens of the Baltic countries the opportunity to choose the form of marriage according to their faith and, if they wished, to have a religious wedding ceremony with the same legal force as a marriage officiated by a civil servant. The change may also be viewed as an attempt to bring more stability into the family.

The civil form of marriage was introduced in Russia only after the Bolshevik coup d'état of October 1917. Before that, all matters connected with the conclusion of marriage fell within the exclusive jurisdiction of the church or other religious institutions. Accordingly, there were different rules on the marriage ceremony for members of different religious confessions and denominations. There was no civil (secular) form of marriage recognized in the country at all,[8] and pre-revolutionary Russia strongly opposed all attempts to introduce any civil form of marriage registration. This was one of the main reasons why Russia did not ratify the Hague Convention of 1902 relating to the Settlement of the Conflict of Laws, which provided recognition of marriages concluded abroad in a civil form (Goikhbarg, 1927, p.177).

The Bolsheviks understood that in order to fulfill one of the main tasks of the new Soviet regime, which was to "smash the pre-revolutionary conceptions entirely" (Berman, 1946/1947, pp. 35–36), one necessary step was to tear down completely and as quickly as possible all the old family-law rules and to take family law out of the jurisdiction of the church. One of the first acts adopted by the new regime, therefore, was the decree (*Dekret*) of December 18, 1917, "On Civil Marriage, on Children, and on the Keeping of Civil Registry Books,"[9] which transferred acts of civil status from the jurisdiction of the church to that of the state, denied legal force to religious marriages, and established that the only legal form of marriage was civil (secular).[10] It declared citizens' freedom to conclude marriage and abolished most of the obstacles presented by the old pre-revolutionary law, thus liberating marriage law from numerous religious and class (*soslovnykh*) conditions. The secularization of marriage directly affected the country's whole population, both urban and rural. It was a true revolution in ideology and the popular mindset (Genkin et al., 1949, p. 396) and "a sharp break with Russia's own traditions" (Carlbäck, 2005, p. 72).

However important the secularization of marriage was for the country at the time, Russia was not first in the world in this regard. It was from France, after the French Revolution, that the civil form of marriage "spread all over the world" (Glendon, 1989, p. 33).[11] Nevertheless, quite apart from the introduction of secular marriage, the post-revolutionary reforms in Russia in 1917–1926 differentiated the new Russian (Soviet) family law entirely from Western law of the same period. To add just the most important changes to those already mentioned, the law provided for equality between men and women; the introduction of no-fault divorce, and later, divorce upon demand (to which I will return below); the abolition of the concept of illegitimacy, which gave all children the same rights vis-à-vis their parents and other relatives regardless of whether they were born in or out of wedlock; and, finally in 1926, legal recognition of *de facto* marriages, or extramarital cohabitation.[12] To a certain extent these changes are comparable only with the Swedish family law reform of 1915, which introduced a mandatory civil or religious celebration of marriage and permitted divorce on no-fault grounds (ibid., pp. 74, 184).[13] Family law in the rest of the Western world was still based on the subordinate position of women, the inequality of children born outside legal marriage, and fault-based divorce. Changes began to take place only after World War II, "at some time between the late 1950s and the late 1970s" (Willekens, 1998, p. 53). Among the first laws to introduce changes were the West German Equal Rights Law of 1957, a French law of 1970 that deprived the husband of his position as "the head of the family," and the 1969 English and California divorce law reforms discussed in the next section below.

After it was abolished in 1917, the religious form of marriage never entailed any legal consequences in the Soviet Union.[14] The only exception was made later for marriages concluded in religious form during World War II in the occupied Soviet territories before the Soviet Civil Registry Offices (*otdel zapisi aktov grazhdanskogo sostoiania*)[15] were restored there. These marriages have been and are still recognized as valid, irrespective of whether they were subsequently officially registered.[16]

The post-Soviet Russian family law—the Family Code of 1995—followed the Soviet tradition and stipulated that the only valid form of marriage was marriage concluded in the state Civil Registry Offices (s. 10). There are no legal rules requiring that a religious marriage ceremony be conducted only after registration in such an office. These issues are regulated by the rules of the relevant religious denomination. However, most of the Christian Orthodox churches, at least in Moscow, perform weddings only after a couple is officially married and can present the marriage certificate to the priest.

Having reintroduced the religious form of marriage, the Baltic countries have returned to the status quo that existed before their annexation by the USSR. As has already been mentioned, there was no civil marriage in the Russian Empire, and accordingly there was no civil marriage in the Baltic territories belonging to it. And in Estonia, for instance, the "Private Law of the Baltic Provinces" of the Russian Empire remained in force until 1940. During the turbulent post-revolutionary years in Latvia, the Soviet government introduced Soviet laws in some of the territories. In particular, the archaic family law of the Russian Empire was abolished and the mandatory state registration of marriage was introduced, yet this legislation was in effect there for only a short time (Vebers, 1997, p. 208). Additional changes came into marriage legislation during the period of independence. In 1921 the Latvian Law on Matrimony was enacted, which made the civil (secular) or religious form of marriage optional. This was most likely due to the influence not only (or, perhaps, not so much) of Soviet secular family legislation, but also of progressive Nordic laws. This law was in force until the adoption of the 1937 Civil Law of Latvia (Civil Code), which entered into legal force in 1938 and also provided prospective spouses with the opportunity to choose between the civil or religious form of marriage. The "new" Civil Law of 1992, as has already been noted, is in fact the re-enacted Civil Law of 1937.

Although the family law as a part of the Latvian Civil Law that is currently in force was significantly revised (for more on this, see, for instance, Fridrihsons, 2001), in many respects it goes back to the law of the era of independence. Thus the Civil Law states that a marriage may be solemnized by the registrar of a General Registry Office or a minister of the denominations set out in the Code (s. 53). Listed under s. 51 of the Code, these are Evangelical Lutheran, Roman Catholic, Orthodox, Old Believers, Methodist, Baptist, Seventh Day Adventist, and believers in Moses (Judaism), currently the major faiths in Latvia (Vebers, 1997, p. 212). Ministers of these denominations may perform wedding ceremonies provided they have been given permission by the leaders of the respective denomination (ss. 51, 53). The Civil Law requires that for each solemnized marriage, the ministers send the information required for the marriage register to the General Registry Office in the area in which the marriage has taken place. If the minister fails to perform this duty within fourteen days, the minister may be held administratively liable (s. 58). As for other denominations not listed in the code, clergy may marry couples only after the marriage has been registered by the civil authorities (ibid.).

The Estonian Family Law Act of 1994 initially did not provide for a religious form of marriage. Although the country needed family law reform, there was not enough time for a complete revision of family law, which would have required thorough research and consideration of new provisions "in light of the legal tradition of Continental Europe" (Kullerkupp, 2001a, p. 96). Therefore, the new Family Law Act of 1994 contained only the most urgent changes, and in its main concepts and scope of regulation it in fact bore "a substantial resemblance to its predecessor, the Marriage and Family Code of the ESSR," which was in force in Estonia during the Soviet period (ibid.). Work on the new draft started in 1996; as was expected, it reflects the main features of European family law and the Continental European legal tradition to which the Estonian legal system belonged "both culturally and historically" (ibid.). Since the adoption of the Family Law Act, the provisions on the registration of marriage have been amended several times, particularly in 2004, when a religious form of marriage was introduced in addition to the secular form. The latest innovations in this regard, however, were incorporated into Estonian family law by the new Family Law Act of 2009 and by the Vital Statistics Registration Act, which came into force at the same time. In accordance with the new provisions, a minister of a religious congregation or association of congregations may be granted the right to act as a Vital Statistics officer for the purpose of marriage registration. In such a case, a properly authorized religious minister may register marriages and issue marriage certificates. If a prospective spouse does not meet the requirements for the conclusion of marriage according to the religion of the church, congregation, or association of congregations, the minister has the right to refuse to register the marriage (Family Law Act 2009, § 6).

There is much more uncertainty with regard to the Lithuanian version of religious marriage. The Lithuanian Civil Code permits the formation of religious marriage in the procedure established by the church (confession) (art. 3.24). Furthermore, in the same article the Civil Code lays down the conditions under which religious marriage entails "the same legal consequences as those entailed by the formation of a marriage in the Register Office." For this purpose the Code also requires that: 1) the conditions for concluding a marriage laid down in the Civil Code be satisfied; and 2) the marriage be formed according to the procedures established by the canons of a religious organization registered in and recognized by the Republic of Lithuania. Among them there is the requirement that the formation of a marriage in the procedure established by the church (confession) be "recorded at the Register Office in the procedure provided for herein." The person authorized by the respective religious organization is obliged to present to the local Register Office notification of the religious marriage solemnized in the procedure set by the church (confession) within ten days of the marriage ceremony (art. 3.304 [1]). If this requirement has been met and the Register Office receives the notification on time, the marriage is considered to be concluded on the day of the religious ceremony. However, if the notification requirement has not been fulfilled on time, "the marriage shall be held to have been contracted on the day when it was registered in the Register Office."

In such a case, the question reasonably arises whether the Lithuanian version of religious marriage is a "true" religious marriage or just a marriage ceremony that acquires all the requisites of lawful marriage and entails the legal consequences of a lawful marriage only after its registration by the civil authorities. If it is not a "true" religious marriage but a religious marriage that "transcends into a civil one" (Keserauskas, 2004, p. 323)—and the wording of the Civil Code suggests such a conclusion—then the Civil Code in this part is not quite in line with the 1992 Lithuanian Constitution, which "provides for the unconditional recognition of religious marriage" (ibid., pp. 322–323). A practical question that could be raised in this regard is whether a person who dies within ten days after a religious marriage ceremony, without having his or her marriage registered in the Register Office, is to be considered lawfully married, with all the legal consequences thereof. There is no answer to this question in the Lithuanian Civil Code, which to clarify the situation would need to specify whether a marriage can be deemed legally valid on the basis of the religious ceremony alone.

The restoration of the religious form of marriage possessing the same legal meaning and consequences as the civil one was accompanied in Latvia and Lithuania by the restoration of the publication (or announcement) of marriage, an ancient religious institution that has now been extended to the civil form of marriage as well. "Before a marriage is solemnized, it shall be published," declares the Latvian Civil Law (s. 40). The announcement of a forthcoming marriage is to be posted one month in advance at the General Registry Office where the marriage application has been submitted (ss. 44–45). In the case of a religious marriage ceremony, the marriage is publicized in accordance with the procedures of the respective denomination (s. 51). The Lithuanian Civil Code also provides for "the public announcement of an application for the registration of marriage" (art. 3.302). The Lithuanian Code specifies that the announcement shall indicate the given names, surnames, and birthdates of the future spouses and the date of the marriage registration. As has long been the case, the purpose of publicly announcing a forthcoming marriage ceremony is to allow objections or knowledge of any legal impediment to the marriage to be voiced. To this "old" goal Vebers (1999: 214) adds another one, namely to generate a more serious attitude to the conclusion of marriage.

Another institution that relates to the conclusion of marriage that was abolished in the USSR and restored as the result of recent reforms in Latvia and Lithuania is betrothal (engagement). The Latvian Civil Law defines betrothal as "a mutual promise to join together in marriage" (s. 26). Lithuanian family law defines engagement as an "agreement to marry" (art. 3.8). It differentiates between private and public engagements made in private and in public, respectively. An agreement to marry is deemed to be public if the parties submit a marriage application to the Register Office.

The betrothal or engagement provisions do not aim to force anyone to marry based on prior consent. "Agreement to marry is not binding and may not be enforced," states art. 3.8 of the Lithuanian Civil Code. Under Latvian law, betrothal does not confer the right to file a suit forcing one of the parties to enter into marriage (s. 26). Under certain circumstances, however, betrothal (engagement) may have legal consequences. The general principle is that if a betrothal is terminated, each of the parties must return everything that has been received in connection with the intended marriage. Under Lithuanian law these consequences apply only in the case of public engagement. Irrespective of whether the engagement was public or private, however, if one of the parties refuses to enter into marriage without good cause, she or he is required to compensate the damages incurred by the other party due to the refusal. In the case of a public engagement, a compensation claim for non-pecuniary damage may be also brought against the party at fault.

The purpose of provisions on engagement seems to be twofold. First, as a traditional institution of Western family law, it has always aimed to protect the property rights of the betrothed (engaged), especially when this person was not responsible for the cancellation of the engagement. Secondly, it may also increase the responsibility for promising to marry or for breaking the promise by imposing sanctions on a refusal without good cause. It is not yet clear whether such a measure will promote a more responsible attitude towards marriage.

Thus having reintroduced the religious form of marriage as an alternative to secular marriage, the Baltic countries have joined Western jurisdictions, where with regard to the marriage ceremony "different variants of what one might call *pluralistic systems* are in force" (Glendon, 1989, p. 67) that allow the prospective spouses to choose the form of ceremony most appropriate to their tastes and beliefs.

Divorce Law

Soviet divorce law has been traditionally considered liberal, even though in the USSR divorced couples were sometimes publicly criticized for their inability to save their marriage (Kelly, 2007, p. 387). Nevertheless, with the exception of a period between 1944 and the early 1960s, it was easy to get divorced—much easier than, for instance, under the 1915 Swedish divorce reform, which at the time was considered to be "the most permissive in Europe" (Antokolskaia, 2006, pp. 315, 317). Interestingly, the liberal Soviet divorce law and particularly early Bolshevik divorce legislation clearly influenced the Swedish family law reform of 1973 (Sundberg, 1975, p. 34).

Marxist theory interpreted freedom of divorce as a precondition for freedom of marriage and its logical continuation. According to Lenin, "in actual fact freedom of divorce will not cause the 'disintegration' of family ties, but, on the contrary, will strengthen them on a democratic basis, which is the only possible and durable basis in civilized society" (Lenin, 1972). Divorce reform was an important part of the Bolshevik reform of family law and an effective tool for the reorganization of society.

The church's exclusive competence with regard to the conclusion of marriage that existed in Russia before October 1917 was paralleled by its exclusive competence in divorce matters. The possibility of divorce, if any, and the grounds for divorce were determined by the rules of the particular confession to which the parties belonged, and divorce cases were handled by ecclesiastical courts. The divorce procedure was complicated and based on fault grounds (adultery being one of the most serious offenses)(for more detail, see Antokolskaia, 2010, p. 92).

Like the above-mentioned decree introducing civil marriage, the divorce reform implemented by the decree of December 19, 1917 ("On Divorce"), was meant to take family matters out of the jurisdiction of the church and, it was thought at the time, "forever put an end to the participation of the church with respect to the termination of marital relations" (Genkin et al., 1949, p. 397). "On Divorce" declared the "freedom of divorce" and abolished the concept of guilt and all the fault grounds. It became possible to dissolve marriage in a local court or, in cases of mutual consent, in administrative bodies under a simplified procedure without any inquiry at all. The subsequent legislation of 1918 and especially of 1926[17] made the divorce procedure even more simple, narrowing it down to mere registration upon demand by one or both spouses. This, unsurprisingly, was received in the Europe of those days as "a shocking extremity" (Antokolskaia, 2006, p. 240). A short folk song even appeared that went roughly as follows: "Now the Soviets are in power, and I no longer fear my husband. If I'm not happy with him, I'll just get a divorce."[18] The result was that in the early 1920s, 14 percent of marriages ended in divorce, which commentators have correctly stated to be "an enormous figure for those times" (Engel, 2004, p. 154). The divorce rate was more than twice that in Germany and was almost three times the rate in France (ibid.). In 1934 in Moscow there were already thirty-seven divorces for every 100 marriages, and this number tended to increase (Berman, 1946/1947, p. 46).

Although it liberated women from the "tyranny of their husbands," freedom of divorce exacerbated the serious social and economic problems accompanying marriage instability in a country where the financial position of the overwhelming majority of the population was poor. Divorced women with children tried to sue their husbands for child support, but they often failed to get the money. Indeed, although freedom of divorce liberated women, by the same token it made it easy for men to get rid of marriages that they considered unhappy or that they were just tired of. Often women filed suits against men who were seeking to end their fourth or fifth marriage; there were reports of men who were divorced "as many as fifteen times, leaving ex-wives and children to fend for themselves" (Engel, 2004, p. 154). In such cases the court could hardly rule that any considerable support be paid to the former wife.

The pro-family policy that Stalin started to pursue in the mid-1930s and which was fully realized in the notorious edict (*Ukaz*) of July 8, 1944, aimed at what was called "strengthening the Soviet family." However, what it actually did was to put the private life of Soviet citizens under more stringent state control (Edict "On Increasing Public Support to Pregnant Mothers, Mothers with Many Children, Single Mothers, Enhancing the Protection of Motherhood and Childhood, Proclaiming 'Heroine Mother' as the Title of Highest Distinction, and Establishing the Order of Maternal Glory and the Medal of Motherhood"). With this goal in view, the edict made the divorce procedure significantly more difficult: it abolished divorce on demand and put it under the strict control of the courts, which also made it rather expensive. Instead of the previous simple administrative procedure, which allowed a divorce to be registered with a state Civil Registry Office upon the request of either spouse alone without citing any reasons, the edict introduced a two-stage divorce procedure in court. The petitioner was obliged to state the grounds for divorce, which sometimes required witnesses to be involved, and approval or denial of the request was left to the discretion of the court. Notice of divorce proceedings was to be published in a local newspaper at the petitioner's expense, and divorce itself was generally accompanied by public condemnation. The result was that it became "more difficult to obtain a divorce in Soviet Russia than in many capitalist countries where civil marriage [was] recognized" (Gsovski, 1948/1949, p. 125).

Divorce law was liberalized by a special edict in 1965 which was later incorporated into the 1968 "Fundamentals of Legislation of the USSR and Soviet Republics on Marriage and the Family." A year later, the RSFR Family Code of 1969 finally repealed the harshest provisions of Stalin's legislation.[19] The Code restored administrative divorce procedure but limited it to cases of mutual consent with no children involved. As for divorce proceedings in court, they were greatly simplified in comparison with the Stalin period but still required the court to inquire into the reasons of divorce and demanded that the petitioner prove that the marriage had broken down irretrievably. The 1969 Russian law with regard to divorce was "more or less released from the extremes" of both post-revolutionary legislation and Stalin's conservative family policy (Antokolskaia, 2006, p. 317). It regarded the breakdown of the marriage and the impossibility of restoring family life as grounds for divorce and was thus more progressive than divorce law of the time in most Western countries, which was still based primarily on the principle of fault.

Coincidentally, 1969, the year when the RSFSR code on marriage and divorce was adopted, was also of special importance in the development of Western family law, as it marked the beginning of a radical revision of divorce law there. In 1969 England adopted the Divorce Reform Act abolishing fault as the grounds for divorce.[20] The same year, California was the first state in the United States to abolish fault-based divorce. After that date, "suddenly, the dam seemed to burst in divorce law [...] The old system collapsed completely" (Friedman, 1984, p. 664). In the ten years that followed, the majority of Western European countries and the overwhelming majority of American states adopted laws that either replaced fault as the grounds for divorce with no-fault grounds (irremediable or irretrievable breakdown, irreconcilable differences, incompatibility, and/or a living-apart requirement) or introduced no-fault grounds but kept traditional fault-based divorce as an alternative. Today, no-fault divorce is permitted in every American state (Bettelheim, 2010).

The Nordic countries represent an interesting exception in this regard because divorce reform took place much earlier there. No-fault divorce was introduced in Sweden in 1915, in Norway in 1918, and in Denmark, Finland, and Iceland in the 1920s. As noted in Antokolskaia (2006, p. 234), for many scholars there is still no convincing explanation as to why the Nordic region was the first in Europe to modernize its family law in a "natural" fashion rather than as a result of political revolution, as for instance, happened in the Soviet Union. Most probably there were several interconnected reasons for such a tolerant attitude to divorce. These included a relatively high level of secularization; a historically relatively liberal family law; the established practice of obtaining royal permission to divorce; the established practice of "Copenhagen divorce" (trips to the closest foreign city, which allowed the spouses, in collusion, to simulate desertion and thus acquire legal grounds for divorce); the frequency of informal, non-registered unions known as "Stockholm marriages," especially among the working class who could not afford the trips to Copenhagen (Glendon, 1989, p. 183).[21] Interestingly, much later, in the mid-twentieth century, before divorce law was liberalized in the rest of the Western world, another type of divorce by collusion became widespread there, when, usually a husband stayed with his girlfriend in a hotel room and that could be witnessed—a practice known as "hotel adultery," described in Irwin Shaw's novel *Evening in Byzantium*.

As for the Soviet Russian Code of 1969, it remained valid for twenty-six years until, in the post-Soviet era, the new Family Code of 1995 was adopted. With regards to divorce, the Code's drafters had two main objectives. First, it was necessary to make the divorce procedure easier for mutually consenting couples. Second—and in contrast with the first point—it was necessary to put child-related matters under stricter control of the court. Thus it is stated in the Code that if the spouses agree that the marriage has broken down, the court issues a divorce decree without ascertaining reasons or attempting to reconcile the spouses. Even if the spouses are silent with respect to their child, however, the court is to solve child-related questions (concerning the child's place of residence and maintenance) (s. 24 [2]). The parents are encouraged to present their agreement concerning their children to the court, but if they fail to come to an accord or if, in the court's opinion, the agreement infringes upon the rights of the children, the court steps in and makes its own decision. Thus, although it has not overcome some shortcomings and inconsistencies in the previous, Soviet-era legislation, the current Russian divorce law remains relatively liberal and is based on the no-fault concept. This sharply contrasts with what can be found in the laws of some newly independent post-Soviet states, particularly in Latvia and even more so in Lithuania.

Technically, the new Latvian law did not reintroduce the fault-based divorce that was originally stipulated in the Civil Law of 1937, but it nevertheless made the divorce procedure much more complicated than it was under the Soviet law. First, it abolished the simplified so-called "administrative" divorce procedure for couples who did not have common children and who were in mutual agreement regarding the divorce itself and its consequences. Second, although it is formally based on a concept of marriage breakdown which itself does not differ from the old Soviet model, the necessity to present grounds to prove the fact of breakdown makes getting divorced more difficult. The main difference is that under the Latvian Civil Law a marriage is presumed to have broken down if the spouses have lived apart for at least three years (s. 72). In such a case it is possible to get a divorce order even without the consent of the other spouse. If the spouses live separately for less than three years, the marriage can be dissolved only in three cases stipulated in the Law (s. 74). The first case is when continuation of the marriage is not possible for the spouse who has requested the dissolution of the marriage, due to reasons that are dependent upon the other spouse and due to which cohabitation with him or her would be intolerable cruelty towards the spouse who has requested the dissolution of the marriage. The second case is when both spouses request the dissolution of the marriage or one spouse consents to the other spouse's request for the dissolution of the marriage. The third case is when one of the spouses has begun cohabitating with another person and in such cohabitation the birth of a child has occurred or is expected.

The Law expressly forbids the dissolution of a marriage before the expiration of the three-year separation period if the other spouse does not consent to divorce and none of the reasons for divorce fits one of the three cases mentioned above (s. 75). Moreover, the court shall not dissolve a marriage—even though it has broken down—if "the preservation of the marriage as an exception due to special reasons is necessary in the interests of minor children born in the marriage" (s. 76). Similarly, the court shall not dissolve a marriage if all divorce-related issues (custody and maintenance of children born in the marriage, division of common property, and so on) have not been resolved before the dissolution of the marriage and are not raised simultaneously with the divorce application (s. 77).

The Latvian Civil Law does not use the term "fault" with regard to divorce or its consequences. However, in accordance with the fault-based divorce logic, Latvian law says that upon the application of one of the spouses, a court may prohibit the spouse who has promoted the breakdown of the marriage from using the surname acquired in marriage after divorce if it does not affect the interests of the child (s. 82). As far as the issues of spousal maintenance after divorce are concerned—another divorce-related consequence that may have fault-based implications—the Civil Law states that the right to claim maintenance is conditioned on the financial status of each of the ex-spouses, and "a former spouse may claim means from the other former spouse commensurate with his or her financial state if the latter by his or her actions has promoted the breakdown of the marriage and the means are necessary to ensure or maintain the previous level of welfare" (s. 80).

Latvian divorce reform made Latvian legislation similar to that in many European countries, where grounds for divorce vary from divorce by mutual consent (with no or minimum inquiry) to fault of one of the spouses in the breakdown of the marriage and to divorce based on a certain period of separation (which varies from country to country: for instance, it is one year in Denmark and Norway, two years in France, three years in Germany, four years in Switzerland, five years in England, and six years in Austria) (for more detail, see Antokolskaia, 2006, p. 355). At the same time, although they established a differentiated approach to divorce, Latvian legislators made the divorce procedure more complicated overall in comparison with how it was regulated under Soviet law and how it is regulated under the current Swedish law. In accordance with the Swedish Marriage Code of 1987,[22] if spouses with no common children agree to divorce, they have a right to immediate divorce upon application (divorce on demand); if there is a child under sixteen years of age in the family, the granting of divorce must be preceded by a reconsideration period of six months. Swedish divorce law does not provide for any fault-based grounds for divorce at all (Jänterä-Jareborg, 2002, pp. 3–4).

The Lithuanian family law reform of 2000 is more straightforward. Although the Code restored fault-based divorce, which demonstrated that the concept had not vanished completely, it also stipulated two no-fault types of divorce. Book III on Family Law of the Lithuanian Civil Code is based to a significant extent on the French Civil Code (Mikelenas, 2000, p. 249), and with regard to divorce, the Lithuanian provisions resemble those that were introduced into French family law by the divorce reform of 1975. Under this 1975 reform fault-based divorce was replaced by several different grounds and offered divorcing couples "a number of avenues to divorce" (Glendon, 1989, p. 162). These grounds, or "avenues," were so varied and so many that the reform was described as having established "divorce *à la carte*" (Glendon, 1989, p. 162). Like the French provisions, the divorce provisions of the Lithuanian Civil Code offer different "avenues" for terminating broken marriages. Apart from divorce based on the fault of one of the spouses, it also provides for: 1) divorce by mutual consent, and 2) divorce on the application of one of the spouses (based on marital separation in one or another form).

Divorce by mutual consent is permitted in accordance with the Lithuanian Civil Code through a simplified procedure, provided that one year has elapsed from the conclusion of the marriage, that the spouses have made a contract covering all the consequences of the divorce (both property and child-related), and that both spouses have full legal capacity (art. 3.51). However, there is still no "automatic" divorce, even if there is mutual consent between the spouses regarding the divorce itself and all divorce-related issues. The spouses must indicate in their mutual application for divorce the reasons for the breakdown of their marriage. The court will issue a divorce order "if it is satisfied that the marriage has broken down irretrievably" (art. 3.53). Separation "from bed and board" for over a year makes divorce much easier, as it serves as a statutory presumption that a marriage has irretrievably broken down.

Divorce on the application of one of the spouses is designed for cases in which there are no fault-based grounds for divorce and the spouses do not apply for divorce by mutual consent. These cases are as follows: 1) the spouses have been separated for over one year; 2) one of the spouses, after the conclusion of the marriage, has been declared legally incapacitated by the court; 3) one of the spouses has been declared missing by the court; or 4) one of the spouses has been imprisoned for over a year for a non-premeditated crime (art. 3.55). The Code establishes a simplified procedure for this type of divorce, too. However, it also sets out what may be called a "hardship clause" that may prevent the spouses from divorcing even after one year of separation. Taking into consideration the age of one of the spouses, the length of the marriage, and the interests of minor children, the court may refuse to grant a divorce decree if divorce "may cause significant harm to the property and non-property interests of one of the spouses or their children" (art. 3.57 [3]).

Divorce through the fault of one of the spouses is based on a traditional understanding of fault grounds for divorce, meaning that a serious breach of family or matrimonial duties must occur. Namely, the Code refers to adultery committed by a spouse, violence towards the other spouse or family members, desertion of the family by a spouse for over one year, or conviction of a spouse of a premeditated crime (art. 3.60). The court may find that both spouses are at fault for the breakdown of their marriage. In such a case, the consequences are the same as in divorce by mutual consent.

In accordance with the fault-based approach to divorce, the Lithuanian Code stipulates that in the case of divorce granted on the fault basis, the spouse at fault loses the right of a divorcee under the law or even according to the terms of a marriage contract, including the right to maintenance (art. 3.70 [1]). Thus the goal of divorce reform was not only to bring back fault grounds as such to divorce law, but also, first, to make the divorce procedure in general more complicated and, second, to punish the party at fault. Moreover, it was intended to have a "preventive and educative effect on society" (Keserauskas, 2004, p. 331). I share the skepticism expressed by Lithuanian scholars (ibid., p. 332), however, as to whether conservative divorce law can achieve this objective of discouraging divorce and promoting stability in the family.

In what has been described as the "significant novelty introduced under the new Code" (ibid., p. 327), Lithuanian legislators also restored legal separation as an institution complementary to the dissolution of marriage by divorce. The revival of legal separation—an ancient institution that originated in canon law and that still exists in many European countries—is undoubtedly attributable to the increased role of the church in post-Soviet society, as it provides a good option to those who for various and above all religious reasons do not consider divorce acceptable. Not surprisingly, legal separation was unknown in Soviet family law.

The separation proceedings and some of the legal consequences are similar to those of the divorce procedure. The Lithuanian Code says that in order to be legally separated, one or both of the spouses must apply to the court. Separated couples are not released from the marriage bonds, however, and they do not acquire the right to marry anybody else. Most importantly, a court judgment on separation releases the spouses "from the obligation to live together" (art. 3.77). Depending on the facts of the case and in particular on who initiated the separation proceeding, who is the party at fault, and whether the spouses have reached agreement regarding property and financial issues, the spouses' rights and duties may or may not be extinguished as the result of the separation judgment.

The changes to the divorce procedure in the Estonian Family Law Act seem to be less substantial than those in Latvia and Lithuania. As in the Soviet legislation and in contrast to the Latvian and Lithuanian legislation, current Estonian law provides for both "judicial" and "administrative" divorce (Kullerkupp, 2001a, p. 103). It has preserved a simplified administrative divorce procedure (in a Vital Statistics Office) for cases in which there is agreement between the spouses on divorce and other (including child-related)[23] matters, providing they reside in Estonia (§ 64) and present a joint written petition. If the spouses disagree concerning divorce or the circumstances related to divorce, or if a Vital Statistics Office is not competent to grant divorce, the divorce case is heard by a court. Initially, in the Family Law Act of 1994, it was stipulated only that a court grants divorce if it "ascertains that continuation of the marriage is impossible" (§ 29 [2]). The current law (the Family Law Act of 2009) makes the procedure a bit more sophisticated. Like the 1994 Act, the Act of 2009 says that a court can grant divorce if conjugal relations have been terminated. However, in contrast to the 1994 Act, it goes into more detail and defines conjugal relations as terminated "if the spouses do not have matrimonial cohabitation any longer and there is reason to believe that the spouses will not restore cohabitation" (§ 67 [1]). Furthermore, the Act of 2009 stipulates that a two-year separation gives a court the grounds to presume that conjugal relations are terminated (§ 67 [2]). A court may adjourn granting a divorce for a period of up to six months to allow the spouses to reconcile, if it finds it appropriate. A separation period that proves the breakdown of a marriage is new to Estonian family law and similar to the provisions on separation in the legislation of Latvia, Lithuania, and some other countries. It means that if the spouses have not been separated for two years by the time of the divorce proceedings, the court must investigate the circumstances of the spousal conflict before it can conclude that there is "reason to believe that the spouses will not restore cohabitation," as the Family Law Act of 2009 requires.

Thus, in contrast with the Latvian and Lithuanian divorce reforms, the main difference between divorce law in newly independent Estonia and that of the Soviet period consists of a simplified divorce procedure in cases of mutual consent between the spouses on divorce and all divorce-related matters. In this situation, divorce can be granted by administrative procedure, even if the divorcing spouses have underage children. This was immediately reflected in the ratio of divorces performed in a Vital Statistics Office (administrative procedure) to those that went to court. For instance, between 1990 and 1994 (when the Soviet family law was in force), 82 percent of divorces were performed by Estonian courts, while only 18 percent went through administrative procedure. In 1995, the first year when the new law was in force, the divorce ratio reversed dramatically to 29 percent performed by the courts and 71 percent in Vital Statistics Offices (Salumaa, 1996, p. 95). It would be interesting to know whether the changes in the divorce procedure in court introduced by the new Estonian family law of 2009 will affect the "judicial" and "administrative" divorce ratio, but it is still too early to draw any conclusions in this regard.

Conclusion

To understand the conservative turn that family law has taken in some of the Baltic countries, we need to bear in mind the context of their historical development and above all, of course, their Soviet past. The secularization of marriage and liberalization of divorce law during the Soviet period were not the result of a gradual development of family law in the Baltic states similar to that in Western countries. That is why the restoration of religious marriage in Latvia, Lithuania, and Estonia may be interpreted as "a partial compensation for the repression" (Keserauskas, 2004, p. 322) that the church experienced under communist rule. Because it is linked to some extent to the revival of the role of the religion in the post-Soviet era, the restoration of fault-based divorce should be also interpreted as a reaction to "the divorce culture" that formed there during the decades of the Soviet regime. It is not surprising, therefore, that many liberal provisions of Soviet family law were ultimately discarded as part of the "Soviet heritage" (Antokolskaia, 2006, p. 271). As they reconsidered their family law and tried to move it forward, the Baltic states had to go back to pre-Soviet times and start from the point where their development was interrupted.[24]

Despite the conservative tone of some of the provisions in the laws of the Baltic countries, there are also signs of movement towards European liberal family law concepts. The most obvious example is the provisions of the Lithuanian Civil Code that regulate property rights of cohabiting but not legally married couples (Chapter XV).

NOTES

1 In Latvia, the Civil Code (Civil Law) of 1937 was restored with some amendments.
2 This replaced the Family Law Act of 1994.
3 RSFSR is an abbreviation for the Russian Soviet Federative Socialist Republic.
4 As was noted in the preface to the English translation of the Code, see *The Civil Law of Latvia*, 2001.
5 The 1987 Swedish Cohabitees (Joint Homes) Act.
6 This was a problem typical of most countries in the socialist bloc in Eastern Europe before 1989. See, for instance, Todorova (2007, pp. 79–95).
7 The Russian Federation joined the Council of Europe in 1996 and ratified the European Convention on Human Rights in 1998.
8 Exception was made only for the "schismatics," those belonging to a religious movement in the Russian Orthodox Church that rejected a reform aimed at unification of the liturgical rank of the Russian Church with the Greek Church, and first of all, the Church of Constantinople (1650–1660). The reform resulted in the split in the Russian Church; the adherents of the old traditions are also called the "splitters" (*raskol'niki*).
9 As well as the Decree on Divorce discussed below.
10 From 1926 until 1944, *de facto* marriage relations (nonmarital cohabitation) entailed the same legal consequences as a marriage concluded at the Civil Registry Office (*otdel zapisi aktov grazhdanskogo sostoiania*).
11 The civil (secular) marriage ceremony was declared mandatory in France by the revolutionary decree of September 20, 1792, and was incorporated later into the Code Napoléon of 1804.
12 The majority of these liberal provisions were abolished under Stalin and were not restored until the late 1960s, with the exception of *de facto* marriages, which had never been recognized after being abolished in 1944. For more detail, see Khazova (1998, pp. 73–76).
13 The civil (secular) form of marriage as an alternative to the religious one was also introduced in Norway in 1918.
14 In later years these provisions were incorporated into the subsequent Soviet Family Codes of 1918, 1926, and 1968.
15 In the following, I use country-specific terminology for this agency: Estonia—Vital Statistics Office, Latvia—General Registry Office, Lithuania—Register Office, and Russia—the Acts of Civil Status Registry Office.

16 The current family law also recognizes the validity of this form of marriage (Semeinyi Kodeks… 1996, s. 169 [7]).
17 Namely, the Code on the Acts of Civil Status, Marriage, Family, and Custody Law of 1918 (*Kodeks zakonov ob aktakh grazhdanskogo sostoiania, brachnom, semeinom i opekunskom prave*) and the Code on Marriage, Family, and Custody 1926 (*Kodeks zakonov o brake, sem'e i opeke*).
18 "Sovetskaia vlast'—muzha ne boiusia. Budet plokho zhit'—poidu razvedusia!"
19 The difference in the courts' attitude to divorce in the 1980s versus the late 1940s, when Stalin's divorce legislation was still in force, may be illustrated by a divorce case that was considered by the USSR Supreme Court twice, in 1949 and in 1985. The latter reflected a much more liberal standpoint towards divorce: in 1949 the facts presented were considered insufficient to prove the breakdown of the marriage, while in 1985 the same facts were ruled sufficient to prove the breakdown of the marriage. For a description of the case in English, see Butler (1986/1987, pp. 239–240).
20 However, its enactment was postponed until 1971, when the law regulating some of the economic consequences of marriage dissolution was to be adopted.
21 For more detail, see Antokolskaia (2006, pp. 234–236), Gendon (1989, pp. 182–184), Rheinstein (1972, pp. 139–142).
22 The rules of the 1973 Swedish reform were transferred to the new Marriage Code of 1987, Book 5 of which regulates divorce.
23 Under Soviet law, divorce could not be granted by the state offices of registration of civil status if the spouses had common underage children (The Fundamentals of Legislation of the USSR and Soviet Republics on Marriage and the Family 1998, s. 14).
24 See, for instance, J. Vebers (1997, p. 209), who notes that the restoration of independence in the Baltic states provided an opportunity to continue the interrupted development of the market economy and institutions of the democratic state.

References

Antokolskaia, Masha, ed. 2006. *Harmonisation of Family Law in Europe: A Historical Perspective*. Antwerp and Oxford: Intersentia.

———. 2010. *Semeinoe pravo: Uchebnik*. Moscow: Norma Infra-M.

Berman, Harold J. 1946/1947. "Soviet Family Law in the Light of Russian History and Marxist Theory." *Yale Law Journal*, no. 56: 26–57.

Bettelheim, Ruth. 2010. "No Fault of Their Own." *New York Times*, http://www.nytimes.com/2010/02/18/opinion/18bettelheim.html (accessed June 28, 2011).

Butler, William E. 1986/1987. "Soviet Union: The Transition to the Gorbachev Era; Annual Survey of Family Law 1985." *Journal of Family Law* 25: 237–243.

Carlbäck, Helene. 2005. "Tracing the Roots of Early Soviet Russian Family Laws." In *Gender Transitions in Russia and Eastern Europe*, eds. Ildikó Asztalos Morell,

Helene Carlbäck, Madeleine Hurd, and Sara Rastbäck, 69–84. Eslöv, Sweden: Gondolin.
Engel, Barbara. 2004. *Women in Russia, 1700–2000*. Cambridge: Cambridge University Press.
Fridrihsons, Imants. 2001. "Court Procedure in Legal Disputes on Family Rights." *Humanities and Social Sciences: Latvia; University of Latvia* 31, no. 2: 75–82.
Friedman, Lawrence. 1984. "Rights of Passage: Divorce Law in Historical Perspective." *Oregon Law Review*, no. 63: 649–670.
Genkin, D.M., I.B. Novitskii, and N.V. Rabinovich. 1949. *Istoriia sovetskogo grazhdanskogo prava 1917–1947* (The history of Soviet civil law 1917–1947). Moscow: Yuridichwskoe izdatel'stvo Ministerstva Yustitsii SSSR.
Glendon, Mary A. 1989. *The Transformation of Family Law: State, Law, and Family in the United States and Western Europe*. Chicago: University of Chicago Press.
Goikhbarg, A.G. 1927. *Sravnitel'noe semeinoe pravo* (Comparative family law). Moscow: Yuridicheskoe izdatel'stvo NKY RSFSR.
Gsovski, Vladimir. 1948/1949. *Soviet Civil Law*. Ann Arbor: University of Michigan Law School.
Jänterä-Jareborg, Maarit. 2002. *Grounds for Divorce and Maintenance between Former Spouses: Sweden; Swedish Report to the Commission on European Family Law*, http://www.ceflonline.net/Reports/pdf/Sweden02.pdf.
Kelly, Catriona. 2007. *Children's World: Growing Up in Russia, 1890–1991*. New Haven, CT: Yale University Press.
Keserauskas, Sarunas. 2004. "Moving in the Same Direction? Presentation of Family Law Reforms in Lithuania." In *The International Survey of Family Law: 2004*, ed. Andrew Bainham, 315–335. Bristol, UK: Family Law.
Khazova, Olga. 1998. "The New Codification of Russian Family Law." In *The Changing Family: International Perspectives on the Family and Family Law*, eds. John Eekelaar and Thandabantu Nhlapo, 73–83. Oxford: Hart.
———. 2007. "Family Law in the Former Soviet Union: More Differences or More in Common." In *Convergence and Divergence of Family Law in Europe*, ed. Masha Antokolskaia, 97–117. Antwerp: Intersentia.
———. 2009. "Property Maintenance and Post-Soviet Family Law." *International Family Law*, no. 3: 160–164.
Kullerkupp, Kai. 2001a. "Family Law in Estonia." In *The International Survey of Family Law: 2001*, ed. Andrew Bainham, 95–110. Bristol, UK: Jordans.
———. 2001b. "Statutory Marital Property Law de lege lata and de lege ferenda." *Juridica International*, no. 6: 78–88.
Lenin, Vladimir I. 1972. *O prave natsii na samoopredelenie* (The right of nations to self-determination). *Izbrannye sochineniia* (Collected works), http://www.marxists.org/archive/lenin/works/1914/self-det/ (accessed June 29, 2011). Translated by B. Isaacs and J. Fineberg.
Mikelenas, Valentinas. 2000. "Unification and Harmonisation of Law at the Turn of the Millennium: The Lithuanian Experience." *Uniform Law Review* 2, no. 5: 243–261.

Rheinstein, Max. 1972. *Marriage Stability, Divorce, and the Law*. Chicago: University of Chicago Press.
Salumaa, Edgar. 1996. "The Family Law Act." *Juridica International: Law Review University of Tartu*: 94–98.
Semeinyi Kodeks Rossiiskoi Federatsii (The Russian Family Code).1996. *Sobranie zakonodatel'stva Rossiiskoi Federatsii* (The Collections of Laws of the Russian Federation), no. 1, st. 16.
Sundberg, Jakob. 1975. "Recent Changes in Swedish Family Law: Experiment Repeated." *American Journal of Comparative Law,* no. 23: 34–49.
Todorova, Velina. 2007. "The Accession of Bulgaria to the European Union: A Path to the Harmonisation of Family Law?" In *Convergence and Divergence of Family Law in Europe*, ed. Masha Antokolskaia, 79–95. Antwerp: Intersentia.
The Civil Law of Latvia (Latvijas Republikas Civillikums), 2001. Translation and Terminology Centre: Riga.
Vebers, Janis. 1997. "Family Law in Latvia: From Establishment of the Independent State of Latvia in 1918 to Restoration of Independence in 1993." In *The International Survey of Family Law*, ed. Andrew Bainham, 207–227. The Hague: Martinus Nijhoff.
Willekens, Harry. 1998. "Long-Term Developments in Family Law in Western Europe: An Explanation." In *The Changing Family: International Perspectives on the Family and Family Law*, eds. John Eekelaar and Thandabantu Nhlapo, 47–71. Oxford: Hart.

CHAPTER 13

Doing Parenting in Post-Socialist Estonia and Latvia

INGEGERD MUNICIO-LARSSON

INTRODUCTION

This chapter is about parenthood, about the rights and obligations that come with being a mother or a father.[1] In order to find out what is thought to be proper for a woman or a man in relation to her/his children, parents who have divorced are interviewed and asked about how they organize their lives. The idea is that when a couple divorces, it becomes necessary to spell out how to share duties and responsibilities that previously did not require explanations. The concept of *doing parenting* in the title denotes a post-structuralist approach to studying differences between women and men as to parental rights and obligations. This is parallel to how the concept of *doing gender* is used in feminist post-structuralism, that is, as opposed to *being* a woman or a man (West and Zimmerman, 1987, p. 137). This approach encourages a study of the processes by which social practice, cultural patterns, and individual identities are constituted.

Post-structuralism differs from structuralism in that, instead of trying to establish law-like structures that order both language and society, it turns to *discourse*. In this context, discourse is about *meaning*, "what we mean and how this influences our acting" (Lenz Taguchi, 2004, p. 15); how we constitute our world, our lives, and our relations in specific ways and in accordance with the meaning indicated by the discourse. In feminist post-structuralism the focus is not only on discourse *per se,* but on the thinking and acting of subjects within discourses and practices (Søndergaard, 2006, p. 67). Thus it is assumed that the way people talk about family life after divorce provides a frame of reference for acting. It is also assumed that studying divorce with a focus on discourse will illustrate family life in general as well as parenting in stable families. The aim is to get access to the discourses on family life and parenting that are present in society. What is possible to say; what is considered to be a problem; and what is a reasonable solution? (Bacchi, 1999).

Here the focus is on the following questions. How is parenthood defined and worked out after divorce when there are children involved? Are the rights and obligations of women defined differently than those of men? How do mothers and fathers understand the obligation to care for their children in relation to the need to provide for them economically? Is there a specific "Eastern" way to understand family life after divorce, in comparison to what is conceived as a "Western" way?

Every naming and acting has to be put into context. In this case it has to do with political, economic, and social transformation, but also the Soviet legacy as to social norms and accustomed ways of organizing everyday life. The assumption is that when people describe their universe of meaning, they relate to both formal and informal practices and institutions and combine ideas and concepts that are seen as new with what is handed down by tradition. In this case the "new" is a turbulent and rapidly changing society, while the "old" consists of well-known strategies of coping with everyday problems. We know from research that in the process of transformation, political and economic issues were given priority by the governments of these years as they set about "establishing a market economy and reinforcing political independence" (Aidukaite, 2004, p. 88). Less effort was invested in solving social problems, and there are many reports that testify to the loss of welfare (Gassman, 2000; Narusk and Hansson, 1999). This resulted "in expanding differences in the living standards" and an increased "risk of falling below the poverty line," especially for families with many underage children and single-mother families (Hansson, 2001, p. 14).

A second context of the naming and acting studied here comes from global discourses on parenting. It is assumed that when parents in Estonia and Latvia talk about family life, children, and divorce, they have access to a wide range of repertoires (Ekström, 2005). Some are specific to their local or national milieu; some are given by tradition, either from Soviet times or from the period of prewar independence, while others reflect interchange with discourses from other post-Soviet countries or from the West. The narratives of the interviews are therefore compared with what other research endeavors tell us about discourses in other countries. Special attention is given to the possibility of a Soviet legacy in the ways in which family life and divorce are talked about today. These comparisons occasionally make reference to family discourses in Spain, where I have previously studied divorced parents.

Theories on Parenting

It is commonplace today to talk about the crisis of the family. In the words of Tabuna (1997, p. 287), "[t]he modern-day European family is experiencing a crisis," the signs of which are low fertility rates, cohabitation instead of marriage, children born outside marriage, and finally, divorce. The cause of this crisis is assumed to be failing family policies, Latvia being a case in point. Beck and Beck-Gernsheim (1995, p. 1) also start from the assumption of the crisis of the family. What is falling apart for them, however, is the "nuclear family, built around gender status." What is happening is that women's emancipation and demands for equal rights "no longer conveniently come to a halt outside our private lives." When women are on a par with men in society, they will not accept a subordinate position in the family. But according to Beck and Beck-Gernsheim, what will take over from the family is the family.

> Only different, more, better: the negotiated family, the alternating family, the multiple family, new arrangements after divorce, remarriage, divorce again, new assortments from your, my, our children, our past and present families. (Ibid., p. 2)

This negotiated family will become the arena for a long and bitter gender struggle (ibid., p. 14). Love may keep a family together, but it may also cause its breakdown. This is because both women and men will seek economic independence and self-fulfillment outside marriage. Furthermore, Tabuna (1997, p. 290) observes that the "traditional family type is being replaced by new family structures in which emotional links are dominant." Giddens (1992), in turn, outlines a possible scheme for reconciliation between women and men, a promise of intimacy in a pure relationship characterized by a democratic order in which rights and obligations are continuously renegotiated in open communication.

If gender relations and family life are characterized by negotiations, it is to be assumed that the need to negotiate intensifies in connection with divorce, especially when there are children involved. It would be a mistake to think that marriage ends with divorce. Instead, the marriage "transforms itself into a new phase of post-marital 'separation marriage'" (Beck and Beck-Gernsheim, 1995, p. 147). We must also assume at the outset that children cannot be divorced from their parents. This means that divorced couples remain linked to each other not only by their shared biography, but also by the children they have in common. The question at issue here is what post-marital negotiations are about. All matters concerning the children have to be negotiated at the moment of legal divorce, but also for many years to come. With whom will the children spend most of their time? Will the absent parent have visiting rights, and how will support payments be settled?

As mentioned above, it is assumed here that people interpret their experiences of everyday life in the light of the repertoires given by discourses present in society. What knowledge do we proceed from when we try to distinguish such repertoires in the interviews? Another question to answer is whether these repertoires are different in former Soviet republics versus countries in the West. Asztalos Morell et al. (2005) advise against overemphasizing the East-West divide. They believe that the concept of Eastern Europe is meaningful in the social sciences, however, because the communist and post-communist legacies provide "certain countries with specific common experiences" (p. 17). Haukanes (2001, p. 2) also points to the shared experiences of the communist period and to "certain structural similarities" produced by communist politics. What is of special interest here is how parenthood was conceived of in Soviet times, when family policy was common to all the countries in the Soviet sphere.

...in the East
Issoupova (2000, p. 30) studies the "changing construction of motherhood in Soviet and post-Soviet Russia" by comparing a journal that was a "mouthpiece for state policy" with the presentation of "contemporary opinion" in the press during the latter period. According to her, Soviet policy emphasized "the links between mother, state and child," while the bond between father and child was "relegated to the level of financial obligation" (p. 38). In her study of men in Russia, Kay (2006, p. 138) also notes that "Soviet family legislation and social provision was constructed overwhelmingly round the mother-child role." In the 1980s the provision of state nurseries and kindergartens and increased maternity leave and child benefits "made reliance on the state rather than the individual man quite feasible" (Issoupova, 2000, p. 39). In the late Soviet period a pronatalist discourse was promoted by the state, which was alarmed by the low birthrate, and again mothers were called upon in a discourse charged with "essentialist language and imagery" and "a cult of maternity" (Kay, 2006, p. 154). Parallel to a discourse that played down men's tasks in the family, the 1980s experienced a discourse in which emphasis was placed on men's roles as providers, with women returning to "primarily domestic and family-oriented roles" (ibid., p. 77). This call for women to be good mothers and

wives was reformulated by Gorbachev during perestroika (Brunovskis, 2001, p. 22) and was then supplemented with an extension of maternity leave and increased child benefits.

A popular image of both sexes in post-Soviet Russia was that of "the feminine, caring, nurturing, home-making, fertile female, partnered by the strong, economically active, dependable husband and father" (Bridger, 2001, p. 14). This was framed within a discourse of anti-communism and was repeated in varying forms also in other post-Soviet countries (Aidukaite, 2004, pp. 122f; Hansson, 2001, p. 75; Haskova, 2005, pp. 32f; Haukanes, 2001, p. 4; Koroleva, 1997, p. 308; Narusk and Hansson, 1999, pp. 15f). Surveys in Estonia and Latvia in the 1990s have shown overwhelming support for traditional gender roles. Thus, for example, around 80 percent agreed with the statement that "it was man's task to earn money, and woman's task to take care of home and children" (Narusk and Hansson, 1999, p. 15; see also Rungule, 1997, p. 313).

Motherhood has been reconceptualized in the post-communist period as a private experience, and the state has retreated somewhat from its former responsibilities. In Russia this has opened the way for "the reclamation of the institution of fatherhood," not only for financial provision, but also for paternal participation in care (Issoupova, 2000, p. 42). Also, in the three Baltic countries, attempts have been made to "promote fatherhood [...] and involve fathers more in the upbringing of their children" (Aidukaite, 2004, p. 159).

To summarize, what we find in the communist and post-communist context is a tradition of emphasis on different versions of the mother-child bond. During the Soviet period this was complemented by state support for maternity and childcare. When fathers were added to this threesome relationship, it was first as providers and later also as carers. By then the state had abdicated its previous ambition to monitor reproduction.

...in the West
In the West as well, there are studies of the promotion of fatherhood in official documents. Sarre (1996) has looked at how fathers were conceptualized in social policy in England from the 1950s to the 1990s. She concludes that the idea of fathers as cash providers "has maintained its ideological importance" throughout this period, though "the growth in child psychology" and a greater emphasis on child welfare in policy "has increased the importance placed on the father as carer" (p. 46).

Atkinson and Blackwelder (1993) have studied descriptions of parenthood in popular magazine articles in the United States from 1900 to 1989.

They conclude that the most dramatic change was "a shift toward gender-nonspecific parenting articles over the century" (ibid., p. 980). Thus "parenting began to be conceptualized as gender-free, rather than as equivalent to mothering." They also find that "fathers were most often defined as nurturers" in the later decades, in contrast to being defined as providers up to the 1940s (ibid., pp. 980–981).

In their study of "law and legal interpretations on custody, support, and paternity" in the United States, Walters and Chapman (1991) also identify a trend toward gender neutrality. Thus on the eve of the twentieth century, the preference for fathers as custodians of children shifted to a preference for mothers. Subsequently, "[r]ationales for preference for mothers as custodians of children have progressed from motherhood as instinct, to the tender years doctrine [the assumption that "young children belong with their instinctively nurturant mothers"], to the standard of best interest of the child" (p. 85). Starting in the late twentieth century, when the notion of the best interest of the child was introduced, a father could be awarded custody, though mothers generally continued to be favored. Walters and Chapman conclude that the latest trend is toward shared custody, with reference to the best interest of the child.

Turning to Western Europe, we find a great diversity of policy models and public discourses with reference to the family. Thus, for example:

> [T]he southern countries share a cultural emphasis on gender division of labor within the family, on the crucial role of mothers' presence and care in the early childhood years, and a high reliance on family for supporting individual and household needs, including childcare needs. (Saraceno, 2000, p. 140)

In this gender division the male is the breadwinner. Also in other Western European countries, the male breadwinner model is still prevalent in practice, if not in official rhetoric. Women's participation in paid labor is generally encouraged, and maternity leave is quite generous. However, childcare services are missing, and women adapt their working life to their caring duties (Meyers et al., 1999, pp. 124f). Therefore, although there has been a change in official rhetoric towards two-earner families and shared parenting, women's activity rates have not reached those of men, and men's participation in care has not reached that of women. The European Union institutions have been paying attention to the problems of "traditional fatherhood" and "encouraging men to embrace new and modern gender roles," which would include the caring role previously left exclusively to women (Tereskinas and Reingardiene, 2005, pp. 5f). Although they point to the new EU countries in particular, the traditional model seems to be a problem in many of the old EU countries as well.

In the Scandinavian countries the state actively supports a two-earner family with shared parenting. Reforms have been created to reduce "the actual hindrances that active fathering meets" (Holter, 2005, p. 122). One example is the introduction of "daddy quotas," that is, a portion of the parental leave that cannot be transferred to the mother.

As described above, in the East the emphasis has been on the mother-child bond. In the 1980s fathers were added to this relationship, mainly as providers, but not until the turn of the century as carers. In the West we find a similar development, though fathers as providers seem to have been present in the discourse throughout the twentieth century, and the change towards fathers as carers in official rhetoric has come sooner than in the East.

To conclude this synopsis of theories on parenting, we may now add a few questions to those specified earlier. If we assume that divorce is a window into the negotiated family, the issue is not only how rights and obligations are defined for mothers and fathers after divorce, but also which discourses are available to negotiate and organize life in families that are not broken. Another question is whether fathers are conceived of mainly as providers or are expected to be carers, as was pointed out above. Is the tight mother-child bond still a node of every discourse—that is, is it the center which is generally not explicitly mentioned but is always taken for granted?

Data and Method

The data needed for studying discourse would have to include some kind of narratives in which the processes of meaning-making can be distinguished and analyzed. For this study, divorced women and men with underage children were interviewed in 2000 and 2001. Sixteen interviews are from Tallinn, Estonia, and an equal number are from Riga, Latvia. There were two steps to the transcription: the recorded text was transcribed and then translated into English. Thus the original interviews have been interpreted twice. The interviews are numbered in the transcription from one to eight for women and likewise for men in Tallinn, and from one to sixteen in Riga.

This transcription obviously limits the information that can be gained from the interviews, since body language, intonation, silences, and moments of hesitation are missing (Kvale, 1988, pp. 97f). The translation from the original languages also means that it is not possible to analyze wording or specific expressions. Here such fine nuances have been set aside, and instead broad analytical themes have been drawn from the recorded narratives of divorce. The meaning of these themes is discussed in relation to the totality of transcribed text, that is, the chorus of voices expressed in the interviews (Kvale, 1983, p. 186). Ultimately it is up to the reader to judge if the analysis adds to our understanding of parenting and divorce.

An Open Door to Success

As mentioned before, the context of the interviews is a turbulent and rapidly changing society. This time was turbulent on a personal level, too. In many interviews the "spirit of freedom" of those years is brought up.

> All around the country, something was in the air. Don't you remember those first years of independence? That was a time when one could imagine that the door to success was open; a new life would start. (Latvia 2, male, 37)

The open "door to success" was situated mainly in the new economy, but on some occasions, the possibility of starting "a new life" also referred to the private sphere. New constellations were formed in the area of family life, where "winners and losers" realigned according to the value criteria of the new societies. Thus, "success" seems to be a key word when describing the new society. Life is about competing for material assets, and the image of "winners and losers" is also used in research to analyze the outcomes of transition (Gassman, 2000, pp. 85f; Narusk and Hansson, 1999).

Accordingly, both kinship and non-kin ties were loosened, either when poverty made it difficult to "be either hosts or guests on a regular basis" (Trapenciere et al., 2000, p. 132), or when the "quickly upward-mobile people" found little interest in keeping contacts with those who were less successful (Hansson, 2001, p. 82). When such expectations of success failed, it was sometimes difficult to keep up a marriage.

> Unfortunately, that was just for some years, and then all the problems started to come. Lots of problems related to business and debts. This affected my family life. My wife didn't understand lots of things, what I was doing and about my business. She started to criticize me and to

push me, saying that the train had already left the station. She thought that I was a loser. And I had to shift from one job to another. My working opportunities changed, and I had to spend more time in Riga, but my wife and my children stayed in X. (Latvia 2, male, 37)

When "change" was the rule in society, "change" was also sought in the family. In their study of poverty in Latvia, Trapenciere et al. (2000, p. 38) have described how families disintegrate under "the continuous anxiety to make ends meet," and when spouses, just as in the above case, blame each other for not "doing as much as he or she could." In both Latvia and Estonia, the divorce rates are among the highest in Europe (Svarckopfa, 2001, p. 144). The number of divorces was already high in the 1980s, and it actually decreased from 1990 to 2000. In both countries, however, the number of marriages declined abruptly in that decade.[2] This does not mean that couples were not formed. Instead, the increasing proportion of children born out of wedlock indicates a high rate of cohabitation, that is, from 27 percent to 55 percent of live births in Estonia, and from 17 percent to 39 percent in Latvia (SOE, 2001, p. 40; Svarckopfa, 2001, p. 144). The share of remarriages in Estonia increased to account for one-third of all marriages. This shows that people were inclined to give "a new relationship a try during this period of transition" (Jacobsen, 1996, p. 35).

MEN AS FATHERS

Kay (2006, p. 73) has pointed out that in media and cultural discourses of the Soviet Union, "work was the centre of the Soviet man's life," while his private, personal, and family life was paid less attention. As has been noted above, this was also a tendency of Soviet policy. In the interviews as well, the issue of whether men are able fathers is often brought up.

> I guess I'm so conservative in my thinking, but I think that children are the meaning of a marriage. But men see things totally differently, at least the men that I've been in contact with. [...] It seems that a man and a child [...], at least in our case, it has turned out that being a father is too difficult for a man. (Estonia 4, female, 38)

Even if this is thought to be "conservative thinking," we shall see that the notion of women and children forming a "natural" unit is the self-evident background to discussions of men. A distinction is made between being a man and being a father. Thus men are men, but being a father is something that men may choose. As we shall see, the demands put on fathers are generally not too high. But even so, it may be "too difficult for a man." Another single mother finishes recounting her experience with men with the remark: "there is a shortfall of fathers, yes" (Latvia 13, female, 31). Consequently, women may decide to do without.

> I'll manage. I won't give up. The main thing is that I have a job and my health won't fail. I can manage by myself, and I don't need anyone by my side. I have an Estonian soul, or rather, the soul of an Estonian woman. I have decided for sure that I do not want a man by my side. At least until the kids are grown. One more experience like I had, and I couldn't take it anymore! (Estonia 4, female, 38)

Kay reports on similar attitudes among divorced mothers in Russia, who were "antagonistic towards the idea of remarriage and were far more negative about men in general, describing them as irresponsible, egotistical and a burden to women" (Luniakova, 2004, cited in Kay, ibid., p. 175). As expressed above, this disappointment with men may take the form of praising women for their capability and sense of responsibility, in contrast with men and their shortcomings. Here the struggle of women for their families is related to the national rhetoric of independence: "an Estonian soul" striving for independence and self-fulfillment.

FATHERS AFTER DIVORCE

The interviews provide a more specific image of the mother/father/child triad after divorce. In this image as well, mother and child form a unit to which the father is less tightly connected. The following citations illustrate this point:

> I think it is the right thing to leave the kids of divorced couples with their mother. But the child has every right to know who his father is. In kindergarten and at school, children like to speak about their fathers, especially boys. My daddy works there, and my daddy has such-and-such a car. And when there is no daddy at home, the kid has the right to know that somewhere there is a daddy for him as well, who cares and whom he could meet every now and then. And so he

also has someone he can be proud of and speak about. A child cannot be brought up with the feeling that he has no father at all. (Estonia 2, male, 26)

In this description the tie between father and child is weak and somewhat distant. The father is thought to be someone to "meet every now and then," but not on a daily or even weekly basis. A father is pictured more as a mental figure than a real person who is present in everyday life. Similar descriptions are given in Latvia; for example, when asked about how often he meets his now-eleven-year-old son, a Latvian man says:

Sometimes. They [the son and his mother] live where my parents live, and I visit them [his parents]. Once I met him in a shop and I asked him: What do you want me to buy for you, son? And he asked me to buy him a packet of potato chips. (Latvia 1, male, 30)

In this description occasional encounters have superseded regular and planned visits. For this man, visiting his parents is more important than keeping in touch with his son from a previous marriage. He goes on to say that his new partner has two sons and "we're raising them together." As in other cases, a new family has taken the place of previous engagements. As for his partner's ex-husband and his visiting habits, his interest is said to be declining.

The next citation goes even further, concluding that fathers are interchangeable and that it might be best for the child to lose contact with the biological father when the mother finds a new partner.

It's difficult to say what the best way is, as there are so many different situations, and people are different. Take my case, for example. My ex-wife and her new partner made a new family, and it's the family for my son. Then there's my partner and me; we are the family for her son. And I know that the father of her son has also made a new family, and he's exactly in the same position as I am.
It's even a bit difficult to explain it. I might like to meet my son three to four times a month, but then if contact with me is too close, he might not accept my wife's new partner as a stepfather. And at present it's just like that—he doesn't call him Daddy; he calls him by his first name. If I considered it very important to meet him as often as possible, then it might make things worse for him. I think that by the

time they are a bit older—I mean the kids—they are able to make their own choice. I mean about who's important and who's not. (Estonia 3, male, 33)

This reasoning illustrates a discourse present in society in both Estonia and Latvia; that is, that fathers are interchangeable. However, what is described here is not the image of a deadbeat dad but a father who gives priority to his social ties of fatherhood rather than his biological ties. Thus he considers himself a dependable father, but to the children of his second family. He inverts the fact that he does not think it "very important" to meet his son "as often as possible" to mean solicitude for his son. It may also well be that the separation is due more to how things came about than the result of a well-founded decision.

This discourse has to be put into context. In this interview and in many others, both men and women talk about their long working hours, sometimes combining two different jobs. Turbulence in the new economy, in which firms appear and often soon disappear, also makes it difficult to make demands of employers concerning working hours or days off (Hansson, 2001, pp. 61f; Trapenciere et al., 2000, p. 63). The stressful lives of adults lead some to rationalize a situation where there is little time to spend with a child from a previous marriage, and any spare time left is spent with the new family.

Mothers and Children after Divorce

The interviewees express no doubts that the biological mothers are their children's social mothers, even after divorce. Instead, what mothers as well as fathers discuss is the father's involvement. Usually mothers accept even sparse and irregular visiting patterns. A mother of two—a twelve-year-old son and a ten-year-old daughter—explains this irregularity as a result of her ex-husband's commitment to his new family.

> Before he had his own children, he visited more often, once every two or three months. He took the children to the beach or went with them to the theater, if admission was free. After his second wife gave birth to a boy for him, he started coming more seldom, only during birthdays and not every year. (Latvia 5, female, 32)

In this case, the mother seems to accept her own explanation as to why the father's not very frequent visits were phased out when he got a new child. It is no use counting on a father—this seems to be accepted as reality and is no cause for complaint or worry for the sake of the children. The demands that women place on their ex-husbands, the fathers of their children, are extremely low.

Newfound interest in a child, coming from a father who has long been distant, may also be interpreted as a threat if it starts just when the mother has found a new partner.

> After we separated, my husband was very supportive, also financially. But then a couple of years passed and he disappeared. And we had to manage on our own. If he doesn't care for us, if he isn't interested in us, I won't force him. He just disappeared, for us he didn't exist any more. And now when I have started a new family, and everything seems to be OK, now he's back again and ready to support us. And as for his support, it's not much after all. Two or three times a year he comes, brings some expensive gifts, and that's all. We are well-off and we are able to buy everything the kid needs, there is no need for any kind of support any more. It looks like he's trying to strengthen his position; someday in the future he could come and say, I have bought this and that, and I have to have some rights. Now when we have found a man who could be a good father for my son, it turns out that there is one father too many. (Estonia 5, female, 29)

Also here we see acceptance of the father's disappearance: "for us he didn't exist any more." This mother seems to include her son in the "us" and later in the "we" who "have found a man." She seems to assume that her son does not miss his father and that a new father is in his interest. Consequently, the fact that the son enjoys his father's attention is a big problem.

> It's quite a problem. And I'm really worried about it. The thing is that my son is old enough to understand who is who and who is his real dad, and by buying all these things the child can be manipulated. Already now he sometimes stresses that he wants to put on the coat his daddy bought.

Strangely absent from the reasoning of both mothers and fathers are comments on how the children might possibly want things to be organized or what their needs might be. Instead, children are expected to adapt to the plans of adults. However, there are comments in the interviews about children seeming to resist the arrangements made by their parents and wanting to hold on to their biological fathers instead.

Children's experience of divorce has been described more thoroughly elsewhere. Thus, for example, Butler et al. (2004, p. 93) conclude that children have strong feelings about their parents' divorce: "the anger, the sense of betrayal, the sympathy for the resident parent, the resentment of her father's new partner, the deep personal hurt and the confusion of many of the children." On the other hand, they note that relationships between parents and children may improve "once any divorce-contingent conflict subsides" (ibid., p. 115). Furstenberg et al. (1987, p. 698) have more specifically studied paternal participation and children's well-being after divorce. They find that "the quality of a child's relationship to his or her outside father" does not seem to matter for the child's well-being, while maternal relationships are important. But they also note: "Children may closely identify with their fathers even though they see them infrequently." In their study of divorce, Wallerstein and Blakeslee (1989, p. 159) also find that children wish to maintain the bond to their (sometimes failing) fathers. Thus, "for the child of divorce," they note, it "represents a grave injustice and a personal tragedy" when remarriage replaces the former family. But they also conclude that in the long run, the quality of the mother's parenting is the single most important factor for a child's well-being. In view of these findings, it seems more important for the children that their mothers are still there for them after divorce than whether their fathers prioritize other engagements.

What we hear in these narratives is a discourse that justifies fathers' cutting ties with their children after divorce. A new family with children is accepted as an excuse for breaking the bond with children from a previous marriage. In this discourse, mothers are supposed to be there for their children, while fathers may choose their degree of engagement. Children have little say in these matters, and their wishes and emotions are not heard. The degree to which fathers share responsibilities for the children is not an issue. Instead, care and keeping the family together are assumed to be something for mothers to manage. This distribution of responsibilities presumably reflects the way family life is organized in non-broken families. Thus the demands on fathers are not high, nor do women who remarry ask much of their new partners. The men whom the children are expected to accept as their new fathers will probably not identify themselves as carers. It is thus mothers who are the managers of family life, and according to the research cited above, it is also their quality of parenting that is most important for children's well-being.

PARENTING IN CONTEXT

If we put this discourse in a global context, a matching example can be found in the cultural values of the Southern European countries noted above. The emphasis there is on a traditional gender division of labor in the family, and women are assumed to be responsible for childcare and other caring duties as well. The official and unofficial rhetoric of other countries stresses instead shared duties within the family and promotes fathers as carers. With reference to divorce, it is generally stated that divorce is not a divorce from the children. An explicit discourse of interchangeable fathers is not to be found. The trend towards joint custody also goes against this idea.

If we instead take a look at practice, we find that men's participation in care does not correspond to the official and unofficial discourses on fathering. For example, in Norway and Sweden, men take only about one-fifth of the available days for parental leave, and more women than men work part-time, which makes childcare still more a duty of women than of men (Holter, 2005, p. 138; Ivarsson, 2008). And in spite of the general emphasis on the desirability of continuing paternal contact with children after divorce, a national survey in the United States reports that 40 percent of the children are not visited by their fathers (Furstenberg et al. 1987, p. 696). Even in Sweden, where there is a strong discourse of fathers continuing as parents after divorce, one-fourth of children of divorced parents have little or no contact with their fathers (Rädda Barnen 2005, p. 7). Similar figures are reported from other Scandinavian countries (Jensen, 1995, p 227).

These trends may be a result of the diversification of family forms that we have experienced during the twentieth century. Thus the crisis of the traditional family and new arrangements after divorce or separation may weaken the biological ties between parents and children and strengthen the social ties. This will mainly affect fathers who leave their children from the first marriage or cohabitation and bond with the children in their new family.

Fathers and Child Support

Women often bring up problems with getting economic support from fathers: "We agreed that he would pay me twenty-five lats [approximately 40 euros] each month for child subsistence. He did pay for about half a year, but then he disappeared somewhere" (Latvia 6, female, 28). When mothers describe fathers' failure to provide for the children after divorce, the reason they often give is that he just disappeared. How do fathers themselves explain their failure to support their kids from a previous marriage? Not earning enough money is one reason often mentioned. Problems with employment and difficulties in coping with the new economy are others.

> At first I didn't pay anything because I had no income. My business had gone bankrupt and I hadn't found a job. I was unemployed for a while. But later on I started to work for the X company [health foods] as a distributor, and I started to pay. But usually it is not a monthly fixed sum or anything. (Estonia 7, male, 49)

Another reason given by the men is that they have a new family to support.

> And again I feel guilty, of course. It is my child, but I have a family. I have two children to bring up. And if I don't have money, I manipulate my ex, I say, I don't have money right now, could you wait for a bit, please. And she waits. (Latvia 1, male, 30)

This situation seems to be both recognized and often accepted by the mothers.

> It's not his fault that the present situation in the economy is bad. Due to the economic crisis in Russia, many companies and entrepreneurs have difficulties. (Estonia 3, female, 29)

The fathers interviewed are generally neither homeless nor penniless. But even when a father is well-off and has a stable income, he might find reasons not to pay, as in the case below, where he thinks the economic agreement after his first divorce was unfair. He also divorced a second time.

> Well, I did buy them clothes and things like that as well, naturally. But well, basically I gave less to the first child, because she got that money when I left home, and I didn't think it was right, because it

> didn't take long until she found another man. And they had more kids, and why should I toil for them as well? If my own kid got the money, then all right. Anyway, they weren't going hungry or anything. (Estonia 5, male, 49)

Another reason that fathers give for not paying child support is that they show their good will in other ways, for example, by buying presents for birthdays or on other occasions.

> We agreed on what child support I should pay. Sometimes I pay more; sometimes I do not pay at all. When I pay more, it is, for example, for birthday gifts. (Latvia 15, male, 30)

This is a recurrent theme when men discuss paying for their children. They want to make sure that the money they bring is only for their own child. The fathers' remarks—about buying clothes and occasional birthday presents instead of paying regular support—may point towards another model of fatherhood, a "fun father" who pretends to be accessible but has no "specific childrearing tasks" in the family (cf. Municio-Larsson and Pujol Algans, 2002, p. 201; Tabuna, 1997, pp. 295f). They do not see themselves as carers or stable providers, but they do not want to disconnect altogether from their biological children.

Fathers who have little or no contact with their children talk about reconnecting sometime in the future: "we will talk about it one day, sooner or later, or when she has graduated from school [...], and she will understand" (Latvia 8, male, 36). This may point towards yet another model of fatherhood—one in which the father is a mentor to a young adult rather than a carer of a child. The image is one of continued connection in some way and an expectation that the child "will understand" when the time comes. These fathers expect to be understood, but they themselves do not attempt to understand their children.

It is possible in both Estonia and Latvia to go to court to demand child support and to have it garnished from the father's salary. However, mothers generally do not see any point in doing so, because they say that their ex-husbands make sure that their earnings are all off the books. They describe different ways men evade payment.

> If a man has some feelings towards his child, he will find a way to support him. And if he doesn't, then the court cannot help either. You see, in our wage system a man can make his official salary very small,

and the rest could be given to him in an envelope. You have heard about these tricks, haven't you? I know that it's very often done that way. And in such a case women really get practically nothing.
(Estonia 5, female, 29)

The father's non-payment of support is regarded as equivalent to a lack of feeling for his child, and the prospects of forcing him to pay are gloomy, however much the mother might need this support. This mother has resigned herself to not getting anything—no affection and no support from the father of her children, and no backing from the outside society. She will manage on her own.

CHILD SUPPORT IN CONTEXT

Here we encounter what Wallerstein and Blakeslee (1989, p. 136) describe as "a continuing sore spot in most co-parenting relationships." It illustrates the fact that divorce does not end marriage. Instead, the stage is set for many years of post-marital negotiations. In the citations above, we hear more resignation and acceptance than gender struggle. This acceptance derives its meaning from a discourse in which mothers are carers but also providers. Thus on the economic side of parenthood as well, mothers are thought to be tightly bound to their children, while fathers may reject both caring and providing.

The turbulent economic situation of these countries is again brought up in the interviews as a cause of non-payment of child support. Another problem is said to be the difficulties the authorities have in monitoring people's income and whereabouts. Chandler (2002, cited in Aidukaite, 2004, p. 67) describes the "shadow economy" of the Baltic countries as a problem in collecting taxes. Obviously, this also makes it difficult to enforce payment of child support. In both Estonia and Latvia, our informants express a deep distrust of the courts' ability to solve this kind of problem. Nor do they expect any assistance from other state or local authorities.

In her study of welfare in Latvia, Gassman (2000, p. 161) concludes that the majority of people in need do not apply for help because they do not expect to get any. This may be an effect of "transitional shock" (Hansson, 2001, p. 13), which led most people to believe that the umbrella of state protection was no longer there. However, Aidukaite (2004, pp. 113f) notes that different measures of state support for families are still in force, but the levels paid are generally too low. Therefore, either people believe that it is not worth applying, or they do not identify themselves as those most in need.

In a global context it is generally assumed that divorce entails economic hardships and that these are biased against women. Beck and Beck-Gernsheim (1995, p. 32) put it bluntly: "after divorce the woman is left with the children and without an income, the man with an income and without children." In many countries the two-earner family has gradually supplanted the traditional male-breadwinner family. However, women's position in the labor market is weaker than men's, and if fathers are reluctant to share child expenses, it is generally recognized that women-headed families risk poverty. State measures to eliminate this risk differ from country to country, depending on the availability of state support for families and on the ability to enforce payment from fathers.

According to Wallerstein and Blakeslee (1989, p. 136), in the United States, child support decided by the courts is generally low. Even so, of "the millions of women who are entitled to child support, fewer than half receive payments as ordered," and one-fourth of the women get nothing. These fathers have difficulties recognizing the needs of their children and may therefore reason that their ex-wife and children will manage on their own. The conclusion is that "out of sight is often out of mind" (ibid., p. 144). This may also be applied to the Estonian and Latvian cases. Thus the discourse of interchangeable fathers supplies arguments excusing loss of contact with the children, and a lack of contact goes hand-in-hand with a low propensity to pay child support.

A final conclusion is that the discourse in Estonia and Latvia is different than in the other countries used here for comparison. However, when we look at practice in the latter, the similarities to how parents in Estonia and Latvia talk about family are striking.

Conclusion: Three Scenarios

If we extrapolate into the future based on what has been described above, we may envisage a social order in which children and women form families without men. Women are the dependable providers and competent carers in these family units. Men have thrown off the yoke of providing and caring for others. They are now free to match the demands of the labor market for mobile and ambitious individuals without any social commitments. Women are available to the labor market, but because of their caring responsibilities, they may have to accept lower salaries and fewer opportunities to reach higher positions. The society will be structured accordingly. In comparison to other households, women-headed families will be poor or very poor, depending on the degree to which the state provides economic support and service. Women and children will lose economically but gain in non-material assets. They will appropriate for themselves this haven of affection, company, and rest, this contrast to the cold outside world—all the things family life is supposed to be. This will be the new matriarchy.

A second alternative is the negotiated family according to Beck and Beck-Gernsham (1995). In this alternative, women and men form couples with or without children and try to negotiate a "good-enough" life together. These negotiations will increasingly be formalized as contracts to be used in case of a break-up. Love will continue to be essential to every life project, and the search for love will lead to successive family arrangements. Children will share their home with varying constellations of sisters and brothers, stepfathers, and sometimes stepmothers. Social bonds will be more important than some biological bonds. This represents an extrapolation of present trends in society.

The third possibility is the reconciliation alternative inspired by Giddens's analysis of modern societies (1992). Women, men, and children living in democratic relationships form families. Each party deserves equal respect and has an equal right to family resources. Mothers and fathers share caring responsibilities and are equally sensitive to the needs of children. Women and men have equal rights to engage in the outside world and to search for self-fulfillment outside the family. This is utopia, a dream shared by feminists and policy-makers alike.

Notes

1 This project was financed by the Baltic Sea Foundation, 1999–2001, reference no. 518/231/00. I wish to thank the editors for their comments to an initial version of this text. I also wish to acknowledge assistance with the interviews from Leeni Hansson and her team at the Institute for International and Social Sciences, Tallinn, and Ritma Rungule and her team at the Latvian Academy of Sciences, Riga.
2 In Estonia there were 11,774 marriages in 1990, or 7.9 per thousand inhabitants, and 5,485 ten years later (2.9 per thousand inhabitants), of which 32 percent were remarriages. There were 5,785 divorces in 1990 (3.6 per 1,000 inhabitants), and 4,230 in the year 2000, or 2.9 per 1,000 (SOE, 2001, p. 49). In Latvia there were 23,619 marriages in 1990, or 8.8 per thousand inhabitants, and 9,399 or 3.9 per thousand inhabitants in 1999. Divorces numbered 10,783 in 1990 and 6,010 in 1999; that is, 4.0 and 2.5 per thousand (CSBL, 2000, Table 4, p. 13).

REFERENCES

Aidukaite, Jolanta. 2004. *The Emergence of the Post-Socialist Welfare State: The Case of the Baltic States; Estonia, Latvia and Lithuania*. Södertörn PhD diss., Stockholm University.

Asztalos Morell, Ildikó, Helene Carlbäck, Madeleine Hurd, and Sara Rastbäck, eds. 2005. *Gender Transitions: In Russia and Eastern Europe*. Eslöv, Sweden: Gondolin.

Atkinson, Maxine P., and Stephen P. Blackwelder. 1993. "Fathering in the 20th Century." *Journal of Marriage and the Family* 55, no. 4 (November): 975–986.

Bacchi, Carol L. 1999. *Women, Policy and Politics: The Constitution of Policy Problems*. London; Thousand Oaks, CA; and New Delhi: Sage.

Beck, Ulrich, and Elisabeth Beck-Gernsheim. 1995. *The Normal Chaos of Love*. Cambridge: Polity Press.

Bridger, Sue. 2001. "Image, Reality and Propaganda: Looking Again at the Soviet Legacy." In *Women after Communism: Ideal Images and Real Lives*, ed. Haldis Haukanes, 13–27. Bergen, Norway: University of Bergen.

Brunovskis, Anette. 2001. "Kvinner og det latviske arbeidsmarkedet – tendenser i siste halvdel av 1990-tallet" (Women and the Latvian labor market—tendencies in the latter half of the 1990s). *Nordisk Østforum. Samfunn og kultur i Russland og Øst-Europa* 15, no. 1: 21–28.

Butler, Ian, Lesley Scanlan, Margaret Robinson, Gillan Douglas, and Mervyn Murch, eds. 2004. *Divorcing Children: Children's Experience of Their Parents' Divorce*. London and New York: Jessica Kingsley Publishers.

CSBL. 2000. *Statistical Yearbook of Latvia*. Riga: Central Statistical Bureau of Latvia.

Ekström, Linda. 2005. *En problemrepresentation i förändring? En diskursiv policystudie av jämställdhetsbegreppets innebörd i svensk jämställdhetsdebatt och svensk jämställdhetspolitik* (A problem representation in change? A discursive policy study of the meaning of the notion of equality in Swedish social debate and equality policy). Annual Meeting of Political Science, Lund, Sweden.

Furstenberg, Frank F., Philip S. Morgan, and Paul D. Allison. 1987. "Paternal Participation and Children's Well-Being After Marital Dissolution." *American Sociological Review* 52: 695–701.

Gassman, Franziska. 2000. *On the Verge of Poverty: Welfare and Economic Transition in Latvia*. Maastricht: UPM.

Giddens, Anthony. 1992. *The Transformation of Intimacy, Sexuality, Love and Eroticism in Modern Societies*. Cambridge: Polity Press/Blackwell Publishers.

Hansson, Leeni. 2001. *Networks Matter: The Role of Informal Social Networks in the Period of Socio-Economic Reforms of the 1990s in Estonia*. Jyväskylä, Finland.

Haskova, Hana. 2005. "Gender Roles, Family Policy and Family Behavior: Changing Czech Society in the European Context." In *Generations, Kinship and Care: Gendered Provisions of Social Security in Central Eastern Europe*, eds. Haldis Haukanes and Frances Pine, 23–52. Bergen, Norway: University of Bergen.

Haukanes, Haldis. 2001. "Introduction." In *Women after Communism: Ideal Images and Real Lives*, ed. Haldis Haukanes, 1–9. Bergen, Norway: University of Bergen.

Holter, Oystein G. 2005. "Can Men Do It? On Men, Caring and Gender Equality in an East/West Perspective." In *Men and Fatherhood: New Forms of Masculinity in Europe*, eds. Arturas Tereskinas and Jolanta Reingardiene, 114–147. Vilnius, Lithuania: Eugrimas.

Issoupova, Olga. 2000. "From Duty to Pleasure: Motherhood in Soviet and Post-Soviet Russia." In *Gender, State and Society in Soviet and Post-Soviet Russia*, ed. Sarah Ashwin, 30–54. London and New York: Routledge.

Ivarsson, A. 2008. "Barnledig gynnas vid vårdnadstvist" (Parent who took leave favored in child-custody disputes). *Dagens Nyheter*, August 2, 2008.

Jacobsen, B. 1996. *Population: Estonia in the Grip of Change*. NORBALT Living Conditions Project: Fafo-report, no. 190.

Jensen, An-Magritt. 1995. "Gender Gaps in Relationships with Children: Closing or Widening." In *Gender and Family Change in Industrialized Countries*, eds. Karen Oppenheim Mason and An-Magritt Jensen, 223–242. Oxford: Clarendon Press.

Kay, Rebecca. 2006. *Men in Contemporary Russia: The Fallen Heroes of Post-Soviet Change*. Aldershot, UK, and Burlington, VT: Ashgate.

Koroleva, I. 1997. "Gender Roles in Family: Perceptions and Reality." In *Invitation to Dialogue: Beyond Gender (In)equality*, 299–309. Riga: Institute of Philosophy and Sociology. Latvian Academy of Sciences.

———. 1983. "The Qualitative Research Interview: A Phenomenological and a Hermeneutical Mode of Understanding." *Journal of Phenomenological Psychology* 14, no. 2: 171–196.

Kvale, Steiner. 1988. "The 1000-Page Question." *Phenomenology and Pedagogy* 6, no. 2: 90–106.

Lenz Taguchi, Hillevi. 2004. *In på bara benet. En introduktion till feministisk poststrukturalism* (Right down to the bone: An introduction to feminist post-structuralism). Stockholm: HLS Förlag.

Meyers, Marcia K., Janet C. Gornick, and Katherin E. Ross. 1999. "Public Childcare, Parental Leave, and Employment." In *Gender and Welfare State Regimes*, ed. Diane Sainsbury, 117–146. Oxford: Oxford University Press.

Municio-Larsson, Ingegerd, and Carmen Pujol Algans. 2002. "Making Sense of Fatherhood: The Non-Payment of Child Support in Spain." In *Making Men into Fathers: Men, Masculinities and the Social Politics of Fatherhood*, ed. Barbara Hobson, 191–212. Cambridge: Cambridge University Press.

Narusk, Anu, and Leeni Hansson. 1999. *Estonian Families in the 1990s: Winners and Losers*. Tallinn: Estonian Academy Publishers.

Rungule, R. 1997. "The Role of Parents—Fathers and Mothers—in the Family and in Society." In *Invitation to Dialogue: Beyond Gender (In)equality*, Riga: Institute of Philosophy and Sociology. Latvian Academy of Sciences.

Rädda Barnen (Save the Children). 2005. *Skilsmässobarn* (Children of divorce). N.p.: Rädda Barnen.

Saraceno, Chiara. 2000. "Gendered Policies: Family Obligations and Social Policies in Europe." In *Gender, Welfare State, and the Market: Towards a New Division of Labour*, eds. Thomas Boje and Arnlaug Leira, 135–156. London and New York: Routledge.

Sarre, Sophie. 1996. *A Place for Fathers: Fathers and Social Policy in the Post-War Period*. Welfare State Program. London: London School of Economics and Political Science, no. 125.

SOE. 2001. *Statistical Yearbook of Estonia*. Tallinn: Statistical Office of Estonia.

Svarckopfa, Anita. 2001. *Latvia: Human Development Report 2000/2001; The Public Policy Process in Latvia*. Riga, Latvia: UNDP.

Søndergaard, Dorte M. 2006. "Destabiliserende diskursanalyse: veje ind i poststrukturalistisk inspireret empirisk forskning" (Destabilizing discourse analysis: Toward post-structuralist-inspired empirical research). In *Kön och tolkning: metodiska möjligheter i kvalitativ forskning* (Gender and interpretation: Methodological possibilities in qualitative research), eds. Agnes Andenaes and Hanne Haavind, 60–104. Stockholm: Natur och Kultur i samarbete med Gyldendal akademisk.

Tabuna, A. 1997. "Equality between Men and Women in the Family." In *Invitation to Dialogue: Beyond Gender (In)equality*, 287–298. Riga: Institute of Philosophy and Sociology. Latvian Academy of Sciences.

Tereskinas, Arturas and Jolanta Reingardiene, eds. 2005. *Men and Fatherhood: New Forms of Masculinity in Europe*. Vilnius, Lithuania: Eugrimas.

Trapenciere, I., R. Rungule, M. Pranka, T. Lace, and N. Dudwick, 2000. *Listening to the Poor: Social Assessment of Poverty in Latvia; Report on Research Findings (March-June 1998)*. Riga: Ministry of the Republic of Latvia.

Wallerstein, Judith S., and Sandra Blakeslee. 1989. *Second Changes: Men, Women and Children a Decade after Divorce*. New York: Ticknor and Fields.

Walters, Lynda Henley, and Steven F. Chapman. 1991. "Changes in Legal Views of Parenthood: Implications for Fathers in Minority Cultures." In *Fatherhood and Families in Cultural Context*, eds. Frederik Bozett and Shirley Hanson, 83–113. New York: Springer.

West, Candace and Don H. Zimmerman. 1987. "'Doing Gender.'" *Gender and Society* 1, no. 2: 125–151.

CHAPTER 14

Gendered Experiences in Entrepreneurship, Family and Social Activities in Russia

Ann-Mari Sätre

Introduction

In the Soviet Union the state took responsibility for a large share of duties traditionally dealt with by families. When the Soviet system collapsed, it was expected that budget-financed, female-dominated sectors such as health care and education would be the first to suffer from the reduction in government funding. Simultaneously, reforms such as those reflected in the constitution of 1993 and the family law adopted in 1995 made it possible for women to opt not to work outside the home by establishing material obligations of family members to each other (*Semeinyi Kodeks...*, 1995, art. 85–87). The abolishment of the Soviet system for planning entailed a reduction in the number of salaried positions. Fewer employment opportunities, along with new possibilities to set up private businesses, implied that men as the main breadwinners were assigned a special role in the Russian family and now would earn money from entrepreneurship. However, although the changes in family policy seemed to suggest that the state had abandoned the norm of a two-income household, it soon became clear that such a policy was not realistic. Women continued to provide a substantial share of family income, and most never got the option of becoming a housewife. In any case, the idea of a sole male breadwinner seemed completely unrealistic for most Russian families.

Thus in post-Soviet Russia, more responsibility for breadwinning and care duties was put on the family. The aim of my chapter is to shed light on the effects of this increased responsibility for gender relations in the family and society. To this end I will relate the gender effects to surviving and changing institutions.[1] My ambition is to explain why the Soviet family model of a dual breadwinner and a female/state caregiver has survived despite considerable pressure. The analytical frame is based on Douglass North (1990), who specifies four main kinds of institutions influencing the way a society develops: legal rules, organization forms, enforcement, and behavioral norms. To this I will add the gender dimension. To gain deeper insights into these questions, I will use interviews with women and men in families where one or both spouses have been active in the business sphere, as well as exchanges with politicians and community officials on their experiences of and views on gender roles in Russian families in post-Soviet Russia.[2] These questions were asked within the framework of the fifty interviews I conducted between 2002 and 2008 in conjunction with the follow-up of a project financed by the Swedish International Development Cooperation Agency (SIDA) aimed at helping individuals to start their own businesses.[3] The interviews were conducted in three communities in one Russian region that represent the situation in sparsely populated areas as well as in neighborhoods near a city.[4] As many of those I have talked to wished to be anonymous, I have not identified the region in which the study was carried out. In general terms the economic development in this region has followed trends on the national level (Sätre, 2007).

Changing Images versus Surviving Norms

The Soviet gender order was strongly determined by the needs of the state and communist ideology. Because women and men were needed to build up the industrialized socialist state, household duties were to be taken care of by childcare facilities and public authorities outside the family (Clements, 1992). In tune with the rhetoric of the 1930s, women were portrayed on tractors, thus mirroring the images of the socialist woman current in that period (Carlbäck, 2005). Because the socialization of households was only partially realized in practice, the image of the "working mother" soon came to dominate the female identity, which became constructed upon the double burden of domestic care duties and full-time paid work (Gradskova, 2007; Khotkina, 2001; Kozina, 2005). The male identity continued to be built around paid work, while men took little role in household work. In particular, the economic reforms of the early 1990s strongly cultivated the ideal of a male breadwinner (Ashwin, 2006; Kiblitskaia, 2000). Simultaneously, there was a changing image of women that could be interpreted as a backlash against women regarding their position on the labor market. The most successful images of the ideal woman in the media were as a housekeeper or a beautiful sex symbol with a rich husband (Bridger et al., 1996; Kudriashova and Koukarenko, 2003).

On the other hand, gender relations in the Russian labor market show remarkable consistency with the Soviet era (Katz, 2001; Kozina, 2005; Sätre, 2001, 2005). Women have preserved their presence in the labor force, and the labor market continues to be heavily segregated by gender. The relative wages of female-dominated and male-dominated sectors have not changed much since the Soviet era. On average, women continue to earn approximately one-third less than men (Hansberry, 2004; Kazakova, 2007). Gender divisions that are characteristic of the Russian labor market can also be identified in the entrepreneurial sector. Trends in gender relations thus appear to be difficult to define. Images do not correspond with development paths in the labor market. This suggests that policy changes with respect to gender lack coherence.

Scholars have also started to devote attention to "the masculinity crisis" (Kay, 2006). Russian academics express the view that, after the open discussion of gender issues in the media in the 1990s, the focus in the Putin era is on "how it should be" rather than on actual problems. "While the media could examine and discuss gender-related issues in the 1990s, under the Putin regime, problems that women actually face are never highlighted."[5] Nor is there any attention in official political speeches or in the media to such problems as the abuse of alcohol or psychological disorders, which are more often attributed to men than women. According to the researchers, certain "male" problems like drug addiction, alcoholism, and smoking are acknowledged, but no official attention is devoted to solving them (see Aivazova, 2004). Furthermore, the gender contract that relies on women's double burden is also characteristic of the contemporary gender order, while the state appears to have resorted to discourses based on the concept of the "working mother" (Ashwin, 2006; Kravchenko, 2008). Women carry the main responsibility for domestic duties and childcare, and they also play a key role in forging and maintaining the family's social networks (Salmenniemi, 2008).

GENDER AND CHANGES IN THE INSTITUTIONAL FRAMEWORK

Well-defined gender roles within the family according to gender stereotypes were well in line with the overall reform package of the 1990s. Coming in the wake of the collapse of the Soviet planning system, those reforms liberalized the economy to enable the flourishing of a market economy based on private entrepreneurship. This, in turn, was compatible with the assumption that males, as the main breadwinners, would increasingly support their families as business developers. Because this model failed to become universal, therefore, it simply became an integral part of overall reforms, which failed to generate the development of small businesses.[6]

Two main types of explanations regarding the failure of reforms have been advanced in the literature. One explanation is that the "shock therapy reforms" as such have been designed the wrong way or have simply not gone far enough due to the lack of well-defined property rights (de Soto, 2000; Leeson and Trumbull, 2006; Roland, 2002). The other approach analyzes the development of informal institutions to attempt to explain why changes in formal institutions have not led to the intended results (North, 1990). The second line of thought will form the point of departure in the present chapter.

According to North (1990), although formal institutions in the form of laws and regulations have changed as a result of political decisions, informal institutions, such as behavioral norms, are not likely to have evolved to the same extent. Two main reasons for this can be identified. Either the informal institutions change more slowly, or they are more deeply rooted culturally and change barely at all or in a direction other than that intended by policy-makers. Adding the gender dimension, gender effects of reforms as such need to be separated from gender consequences arising from the survival and evolution of informal institutions. The latter aspects are directly related to how people react or adapt to reforms, and they are also connected with the kind of organization individuals have formed and their faith in the enforcement of rules, norms, behavior, and attitudes. According to this approach, the sole-male-breadwinner model failed because, due to their relatively high priority and low efficiency during the Soviet era, male-dominated branches face severe problems when they confront market realities (Sätre, 2001, 2009). Given that the sole male breadwinner model has not been realized in a general sense, it also seems unrealistic that women would be able to take on an increased burden for care work, as this is placed upon their shoulders on top of the "double burden" they are already carrying.

In broad terms, the Soviet system might be characterized as prioritizing industrial development over social infrastructure. Formally, while industry was completely integrated in the state system of planning, social services were only partially integrated. As a result, social issues remained partly outside of the planned target system and were to be dealt with in the informal sphere. Actors were left to look for entrepreneurial solutions outside the hierarchical structures for planning. Adding the gender dimension and the prevailing family model of "dual-earner/state and female caregiver," this meant that women had to be entrepreneurial in the Soviet system. Thus—adhering to North's framework—the survival of norms provides the basis for the analytical approach that needs to be developed here.

In my chapter I interpret persistent gender stereotypes against the background of informal institutions in order to highlight the different components of the institutional framework. As I demonstrate, although remaining features of the Soviet system can prevent development, they can also facilitate a family's economic survival. Although different tendencies might be intertwined in my study for analytical reasons, I bring up norms, behavior, and organizations one by one without excluding the possibility that gender stereotypes are affected by more than one of these. First, possible changes in legal rules with respect to gender stereotypes are highlighted. I then investigate the male role as main breadwinner in relation to the survival of Soviet-type hierarchical organizations and uncertainty with respect to enforcement of changes, respectively. My point of departure is that men were expected to fulfill their breadwinning duties by setting up private businesses, which meant they were assigned a role that was difficult to live up to (Kiblitskaia, 2000). In the third part of my chapter, I focus on the following question: How does the survival of norms and horizontal networks contribute to an explanation of women's ability to solve questions related to their assigned role of caregiver?

Changes in Legal Rules and Their Relations to Gender Stereotypes

There are a few important changes in the legal rules facing families that promote gender stereotypes. One such example is the 2006 law that provides a lump-sum benefit to mothers who adopt or bear a second child; this benefit cannot be claimed by the father (unless the mother dies or loses her parental rights, or if the father is the sole adopter). A new law on the monetization of social benefits, which converted in-kind benefits into cash allowances and transferred responsibility for welfare from central to local authorities, was introduced in 2005.[7] As women are responsible for the household and the general care of the extended family, this law is generally thought to increase their workload.

Changes in legal rules have also given rise to a responsibility for self-financing at the local level.[8] Because this is expected to increase the need for voluntary work in the social sphere, which tends to be a female responsibility, it is likely to increase the workload on women as well. Local initiatives among women have increased and independent women's organizations have been formed to address current social, political, and economic problems (see Cook and Vinogradova, 2006; Hemment, 2007; Kulmala, 2008;

Salmenniemi, 2008; Sperling, 1999). For many women this means at least a partial transfer from paid work in the state sector to low-paid or unpaid work in the voluntary sector (Sätre, 2000). This also entails the risk that the women's workforce will be exploited in civic organizations (Salmenniemi, 2008).

As targets for support were diverted from families to general groups in the 1990s (Kravchenko, 2008), there were other legal changes that made it more difficult for women as the main care providers within families. The changed view of women since then, however, is reflected in the fact that the need for state support to working mothers that had disappeared in the 1995 family code was reinstated in 2007 (Chandler, 2008; Teplova, 2004).

The privatization reforms in 1993 opened up the possibility for individuals to become owners of firms. As directors in state enterprises were more often men, more men than women became owners as a result of privatization, which facilitated their assigned breadwinning role at the time (see Sätre, 2009). This presumably meant that men could more easily get bank loans, since they would more often be able to provide security. The privatization of property meant that men became the sole owners of apartments, which provided them another opportunity to accumulate capital (Schleuning, 1998; Turbine, 2008). On the other hand, it might be argued that social welfare policy was not designed to facilitate everyday life for families (Chandler, 2008). If policies actively promoting stronger families cannot be identified, this reinforces the impression that there is also no real goal to promote gender stereotypes as such, or for that matter gender equality. Decentralization as such does not mean that the state abandons responsibility for social affairs but that it simply transfers responsibility to the local level. Thus the effect on families is more indirect.

Breadwinning, the Enforcement of Legal Rules and the Size of Firms

It might be argued that reforms on a societal level have promoted an image of male breadwinners that is increasingly based on private entrepreneurship. Following North's analytical framework, the fact that this image is not compatible with existing norms means that political efforts to grow the economy by developing the small business sector are not likely to be realized in the short term. On the contrary, it seems reasonable to assume that the survival of hierarchical decision-making in male-dominated branches is reflected in the business sphere, in organizations as well as in enforcement, and in the behavior of male entrepreneurs. Because men have set up businesses in traditionally male sectors, they have continued to be active in the branches prioritized in the Soviet era; these branches have retained hierarchical structures that do not promote entrepreneurial thinking (Sätre, 2001).

Vertical rather than horizontal integration means that it is difficult to set up new firms. Because the markets are controlled by already solvent entrepreneurs, newcomers are likely to be forced into existing hierarchical structures. Both the statistics and interviews reflect the general difficulties encountered in developing small enterprises in male-dominated branches such as heavy industry and metalworking (Sätre, 2009). Several entrepreneurs held the view that setting up businesses may have become more difficult recently, compared to just after the privatization reform in 1993. It was possible then to take over state firms or equipment from firms that were closing down. In the early years of perestroika, those who were able and perhaps lucky enough to take chances at the right time seized whatever opportunities they had, turning to the mayor and asking for privatization of the state enterprises of which they were in charge.

Interviewees also express a fear of getting involved in dangerous businesses. The attitude towards male business simply reflects family members' fear that their son or husband will get mixed up in some dangerous activity, will "fall into the hands of criminals," be "subject to mafia methods," and so on. "They would be risking not only their money, but also their lives." One example is a person who wanted to start a dairy. In order to earn some capital to get started, he borrowed some money from a timber-cutting firm and signed a contract with the firm to deliver timber. He was then unable to fulfill the contract, as he put it, "due to too much snow and unskilled workers on his timber cutting team." The situation he ended up in, he remarked, was "similar to serfdom," as the firm took his machines while he himself had to work eleven hours per day.[9] Another example is a man who ended up as a nightwatchman for one of the larger entrepreneurs after he had failed to set up a tourism business.[10] A third example is the two men who turned an empty building into a café, a sewing room, and a room with bath facilities, but who had to close their premises when the heating and electricity were cut off by the new owner of the only larger firm in the vicinity.[11]

Although male as well as female entrepreneurs expressed the fear that they would be "swallowed up" by larger firms, the general view seemed to be that this was a danger more for males than for females, depending just as much on expected behavior as on actual behavior and on what branch they got involved in. Some of the interviewed men were, however, aware of this "danger" and said they tried to avoid the trap. One example is a timber cutter who said he preferred to earn less and sleep at night. "If you get a little bigger, somebody will come and tell you to leave."[12] According to him, it is easier for the mafia to control a more profitable business, while for him it is easier to have control if the business is smaller and has fewer employees. "As long as the firm is small, it is your own, but if you start to grow, some person who works close to the government will come and buy you up." Similar views were also articulated by entrepreneurs in the tourism industry.[13]

It seems reasonable to assume that leaders of large firms are more powerful than those of small ones, since the former are in a position to bargain with local community officials and have more power to disobey rules and legislation or simply set their own laws (Braginsky and Myerson, 2007). Interviews confirm this view; local authorities are described as "being in the hands of local oligarchs." So it seems that larger firms that are more solvent than smaller ones dare to trust the legal system and "the market" and are more likely to do business based on market relations, while smaller ones would prefer to stick to personal relations (Bruno, 1997; Radaev, 2001; Sätre, 2010; Ylinenpää and Chechurina, 2000). Furthermore, previous research supports the impression that authorities would rather deal with a few large firms than many small ones (Oganian, 2002; Skvoznikov and Azarenkova, 2001; Wells, 2003). The larger ones are better able to negotiate in the event of disagreements on the terms of trade, and they have some reserves in the event of failures, miscalculations, legal troubles or dishonest behavior.

There may also be differences in the enforcement of legal rules that benefit large organizations (Hitt et al., 2004; Polishchuk and Savateev, 2004). In a survey cited by Radaev (2001), for example, due to difficulties with registration and licensing, small entrepreneurs rank the bureaucracy as the most important problem they face. Because of limited experience of (or lack of interest in) self-managed organizations, the institutional framework is not likely to be adapted to their needs. Interviewees told of administrators and officials who act differently at various levels, and as there are many hierarchies to go through, it seems easy to believe that obstacles will appear on at least one of the levels. The general feeling among small entrepreneurs seems to be that legislation changes frequently, especially at the local and regional levels. Many also feel that the rules frequently contradict one another. This makes it impossible to comply with all of them and potentially leaves much power in the hands of the administrative official.

Interviewees told me of signs that a situation was developing in which only a few large entrepreneurs dominate the scene and are more or less governed by their own laws: "the community was only interested in cooperation with large entrepreneurs who have divided power and wealth among themselves, including the right to cut down forests." Confirming this view, one mayor told me that since it is easier to have to deal with just a few strong firms, he promoted a process in which larger firms took over the smaller ones. He admitted that he could "turn a blind eye if these companies create large agricultural firms that can employ women and contribute to fulfilling social needs in some of the villages."[14]

The overall impression from interviews is that performance varies more among male entrepreneurs than among females. A female former vice-mayor said that heavy pressure on young males to succeed as entrepreneurs, combined with little experience and unrealistic plans, big risks, impatience, and an ambition to make fast money, contributed to their failure. Earlier research confirms that the polarization among Russian men is more pronounced than among women: men predominate both among the deeply marginalized groups marked by heavy drinking and early death and among the political and economic elites (Ashwin, 2006). The picture that emerges from the interviews is one of increasing discrepancies among men, in which a few gradually manage to build up fortunes but the vast majority fail to do so. Many interviewees spoke of hard conditions, where the stronger buy up or otherwise defeat the weaker. Mafia methods are taken for granted, and even the most successful businessmen are thought to be "in the hands" of dominant forces in Moscow.[15]

Interviews also reveal, however, that some have been able to start "from scratch" and develop their businesses little by little, using timber or trade as capital to launch any business. "You have to be brave to get started" and enter one branch after another "to ensure a more stable position" and "not put everything in one basket." As one of the successful interviewees put it: "Because the risk of failure is so big, in order to succeed you have to start at least ten firms."[16] Tourism, textiles, handicrafts, and food are examples of branches in which it has been possible to run small-scale as well as large-scale businesses. In any case, starting a private firm is a new undertaking that was not possible in the Soviet Union. This opens the way for non-hierarchical decision-making, a development that indicates that norms have changed somewhat. Men start firms in branches in which women were dominating from the beginning, such as trade, where actual behavior differs from traditional hierarchical structures. Interviews revealed, however, how extremely difficult it is to start on your own. The overall high level of uncertainty involved in the venture demands strong solidarity between partners, which encourages business development based on personal family ties rather than on impersonal market relations. One result of this situation is the emergence of family businesses, a rather new phenomenon in post-Soviet Russia.

Care Duties and Surviving Norms

Interpreting the gendered nature of responsibility for care duties in terms of the survival of norms helps establish a multi-dimensional framework for explaining how an increased burden for care work is handled within the context of the general survival of the "double burden." In this case, where the breakdown of the Soviet system has caused increased responsibility to be shifted to families, the persistence of slow-changing norms can prevent serious consequences for them when the formal institutions they have relied upon fall apart. This is a rather complex issue, since the meaning of privatizing responsibilities for care is in itself unclear, given the simultaneously widespread insecurity of overall transformation trends. It also has to do with the survival of the state policy that prioritizes production over social security. Such a priority implicitly accepts the image of the "working mother" and thus imposes the "double burden" as a residual element. Not really an active policy in itself, the approach bespeaks the absence of a gender equality policy. As such, it seems to be more a question of the persistence of a general female responsibility for both the individual household and social affairs.

To return to North's analytical framework, what is involved here is the survival of entrepreneurial behavior necessary to deal with shortcomings resulting from the low-priority status of social issues in the Soviet system that were solved by women's horizontal organizations based on informal networks of mutual support or care. In this process various combinations of women's formal and informal organizations have survived. These are activities in which women have engaged within the state or in the private sphere. A combination of strategies is needed to overcome various deficiencies arising in the processes of post-Soviet transformation and decentralization. In any case, given the gendered nature of the responsibility for the provision of care in both state and non-state contexts, women are responsible both for organizing care within households and in society and for empowering voluntary work and self-help strategies.

GENDER ROLES WITH RESPECT TO HOUSEHOLD DUTIES

Earlier research has argued that Russian women do not tend to question the gender division of household duties and that they view the domestic sphere as a natural female responsibility (Afontsev et al., 2008; Kay, 2002). The dominant gender contract that emerges in the interviews is of a "working mother," which was also characteristic of the Soviet era (Kravchenko, 2008). The majority of women interviewees either ran the household themselves or at least were responsible for organizing it. A few of the older women mentioned that they helped their daughters, while the younger women said they got help from their mothers. Some interviewees reported their husbands as being actively involved in running the household, while others said they got help from their husbands when they asked for it. The majority of interviewees reported receiving great practical support and help from their spouses with the housework and childcare. For example, one entrepreneur said that her husband stayed at home with the newborn baby when she returned to run her enterprise a couple of days after giving birth.[17]

The interviews show that although gender roles within families survive, some changes in attitudes seem to be taking hold. One woman who is running a textile business said that she does not like to cook. She explained that her husband does the cooking and that he also takes on most of the care responsibility for their two children. The woman and man do not receive any help from their parents, although they live nearby. The older son takes a lot of responsibility for the younger son, and they have also hired a girl to help with childcare. The husband, the girl, and the eleven-year-old son took turns bringing the baby to her office so that she could feed him until he was one month old. Then she stopped nursing, as she did not feel she could spare the time for it.[18]

The interviews show that the private business in itself sometimes helps ease household work. One woman's development of a tourism business, for example, shows how the gradual increase in the number of employees has benefited the household. One component is the cafeteria. Good cooking for guests also benefits the family, who take the opportunity to cook for themselves when the *babushka* is not taking care of them. Thus given low labor costs, labor-intensive activities can contribute to the private household, which can benefit from cooking, cleaning, building repairs, vehicle maintenance, and even occasional childcare. Childcare is secured through a private preschool a few hours per day; the grandmother also helps, and sometimes the child follows her mother while she is working.[19]

After many years of fighting various obstacles, the mother in another family finally had her business registered, "although in her daughter's name." In this case all three generations helped in the business. The mother did most of the cooking for her daughter's family as well and helped her daughter with the housework and taking care of the grandchildren. The father and the daughter's husband performed traditional men's duties within the households, such as driving and making furniture. Some work, like picking mushrooms and berries, was shared by the entire extended family.[20]

In another "family model" the mother and daughter collaborate in the making of cheese. While the daughter produces cheese in her own kitchen in the city, the retired mother is responsible for selling this cheese and other dairy products from her own farm. As a widow from an early age and the single mother of three children, she always supported her family through various entrepreneurial activities. Since retirement she has continued with her business, and she also works as a massage therapist. She lives in a kind of extended family in a big, newly built house (after the old one burned down twice) with homeless couples, former alcoholics who perform various duties at her farm in return for free housing, food, and some pocket money. A good friend of hers, also a widow for many years, is involved in the cooking.[21] In the region where the field work for this study was carried out, in one of the communities with 35,000 inhabitants, for example, there were four orphanages. While some of the children were there permanently, others came from families with "temporary" social problems, which indicates that some families fail to take care of their children.[22]

Interviews also reveal that the father is taking on an increased role in the household. One view is that it has become more common for men to cook and take care of children. "As society is changing, men have to take more responsibility for childcare as well." There are of course differences between generations and between rural versus urban families. Interviews with female local politicians give the impression that it has become less common for grandmothers to look after the children. The *babushka* tradition seems to be disappearing. One reason is that grandmothers have to work because their pensions are no longer large enough to support them. Women in urban areas with higher education do not want to take the role of a grandmother at the age of fifty, the official retirement age for women in northern regions. They prefer a more active life. Another reason is a changing attitude among parents. Due to the child-raising approach of their grandmothers, they do not want their children to be brought up by the older generation.[23] They hire female caretakers or teachers instead through special firms. Women who take on such jobs are usually between thirty and forty years old and have lost their jobs when their workplaces shut down. These are the women who according to Posadskaya (1996) are likely to suffer as a new, special labor market, with limited opportunities and insecure, poorly paid, and low-status employment, was established in the service sector. Sometimes they are relatives from the countryside who take the opportunity to move to a city or town to live in the family they work for.

SOCIAL MOTHERS

Earlier research has documented how women seem to take on the role of "social mothers" whose duties include taking care of the village or the local community (Kulmala, 2008; Salmenniemi, 2008). My interviews with female politicians support the view that being "social mothers" is a female responsibility. On the question of where women get their strength, a former female vice-mayor responsible for social issues replied: "Women are focused on how to survive, they are not aggressive and they do not have to prove anything."[24] Another answer was: "Women have themselves and their own strength; they do not count on anything else."[25] One female vice-mayor emphasized that her grandmother had been her best teacher. From her she learned how to use different bargaining strategies, when to be a diplomat, and how to avoid problems. She said: "It is about being able to talk in front of other people and to know your history. It is what you actually do that matters. As a Russian woman you are used to surviving, you simply have to be. It is not about experience from your working life, training or education; it is an instinct, a habit."

It is well-documented that female politicians were commonly responsible for social policies in the Soviet Union and that women continue to take this responsibility at all political levels in post-Soviet Russia (Clements, 1992; Kudriashova and Koukarenko, 2003; Lapidus, 1975; Moses, 2008; Shevchenko, 2002). It also seems clear that women officials view women's organizations as potential allies in the social sphere, as potential providers of social services that fill gaps in the badly shredded Russian safety net (Lipovskaya, 1997; Salmenniemi, 2008; Sätre, 2000). My interviews reflect how female politicians have initiated social projects and cultural activities in the local communities. One example is the "House of Culture," which receives children from distant villages. One measure that a former vice-mayor described was that women took turns going with the cutting team to the timber-cutting area in order to prevent them from getting drunk on the bus. With regional-level financial support, women have created local jobs in sewing workshops and in cafés.[26] There are also examples of young people starting their small businesses with the help of retired women. Or as a local social activist put it: "In the villages women provide concrete ideas, and behind them are the men with their toolboxes." Earlier research confirms that social networks and subsistence entrepreneurship are important to the survival of villages (Nikula and Granberg, 2006; Svensson, 2008).

Few studies, however, have looked deeper into the apparent contradiction here. Women continue to carry the double burden on their shoulders. They are responsible for households and, in addition, appear to be overloaded with increased responsibility for social duties. Women seem to be in charge in situations where there is no money. "Sometimes I am standing in the same place, but this is something you just have to endure." This is how Violetta, who has been in charge at the lowest political level for eight years, describes a "normal working day."[27] In the morning she receives visitors from the local population. They come to see her when they have complaints about practical matters. Then she spends all day in meetings "begging for money." It seems clear that her job is not really a matter of ideology or political strategies but about finding practical solutions to people's ordinary problems in their everyday lives.

Violetta describes how she has to find ways to get hold of resources by asking for funds from higher political levels, by asking the local entrepreneurs for support or by mobilizing local people to either contribute voluntarily or engage in a process of bargaining. In effect, what Violetta describes is how decentralization affects her own working situation and how difficult it can be at times. She also, however, emphasizes that she feels more powerful, with more possibilities than before to implement measures. Thus although "women continue to solve the problems that fall between the chairs as they did in Soviet times," there seem to be more options now, and Violetta is proud of her achievements in recent years.

Interviews with female politicians at the community level confirm Violetta's experiences of how survival and development are facilitated both by strong norms originally established as an integral part of the Soviet system and new possibilities resulting from reforms.[28] One example is of a mayor in a rural community and the director of the department of cultural affairs, both females, encouraging entrepreneurship and local development by advising people how to apply for funds for projects.[29] In another community, officials try to stimulate cultural activities and education and local development groups to raise satisfaction levels and foster a changed mentality that sees opportunities and is prepared to take action.[30] Politicians are actively taking part in starting cultural organizations, trade unions, and women's councils. They advocate extending to the local community the norm from Soviet times, when big firms took social responsibility for their employees.[31] This phenomenon is confirmed in the work of other scholars (Kulmala, 2008; Lazareva, 2009; Nikula and Granberg, 2006; Shubin, 2007).

Conclusions

This chapter has examined the experiences and perceptions of gender roles in Russian families and society in the context of the increase that has occurred in the household and employment workload families must bear. The result of the analysis shows that although the "double burden" has been extended to include local society and social affairs, gender roles in breadwinning and within households do not seem to have changed much. Although subject to reforms, strong norms established as an integral part of the Soviet system have survived and are difficult to change, as they are deeply rooted in people's attitudes. My study, however, has shown that the increased responsibility on families has had various effects on gender, albeit indirectly.

One effect highlighted here is the way in which labor market transformation and privatization tend to widen gaps between performances of males as main providers. My study indicates that the increased expectations on males to earn money from entrepreneurial activities can be difficult to meet, given the difficulty of setting up new firms in male-dominated sectors characterized by hierarchical organizations. Second, although my study provides some indication of men's deeper involvement in the household, the domestic sphere remains mainly a women's realm. Among women, however, a new division of labor also seems to be emerging in which those who are able to develop private businesses use hired help to ease their own double burden.

Third, my study points to a widening gap both between and within communities, which implies that the ability to support weak families differs from place to place. State policy towards families was highlighted indirectly. Although pronatalist in rhetoric, policies focus on easing the difficult situation of ordinary people, not necessarily on improving the situation of individual families. Economic recovery in the new decade means money will be coming into the state budget, some of which is earmarked for social issues. However, rather than the support going directly to families, it is given to local authorities, both directly for certain earmarked tasks and indirectly, on the basis of submitted project applications. Although social policy continues to be financed by the state to some extent, the way it is organized is partly new.

The female politicians responsible for organizing social care said they use various strategies. This means that solutions are likely to be more heterogeneous than before. The present study indicates that female politicians who are responsible for social affairs have to negotiate with local firms and voluntary organizations, beg, or find solutions in other ways. On the other hand, we have also seen that women in charge feel more powerful and better able to implement measures than before. One important explanation of the variations within communities appears to be the existence of large local firms. With them, however, comes the risk that the distribution of social welfare at the local level will be decided by rich businesspeople, who most commonly are men, rather than the local female politicians responsible for social affairs.

Notes

1 Institutions are all the regulations that humans have created to form interaction in society. While formal rules can be changed by political decisions, informal rules, such as behavioral norms that are rooted in society, are not quickly changed (see also North, 1990, for the role of institutions in societal development).
2 Most of the empirical material for this study was collected during my visits to three communities in one of Russia's eighty-nine regions in May 2002, November 2003, December 2005, October 2006, and October–November 2008.
3 Fifteen people took part in a SIDA-financed project aimed at helping individual entrepreneurs start their own businesses. I interviewed eleven women, three men, and the mother of a woman who was not interviewed. The project involved education in business development, including help for the participants to develop their own business plans in 2001, and a study trip to Sweden, where they visited individual entrepreneurs within the same business field. In 2008 one of the three who was running a business, a woman, had been running her textile firm since 1993. Another woman had in 2006 finally managed to register her firm as a "self-employed entrepreneur." A third woman had, after a long struggle, succeeded in having her berry-and-mushroom-processing firm registered in 2007, although in her daughter's name. One of the men had been able to set up a Swedish-Russian timber-cutting firm in 2003 with a Swedish partner, but he was out of business by 2008. Some of the others who had tried were running their businesses without registering them. One of the men had died, and one of the women had moved to St. Petersburg.

4   Apart from the participants in the project, interviews in three communities were carried out with other individuals who have attempted, successfully or unsuccessfully, to start their own firms, as well as with politicians and community officials. In 2003 interviews were conducted with the mayors in all three communities, as well as with one vice-mayor and one former vice-mayor. In 2005 interviews were conducted with the new mayor and the new vice-mayor in one of the communities, where those in charge had been replaced in 2003. In 2006 and 2008, interviews were carried out with the mayor and the vice-mayor in two of the communities and with four politicians at the lowest local level. At the regional level I talked to a vice-governor, a vice-chairman, and a member of the regional Duma.
5   Interviews at the Centre of Gender Studies at Pomor University in Arkhangelsk, October 25, 2008.
6   There is no general agreement among scholars on this issue. The official view of the Putin administration is to see Yeltsin's reform, the "shock therapy," as a failure. Problems in developing small and medium-sized firms, for example, have been highlighted through repeated statements by President Medvedev on the news program *Vremia*.
7   Federal'nyi Zakon No. 122-FZ (Federal Law No. 122-FZ) *O vnesenii izmenenii v zakonodatel'nye akty Rossiiskoi Federatsii* [...] (On introducing amendments into legislative acts of the Russian Federation [...]), August 22, 2004. A key task was to divide administrative and financial responsibility for providing benefits (*l'goty*) between the central level and the regions, which means that regions support two-thirds of the recipients. See Wengle and Rassell (2008, pp. 743–744).
8   Federal'nyi Zakon No. 131-FZ (Federal Law No. 131-FZ) *Ob obshchikh printsipakh organizatsii mestnogo samoupravleniia v Rossiiskoi Federatsii* (On the general principles of organization of local self-governance in the Russian Federation), October 6, 2003, with the latest amendments introduced on January 1, 2006. A key task involved increased responsibility for self-financing of costs along with the introduction of a fourth level of administration (*poselenie*) within each community.
9   Interviews, November 24, 2003, and December 10, 2005. According to his former partners, he had run into serious problems and was still alive only because his father-in-law, the director of one of the largest forestry firms, had saved him (interview, October 30, 2008).
10 Interview with a man who tried and failed to set up his own tourism business, October 25, 2008.
11 Interview with two men who work as employees at a shipyard, while they also tried to develop their own business on the side, October 6, 2006.
12 Interview with the owner of a timber-cutting firm, October 7, 2006.
13 Interview with the female owner of a tourist business, October 10, 2006.
14 Interview with a mayor, November 24, 2003.
15 Interview with the owner of a timber-cutting firm, October 29, 2008.

16 Interview with a businessman in the city who told me how he built up a business "from scratch," how he was cheated and lost everything, and how he started all over again, October 6, 2006.
17 Interview with the female owner of a textile firm, October 29, 2008.
18 Interview with the female owner of a textile firm, October 9, 2006.
19 Interview with the female owner of a tourism firm, October 31, 2008.
20 Interview with a female entrepreneur in the berry-and-mushroom-processing business, October 30, 2008.
21 Interview with an elderly woman who, along with her daughter, is running a business based on cheese processing, October 26, 2008.
22 Interview with a male vice-mayor, November 23, 2003.
23 Interviews with three female politicians at the lowest level of political administration, October 24–25, 2008.
24 Interview with a former vice-mayor, December 9, 2005.
25 Interview with a vice-mayor, October 10, 2006.
26 Interview with a retired person who works without pay for a voluntary organization, December 9, 2005.
24 Interview with the head of the lowest level of political administration, October 28, 2008. This administration, consisting of several villages, used to be denoted *sel'sovet*. Since the new federal law No. 131 came into force in 2006, it has been called *poselenie* (the difference between a *sel'sovet* and a *poselenie* is that the latter is responsible for its own budget).
25 Interviews with a female mayor, November 26, 2003, a female vice-mayor and a female former vice-mayor, October 28–29, 2008.
26 Interviews with the mayor and director of cultural affairs (*glava kul'tury*) in a rural community, both females, November 26, 2003.
27 Interview with a female former vice-mayor, December 9, 2005.
28 Interview with a female vice-head of a *poselenie*, November 1, 2008.

REFERENCES

Afontsev, Sergey, Gijs Kessler, Andrei Markevitch, Victoria Tyazhelnikova, and Timur Valetov. 2008. "The Urban Household in Russia and the Soviet Union, 1900–2000: Patterns of Family Formation in a Turbulent Century." *ScienceDirect* 13: 178–194.

Aivazova, Svetlana. 2004. "Gender i rossiiskaia politika: konflikt makro- i mikro-urovnei vlasti" (Gender and Russian policy: The conflict between micro- and macroauthorities). *Gendernye issledovaniia* 10: 87–88.

Ashwin, Sarah. 2006. "The Post-Soviet Gender Order: Imperatives and Implications." In *Adapting to Russia's New Labour Market: Gender and Employment Behaviour*, ed. Sarah Ashwin, 32–56. London and New York: Routledge.

Braginsky, Sergey, and Roger Myerson. 2007. "A Macroeconomic Model of Russian Transition." *Economics of Transition* 15, no. 1: 77–107.

Bridger, Susan, Rebecca Kay, and Kathryn Pinnick. 1996. *No More Heroines? Russia, Women and the Market*. London: Routledge.

Bruno, Marta. 1997. "Women and the Culture of Entrepreneurship." In *Post-Soviet Women: From the Baltic to Central Asia*, ed. Mary Buckley, 56–74. Cambridge: Cambridge University Press.

Carlbäck, Helene. 2005. "Tracing the Roots of Early Soviet Russian Family Laws." In *Gender Transitions in Russia and Eastern Europe*, eds. Ildikó Asztalos Morell, Helene Carlbäck, Madeleine Hurd, and Sara Rastbäck, 69–84. Eslöv, Sweden: Gondolin.

Chandler, Andrea. 2008. "Citizen, Family and State in Russian Social Policy since 2000: Reform or Restoration?" Paper presented at the Aleksanteri Conference "Welfare, Gender and Agency in Russia and Eastern Europe," December 10–12, 2008, Helsinki.

Clements, Barbara Evans. 1992. "The Utopianism of the Zhenotdel." *Slavic Review* 51, no. 3: 485–496.

Cook, Linda J., and Elena Vinogradova. 2006. "NGOs and Social Policy in Russia's Regions." *Problems of Post-Communism* 53, no. 5: 28–41.

Gradskova, Youlia. 2007. *Soviet People with Female Bodies: Performing Beauty and Maternity in Soviet Russia in the Mid 1930–1960s*. Stockholm: Acta Universitatis Stockholmiensis.

Hansberry, Rita. 2004. *An Analysis of Gender Wage Differentials in Russia from 1996–2002*. William Davidson Institute Working Paper Number 720, Social Science Research Network, http://ssrn.com/abstract=615801.

Hemment, Julie. 2007. *Empowering Women in Russia, Activism, Aid, and NGOs*. Bloomington and Indianapolis: Indiana University Press.

Hitt, Michael A., David Ahlstrom, M. Tina Dacin, Edward Levitas, and Lilia Svobodina. 2004. "The Institutional Effects on Strategic Alliance Partner Selection in Transition Economics: China vs. Russia." *Organization Science* 15, no. 2: 173–185.

Katz, Katarina. 2001. *Gender, Work and Wages in the Soviet Union: A Legacy of Discrimination*. Basingstoke, UK: Palgrave.

Kay, Rebecca. 2002. "A Liberation from Emancipation? Changing Discourses on Women's Employment in Soviet and Post-Soviet Russia." *Journal of Communist Studies and Transition Politics* 18, no. 1: 51–72.

———. 2006. *Men in Contemporary Russia: The Fallen Heroes of Post-Soviet Change*. Aldershot, UK, and Burlington, VT: Ashgate.

Kazakova, Elena. 2007. "Wages in a Growing Russia: When Is a 10 Percent Rise in the Gender Wage Gap Good News?" *Economics of Transition* 15, no. 2: 365–392.

Khotkina, Zoya. 2001. "Female Unemployment and Informal Employment in Russia." *Problems of Economic Transition* 43, no. 9: 20–23.

Kiblitskaia, Marina. 2000. "'Once We Were Kings:' Male Experiences of Loss of Status at Work in Post-Communist Russia." In *Gender, State and Society in Soviet and Post-Soviet Russia*, ed. Sarah Ashwin, 55–70. London: Routledge.

Kozina, Irina. 2005. "The Significance of Gender Stereotypes in the Russian Labour Market." In *Gender Transitions in Russia and Eastern Europe*, eds. Ildikó Asztalos Morell, Helene Carlbäck, Madeleine Hurd, and Sara Rastbäck, 219–231. Eslöv, Sweden.

Kravchenko, Zhanna. 2008. *Family (versus) Policy: Combining Work and Care in Russia and Sweden*. Stockholm: Acta Universitatis Stockholmiensis.

Kudriashova, Elena, and Natalia Koukarenko. 2003. "The Political Participation of Women: Is It Really Easier for Women in the Municipalities?" In *Women's Strategies and Politics in Transition: Dialogue Across the East-West Divide*, eds. Irina Yukina, Aino Saarinen, and Elena Kudriashova, 11–27. Archangelsk, Russia: Pomor University Press.

Kulmala, Meri. 2008. *Women Rule the Country: Women's Social Activism in Rural Karelia*. Paper presented at the Aleksanteri Conference "Welfare, Gender and Agency in Russia and Eastern Europe," December 10–12, 2008, Helsinki.

Lapidus, Gail Warshofsky. 1975. "Political Mobilization, Participation, and Leadership: Women in Politics." *Comparative Politics* 8, no. 1: 90–118.

Lazareva, Olga. 2009. *Labour Market Outcomes during the Russian Transition*. PhD diss., Stockholm School of Economics.

Leeson, Peter T., and William N. Trumbull. 2006. "Comparing Apples: Normalcy, Russia, and the Remaining Post-Socialist World." *Post-Soviet Affairs* 22, no. 3: 225–248.

Lipovskaya, Olga. 1997. "Women's Groups in Russia." In *Post-Soviet Women: From the Baltic to Central Asia*, ed. Mary Buckley, 186–199. Cambridge: Cambridge University Press.

Moses, Joel C. 2008. "Who Has Led Russia? Russian Regional Political Elites, 1954–2006." *Europe-Asia Studies* 60, no. 1: 1–24.

Nikula, Jouko, and Leo Granberg. 2006. "Förändring och kontinuitet på den ryska landsbygden" (Change and continuity in the Russian countryside). *Nordisk Östforum* 20, no. 3: 267–281.

North, Douglass. 1990. *Institutions, Institutional Change and Economic Performance*. Cambridge: Cambridge University Press.

Oganian, Oganes. 2002. "O gosudarstvennoi podderzhke malogo biznesa v Rossii" (On state support for small business in Russia). *Ekonomist* 8: 45–51.

Polishchuk, Leonid, and Alexei Savateev. 2004. "Spontaneous (Non)emergence of Property Rights." *Economics of Transition* 12, no. 1: 103–127.

Posadskaia, Anastasia. 1996. "Zhenskie issledovaniia v Rossii: perspektivy novogo videniia" (Research on women in Russia: Prospects of a new vision). In *Gendernye aspekty sotsial'noi transformatsii* (Gender aspects of social transformation), ed. Marina Malysheva, 11–24. Moscow: ISEPN.

Radaev, Vadim. 2001. *The Development of Small Entrepreneurship in Russia*. Discussion Paper No. 135, World Institute for Development Economics Research, http://ideas.repec.org/p/unu/wpaper/dp2001-135.html (accessed June 24, 2011).

Roland, Gérard. 2002. "The Political Economy of Transition." *Journal of Economic Perspectives* 16, no. 1: 29–50.

Salmenniemi, Suvi. 2008. *Democratization and Gender in Contemporary Russia*. London and New York: Routledge.

Schleuning, Neala. 1998. "Family Economics in Russia: Women's Perspectives on the Transition to a Market Economy." *Journal of Consumer Studies and Home Economics* 22, no. 1: 51–64.

Semeinyi Kodeks Rossiiskoi Federatsii (The Russian Family Code). 1995. Published in *Rossiiskaia gazeta* (January 27, 1996), http://base.consultant.ru/cons/cgi/online.cgi?req=doc;base=LAW;n=60687 (accessed June 30, 2011).

Shevchenko, Julia. 2002. "Who Cares about Women's Problems? Female Legislators in the 1995 and 1999 Russian State Dumas." *Europe-Asia Studies* 54, no. 8: 1201–1222.

Shubin, Sergei. 2007. "Networked Poverty in Rural Russia." *Europe-Asia Studies* 59, no. 4: 591–620.

Skvoznikov, Vladimir, and N.V. Azarenkova. 2001. "Problemy otsenki tenevoi ekonomiki" (Problems of evaluating the shadow economy). *Voprosy statistiki* 12: 18–26.

Soto, Hernando de. 2000. *The Mystery of Capital: Why Capitalism Triumphs in the West and Fails Everywhere Else*. New York: Random House.

Sperling, Valerie. 1999. *Organizing Women in Contemporary Russia: Engendering Transition*. Cambridge: Cambridge University Press.

Svensson, Bengt. 2008. *Seven Years that Shook Soviet Economic and Social Thinking: Reflections on the Revolution in Communist Economics 1985–91*. PhD diss., Stockholm University.

Sätre, Ann-Mari. 2000. "Women and the Social Economy in Transitional Russia." *Annals of Public and Cooperative Economics* 71, no. 3: 441–465.

———. 2001. "Women's and Men's Work in Transitional Russia: Legacies of the Soviet System." *Post-Soviet Affairs* 17, no. 1: 56–79.

———. 2005. "Women and Women's Work in Transitional Russia: Impacts from the Soviet System." In *Gender Transitions in Russia and Eastern Europe*, eds. Ildikó Asztalos Morell, Helene Carlbäck, Madeleine Hurd, and Sara Rastbäck, 195–217. Eslöv, Sweden: Gondolin.

———.2007. *Vild kapitalism och gammal byråkrati. Om småföretagare i Ryssland* (Wild capitalism and old bureaucracy. On small entrepreneurs in Russia). Stockholm: Premiss förlag.

———. 2009. *Political Strategies for Development and Survival in Russian Regions*. Working Paper 121, Department of Eurasian Studies, Uppsala University, http://www.eurasia.uu.se/docs_publikationer/AR121AS.pdf, accessed April 24, 2011.

———. 2010. "Women's Work in Transitional Russia: Women's Strategies for Entrepreneurship and Survival in Russian Regions." In *Perestroika: Process and Consequences*, eds. Markku Kangaspuro, Jouko Nikula, and Ivor Stodolsky, 330–350. Helsinki: Finnish Literary Society.

Teplova, Tatyana. 2004. *Social Reforms in Russia: Labour Market Implications*. Paper presented to the ISA RC19 annual conference "Welfare State Restructuring: Processes and Social Outcomes," September 2–4, 2004, Paris.

Turbine, Vikki. 2008. "Legal Advice Columns in Contemporary Russia: Legitimising New Forms of Women's Agency and the Privatisation of Welfare?" Paper presented at the Aleksanteri Conference "Welfare, Gender and Agency in Russia and Eastern Europe," December 10–12, 2008, Helsinki.

Wells, Betty L. 2003. "Russian Women Business Owners: Evidence of Entrepreneurship in a Transition Economy." *Journal of Developmental Entrepreneurship* 7, no. 2: 1–7.

Wengle, Susanne, and Michael Rasell. 2008. "The Monetisation of L'goty: Changing Patterns of Welfare Politics and Provision in Russia." *Europe-Asia Studies* 60, no. 5: 739–756.

Ylinenpää, Håkan, and Maya Chechurina. 2000. *Perceptions of Female Entrepreneurship in Russia*. Working paper, Luleå Tekniska Universitet, http://pure.ltu.se/portal/sv/publications/perceptions-of-female-entrepreneurship-in-russia(2729a8c0-6792-11dc-a0c3-000ea68e967b).html, (accessed June 28, 2011).

Notes on Contributors

Ildikó ASZTALOS MORELL (Sweden) is Associate Professor in Sociology at Uppsala University and Senior Research Fellow at Södertörn University. She is the author and editor of several books and articles on gender and welfare issues in Sweden. She is currently involved in the research projects *Family and the Strong State: Emancipation or Coercion?* (Södertörn University) and *The organization of Care: Local care regimes in the context of rural transformation and welfare governance* (Uppsala University).

Helene CARLBÄCK (Sweden) is Associate Professor in History at Södertörn University. She has published and edited several books and articles on Soviet–Swedish relations in the 20th century, as well as on Russian family and gender history. She is currently involved in the research project *Family and the Strong State: Emancipation or Coercion?* (Södertörn University).

Christine FARHAN (Sweden) is Associate Professor in German Studies, at Södertörn University. She is the author of several works on comparative studies of Swedish and German literature with special reference to gender issues. Currently she is taking part in the project *Family and the Strong State: Emancipation or Coercion?* (Södertörn University)

Yulia GRADSKOVA (Sweden) holds a Ph.D. in History from Stockholm University (title of dissertation: *Soviet People with Female Bodies: Performing Beauty and Maternity in Soviet Russia in the mid1930–1960s.*) She is currently lecturer in History at Södertörn University. She has published several articles on femininity constructions, maternity and beauty in the Soviet and contemporary Russian context. She is also involved in the research project *Family and the Strong State: Emancipation or Coercion?* (Södertörn University).

Elena IARSKAIA-SMIRNOVA (Russia) is Professor of the Department of Social Anthropology and Social Work, Saratov State Technical University (Russia). She is advisor to an independent research organization, the Center for Social Policy and Gender Studies and co-editor of a *Russian Journal of Social Policy Studies*.

Katja KESSELI (Finland) is a Researcher at the Rehabilitation Foundation in Finland. She prepares her doctoral dissertation at the University of Helsinki on first birth and union formation in Russia and Estonia.

Zhanna KRAVCHENKO (Sweden) holds a Ph.D. in Sociology from Stockholm University (title of the dissertation: *Family (versus) policy. Combining work and care in Russia and Sweden*). She is currently Research Fellow (postdoc) at the School of Social Work, Lund University. Her research interests include family sociology, social policy, and housing planning.

Olga KHAZOVA (Russia) is Associate Professor of Law at the Russian Academy of Sciences Institute of State and Law. Her main field of expertise concerns comparative family law. Apart from teaching family law, she serves as expert on family matters for governmental bodies, courts and law firms. She is a member of the Executive Council of the ISFL.

Dalia LEINARTE (Lithuania) is Professor in History at the University of Vilnius (Lithuania). Her research interests include the history of Lithuanian family and oral history.

Ingegerd MUNICIO-LARSSON (Sweden) is Associate Professor Emeritus in Political Science at Södertörn University (Sweden). She is the author of numerous works on migration policies, as well as family and gender issues.

Pavel ROMANOV (Russia) is the director of an independent research organization, Center for Social Policy and Gender Studies in Saratov (Russia), and co-editor of the *Journal of Social Policy Studies*.

Anna ROTKIRCH (Finland) is Associate Professor in Social policy and Women's studies at the University of Helsinki and currently a special researcher at the Population Research Institute, Väestöliitto (Finland). She has published and edited numerous works on gender, families and sexuality and in Russian studies, as well as several translations and articles in various popular newspaper columns and journals.

Maija RUNCIS (Sweden) is Associate Professor in history at Stockholm University and Södertörn University. Runcis's research has focused primarily on the Swedish welfare state and Swedish social policies from the perspective of minorities (e.g., the sterilization of deviants, forced removal of children from the home, educational programs for immigrants). At present, she is a member of the research project "The Family and the Powerful State: On Family Politics in an East European Perspective", in the context of which she is writing on family politics in Soviet Latvia.

Aino SAARINEN (Finland) is Senior Researcher at the Aleksanteri Institute, Helsinki University and Adjunct Professor in Women's Studies and Sociology at Tampere University and Oulu University (Finland). She has led several international research and networking projects on matters of migration, gendered violence and welfare policies.

Ann-Mari SÄTRE (Sweden) is Associate Professor, an economist specialised in the structure and performance of the Soviet/Russian economy. She is a senior lecturer at UCRS—the Centre of Russian and Eurasian Studies at Uppsala University and a research associate at Södertörn University. Her most recent publications include articles, a book and book chapters on women's work, household strategies for survival and poverty in contemporary Russia. Since 2002 she has conducted field work in three communities in the Archangelsk region where she is following the development mainly through interviews with local actors. Since March 2010 she is engaged in a project about poverty in Nizhny Novgorod.

Elena ZHIDKOVA (Russia) holds an MA degree in History from the Central European University in Budapest. She is currently Deputy Director of the Municipal Museum in Samara (Russia). She has been involved in numerous research projects in the labor market and gender in Russia, and has published widely on these topics. She is the contributor to *Adapting to Russia's New Labour Market* (Routledge, 2006).

Index

abortion (see also *contraception*), 5, 10, 28, 42 n. 31, 50, 93, 237
agency 68–69, 233
 social welfare agency, 212–15, 218, 221, 222
 women's agency, 16, 73, 78, 79, 81, 82n1, 85, 95, 244

birthrate(s) (see also *fertility rate*), 4, 10, 57, 101, 105–6, 128, 151, 167, 236, 237, 238, 245, 246n7, 276
breadwinner (see also *female breadwinner*), 11, 17, 28, 51, 58, 66–67, 75, 100, 123, 125, 236, 278, 291, 297, 298–302

career opportunities, 195, 210, 224
 female working career, 91, 100
career-oriented women, 95, 100n2, 146
career break, 194
caregiver, 7, 66, 67, 76, 168, 175, 179, 186, 194, 199, 297, 300, 301
childbearing, 4–6, 15, 102, 147, 149, 151, 154, 155
childbirth, 3–6, 15, 28, 90, 102, 156, 193, 214
childcare
 norms and practices (see also *nursery schools* and *preschool organizations*),15–16, 74, 76–77, 80, 170, 178, 179, 195–97, 198, 201–2, 238, 287, 298
 domestic, 59, 81, 198, 299, 307–8
 allowance, 195
 in Western Europe, 278

 in GDR, 102n9
 in Hungary, 66–67, 74, 76–77, 79–81
 in Latvia, 133, 134, 135
 in Russia,158, 160, 161, 165, 166, 167, 169–170, 172, 174, 178, 179, 180n7, 189–90, 210, 214
 subsidy, 66–67
 public provision, 1, 9, 12, 50–51, 79, 101, 102n9, 165, 172, 175, 217, 224, 238
 private provision (see also *nanny*), 231
 in the Soviet Union, 184, 209, 277
childhood, 67, 105, 130–33, 139, 165, 171, 174, 178, 261, 278
childlessness, 3, 145, 149
childrearing, 6, 15, 90, 99, 289
cohabitation (see also *extramarital relations*), 3, 4, 27, 113–14, 202n3, 252, 254, 263–64, 267, 269n3, 275, 281, 287
comrades' courts, 47, 49, 52, 54–56, 60
collectivization of private farms, 15, 16, 25, 53, 55, 65–70, 73–74, 76, 78, 82, 124, 133, 139n2
communism, 53, 165
 anti-communism, 272
 building of, 47, 50, 52,
contraception (see also *abortion*), 151, 237

demographic behavior, 3, 5, 6, 25–26
 change, 4, 25, 49, 234
 policies, 5, 15, 191, 237, 244
 problems, 16, 57, 189, 232, 235–26, 245

position, 68–70
transition, 3, 150, 152, 189
discrimination, 89, 98, 216, 217, 231, 235
discriminated against, 91
non-discrimination, 222, 224
divorce legislation, 5, 27, 31, 252–55, 259–63, 268
divorce practices, 3, 6, 13, 16, 26, 27, 252, 273–76, 279–280, 282, 286–88, 290–91
   in Estonia, 267–68, 274, 281
   in GDR/East Germany, 97, 101n7
   in Latvia, 263–64, 274, 281
   in Lithuania, 285–86
   in Russia, 158, 262–63
   in the Soviet Union, 27, 30–32, 42n6, 42 n. 13, 57–58, 61, 259–60, 268
divorced men, 30–31, 32, 282–83, 260
divorced women,10, 114, 130, 135, 155, 209, 260, 282, 284–85
divorce statistics, 3, 4, 27, 58, 260, 268, 281, 292n9

extramarital births (see also *lone mothers, lone motherhood, single mothers*), 3, 25–26, 41n1
extramarital relations (see also *cohabitation*), 54, 60, 254

fatherhood, 1, 7, 11, 13, 17, 26–29, 37, 39, 40, 57, 209, 238, 277, 278, 284, 289
female breadwinner, 91, 100
feminism(see also *women's emancipation*), 91–92
feminist, 9, 10, 86, 91, 92, 98–100, 186, 207, 239, 243–44, 273, 292
   anti-feminist, 138
fertility, 4, 102, 145, 149, 150–52, 160, 161, 200
   crisis, 232, 236, 238, 245
   rate(s) (see also *birthrates*), 3, 15, 105, 150–51, 160, 179n2, 193, 210, 275
   intentions, 146, 156, 160, 210

gender equality, 9, 85, 91, 96, 98, 99, 137, 167, 168, 231, 232, 234, 239, 242, 244, 246n2, 246n7, 302, 306
gender roles, 1, 4, 6, 12, 50, 61, 91, 127, 129, 130, 132, 133, 136–38, 223, 238, 277, 298, 299, 307, 311
generations, 4, 7, 11, 33, 61, 69–70, 76, 80, 85, 91, 102n9, 151, 308
   intergenerational relations, 29, 65, 67, 149, 197
grandmothers, 59, 90, 94, 131, 134, 175, 198, 307–9

housewife, 16, 59, 62n3, 85, 87, 88, 90, 92, 94–96, 101n3, 125, 130, 131, 134, 147, 158, 297
housework, 88, 92, 94, 99, 131, 136, 199, 202, 307, 308

individualism, 93
ideology, 10, 48, 50, 79, 96, 160, 187, 193, 221–22, 254, 310
   communist/Soviet, 4, 124, 127, 129–130, 138, 298
   family, 10, 48, 124, 200
   gender, 10, 158

lone motherhood (see also *single mothers, extramarital births*), 13, 25–26, 34, 39–40, 41n2
lone mothers, 25–27, 29, 31–43
love, 65, 90, 92, 95, 135, 155, 165, 171, 275, 292

marriage legislation, 26, 27–28, 30, 32, 36, 38, 41, 251–60, 263, 268–70
marriage practices, 1, 4, 5, 6, 13, 27, 29, 31, 32, 57, 67, 72, 92, 93, 114, 115, 125, 189, 275
   attitudes towards, 29, 34, 40, 280, 282
   first marriages, 3, 26, 287
   in Estonia, 256–57, 267–68, 281, 292n2
   in GDR/East Germany, 92, 93, 97, 101n6

in Latvia, 134, 136, 255–56, 258, 263–64, 281, 292
in Lithuania, 257–59, 265–57
in the Soviet Union,151, 168, 253, 261–62
norms, 7, 25, 27, 39, 113, 281
remarriage, 275, 281, 282, 286, 288
memory as a source, 69, 70, 73, 82 n. 73, 85–86
modernization, 3, 26, 50, 54, 58, 87, 99 124, 222
motherhood (see also *lone motherhood, single motherhood*), 11, 13, 15, 25, 27, 78, 82, 105, 123, 278
  extended (see also *grandmothers*), 29
  in Europe 27–28, 40
  in GDR/East Germany 96
  in Hungary, 78, 82
  in (Soviet) Russia 28–29, 40, 41n 4, 42, 151, 160, 167, 174, 176, 276, 277
  working motherhood 85, 89, 90, 95, 98-100, 102n9, 245

nanny, 147
nationalism, 124
NGO, 231–50
nursery-schools, 90, 133, 134, 165, 168, 172, 175

parenthood, 15, 17, 101, 102, 145, 159, 178, 273, 276, 277, 290
  shared,15, 160
parental practices, 1, 15, 59, 97, 154, 159, 170, 171, 175–79, 185, 194–200, 202, 216, 218, 273, 275, 283, 301, 307
  norms on parenting, 1, 7, 10, 15, 17, 33, 39, 55, 58, 81, 90, 94, 98, 150, 166, 167, 170, 172–77, 254, 278, 308
  forms of parenting, 4, 14, 17, 27, 30, 97, 101n7, 114, 148, 161, 165, 208–11, 216, 290
  attitudes towards parents, 5, 58, 60
  state regulations of parenting, 5, 7, 8, 9, 10, 58, 60, 92, 160, 168, 180, 188–190, 193, 202n5, 213, 238, 246, 279, 287
partnership (see also *marriage*), 3, 5, 17, 92–93, 96, 97, 98, 101n6
partners, 15, 27, 68, 95, 155, 161, 168, 172, 192, 199, 200, 201, 208, 283, 285, 286–87, 306, 312n3
patriarchy, 9, 10, 66, 67, 81, 87, 186
patriarchal family, 9, 53, 79, 123, 128
patriarchal dependency, 16, 53, 79
patriarchal subordination, 58
patriarchal oppression, 123
preschool organizations, 9, 15, 165–66, 168–170, 172–74, 176–79, 189
private sphere, 10, 40, 51, 58, 61, 81, 86–7, 92, 96, 99, 138, 186, 188, 191, 194, 238, 239, 280, 306
private entrepreneurship, 15, 17, 297, 299, 301, 302, 305, 307, 311
private life,11, 14, 47, 48, 51, 61, 135, 191, 261, 275, 281
private property, 10, 29, 79, 127
private relationships, 67, 68, 81, 128, 200, 232, 236
propaganda, 5, 51, 55, 106, 108, 123, 126, 128, 138, 150, 165, 194, 212

sexual life, 39-40, 41 n. 1, 50, 51, 93, 128, 135, 232, 233, 237, 244
sexuality,11, 25, 129, 146
single motherhood (see also *lone mothers/ motherhood, extramarital births*), 1, 97
  attitudes towards single mothers, 10, 35–36, 37, 60, 218, 221–23
  discrimination of single mothers, 41n4, 211, 216–18, 224
  in GDR/East Germany, 40, 94, 97, 101n7
  in Latvia, 127–28, 138, 282
  in Lithuania,14, 105–7, 110, 113–16, 118
  in Russia 113, 207–12, 214–18, 221–24, 225n7, 241, 308

in Soviet legislation, 41, 128, 168, 261, 274
support to single mothers, 14, 50, 56, 106–7, 110, 113–16, 127, 209, 211, 223, 224
social policy, 5, 7, 8, 14, 17, 186–88, 192, 201, 223, 277
   in GDR/East Germany, 97, 98
   in Russia, 152, 160, 185–88, 207–12, 231, 311–12
   in the Soviet Union, 48, 50, 54, 61, 62, 126, 309
social transfers
   alimony, 56, 168, 209, 210
   allowances, 8, 10, 14, 28, 36, 107–15, 117–18, 127, 132, 189, 195, 209, 210, 211, 213–14, 217, 224n4, 225n7,
   cash benefits, 7, 202, 207, 209, 301
   in-kind benefits, 6, 7, 198, 224n1, 301
   maintenance, 13, 263, 264, 266
   means-tested benefits, 8, 8, 189
   paternal (maternal) benefits, 7, 50, 66, 67, 105–7, 109, 111, 112, 113, 114–18, 193, 209, 213, 276, 277, 301
   social benefits, 52, 169, 188, 190, 192, 195, 214–19, 224n1, 301, 313n7
societal transformation, 2, 4, 6, 8, 9, 13, 15, 16, 17, 67, 69, 71, 102n10, 166, 185, 197, 201, 245, 274, 306, 311

economic reforms, 168, 210, 298, 303, 311, 313n6
Khrushchev's reforms, 61
land reform, 139n2
legislative reforms, 240, 242–43, 251–53, 255–70, 297
(neo)liberal reforms, 165, 179n2, 207, 302, 303
monetary reform, 119n8
policy reforms, 11, 200, 231, 236–37, 299–300
social and economic transition, 65, 70, 85, 86, 95, 99, 100n2, 100n3, 151, 223, 233, 236, 238, 241, 244, 246n6, 246n6, 280, 281, 290
sovietization, 13, 123–30, 132, 133, 136, 137–38, 139n2

trade unions, 14, 47, 49, 52, 61, 91, 106, 117, 126–7, 129, 134–5, 138, 311

voluntary organizations, so called, during Soviet period, 61

women's emancipation, 2, 16, 28, 47, 61, 65–66, 79, 92, 275
women's rights, 16, 238, 244
women's movement, 10, 91, 245
women's labor force participation, 49, 195, 291